Beer Lover's Southern California

First Edition

Kristofor Barnes

Enjoy the Book! Follow the LAAW! Cheers to Beers!

gpp

Guilford, Connecticut

Dedicated to the Fizz in My Beer Glass,
Katie McKissick

All the information in this guidebook is subject to change.
We recommend that you call ahead to obtain current information
before traveling.

Copyright © 2014 Morris Book Publishing, LLC

All photos by the author unless otherwise noted.

Editors: Kevin Sirois and Tracee Williams
Project Editor: Staci Zacharski
Layout Artist: Casey Shain
Text Design: Sheryl P. Kober
Maps: Alena Pearce © Morris Book Publishing, LLC

ISBN 978-0-7627-9200-9

Printed in the United States of America
10 9 8 7 6 5 4 3 2 1

Contents

About the Author

I first got into beer on a camping trip at Sequoia National Forest in 2008. My friend, now business partner, John and our mutual friend Matt had brewed up a Scotch ale called General Grant, a beer that would change my life. My brain exploded with silky, smoky caramel flavor overload. Scotch ale was a style I had never experienced before, and so I set out not only to try every beer I could, but also to brew my own.

Unbeknownst to me, there was a craft revolution brewing in not only Los Angeles, but the rest of the US (and world) as well. As John, Matt, and I progressed with our home brewing, we also experienced the rise of the LA beer scene, meeting inspirational mentors like Jeremy Raub and the team at Eagle Rock Brewery, who not only helped us home brew, but also propelled our imaginations further. I started a home brew blog, Bierkast.com, that eventually turned into an LA beer website focusing on industry events and craft beer professionals.

John and I founded Los Angeles Ale Works in December 2010 and started planning our brewery and what we wanted it to be. We currently brew gypsy-style out of a local LA brewery called Ohana and produce one boutique beer a month while we raise money for our own facility. Over the last five years, I've become incredibly involved with LA beer media and founded the LA Beer Bloggers with a cast of fellow bloggers and writers. In addition to meeting bimonthly, we present attendees with guest speakers, networking, and opportunities for professional development. My newest project, Ziggy The Beer Yeast, is a mobile beer game currently available for Android and iPhone platforms.

Although I grew up in the Pacific Northwest, my home is Los Angeles. I live with my lovely wife, Katie, and guinea pig, Ziggy. It's been an exciting ride watching the city grow its craft beer scene, and the community of enthusiasts I've met here are some of the most interesting, talented, and inspirational people in the industry. This book project has taken me through most of Southern California, and during my travels I've learned more about beer than I ever thought possible and have met incredible people along the way. The craft brewers who devote their lives to making amazing beer cannot be thanked enough.

Acknowledgments

Katie McKissick—whose advice, support, unwavering patience, wisdom, and assistance with this project made it possible. You always believe in me, and that is something for which I can never thank you enough.

John Rockwell—for his friendship, always sage advice, designated driving, and assistance with the project.

My parents and grandparents—without their incredible love and support, I would not be here today. Mom and Dad, you always have the best advice.

Godfather Mike—The start of the beer adventure can be traced back to you. Thank you.

John Verive of Beer of Tomorrow—for listening and offering me feedback on my writing.

Greg Nagel of OC Beer Blog—for his awesome feedback on Orange County.

Kelly Erickson—for offering me advice and helping me get things together at the end.

Derek and JJ Springer—for advice on San Diego and letting me stay with them on my frequent research trips down south.

Pipe Dream Brewery—Brian and Kinglsey, you guys were there for me during these stressful times.

LA River Brewing Co—thank you, thank you for your help.

Beer Paper LA—for believing in me while assisting during my frequent trips into the Inland Empire and Orange County.

Bernie Wire—You, my friend, are a gift sent from above. You're LA's greatest beer event photographer and a true inspiration to me.

Jeremy Raub—This beer adventure wouldn't have been possible without you taking the first step to open in LA. I look up to you and appreciate your mentorship.

Jonathan and Laurie Porter—kumquat tree, chickens, great beer, and sage advice —gracias.

The Beeroness (Jackie) & The Beeronista (Aften)—For your awesome help and recipes.

Beer Search Party, Food GPS, Beers in Paradise, LA Beer Blog, The Beer Goddess, and The LA Beer Bloggers—Thank you to each and every one of you for being awesome, spreading the word about beer, and keeping up the LA craft momentum.

My friends, family, and the LA beer community—there are too many names to write, you are all amazing and awesome.

All the brewers and breweries that opened their doors, donated their time answering my asinine questions, and shared their infinite wisdom, knowledge, and amazing beer stories with me—cheers to all of you.

Introduction

It is an amazing time to be a craft beer lover, especially in California. The massive surge in the popularity of craft beer has sparked a wave of new microbreweries opening all over the state, producing more than 2.2 million barrels a year for thirsty consumers. Not only is beer production in California higher than any other state, but it represents about 20 percent of all craft beer in the nation. California has over 325 brewers, a number that rises every day, and is home to 12 of the 50 largest craft breweries in the United States. Beer love is growing at an exponential rate and so is the demand for top-shelf product. As craft beer gains momentum, more and more people are shifting away from mass-produced macro lagers and willingly educating themselves on the bubbly stuff, increasing demand for high-quality artisanal products.

Southern California is home to one of the largest craft beer communities in the world, San Diego. San Diego County alone showcases over 80 breweries, each with its own unique take on the craft. Other areas like Temecula, Orange County, and Ventura County are also seeing tremendous growth as breweries open their doors. Perhaps one of the most interesting areas in Southern California when it comes to craft beer is Los Angeles, which has up until recently been beer-less save a few classic breweries. With the opening of Eagle Rock Brewery starting to sell beer in 2009 and opening their taproom in 2010, that all changed, and the greater LA area now has over 20 new breweries and brewpubs, with dozens more in planning, supplying the area with craft beer. With so many breweries opening, there is widespread talk about a potential bubble bursting, but only time will tell. One thing for certain, though: No matter where you live, today is a great day to be a beer lover in Southern California.

How to Use This Guide

This guide is meant to be as comprehensive as possible in this turbulent time of craft beer popularity. There will more than likely be places in this book that close and more that pop up at the time of publishing. I aim to give recommendations and a taste of what each place has to offer. Not every place will be for everyone, but I feel that every place has a least one if not more beers, food items, or positive points that can be gleaned by any reader/taster.

Each brewery listing is broken into three parts: general information at the top, brewery description in the middle, and a Beer Lover's Pick at the bottom. I consider myself a beer enthusiast and somewhat of a connoisseur, but I aim to remove the snob as much as possible, as beer is meant to be enjoyed. The Beer Lover's Pick is one beer that you should try if you can only try one, but there are far more on each tap list and I encourage you to order tasters, flights, and growlers/bottles to go. Have fun, enjoy the vibe, talk to the owners/brewers, and revel in the fact that we are here in a nation—and state, for that matter—of craft beer.

Brewery vs. Brewpub: Not every brewery, brewpub, and beer bar is created equal. It's difficult to pigeonhole many of these places into one of these categories. The most difficult is the brewpub. With the modernization and growing popularity of craft beer, the term *brewpub* is being redefined. Restaurants with nanobreweries and breweries with nanokitchens are becoming more commonplace. The '90s-style brewpub with lackluster vanilla beer styles is becoming a thing of the past, but they do exist. I've visited manufacturing/packaging breweries with forgettable beer and brewpubs with brain-bendingly awesome examples of creativity. Some of these places bottle, some don't. I encourage you to read the full description of every brewery and brewpub location to decide if you want to visit.

Beer Lover's Pick: Each Beer Lover's Pick is a highlight beer. These beers are chosen in a variety of ways, ranging from my personal favorite to the brewery's crowning achievement. In some cases, it's their flagship or the brewers favorite beer. Everyone's tastes are different, so order a taster of the Beer Lover's Pick first and decide if you want go back for a full pint.

Tasting Beer

There is no one right way to enjoy beer, but there are things you can do that will heighten enjoyment. From correct glassware to suggested food pairings, just like wine, beer has a wide versatility and can be an infinitely rewarding experience. An entire book could be spent on this subject, and as it turns out there are a few. The best one I've found is Randy Mosher's *Tasting Beer*. It's a great resource that goes over everything in depth in a fun and entertaining way.

After the brewery, brewpub, and beer bar listings, you'll find chapters on:

Beer Festivals: A look at a few of the larger beer festivals in Southern California that occur annually.

Home Brewing & Home Brew Scene: Part of Southern California's growth of breweries has stemmed from a high number of home brewers. In this chapter you'll find a few suggested home brewshops as well as clone recipes of the region's beers you can brew at home.

In the Kitchen: Did you know that beer is the perfect ingredient for a lot of foods? This chapter is all about recipes you can cook at home using Southern California beers. Cooking with Beer will take you into the kitchen with some tasting treats using your favorite pint and Cooking with Grain will challenge home brewers to recycle their leftover spent grain.

Pub Crawls: If you're visiting a city or want to experience multiple places at once, a pub crawl is the way to go. There are four itineraries from around Southern California that will have you jumping into the local beer scene.

Glossary of Terms

ABV: Alcohol by volume—the percentage of alcohol in a beer. A typical domestic beer is a little less than 5 percent ABV.

Ale: Beer brewed with top-fermenting yeast. Quicker to brew than lagers, most every craft beer is a style of ale. Popular styles of ales include pale ales, amber ales, stouts, and porters.

Altbier: A German style of ale, typically brown in color, smooth, and fruity.

Barleywine: Not a wine at all but a high-ABV ale that originated in England and is typically sweet. American versions often have large amounts of hops.

Barrel: Production of beer is measured in barrels, also refered to as a BBL. A barrel equals 31 gallons.

Beer: An alcoholic beverage brewed with malt, water, hops, and yeast.

Beer bar: A bar that focuses on carrying craft or fine imported beers.

Bitter: An English bitter is an English-style ale, more hoppy than an English mild but less hoppy than an IPA.

Bock: A German-style lager, typically stronger than the typical lager.

Bomber: Most beers are packaged in 12-ounce bottles. Bombers are 22-ounce bottles.

Brewpub: Typically a restaurant, but sometimes a bar, that brews its own beers on the premises.

Cask ale: Also known as *real ales,* cask ales are naturally carbonated and are usually served with a hand pump rather than forced out with carbon dioxide or nitrogen.

Clone beer: A home brew recipe based on a commercial beer.

Contract brewery: A company that does not have its own brewery and pays someone else to brew and bottle its beer.

Craft beer: High-quality, flavorful beer made by small breweries.

DIPA: A double India pale ale is a strong version of the classic style India pale ale. These usually include higher hopping rates, a thicker body, and more alcohol.

Double: Most often means a higher-alcohol version of a beer, most typically used in reference to a double, or imperial, IPA. Can also be used as an American translation of a Belgian dubbel, a style of Belgian ale.

ESB: Extra-special bitter. A traditional malt-heavy English pub ale with low bitterness, usually served on cask.

Ester: An ester is a chemical compound created by yeast during fermentation. They often take on the fruity notes in the aroma and flavor ranging from banana, to bubble gum, to dark raisins.

Flagship beer: Flagship beers are traditionally the beer that put the brewery on the map. These are beers that each brewery is most well known for. This is a classic brewery term, but today the term flagship is less common with newer breweries. Flagship can mean best-selling beer that month or year. Many breweries in today's climate specifically opt out of the term *flagship*. For the purposes of this book flagship means best-selling beer or most widely known beer.

Gastropub: A beer-centric bar or pub that exhibits the same amount of care selecting its foods as it does its beers.

Growler: A half-gallon jug of beer. Many brewpubs sell growlers of their beers to go.

Gypsy brewer: A company that does not own its own brewery, but rents space at an existing brewery to brew it themselves.

Hard cider: An alcoholic drink made from fermented fruit juice, traditionally apples.

Hops: Flowers used in beers to produce aroma, bitterness, and flavor. Nearly every beer in the world has hops.

IBU: International bittering units—used to measure how bitter a beer is.

Imperial: A higher-alcohol version of a regular-strength beer.

IPA: India pale ale. A popular style of ale created in England that has taken a decidedly American twist over the years. Often bitter, thanks to more hops used than in other styles of beer.

Kölsch: A light, refreshing German-style ale.

Lager: Beer brewed with bottom-fermenting yeast. Takes longer and is harder to brew than ales. Popular styles of lagers include black lagers, Doppelbocks, pilsners, and Vienna lagers.

Malt: Typically barley malt, but sometimes wheat malt. Malt provides the fermentable sugar in beers. The more fermentable sugar, the higher the ABV in a beer. Without malt, a beer would be too bitter from the hops.

Mead: An alcoholic drink made from fermented honey.

Microbrewery: A brewery that brews less than 15,000 barrels of beer a year.

Nanobrewery: A brewery that brews four barrels of beer per batch or less.

Nitro draft: Most beers that are served on draft use kegs pressurized with carbon dioxide. Occasionally, particularly with stouts, nitrogen is used, which helps create a creamier body.

Pilsner: A style of German or Czechoslovakian lager, usually light in color. Most mass-produced beers are based on this style.

Porter: A dark ale, similar to stout but with fewer roasted characters.

Pounders: 16-ounce cans.

Quad: A strong Belgian-style ale, typically sweet and high in alcohol.

Regional brewery: A brewery that brews up to six million barrels of beer a year.

Russian imperial stout: A stout is a dark, heavy beer. A Russian imperial stout is a higher-alcohol, thicker-bodied version of regular stouts.

Saison: Also known as a Belgian or French farmhouse ale. It can be fruity and can also be peppery, and is usually refreshing.

Seasonal: A beer that is brewed only at a certain time of year to coincide with the seasons.

Session beer: A low-alcohol beer, of which you can have several in one long drinking "session."

Stout: A dark beer brewed with roasted malts.

Strong ale: A style of ale that is typically both hoppy and malty and can be aged for years.

Tap takeover: An event where a bar or pub hosts a brewery and has several of its beers on tap.

Triple (Tripel): A Belgian-style ale, typically lighter in color than a dubbel but higher in alcohol.

Wheat beer: Beers, such as Hefeweizens and Witbiers, that are brewed using wheat malt along with barley malt.

Yeast: The living organism in beer that causes the sugars to ferment and become alcohol.

Ventura & Santa Barbara

BREWERIES
11 Enegren Brewing Company
1 Figueroa Mountain Brewing Company
2 Firestone Walker Barrelworks
7 Island Brewing Company
10 Surf Brewery
4 Telegraph Brewing Company— Santa Barbara

BREWPUBS
8 Anacapa Brewing Company
6 The Brewhouse
3 Hollister Brewing Company
5 Santa Barbara Brewing Company

BEER BARS & BOTTLE SHOPS
9 Barrelhouse 101
12 Draughts Restaurant and Bar

Inset

Nopal St.
Quarantina St.
Cesar Chavez
Calle
Olive St.
4
Chase Palm Park
Laguna St.
Garden St.
Gutierrez St.
Yanonali St.
Cabrillo Blvd.
Santa Barbara
State St.
Cota St.
Hadley St.
5
Bath St.
Castillo St.
6
Ortega St.
Montecito St.

0   0.2   0.4 mile

Los Padres National Forest

Lake Cachuma

Lake Piru

Lake Casitas

Buellton
2
1

Goleta
3

Carpinteria
7
4-6
See Inset

Ventura
8, 9
10

Moorpark
11

Thousand Oaks
12

Channel Island National Park

San Miguel Island
Santa Rosa Island
Santa Cruz Island

N

0   10   20 miles

Ventura & Santa Barbara

Depending on which map you are reading, Ventura County is either the northern tip of Southern California or part of Central California. For the purposes of this book, we'll go with the former. Keep in mind that a diligent, no-nonsense beer lover can do all of the breweries, brewpubs, and bars in this chapter in one day—with the help of a designated driver, of course—but that's no fun. Take your time, enjoy the coast and the town vibe, and relax. Most of these places are fairly close to the beach, so you could easily make a beach or surf day bookended by beer tastings and great-quality food. Santa Barbara, Ventura, and Agoura Hills all have their charm, not to mention amazing beer.

Breweries

ENEGREN BREWING COMPANY

680 Flinn Ave., Moorpark, CA 93021; (805) 552-0602; enegrenbrewing.com;
@EnegrenBrewing

Founded: 2011 **Founder:** Chris Enegren, Matt Enegren, and Joe Nascenzi **Brewer:** Chris Enegren, Matt Enegren, and Joe Nascenzi **Flagship Beer:** Valkyrie California Altbier **Year-round Beers:** Valkyrie California Altbier, Protector Imperial IPA, Hop Project IPA **Seasonals/Special Releases:** Golden Spur Saison, Daniel Irons Oatmeal Stout, Captain Summer Session, Foliage Pale Ale, Dean Hickman English Bitter, Captain Patrick Irish Stout, Shorts Day Spring IPA **Tours:** Yes **Taproom:** Yes; limited weekend hours

You would be hard-pressed to find a more devoted brew crew than the folks at Enegren Brewing Company in Moorpark. Here, far from the hustle and bustle of the city, through the farmland, you'll find a small industrial park with a three-person brew crew manning a 3 BBL nanobrewhouse. Brothers Chris and Matt Enegren and college friend Joe Nascenzi started Enegren Brewing July 2011, and since then

it has picked up notoriety among local and Los Angeles–area beer bars. Enegren is an incredibly small operation, but it is intensely time-consuming for the young friends who all work day jobs during the day only to hightail it to their brewery and knock out a batch or two at night. A solid engineering background for all three not only has given them the ability to brew consistent batches of their flagships, but also allows them to custom program everything in the brewery from brewing to fermentation temperatures. Chris can even control the conical tank temperatures remotely from his iPhone! Enegren is an incredibly passionate, dedicated, and innovative crew.

Beer Lover's Pick

Valkyrie California Altbier
Style: German Altbier
ABV: 6.2%
Availability: Year-round
A delicious German-style Altbier is hard to find nowadays, but Enegren aims to change that. Valkyrie California Altbier is their flagship and has proved mighty successful for the small crew. Rich melanoidin flavors from the Munich malt used in the batch dominate, and a clean but subdued, hoppy bite finishes the beer out. It's a refreshingly complex German beer and one that is done very well. It pours a dark amber color with an off-white head and clocks in at 6.2% so you can have more than one, but you'll probably also want to try Enegren's other brews because they are all great.

Enegren focuses on German and European styles, but also dabbles in the American IPA and Double IPA craze. Their flagship beer is **Valkyrie,** an Altbier, which is a style you don't see too often. The **Golden Spur Saison** is a crowd favorite and makes its way to many local beer bars during the spring and summer season—and it's the Enegren crew that hand-delivers it there. Other noteworthy beers include their **Protector IPA,** a solid fruity-citrus-resiny IPA with light carbonation, and the **Dean Hickman English Bitter,** also a seasonal. Enegren brews are detail-oriented small batches with home-brewing creativity and precision that can only be attributed to their engineering background.

The taproom is modestly sized for the space, with a nice wooden bar and a high-top picnic table. The brewhouse is directly adjacent and in use during taproom hours, so you can watch the action happen while you enjoy your beer. The brewery is clean and polished even during use, and the vibe is small-town beer enthusiast. It's a family-run operation, so you'll likely see Brianne, Chris's wife, pouring pints and answering questions. It's definitely worthy of a visit, but taproom hours are limited to weekends so make sure you call ahead.

FIGUEROA MOUNTAIN BREWING COMPANY

45 Industrial Way, Buellton, CA 93427; (805) 694-2252; figmtnbrew.com; @FigMtn
Founded: 2010 **Founder:** Jaime and Jim Dietenhofer **Brewer:** AJ Stoll **Flagship Beer:** Hoppy Poppy IPA **Year-round Beers:** Paradise Road Pilsner, Wrangler Wheat, Figueroa Mtn Pale Ale, Danish Red Lager, Hoppy Poppy IPA, Hurricane Deck Double IPA, Davy Brown Ale, Stagecoach Stout **Seasonals/Special Releases:** First Anniversary Ale, Scotch Ale, Big Cone Black, Magpie Porter, Jalama Beach Blonde **Tours:** Yes **Taproom:** Yes

Figueroa Mountain, located in a Buellton industrial park next to a winery, distillery, and mountain range, is one of the fastest-expanding new breweries in Southern California. Proprietors and father-and-son team Jaime and Jim Dietenhofer opened their doors, after 16 years of planning, in November of 2010 to a large thirsty crowd. They hired award-winning brewmaster and chemist AJ Stoll, and together they focus mainly on classic styles with slight twists and variations. The resulting beers are excellently executed. Jaime comes from a construction background and still owns his own contracting business. His experience in this area has allowed him to expertly scale the business and steadily expand the Figueroa Mountain Brewing facility as well as the operation as a whole. The resulting success has even spawned the opening of a second location in Santa Barbara, which brews and serves more experimental beers so the main facility can focus on the core brand offerings.

Davy Brown Ale
Style: American Brown Ale
ABV: 6.0%
Availability: Year-round

American brown ales are sometimes hard to find, but there seems to be a resurgence of them lately. It's not a surprise, with the accompanying strong lineup of classic styles, that Figueroa Mountain's brown ale is exceptional. The extremely drinkable beer is a rich combination of dark malts and a delightfully creamy effervescence. As the beer warms, notes of toasted Irish brown bread dominate along with dark chocolate. Also recommended are the multi-award-winning Stagecoach Stout and the barrel-aged second anniversary Grand Cru with Grenache grapes. These beers, depending on how you look at them, can be simple and tasty or complex and thought-provoking.

The taproom is beautiful, separating itself from the brewery with a nice stone bar overlooking the 15 BBL brewhouse where beer lovers can sit down and watch the magic happen while having a pint. It's medium-large with a wooden facade over the bar that makes it look like a pioneer mining town. Mug Club mugs can be seen hanging in the background, and if there are openings, you can even sign up for a membership. The entire space can accommodate large groups with both sitting and standing areas. They also have a huge outdoor beer garden complete with bocce, picnic tables, and local food trucks, and will be working with a local restaurateur in the near future to put in full food service.

Ventura & Santa Barbara

Figueroa Mountain created the brand image with the help of TapHandles.com and is one of their flagship customers; because of this, the labels, tap handles, and artwork accompanying the brewery's impressive beer line are beautiful. **Hoppy Poppy IPA, Danish Red Ale, Stagecoach Stout, Davy Brown,** and the recently released second anniversary **Grand Cru** are among some of the recommended beers to try, but you really can't go wrong with any of them. **Hoppy Poppy,** their dank West Coast IPA, is the flagship and most popular with the locals. If you can't make a decision, you can order mixed flights, which come with tasting notes, and you can also take home brew in nifty Figueroa Mountain growlers. Figueroa Mountain has wide distribution throughout California. Their bottles are easy to find in both high-end and large-scale bottle shops, and draft beers are located in most craft-centric gastropubs.

FIRESTONE WALKER BARRELWORKS

620 McMurray Rd., Buellton, CA 93427; (805) 686-1557; firestonebeer.com/barrelworks; @FirestoneWalker

Founded: 2013 **Founder:** David Walker and Adam Firestone **Brewer:** Matt Brynildson **Cellarmaster/Barrel Guy:** Jim "Sour Jim" Crooks **Flagship Beer:** Bretta Weisse **Year-round Beers:** Bretta Weisse, Lil' Opal **Seasonals/Special Releases:** Agrestic, Lil Mikkel, Sour Opal, Vessel 8, SLO-Ambic, Parabola, Helldorado, §ucaba, Double DBA, Bravo, Velvet Merkin **Tours:** Yes; call ahead **Taproom:** Yes; pub attached

Buellton isn't the main site of Firestone Walker, but it is where they barrel age all of their sours. The Barrelworks opened in January of 2013 and is located at the site of the Buellton pub and taproom. Previously the Barrelworks was just extra storage, but now it's a full-fledged souring program with walls and walls (part of the 1,500-plus collection) of barrels aging various styles which will eventually be blended together. Sours and wild beers are stored in Buellton, far away from the Paso Robles brewery, to reduce the risk of unwanted contamination of other Firestone Walker beers.

Getting into the Barrelworks might be kind of confusing, even though there is a large sign in front. The entrance to the Barrelworks is a new addition to the taproom, so if you've been there in the past, you'll now be entering through a different door on the side. You can still get to the Barrelworks taproom from the original front door, but you'll have to walk through the pub. The taproom is small and is directly adjacent to the barrel room. There's a small stainless bar with an attractive tap setup mimicking pouring straight from the cask. If you are looking for grub and not in the mood for sours, check out the pub next door with burgers, fries, salads, and more.

Bretta Weisse
Style: Young Wheat
     Berliner Weisse
ABV: 3.4%
Availability: Only available at
     Barrelworks tasting room

I recently got a taste of the so-called Firestone Walker sour program flagship simply called Bretta Weisse. It is an extremely low ABV, 3.4%, wheat Berliner Weisse, which most likely uses the Firestone Hefeweizen, Solace, as its base. It's very quaffable and extremely refreshing. Light tartness and the citrus element make it the perfect beer for a hot day in the fields and would make an exceptionally appropriate pairing for fish or a light salad. Drinking this beer only made me want more, and learning that I couldn't take a growler home brought a tear to my eye. Luckily, this beer is due to be one of the first bottled out of Barrelworks and will also be available year-round, which means I'll soon be able to get it whenever I want. And because Firestone Walker has a larger distribution circle, you'll likely be able to get it wherever their products are sold. Good deal!

The Buellton pub is generally moderately crowded depending on the day, so reservations are sometimes suggested but probably not required. It's a small-town feel, but city slickers are always welcome.

You can order flights or larger pours, but be warned, some of these lengthy aged products come with a price. **SLO-Ambic,** their lambic, is $2 an ounce, but it's worth it if you are in the mood for complex sours and Olalla berries. A fridge in the back showcases the high-octane Firestone Walker barrel beers like **Parabola, Anniversary verticals,** and **§ucaba.** Growler fills and bottles are available at the pub bar, and merchandise is nearby, too, if you need a hat to cover your noggin. If you have more time and you like Firestone Walker beers, you should definitely head up to Paso Robles to see the brewery—it's awe-inspiring.

ISLAND BREWING COMPANY

5049 Sixth St., Carpinteria, CA 93013; (805) 745-8272; islandbrewingcompany.com; @islandbrewingco
Founded: 2001 **Founder:** Paul Wright **Brewer:** Paul Wright **Flagship Beer:** Island Blonde **Year-round Beers:** Island Blonde, Paradise Pale Ale, Island Pale Ale, Jubilee Ale, Blackbird Porter **Seasonals/Special Releases:** Starry Night Stout **Tours:** Yes—limited; call for availability **Taproom:** Yes

Island Brewing Company is a great place to enjoy a beer with a beautiful view of the beach. Paul Wright, originally a brewer for Marin Brewing Company in Marin, CA, moved down to Carpinteria to establish IBC in 2001. Since then it has expanded in popularity and is now an incredibly busy beer hot spot. Walking in on the weekend you'll find it very crowded, and you'll likely need to wait in line for a few minutes to get a beer. Patrons in beach and bike attire flood the taproom and outside patio, filling growlers, taking home bottles, and relaxing after a hard day of recreational activities. The location is a bit hard to find if you are using a mobile phone mapping system, but you just have to persevere and follow the noise of the crowd and the smell of the ocean.

Island Brewing Company has a very focused set of beers available in their taproom, and each one is to style. Their **Starry Night Stout,** a 6.8% foreign extra-style stout, is silky smooth like chocolate and coffee and is also a recent Great American Beer Festival (GABF) winner. The **Blonde Ale** and **Island Pale Ale** are popular with the surfers that want to relax, but if they are looking for something a bit more powerful, the **Jubilee Ale** is where it's at. IBC is a great stop for anyone in the area doing a brew tour; it's a classic-style manufacturing brewery with a fully functioning tasting room and an island vibe. If you enjoy the beach and like beer, you can't do wrong by going to Island Brewing.

Jubilee Ale
Style: Old Ale
ABV: 7.2%
Availability: Year-round
I went into Jubilee Ale thinking it was going to be a spiced holiday beer, but was surprised to find an incredibly malty old ale. Jubilee has a huge silky mouthfeel with a sweet bready aroma. There isn't rye in the malt bill, but the spicy breading sure fooled me. There is a slight doggy hoppiness to it and a pleasant caramel toffee aftertaste. Jubilee is apparently one of the most popular beers among the locals and is even used in a counting system: "We'll give this guy three Jubilees so he can relax."

Ventura & Santa Barbara

SURF BREWERY

4561 Market St., Ventura, CA 93003; (805) 644-2739; surfbrewery.com; @surfbrewery
Founded: 2011 **Founder:** Bill Riegler and Doug Mason **Brewer:** Chas Cloud **Flagship Beer:** County Line Pale **Year-round Beers:** Mondo's Cream Ale, County Line Pale, Surf Black IPA Style Ale, Oil Piers Porter, South Swell Double IPA, Strawberry Wahine Wheat, Shaka XPA Extra Pale Ale, Extra Special Rye **Seasonals/Special Releases:** Cask **Tours:** Yes; call for availability **Taproom:** Yes—large

Surf Brewery has a great name and vibe. Walking into the taproom you'll likely pass by a food truck and hear the sounds of a local surf band playing to the patrons. The taproom is large for a 15 BBL brewery, but UCSB grad and cofounder Bill says that they wanted to focus on having a large space for people to drink and

Oil Piers Porter
Style: Nitro Porter
ABV: 5.3%
Availability: Limited year-round

Oil Piers Porter is a classic porter all the way. It's an excellently roasty, creamy, quaffable representation of the style, and this one is especially silky smooth as it's served on nitro. From tap to glass it looks like a Guinness, complete with tan head and jet

black body. Diving in further you'll find thick toasted coffee and bitter chocolate and a well-attenuated dryness. If you are lucky enough to be there during a cask day, you may even find a variation of Oil Piers that you can compare side by side with the original. The version I had was casked with oak

chips and Palisade hops, which gave it a slight tartness. The signature low carbonation of a cask ale gave this beer a completely different feel, with fruity floral hop notes with a rush of roast at the end. These types of comparisons, variations on a single beer, are what make tastings truly fun.

congregate. There is even a home brew store in the brewery, so if you like making your own beer and live in Ventura, this is the place to visit. Get a Surf pint, then get ingredients to make your own. The vibe is beachy and relaxed. There is a large bar in the back where the Surf beers are served, and the staff is very friendly. Be careful of the cellar man, though—he's a bit surly after a hard day's work, but that's just his nature.

Surf Brewery beers have a classic-style focus with twists that make them very interesting. With thematic names like **County Line Pale, South Swell Double IPA,** and **Strawberry Wahine Wheat,** if you aren't coming to the brewery after a long day's surfing, you'll definitely want to go out afterwards. You won't find a bad beer at Surf, and that's because brewer Chas Cloud is a beer veteran. Originally studying under Ladyface's David Griffiths while at BJ's, Chas has mastered classic beer styles and is now able to add his own take on each to make Surf Brewery stand out. Popular at the taproom are **Mondo's Cream Ale,** a blonde/Kölsch light beer, and the **Strawberry Wahine Wheat,** which celebrates Ventura's passion for strawberries, along with the **County Line Pale.** You'll also find the bar staff mixing styles together to create their own twists, and you can grab a craft spritzy lemonade if you want to take a break from beer.

Surf Brewery has made a name for itself in the last two years and has become synonymous with California quality craft. Their signature monochromatic surfboard taps can be seen everywhere from Ventura to San Diego, and their bottles are also widely available. It wouldn't be surprising to see Surf expanding their production in the next few years and it would a good thing, too, because Surf beers are wicked, brah.

TELEGRAPH BREWING COMPANY—SANTA BARBARA

416 N. Salsipuedes St., Santa Barbara, CA 93103; (805) 963-5018; telegraphbrewing.com; @telegraphbrew

Founded: 2005 **Founder:** Brian R. Thompson **Brewer:** Scott Baer **Flagship Beer:** California Ale **Year-round Beers:** California Ale, Stock Porter, White Ale, Reserve Wheat Ale **Seasonals/Special Releases:** Obscura Cacao, Rhinoceros, Gypsy Ale, Cervesa de Fiesta, Ravena Stout, Winter Ale, Telegraph Obscura Series **Tours:** Yes **Taproom:** Yes

Telegraph Brewing Company is a must stop if you are in the area, and if you are a biker or beach-goer, you should make sure it's on your destination list. You can even hit up the wine-tasting room next door if you're in the mood. The custard-colored industrial building is emblazoned with "Telegraph Brewing Company," and there is a van out front with the same that'll help you find it, no problem. The brewery is small with an equally small tasting room, but what they lack in space, they make up for in quality. The brewhouse is crammed into the back of the facility, and kegs are organized but packed into any available space. Telegraph will be going through an expansion and move in 2014, which will allow them to brew more beer and have more people in the tasting room.

They usually have four beers on tap at any one time, but they rotate beers seasonally so visiting often will likely net you some diverse options. Beers can be

California Ale
Style: Nonspecific Cal/Belgian
   Hybrid
ABV: 6.2%
Availability: Year-round
Their flagship and one of their strongest offerings, the California Ale is deep, complex, and defies classic style. At its simplest it's a malty Belgian amber-colored beer, with an earthy hoppiness. The body of the beer is medium, with a silky head and a potpourri lavender nose. As it warms, the caramel malts come out, exposing a toffee sweetness that plays very nicely with the citrusy Belgian yeast. It's earthy, thought-provoking, and a pleasure to drink. It's no surprise that it's a GABF gold medal winner.

ordered in tasting flights or by the pint, and since you'll likely want to take beer home, they also sell 750 ml Belgian-style corked bottles and growlers. The beers themselves are eclectic. Their flagship **California Ale** is an incredibly complex and deep amber-colored Belgian beer. It's worth a try and a bottle. The **White Ale** is their interpretation of a Witbier with earthy yeast and citrus notes, and their seasonal Obscura series runs the gamut from reds to sours to the recent cacao-infused **Obscura Cacao.** Another solid choice is the **Stock Porter,** an incredibly deep yet simple dark beer that you won't want to share.

Brewpubs

ANACAPA BREWING COMPANY

472 E. Main St., Ventura, CA 93001; (805) 643-2337; anacapabrewing.com; @AnacapaBrewCo

Founded: 2000 **Founder:** Danny Saldana **Brewer:** Jason Coudray **Flagship Beer:** Pierpont IPA **Year-round Beers:** Mirage Rye Pale, Espresso Stout, White Cap Wit, Pierpont IPA, Santa Rosa Red, C-Street Wheat **Seasonals/Special Releases:** Pissy Pelican Pale, Adobe Mexican Lager, Two Trees Double IPA, A Face For Radio IPA **Tours:** No

Anacapa is currently the only brewpub in the city of Ventura, and it's fairly easy to find. Just look for the lighthouse logo on the door with the large "Anacapa" above, nestled between a few other restaurants and bars on Main Street. The brewhouse and fermentors are crammed behind the bar, with a large dining area to the right of the restaurant. The vibe is friendly and family-oriented, and you'll likely see owner Danny Saldana walking around making sure everyone's happy with their meals and beers. Rustic wood tables, a stone bar, and lots of stainless pretty much describe the interior of Anacapa, and there is a large board above the bar displaying the latest brews on tap.

Santa Rosa Red
Style: American Red Ale
ABV: 6.2%
Availability: Year-round

I feel like I don't see American red ales anymore unless I'm at a brewpub. It's a shame, really, because they are delicious and go well with food. Anacapa's Santa Rosa Red is a crowd pleaser and it's easy to see why. It's a straightforward offering not too intense in any direction, with a medium to light body, nice malty caramel notes, and enough hop bitterness to give it a crisp bite without obliterating the taste buds. It's an above-session beer at 6.2% so you can have a few, but you will feel it. Definitely order this beer with

the Angus burger if you are hungry for lunch or dinner.

Anacapa is focused on classic West Coast American styles. You'll find plenty of year-round hoppy beers and seasonal IPAs. The **Pissy Pelican Pale** is a hoppy pale that would be excellent with those fish tacos or Icelandic cod on the menu. The **Santa Rosa Red,** a crowd favorite, is best paired with the half-pound Angus burger. You won't find anything crazy at Anacapa, but if you are stopping by Ventura and are looking for a brewpub with classic styles and food, you can't go wrong here.

THE BREWHOUSE

229 W. Montecito St., Santa Barbara, CA 93101; (805) 884-4664; brewhousesb.com
Founded: 2003 **Founder:** Gary Jacobson and Barb Long **Brewer:** Pete Johnson
Flagship Beer: Condor Pilsner **Year-round Beers:** Nirvana Pale Ale, West Beach
IPA, Honey Brown Ale, Condor Pilsner, Montecito Street Wheat, Apricot Wheat, Vow of
Blindness, Baseball Saison, Breakwater Wit, Habanero Pilsner, Saint Barb's Abbey Ale,
Saint Barb's Dubbel, Saint Barb's Tripel **Seasonals/Special Releases:** Habanero Pilsner,
10W30 Stout, Harry Porter, Rebel Red, Buster Brown **Tours:** No formal tours offered. Call
for private tour availability.

The vibe of the place is beach all the way. Shorts, flip-flops, tank tops, and sunburns. Although it's a beer establishment, it's incredibly family-friendly and there are even crayon drawing contests posted on the walls leading into the bathroom. The Brewhouse has 16 taps, which are supplied with beer from boisterous brewmaster Pete Johnson's 7 BBL copper pub system. You'll find everything from stouts and IPAs to Belgian–style beers on tap. If you are adventurous you can even try the habanero-infused pilsner, but be warned, it's no joke—it's unbelievably hot and meant as a novelty.

Saint Barb's Belgian Tripel (XXX)
Style: Belgian-Style Tripel
ABV: 9.0%
Availability: Year-round

I want so badly to recommend the Habanero Pils here as the novelty is well worth it, but the tasting notes would simply be "Fire," so I'll simply recommend that you taste and then experience it. Habanero Pils is best paired with water. Brewmaster

Pete is a big fan of Belgian-style ales, and has a series of abbey beers he calls Saint Barb's. The most recent release in the series is the Saint Barb's Belgian Tripel, which clocks in at 9.0% ABV; however, it hides the alcohol very well. The beer is sweet and estery, with a very refreshing yeast character. It is well balanced and has a bit of a citrus quality to it. Saint Barb's Tripel easily paired with fish dishes like fish tacos, but would also be nice with a citrusy dessert or sorbet.

The Brewhouse may offer your typical brewpub menu items, but the food is the real deal. Fish tacos, pizza, brunch on weekends, and solid appetizers like grilled artichoke hearts are all cooked to perfection. The beers at The Brewhouse are well paired with anything you can order, and if you aren't sure what to pair it with, the server will give you suggestions. If you aren't in the mood for beer, there's also a full bar. If you happen to be there on a day when Pete Johnson is hanging out, try to get a tour of the facility. It's small but fun, and he may even give you a taste of whatever new beer he's working on. He just released a new Belgian-style **Tripel** in his Saint Barb's line, and it's a powerhouse of yeasty Belgian goodness.

HOLLISTER BREWING COMPANY

6980 Marketplace Dr., Goleta, CA 93117; (805) 968-2810; hollisterbrewco.com;
@Hollisterbrewco
Founded: 2007 **Founder:** Marshall Rose **Brewer:** Eric Rose **Flagship Beer:** The Pope
Year-round Beers: Beachside Blonde, Orange Blossom Special, The J, Ctrl Alt Dlt, Table
24 Red, Southern Chaos, The Pope, Hollister Hefeweizen, rotating IPAs **Seasonals/
Special Releases:** 6th Anniversary Ale **Tours:** No

Hollister Brewing, right off the 101 Ventura Freeway, is located in a suburban strip mall next to a Chile's. The place itself is a pretty standard brewpub, with large indoor seating areas and booths. The bar has a large backlit Hollister sign, and each fuzzy dice–size tap handle looks like a gearshift with a large H emblazoned on it. Walking in after making a reservation will get you seated quickly so you can order brewpub food. It's relatively family-friendly and should be enjoyed with friends. The Kölsch-battered fish tacos come highly recommended, along with the pulled pork, burger, and duck fat fries. If you are there on a weekend and bartender Mike is on shift, you'll be well taken care of.

Southern Chaos
Style: IPA
ABV: 5.8%
Availability: Year-round
Nelson Sauvin hops dominate this beer in both aroma and flavor. Forward notes of grapefruit, lemon peel, and white grape juice along with a crisp attenuated dryness make it very refreshing. The hop character also comes through a bit dank, with some doggy and catty notes. Southern Chaos won brewer Eric Rose a silver medal at GABF, which is proudly displayed in the restaurant near the brewhouse.

The beers at Hollister are pretty solid. **Southern Chaos,** the 5.8% ABV IPA, is a local favorite and was even recommended by several other breweries. Brewmaster Eric Rose studied under Vinny from Russian River, where he developed his brewing chops. Hoppy beers seem to be his focus, which is why beers like **Southern Chaos** and **The Pope** reign supreme.

SANTA BARBARA BREWING COMPANY

501 State St., Santa Barbara, CA 93101; (805) 730-1040; sbbrewco.com; @SBBrewCo
Founded: 1995 **Founder:** Wayne Trella and Steve Hovdesven **Brewer:** Kevin Pratt
Flagship Beer: Santa Barbara Blonde **Year-round Beers:** Santa Barbara Blonde, Gold Coast Wheat, Pacific Pale Ale, India Pale Ale, Double IPA, State Street Stout **Seasonals/ Special Releases:** Doppelbock, Belgian IPA **Tours:** No

A very traditional-style brewpub, Santa Barbara Brewing Company is relatively easy to find on State Street, one of the main drags through downtown Santa Barbara. The brewpub actually has two separate sections, one being the lounge, which is not the brewery, and the other being the pub with the brewhouse. It's

Rincon Red
Style: American Red Ale
ABV: 6.4%
Availability: Year-round

Named after the famous surf beach not too far from the brewery, Rincon Red is a straightforward classic American red ale. You won't find anything crazy out of the ordinary for this beer, but you will find that it goes well with food and you can drink a few of them, although at 6.4% it's not exactly sessionable. It has a malty backbone with a forward hop bitterness. The characteristic ashiness of the Victory malt present in the beer

is very reminiscent of flavors you'll find in Fat Tire, and the Warrior and Cascade hops are as West Coast as you can get. It's a great beer post-surfing.

easy to tell the difference—just look for the giant copper pub system in the back. Inside you'll find a large bar to the left, with mixed seating to the right. The 15 BBL brewhouse directly ahead in the back and the fermentation tanks are crammed together on the mezzanine above. Still, there is a lot of space for crowds, and the pub is family-friendly.

SBBC makes very "to-style" beers and the restaurant offers some classic brewpub options like pizza, burgers, and salads. Make sure to order the pulled pork nachos—they are great. The sweet chili glaze, queso, cilantro, avocado, and barbecue-infused pork really hits the spot and goes nicely with a darker beer or the red ale. If you aren't sure which beer to get, you can order a flight, and they also have a few guest beers on tap as well. The surrounding area is very walkable, so stop in for lunch after walking the streets of Santa Barbara.

Beer Bars & Bottle Shops

BARRELHOUSE 101

545 E. Thompson Blvd., Ventura, CA 93001; (805) 643-0906; barrelhouse101.com; @barrelhouse101

Draft Beers: 101 taps plus beer engine and root beer **Bottled/Canned Beers:** Focused on draft, but will have bottles soon

Barrelhouse 101 is a premier gastropub stop for any beer enthusiast or beer lover. They have an incredible lineup of craft beer with 101 taps that are expertly maintained, and what's more, it's right off the freeway if you are just aiming for a pit stop. Looking at the list might be a bit daunting, but the staff is there to help you. The owner, Joby M. Yoby, is hands-on; you'll often see him walking around, and he may just sit down with you and talk beer. The food at Barrelhouse is solid. Burgers are made with quality ingredients and are, for lack of a better word, huge. Try the salmon burger if you are in the mood for fish, but if you are looking for spicy, turn your attention to the hot wings. The Barrelhouse 101 hot wings are some of the best around town, and with several flavors—BBQ, Buffalo, Spicy, Blazing Hot—you can choose your heat. Blazing Hot is very, very hot; however, if it doesn't do it for you, you can sign a waiver and take the ghost pepper wing challenge, but be warned, you may not survive.

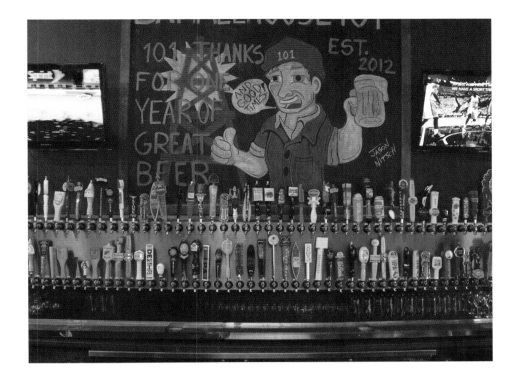

DRAUGHTS RESTAURANT AND BAR

398 N. Moorpark Rd., Thousand Oaks, CA 91360; (805) 777-7883; draughtsrestaurant.com; @draughtsrb
Draft Beers: 31 beers on tap **Bottled/Canned Beers:** 5-10 domestic and craft

Located in a strip mall near a grocery store, Draughts has been around for 10 years. It's in an odd spot for a craft beer bar, but is one of the only places in Moorpark that offers revolving craft taps. In addition to the craft options, they have some domestics and a full bar. Events are regular.

Draughts recently went through a facelift and rebranding to attract a hip crowd. Catering to college-age kids and craft beer drinkers alike, Draughts houses 31 taps with 7 house beers, contracted via Firestone Walker. Pizza, sandwiches, and a slew of other pub food dot the expansive menu. Their specialty, though, is pizza. It's an open space with nothing too fancy sticking out. The bar is to the right as you walk in, and booths and dining tables fill up a majority of the room. There is a large chalkboard over the kitchen detailing beer specials and news. Draughts is family- and group-friendly and gets moderately busy around dinnertime.

The Valley & Northwest LA County

BREWERIES

1. Malibu Sundowner Brewery

BREWPUBS

2. The LAB Brewing Co
3. Ladyface Ale Companie—Alehouse & Brasserie
4. Wolf Creek Restaurant & Brewing Company

BEER BARS & BOTTLE SHOPS

5. Tony's Darts Away
6. Vendome Liquor

Angeles National Forest

Rock Peak Park

Happy Camp Canyon Park

Burbank

North Hollywood

Magnolia Blvd.

Calabasas

Agora Hills

Westlake Village

Santa Monica Mountains National Recreation Area

N

0   3   6 miles

The Valley & Northwest LA County

The Valley isn't host to any breweries yet, but there are a few in planning and opening soon. Northwest LA County's Augora Hills and West Lake Village area, however, have a couple really great brewpubs and a cool nanobrewery set inside a wine shop. There are plenty of places to eat great food and enjoy amazing local craft beer. In this chapter we'll focus more on the beer bars that are pushing craft and educating the public about great local beer.

Breweries

MALIBU SUNDOWNER BREWERY

30961 Agoura Rd., Westlake Village, CA 91361; (818) 597-9463; malibusundowner.com/
the-brewery; @MalibuSundowner
Founded: 2012 (Brewery) **Founder:** Wades Wines, Wade Schlosser; Sundowner Brewery,
Alyssa Schlosser **Brewer:** Todd Slater **Flagship Beer:** Blonde, 30K and 31K IPA **Year-
round Beers:** Constantly changing **Seasonals/Special Releases:** Constantly **Tours:**
Yes—limited; call for availability **Taproom:** Yes

What the heck is a wine bottle shop doing in the brewery section? Well, in addition to the impressive collection of wine, whiskeys, other spirits, and bottled craft beer, Wades Wines is host to an ambitious wine and beer tasting room—oh, and they also have a nanobrewery. Founded by Wade Schlosser, Wades Wines has been a popular bottle shop for well over 10 years. They expanded into spirits and eventually craft beer, and the popularity of the latter led them to opening a taproom with over 100 taps. They also have a wine-tasting room with 42 taps, so if you are traveling with a wine aficionado, you can park them there while you enjoy the beer. The bottle portion of the store is organized and clean, and the taproom portions are warm and rustic with reconditioned wine-crate wood making up the walls.

Sundowner Brewery was started by Wade's daughter, Alyssa Schlosser. With the help of brewmaster Todd Slater, they create a constant lineup of nanobrewery-style

Sailor
Style: Belgian Stout
ABV: 5.7%
Availability: Extremely limited

As mentioned above, the beers here are extremely limited. I was able to order a flight of the six beers they had on tap, but those will most definitely be different from the six you'll order when you visit. The star of the flight was a beer called Sailor, a Belgian-style stout. At the height of the IPA and

double IPA craze, it's great to see other innovative beers pop up. Belgian-style dark beers are always very complex, and a Belgian-style stout occurs very seldom. Malibu's version is a light-bodied version with a very light mouthfeel. There is a nice balance between the Belgian yeast esters and roasted malt character, and at 5.7% you can enjoy more than one. This is one of those beers you can easily give someone who states that they "don't like dark beers" and I'm sure they will be pleasantly surprised. Toasted bread, floral notes, honey, and citrus dominate this beer.

beer. The brewery is tiny, making 55 gallons at a time, but multiple fermentors allow them to have around six beers on tap on any given day. They don't have traditional flagship, year-round, or seasonal beers, so expect to be pleasantly surprised each time you visit. There are often food trucks outside to help you get some grub in your belly before or after a tasting, and Sundowner also offers some charcuterie-style plates.

Sundowner Brewery is a great example of the individuality and inspiration that comes with the craft beer boom. Not everyone wants to open a large-scale manufacturing facility or brewpub, and for Sundowner it's a passion project. If you happen to visit, try the **31K IPA** (though it may be 32, 33, 34, or 40K by that time) as well as the **Jupiter Belgian IPA.** Growlers are available, and you'll likely also be tempted to taste some of the other great beers (or wines) that they have on tap.

Brewpubs

THE LAB BREWING CO

30105 Agoura Rd., Agoura Hills, CA 91301; (818) 735-0091; labbrewingco.com;
@LABBrewing
Founded: 2011 **Cofounder:** Roger Bott **Brewer:** Roger "Dr. Hops" Bott **Flagship Beer:**
Bad Influence IPA **Year-round Beers:** Bad Influence IPA, Big Ass Red, Schwarz Schaf
Schwarzbier, Honey I'm Home Blonde, Hop Solution, Take Her Home Tripel **Seasonals/**
Special Releases: Imperial Hoppy Hefeweizen, Cold Fusion Java Porter, After Midnight
Moo, Dunk in The Trunk **Tours:** Yes—limited; call for availability

The LAB Brewing Co is fairly new to the Agoura Hills area, having opened in late
2011. Brewmaster Roger Bott is a home brewer gone pro and has an impressive
science background, which helped him earn the nickname "Dr. Hops." The science
theme can be seen throughout the lab, from beer names to menu items to the iconic

Beer Lover's Pick

Schwarz Schaf Schwarzbier
Style: Schwarzbier—German Black Lager
ABV: 5.2%
Availability: Year-round
An iconic German style that many beer
drinkers are not widely familiar with, the
Schwarzbier German black lagers are quaffable with a medium alcohol level. This
is true for Schwarz Schaf as well, which
clocks in at 5.2% ABV. It's a simple,
clean, forward roasted lager. The yeast
profile is low, and there is slight bitterness from the hops in combination with
roasted malts. This falls more in line with
an American-style black lager, as the hop

presence is less subdued—so I would say this is classic German beer with a dose of
America.

DNA helix tap handles adorning the bar. The 15 BBL brewhouse can be seen next to the bar area of the restaurant, and there are four large copper fermentation tanks located in the dining area. The vibe is that of a hip gastro club. On weekend nights the lights are low and the music is loud, but during the day it's low-key and relaxed.

Food is definitely a major strength of the brewpub. Pizza, burgers, salads, large cuts of meat, and gourmet sides all feature. Try the white bean hummus with roasted kale, bacon-date Brussels sprouts, or the french fries with blue cheese and habanero. Tasty and filling. The dining experience is good with quick, knowledgeable servers, but as the music gets louder, it's a bit hard to hear your neighbor without yelling. It's fun, though, if you're looking for a night out.

The beers are standard brewpub fare: quaffable, low in alcohol, easily paired with food, and not too adventurous. It's definitely a place you can take the family for a birthday or special occasion. The **Java Porter** is a nice, nuanced style and the **After Midnight Moo Milk Stout** is an interesting style you don't see every day. Growlers are available for takeout, and tours can be arranged as long as you call ahead.

LADYFACE ALE COMPANIE—ALEHOUSE & BRASSERIE

29281 Agoura Rd., Agoura Hills, CA 91301; (818) 477-4566; ladyfaceale.com; @LadyfaceAle
Founded: 2010 **Proprietor:** Cyrena Nouzile **Brewer:** David Griffiths **Flagship Beer:** Blind Ambition **Year-round Beers:** La Blonde, La Grisette, Blind Ambition, Dérailleur Bière de Garde, Trois Filles Tripel, Ladyface IPA, Chesebro IPA, Picture City Porter **Seasonals/Special Releases:** Palo Camado XPA, Blue-Belly Barley Wine, Truth or Dare Strong Ale **Tours:** Yes—limited; call for availability **Taproom:** Yes

Proprietor Cyrena Nouzile opened Ladyface Ale Companie in 2010 in the rustic community of Agoura Hills. Cyrena started out as a home brewer and focused mostly on Belgian styles. She's a member of the Maltose Falcons, a home brew club located in Woodland Hills, and she has since become one of the most well-known local beer advocates for women and craft beer in the greater LA area. She works hand-in-hand with Brewmaster David Griffiths, who started dreaming of a Ladyface brewery after several years of professional brewing at BJ's Brewhouse. Together, they create quality and inspired beers which tend to be focused on the Belgian variety, but hop-focused beers are also present. The brewery portion produced 850 BBLs in 2013, with distribution across the most of the greater Los Angeles area. The brasserie portion of Ladyface, also managed by Cyrena, focuses on Euro-inspired gastro fare.

Blind Ambition
Style: Belgian Abbey Amber
ABV: 8.0%
Availability: Year-round

Let's start this off by saying that I love saisons, and Ladyface's 5.6% La Grisette farmhouse ale is fantastic. That being said, Blind Ambition is a beautiful beer and needs to be high-lighted. This award-winning Belgian abbey–style amber is rich and complex. The Belgian yeast dominates the copper-colored ale. A nice off-white head complements the overall visual appeal of the beer, but the complex dark fruitiness will keep you going back sip by sip. At 8.0% it is relatively higher in alcohol, so it's best to enjoy this one slowly, and you can easily pair it with your meal, be it burger or *moules-frites*. This Belgian-style ale is the real deal.

Ladyface Ale Companie is a beautifully rustic location set next to Ladyface Mountain in Agoura Hills. The view is splendid and the setting is perfect for a hot summer day brunch or early dinner. The menu, by Executive Chef Adrian Gioia, is diverse with a focus on gourmet brasserie-style offerings. If you are looking for a great pairing, order the *moules-frites* (mussels in ale sauce with fries) with **La Grisette** farmhouse ale or **La Blonde.** The vibe is upscale gastropub, but it's also family-friendly. The bar is a beautiful horseshoe shape at which I would recommend sitting. It puts you intimately close to the taps, bartender, and serving tanks, which is a really cool experience. The 7 BBL brewery is not visible from the restaurant, but you can see it through the hallway that leads to the restrooms. Serving and fermentation tanks are located next to the bar—they are shiny and pretty. Events are frequent at Ladyface and well worth the trip out. Cyrena also heads up a ladies' beer gathering monthly, which often includes a hike up Ladyface Mountain and a picnic. This comes highly recommended to all females interested in beer, as both

Cyrena and Ting from Eagle Rock Brewery are highly involved in the women's beer scene in the greater LA area.

Ladyface beers are globally inspired, often using local ingredients, international spices, and traditional brewing techniques. **La Grisette,** a Grisette farmhouse ale, is a light, spritzy, and flavorful Belgian with a dry finish. It pairs nicely with fish and most lighter items on the menu. Ladyface also has a really nice Bière de Garde called **Dérailleur,** which pours a deep golden brown with a nice caramel maltiness and spicy yeast notes. Dave likes to put a West Coast spin on traditional ale recipes and techniques from around the globe. Although they focus primarily on Belgians, their IPAs are also popular, so if you are a hop head, make sure to try the **Ladyface, Chesebro,** or **Cataclysm IPAs.** Each one is different and will provide you with a great tasting side by side if you order them in a flight. You can pick up a growler for takeaway, but there aren't any prepackaged bottles available yet.

WOLF CREEK RESTAURANT & BREWING COMPANY
26787 Agoura Rd., Calabasas, CA 91302; (818) 880-6300; wolfcreekbrewingco.com; @wolfcreekbrew
Founded: 1997 **Founder:** Rob and Laina McFerren **Brewer:** Rob McFerren **Flagship Beer:** Golden Eagle Ale **Year-round Beers:** Little Red Ryeding Hood, Big Bear Brown Ale, Desperado I.P.A., Midnight Howl I.P.A., Surfin' Monk's Triple, Don't Tread Red, Dogtown Dunkelweizen, Golden Eagle Ale, Howlin' Hefeweizen **Seasonals/Special Releases:** Hopdazed Imperial I.P.A., Alpha Wolf India Pale Ale, Irish Red Ale, Mountain Hawk Red Ale, Punkinweizen, Werewolf Harvest Ale, Timber Wolf Bourbon-Oaked Red Ale, Wild Angels Dubbel Trubbel, Winter Wonderland Ale, Wolf Dog Amber Ale, Wolf Pack Pale Ale, Yellowstone Wolf Pale Ale. **Tours:** No

Wolf Creek Brewing Company, located in Calabasas, near Agoura Hills, is a brewpub featuring a full-size catalogue of rotating beers along with a gastro/comfort-food menu. Founded by Rob and Laina McFerren, Wolf Creek first opened in Santa Clarita, where the original brewpub system is, back in 1997. Since then Wolf Creek opened a second location in Calabasas, and due to the popularity of both locations, a third has been opened in Valencia. The Valencia location is actually the site of the new manufacturing brewery, which opened in mid-2013.

The first thing you'll notice is the Alaska/Pacific Northwest theme. Wolf Creek has a rustic interior utilizing a lot of wood and a giant copper brew kettle. The kettle is display-only and is imprinted with their signature wolf footprint logo. The space has a cool vibe and is unlike most Southern California gastropubs and breweries. The building has a huge glass front, which make the space seem very open. They also have a large outdoor patio in the back. The bar is in the back of the restaurant,

Golden Eagle Ale
Style: Blonde Ale
ABV: 4.5%
Availability: Year-round
Golden Eagle is a highly traditional blonde ale that doubles
as their flagship. It clocks in at
a sessionable 4.5% and has a
relatively low bitterness at 20
IBUs. Golden Eagle is very light
in every regard, from its malt
character to its bitterness to its body. It pours with a thick white head and has a
pilsner/Kölsch light-grain nose to it. The fruit esters are relatively high, but are balanced at the same time with the overall feel of the beer. Golden Eagle Ale is one of
the first beers to make it out through wide distribution and is starting to appear on
taps in LA-area bars. Pair this beer with pizza, a fish sandwich, or Mexican food. Its
light breadiness makes it go well with many dishes.

and several booths and high-top tables are available for mixed seating. The menu
is pretty solid, and if you can't decide what to get, go for the pizza, the mac and
cheese, or the pesto brie crostini.

Wolf Creek is a '90s-style brewpub rebranded for modern times. They have a
range of classic styles, which are brewed traditionally without too much deviation.
The tasting flight is a great place to start, and it'll give you a good idea of what
you want to continue with. Their most popular beer is **Golden Eagle Ale,** an award-
winning blonde ale. They recently won awards for their barrel-aged **Timber Wolf
Red Ale** as well as the **Big Bear Brown.** The focus of these beers is definitely to be
paired with food, so all offerings have an emphasis on approachability. In addition
to the beers they have on tap, they also have guest taps featuring other local brews.

Beer Bars & Bottle Shops

TONY'S DARTS AWAY

1710 W. Magnolia Blvd., Burbank, CA 91506; (818) 253-1710;
tonysda.com; @tonysda
Draft Beers: 38

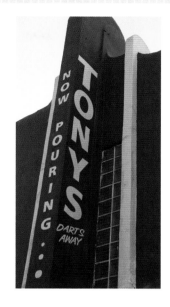

Part of the Mohawk Bend and Golden Road Brewing family, Tony's Darts Away was originally a well-known dive bar established in 1978 and reopened/rebranded by Tony and Amy Yanow in 2010. It's hard to miss with its large movie theater–style vertical sign and outdoor patio with Golden Road Brewing umbrellas. Inside you'll find a bar to the right that features 38 regularly rotating California-only taps including a few Golden Road mainstays. Tony's Darts Away is a low-waste facility so, in an effort to reduce packaging waste, you won't find any bottles or cans. Tony, a well-known Los Angeles restaurateur, is vegan, so although you can find meat dishes on the Tony's Darts Away menu, there is a wide selection of vegan and veggie options. Their specialty is sausages served on locally baked bread. Tony's has a local vibe to it and gets very busy during evening drinking hours. Be prepared to wait for a seat, as it's first come, first served. Tuesday nights feature a new brewery or beer style on tap, so come and get educated. Tony's is a great neighborhood craft beer bar and is definitely worth the drive.

VENDOME LIQUOR

10600 Riverside Dr., North Hollywood, CA 91602; (818) 766-9593; vendometolucalake
.com; @vendomeTL
Bottled/Canned Beers: 1,000+

Vendome Liquor may seem like a divey liquor store from the outside, but on the inside it's actually a high-end wine, spirits, and craft beer vendor. They keep most everything refrigerated, but there is also a large selection of international beers held at room temperature. To be extra helpful, Vendome displays both Ratebeer.com and BeerAdvocate.com scores next to certain beers. If you're a fan of community-rated beer geek sites, you'll definitely feel at home. Vendome offers everything from international to regional to local craft beers with a regularly rotating selection. They also keep some limited specialty releases in the back, which you can usually peruse if you ask nicely.

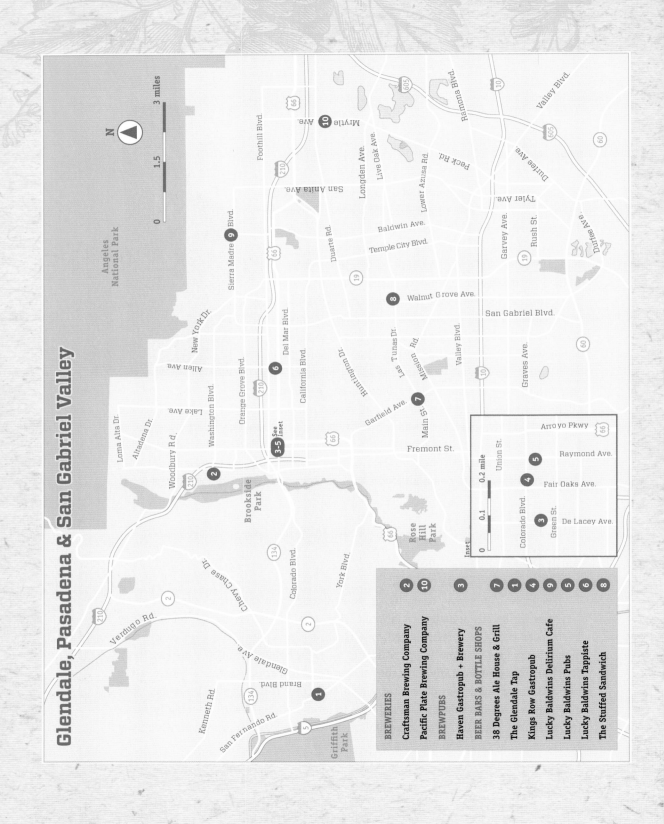

Glendale, Pasadena & San Gabriel Valley

N

0   1.5   3 miles

BREWERIES

2 Craftsman Brewing Company
10 Pacific Plate Brewing Company

BREWPUBS

3 Haven Gastropub + Brewery

BEER BARS & BOTTLE SHOPS

7 38 Degrees Ale House & Grill
1 The Glendale Tap
4 Kings Row Gastropub
9 Lucky Baldwins Delirium Cafe
5 Lucky Baldwins Pubs
6 Lucky Baldwins Tappiste
8 The Stuffed Sandwich

Inset

0   0.1   0.2 mile

Arroyo Pkwy
Raymond Ave.
Fair Oaks Ave.
De Lacey Ave.
Union St.
Colorado Blvd.
Green St.

Glendale, Pasadena & San Gabriel Valley

Pasadena, Glendale, and the San Gabriel Valley is a growing region of beer love, although most of the current beer growth is in Pasadena, which used to be the home of Crown City Brewing (now closed), a traditional-style brewpub. Pasadena is also the home to one of the oldest breweries in the Los Angeles area, Craftsman Brewing Company. With new beer-centric bars, brewpubs, and nanos popping up every day, and multiple breweries in planning, this area is ripe for the picking and has plenty of thirsty patrons waiting for more beer. Take time to enjoy Pasadena—it's a great, walkable town and is prime for a beer crawl.

Breweries

CRAFTSMAN BREWING COMPANY

Unlisted address; craftsmanbrewing.com
Founded: 1995 **Founder:** Mark Jilg **Brewer:** Mark Jilg, Todd Peterson, Patrick Curran, and Oscar Pleitez **Flagship Beer:** 1903 Lager **Year-round Beers:** 1903 Lager, Heavenly Hefeweizen, Poppyfields Pale Ale **Seasonals/Special Releases:** Triple White Sage, Old California Lager, Cabernale, Maximiliano House Beer, Angelino Weisse, Fireworks, Sour Grapes, Persimmon Sour, other specialty aged sours **Tours:** No—not open to the public **Taproom:** No; see Maximiliano listing

Not open to the public, Craftsman Brewing Company, the oldest active brewery in the greater Los Angeles area, is a production brewery in Pasadena. Although they do not offer tours, tastings, or drop-bys, Craftsman beers can be found all over LA. Mark Jilg, the founder and brewer and a former NASA JPL employee, opened the brewery in 1995 and is a true beer artisan. He takes exceptional care in the creation of all of his beers, making sure to release them only when he feels they are ready and living the mantra that "beer has an enormous possibility." Craftsman is known for its unique, traditional, and nontraditional styles and as such, continues to be one of the most influential breweries in Pasadena and Los Angeles.

The brewery itself, which houses a 15 BBL brewhouse, has been hand-constructed by Mark and his team. They also house an impressive barrel-aging room complete with oak Foudre tanks, which they use to age some of their more complex and interesting beers. Plans on the horizon are moving towards bottling in 375 ml corked Bordeaux wine bottles. There is a long waiting list of bars that want to serve Craftsman beers. Due to the limited availability of many of their special releases, bars are hand-selected to carry Mark's taps.

Craftman's flagship beer is their **1903 Lager,** which is an incredibly complex and enjoyable pre-Prohibition-style lager. The 1903 drives over half of Craftsman's sales and allows Mark and his team to also focus on other beer experimenting. **Cabernale** is another widely known beer, artfully blending the lines between wine and beer. It is dark, complex, has forward notes of red grape and dark fruits, and comes complete with lively carbonation. Mark and his team focus on tart beers like their **Angelino Weisse,** a 6.0% Weisse beer; more herb-centric beers like **Triple White Sage;** and the **House Beer** at Maximiliano, the unofficial tasting room of Craftsman beer. The House Beer, coined the "Pizza Beer," incorporates traditional Italian spices with a solid pre-Pro lager backbone and pairs incredibly well with the delicious Italian fare at Maximiliano. Craftsman beers are all unique, all worth trying, and should be enjoyed, savored, respected, and remembered.

1903 Lager
Style: Pre-Prohibition-Style Lager
ABV: 5.4%
Availability: Year-round

While Craftsman releases over 24 beers a year, 20 of them being specialty beers, 1903 has been their flagship and accounts for a majority of beer sold. The beer itself pours a crystal-clear straw color, with a thick and fluffy white head. The beer is spritzy with hints of lemon zest and a nice maltiness reminiscent of French bread. At 5.4%, 1903 Lager is a beer that is perfect for pairing with fish, salads, and warm Pasadena days. It also makes up the base beer in the famous Maximiliano House Beer, or "Pizza Beer" as it's lovingly called. The House version incorporates basil, oregano, and other provincial spices, which go incredibly well with Maximiliano's sourdough pizzas. The 1903 is a versatile beer and is one of the few well-made traditional lagers in the area. It's definitely worth seeking out.

PACIFIC PLATE BREWING COMPANY

1999 S. Myrtle Ave., Monrovia, CA 91016; (626) 239-8456; pacificplatebrewing.com; @Pacific_Plate
Founded: 2012 **Founder:** Stephen Kooshian, Jonathan Parada, and Steven Cardenas
Brewer: Stephen Kooshian, Jonathan Parada, and Steven Cardenas **Flagship Beer:** N/A
Small-Batch Special Releases: Mango IPA, Horchata Stout, Copa De Oro, Cardamom Ginger Saison, Widowmaker IPA **Tours:** Yes; call for availability **Taproom:** Yes

Founded by home-brewing friends Stephen Kooshian, Jonathan Parada, and Steven Cardenas, Pacific Plate Brewing is the first and only nanobrewery in Monrovia. The brewery officially opened its doors in August of 2013. Stephen and Jonathan used to work with each other at LegalZoom. Stephen was a home brewer

Mango IPA
Style: IPA with Fruit
ABV: 6.5%
Availability: Year-round

Pacific Plate Brewing Company's Mango IPA is one of their flagships and one that they hope to have on tap more regularly. As with everything else at Pacific Plate, the mangos are peeled and cut by hand, then blended to make the freshest mango puree possible. The mango is added to both the whirlpool

PHOTO COURTESY OF STEPHEN A. KOOSHIAN

and secondary, and the result is an intensely tropical aromatic beer with a complex citrusy hop profile. The malt backbone is subdued but definitely present, and notes of caramel and light toffee can be detected. The main feature is the fruit and hop synergy, though, which tastes amazingly fresh. It pours a golden amber with a thick white head, and makes a great start to a tasting flight.

at the time and got Jonathan into the hobby. They started brewing together regularly, and when they brought on biochemist Steve Cardenas, the trio decided it was time to turn their hobby into a career change. They do everything themselves, with generous support from friends and family, a fact they are proud of. From the construction of their taproom to the retrofitting of their fermentation tanks, it's all done by hand. Everything is done on a small scale and they are incredibly passionate, donating every second of their waking lives to the brewery.

The team operates a 1 BBL brewhouse with several 3 BBL fermentors in a small industrial building off Myrtle Avenue. They are about 3 miles from where the 210 and 605 cross and about a half mile away from the 210 off-ramp. There isn't much around except for heavy industrial buildings, residential areas, and a few small food places. Parking at the complex is limited, but there's plenty of space on the surrounding streets. The taproom is modest and nano, just like the brewery. A large mosaic of reclaimed wood makes up the backsplash for the tap feature, which will pour up to eight Pacific Plate Brewing Company beers. There is a standing area in front of the bar and a seating/congregation area to the right. The bar is hand-built, and the glowing Pacific Plate sign was water-cut by a friend in one of the neighboring business complexes. It's a fun space with chalkboard walls and a friendly vibe, and says "bootstrap grassroots" all the way.

Pacific Plate Brewing Company creates inspired beers with a focus on Latin flavors. The three friends all share Latin American roots, and they plan to make this a major part of their overall identity as a brewery. Their "27 hour" brewdays create everything from **Horchata Stout** to **Cardamom Ginger Saison.** They have a beer called **Copa De Oro,** which is a 6.5% Belgian golden ale with fresh coriander and orange zest. The beers are boutique, inspired, and constantly changing to keep up with their creativity. A crowd favorite is the **Widowmaker IPA,** a West Coast–style IPA with assertive hoppiness and a slightly sweet malt profile. Pacific Plate Brewing is very new and will likely have even more beer throughout 2014, which will be worth checking out. They offer pint glasses, merchandise, and growlers to go.

Brewpubs

HAVEN GASTROPUB + BREWERY

42 S. De Lacey Ave., Pasadena, CA 91105; (626) 768-9555; havengastropub.com; @HavenGastropub
Founded: 2012 **Founder:** Wil Dee, Greg Daniels, and Ace Patel **Brewer:** Brian Thorson
Flagship Beer: Simcoded **Year-round Beers:** Lenny G., O Face, Hops INC, Jimmy Hafen, Simcoded, Hefeweizen, P.E.D., More Please Kölsch **Seasonals/Special Releases:** Disco Pants, Double Hubble, More Hops **Tours:** No formal tours offered. Call for private tour availability. **Taproom:** Yes

The Haven Collective—Wil Dee, Greg Daniels, and Ace Patel—opened their first gastropub restaurant concept in Old Towne Orange under the same name. The Pasadena location incorporates a 10 BBL brewing system piloted by experienced Drake's brewer Brian Thorson. The menus at both locations are largely similar, with some small seasonal differences. A big focus is put on pork dishes and juicy gastro burgers. If you're adventurous and have a group of eight or more, you can even order a whole roasted suckling pig, provided you give them one-week notice. Food is a focal point for Haven, and the pairing of food with the excellent beers from brewer Brian cannot be understated.

Haven is a beautiful establishment capitalizing on redbrick walls, dark polished wood floors and bars, and wrought-iron chandeliers. The location has an interesting expansive layout, complete with a mirrored draft system in the center with a separate bar on each side. The restaurant has the capacity to entertain large groups and parties, while also catering to regular locals. It has a warm, rustic, and retro/modern feel to it that seems inspired by traditional European pubs. It's elevated dining, but friendly and casual as well.

Haven's Pasadena location has a full lineup of 40 craft beer and 8 wine taps. They are 100 percent craft-focused, so if you're looking for big macro lagers, definitely look elsewhere, or come over to the enlightened side and enjoy a phenomenal burger with local beer. Brian Thorson has focused his beer offerings at Haven on the pairing, sessionable, and balanced nature of craft. **More Please,** a dry, bready Kölsch-style ale, features Saaz hops, which give it a nice citrus element, and easily pairs with most menu items. **Disco Pants** is a black ale with Rauchbier smoke elements that complements some of the denser protein offerings. **Simcoded** is a

P.E.D. (Performance Enhancing Drink)
Style: Coffee Brown Ale
ABV: 4.5%
Availability: Year-round

Inspired by baseball, Performance Enhancing Drink, or P.E.D., is a creamy light-brown copper ale with a cold coffee infusion added. The coffee roast is dominant in the nose and overall flavor of the beer, but the head—and make sure you get a pour with a proper ½ to 1 inch—adds a silky creaminess. The coffee comes from Portola Coffee Lab, one of the most

respected coffee roasters in California. Brian does a cold press of this South American roast and adds it to secondary. The result is a rich, caffeinated pleasure bomb that can be consumed morning, noon, and night. Definitely a great pairing with dessert, this beer also goes surprisingly well with the house Haven Burger.

sessionable pale ale that predominantly features one hop, Simcoe, while emphasizing the drinkable nature of the pale. It's not overly bitter, but has an amazing floral bouquet and balanced middle. These beers will undoubtedly keep evolving and are all worth trying, especially alongside rich food.

Beer Bars & Bottle Shops

38 DEGREES ALE HOUSE & GRILL
100 W. Main St., Alhambra, CA 91801; (626) 282-2038; 38degreesalhambra.com;
@38degrees_LA
Draft Beers: 38 taps plus 1 cask **Bottled/Canned Beers:** 200+ bottles

Opened in June 2009 by cofounders Clay Harding, Brian Sugita, Chuck Fata, and Mike Fata, 38 Degrees Ale House & Grill is a craft beer oasis in the city of Alhambra. Named for the iconic "perfect beer serving temperature," 38 Degrees offers 38 taps and 1 cask. Although a relatively new craft beer restaurant, Clay's family has been part of the Los Angeles craft beer movement for some time, his father being part of the famous Crown City Brewery in Pasadena that eventually closed in 2008. Like Blue Palms, Verdugo Bar, City Tavern, and Beer Belly, 38 Degrees is one of LA's greatest beer bars and should definitely be on the top of the list. Clay is a huge craft beer advocate in Los Angeles and is an outspoken supporter of local breweries and beer bloggers.

38 Degrees is located on W. Main Street, in Alhambra's hopping restaurant and bar district. It's hard to miss—just look for the massive sign over the front door. Inside you'll find large communal bar tables on the left, the long bar in the center, and a more formal dining experience to your right. The space can easily accommodate any group size, and Clay often holds special keg tappings, brewery tap takeovers, and craft-focused events. Choose from any one of the 38 craft-only taps and sample some of the best beers around. If rare beer is your thing, get ready to choose from over 200 of the rarest. As for food, try the cider mussels, tuna niçoise salad, Menage o' Pork burger, and chocolate stout mousse, local favorites. Everything on the menu is good, and the vibe is perfect for enjoying some of the best beers LA has to offer.

THE GLENDALE TAP
4227 San Fernando Rd., Glendale, CA 91204; (818) 241-4227; @GlendaleTap
Draft Beers: 52 **Bottled/Canned Beers:** 24–30 (six-packs and large-format bottles available to go)

Opened in October 2012 by craft beer fanatics Steve Skorupa and Glyn Samuel, the Glendale Tap, or "GT," houses 52 hand-selected craft taps and 24 to 30 assorted craft bottles. The location used to house a notorious dive bar that saw bikers, brawlers, and the occasional drive-by. Today the tap, after a very impressive facelift, resembles a '50s vintage motor garage complete with antique beer cans (one of Steve's hobbies), pool tables, and lots of cool automobile and motorcycle

paraphernalia from both Steve's and Glyn's collections. It's a hip place to drink and draws a mixed crowd of both young and older beer enthusiasts.

The Glendale Tap is located on San Fernando Road almost exactly halfway between Eagle Rock Brewery and Golden Road Brewing, which makes it a great stop going to or coming from either of those spots. They do a cask night every third Thursday of the month, and they sell six-packs to go. If you're feeling hungry, giant deli-style pickles, locally made empanadas, and Bavarian-style pretzels can be purchased. Another claim to fame, a unique twist on the fizzy yellow stuff, is the presence of Miller High Life on tap, and it's served on nitro. The Glendale Tap is a great beer bar and definitely worth visiting if you are touring the area. There are even rumors of Steve opening a nanobrewery next door.

KINGS ROW GASTROPUB
20 E. Colorado Blvd., Pasadena, CA 91103; (626) 793-3010; kingsrowpub.com; @KingsRowPub
Draft Beers: 24 craft taps plus 2 casks **Bottled/Canned Beers:** 10+

Kings Row Gastropub is just a short walk down the alley from Lucky Baldwins, but you can also enter through the small entrance on W. Colorado Boulevard. This elevated Euro-style gastropub is relatively new, having opened in 2011. The space has high ceilings, a beautiful bar to the left, a large and open eating area to the right, and an outdoor patio. The place is actually two units connected, so there is a lot of room. The main bar showcases some 16 taps with the addition of 2 casks, and the side area has an additional 8 taps. Pinball machines, mini shuffleboard, high tables, brickwork, and an overall industrial feel give Kings Row a very modern feel. It's pretty cool.

The thematic element points to the European-style pub, but the menu is more Euro-American fusion and includes fried fare like Scotch eggs and gourmet burgers. Salads, mac and cheese, and a delicious tandoori chicken pizza are also available to share. Their 16 taps feature regularly rotating craft beer with mostly local offerings, but also offer beers like Epic and Baltimore Brewing. It's a friendly, casual vibe and a great place to meet with friends. They have regular beer events featuring local breweries and also have live music on weekends. There is an underground speakeasy-type gathering area with a flat-screen TV that is perfect for private parties and game watching. As with other modern gastropubs, like Haven, Kings Row fits right into the Old Town Pasadena feel. It's a slight walk, but you can also hit up the Stone Company Store and Congregation Ale House if you're so inclined.

Los Angeles Beer

The Los Angeles beer scene is experiencing incredible growth right now. Starting with the opening of Eagle Rock Brewery in 2010, there seems to be a new brewery, brewpub, or beer bar in planning every day. It's a great time to be a beer drinker in LA, and as the scene matures and acquires more fans, many people are beginning to worry about the market becoming saturated. A brewery bubble bursting is a hard thing to predict, but one thing's for certain: By the time you read this, there will likely be a few more breweries, brewpubs, and beer bars in the area. More breweries means more choices, better beer, and a more valuable beer culture. The more the merrier.

LUCKY BALDWINS PUB

17 S. Raymond Ave., Pasadena, CA 91105; (626) 795-0652; luckybaldwins.com; @luckybaldwins, @luckybaldwinsCA
Draft Beers: 63 Belgian craft taps **Bottled/Canned Beers:** 160+ assorted craft and Belgian

Lucky Baldwins Pub, which was opened in 1996 by David Farnworth and Peggy Simonian, is an international beer mecca in Pasadena. The original Old Town Pasadena location still exists in all its glory. David Farnworth passed away recently, but he leaves behind a legacy of not only craft beer but also international beer appreciation. His pubs prominently feature great English, Belgian, and European beers with the addition of regional and local craft. Their tagline "Think Globally . . . Drink Locally" about sums up the small pub chain's motto, and all three locations are frequented by locals and nonlocals alike.

The Lucky Baldwins pub in Old Town is an old-style English pub complete with a second-level mezzanine. International flags, massive Belgian beer bottles, the hum of a reveling crowd, and the smell of pub fare and years of happiness permeate the senses. There is a large outdoor patio for those that want to enjoy the beautiful Pasadena weather. Lucky Baldwins has been serving in Old Town since 1996 and has seen a lot of beer, many of them rarities before the craft beer boom. The second pub, called Delirium Cafe, is in Sierra Madre and opened in 2005. It's a smaller space, but also includes a bottle shop where patrons can buy large- and small-format bottles, English snacks, and beer merchandise. This spot has a more local feel to it and is frequented by people who live in the area. The third location to open, Trappiste, is on Colorado Boulevard, and it's a step up in terms of presentation. The newest of the pubs, it has a more modern look to it, but still has that Euro-pub charm. There is a Peet's Coffee tucked away in the back if you need caffeine.

Lucky Baldwins has a house beer called Lucky Baldwins Red Ale, which is a 7.0% semi-sweet Belgian red ale contract brewed by Van Steenberge. The tap list is different at each location, but the food menu is generally the same: English pub fare, fish-and-chips, meat pies, peas, and fried food. Trivia Nights are on Monday, Lucky Hours are weekdays from 4 to 6 p.m., and an annual Oktoberfest festival is held in August. Like other beer bars, they feature brewery tap takeovers, special tappings, and seasonal events. Lucky Baldwins in Old Town is a classic landmark in Pasadena, but the other pubs are also well worth the visit and are located nearby. An up to date tap list for all three locations can be found on their website and also TapHunter.com.

Other Lucky Baldwins Locations

Lucky Baldwins Trappiste, 1770 E. Colorado Blvd., Pasadena, CA 91106; (626) 844-0447. Founded: 2011; Draft Beers: 65 international craft, local craft, and imports; Bottled/Canned Beers: 100+

Lucky Baldwins Delirium Cafe, 21 Kersting Ct., Sierra Madre, CA 91024; (626) 355-1140. Founded: 2005; Draft Beers: 46 international craft, local craft, and imports; Bottled/Canned Beers: 100+

THE STUFFED SANDWICH

1145 E. Las Tunas Dr., San Gabriel, CA 91776; (626) 285-9161; stuffedsandwich.com
Draft Beers: 7 handles, primarily Craftsman Brewing Company **Bottled/Canned Beers:** 700+ assorted craft and vintage bottles

The Stuffed Sandwich is one of Los Angeles's original if not *the* original craft beer bar. The restaurant was opened in 1976 by beer lovers Sam and Marlene Samaniego. Sam, often referred to as "The Beer Nazi," is largely credited with bringing international beer to the greater Los Angeles area. He started at first with larger lagers, made his way into Belgian beers, and before too long had amassed an amazing collection of bottles, both small and large format. Sam has been called "The Beer Nazi" largely because he has taken it upon himself to tell people what to drink, not the other way around. He feels that educating people this way helps them expand their beer knowledge, and it's been working since 1976.

The Stuffed Sandwich is a small establishment located off E. Las Tunas Drive in San Gabriel. The shop is modest, with a kitchen in back, seating to the right, and beer coolers on the left. Bottles upon bottles overflow in every direction along with vintage beer glasses and merchandise. Specials can be viewed online on both their Facebook page and the main website. The Stuffed Sandwich offers deli-style food including, but not limited to, barbecued meat, stuffed spaghetti, stuffed meatballs, and stuffed sausage sandwiches. Think of it as deli comfort food. Due to recent health issues, Sam has been absent from the store lately. Loyal fans of the "The Beer Nazi" send well wishes and long for the return of the beer baron that helped usher in great beer for Los Angeles.

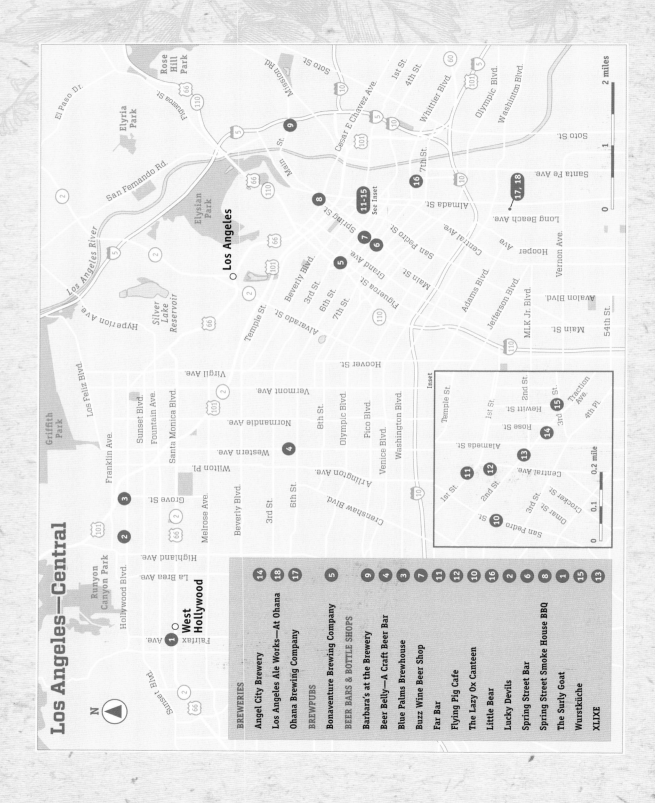

Los Angeles—Central

N

BREWERIES

14 Angel City Brewery
18 Los Angeles Ale Works—At Ohana
17 Ohana Brewing Company

BREWPUBS

5 Bonaventure Brewing Company

BEER BARS & BOTTLE SHOPS

9 Barbara's at the Brewery
4 Beer Belly—A Craft Beer Bar
3 Blue Palms Brewhouse
7 Buzz Wine Beer Shop
11 Far Bar
12 Flying Pig Cafe
10 The Lazy Ox Canteen
16 Little Bear
2 Lucky Devils
6 Spring Street Bar
8 Spring Street Smoke House BBQ
1 The Surly Goat
15 Wurstküche
13 XLIXE

Inset

See Inset

Los Angeles— Central

Downtown Los Angeles has seen a massive revitalization in the last five years. Areas like the old Pabst Brewery art colony and FIGat7th are poised to gentrify the once-bland city streets. Beer bars, speakeasies, gastropubs, food trucks, and now breweries are starting to crop up. And don't think that just because the Wolfgang Puck brewpub failed, LA doesn't like beer—that couldn't be further from the truth. The city is still warming up to the idea of beer manufacturing, and although Los Angeles is far behind the curve of most metropolitan areas when it comes to suds, efforts are being made and trails are being blazed that will make it easier for it to become the beer town it was destined to be.

Breweries

ANGEL CITY BREWERY

S216 S. Alameda St., Los Angeles, CA 90015; (213) 622-1261; angelcitybrewery.com; @AngelCityBeer

Founded: 1997; reopened in 2012 under new management **Founder:** Alan Newman **Brewer:** Dieter Foerstner **Flagship Beer:** Angeleno IPA **Year-round Beers:** Angeleno IPA, Eureka! Wit, Angel City Pilsner **Seasonals/Special Releases:** The French Sip, Angel City Amber, Belligerent Bloke, Berliner Weisse, Pomegranate Saison, Schwarzbier, All Night IPA, White Nite, Pickle Berliner Weisse, Avocado Kölsch **Tours:** Yes; Mon through Fri at 5 and 6 p.m., Sat and Sun at 1, 2, 3, and 4 p.m. **Taproom:** Yes

Angel City Brewery has a very interesting and event-filled history. The brewery, original called Angel City Brewing, was founded in 1997 by award-winning Pacific Gravity home brewer Michael Bowe. In 2004 the brewery expanded its operation and procured a 30 BBL German microbrewery, which it housed in its Alpine Village location until it relocated to downtown Los Angeles in 2010 in a historic

The French Sip
Style: Spiced Ale
ABV: 5.2%
Availability: Seasonal

The French Sip is described as an "au jus inspired ale brewed with black pepper, pink salt, rosemary, and seaweed" and honestly, that's exactly what it is. Before you turn your nose up and scoff it off as a gimmick beer, you need to try it. The French Sip is a very well-balanced spiced beer. The rosemary and black pepper are forward and dominate the taste, but at the same time, the malt profile shines through and everything rounds out into a very tasty package. Too many rosemary or old-style gruit beers overdo rosemary—it's easy to do. Sip isn't overdone and it's one of the most popular beers on tap; too bad it's only seasonal. The beer pours a ruby brown with an off-white head. It's a great beer to cook with, and using it as a braise for chicken or fish would be a delicious way to utilize the spice profile.

bridge cable factory. In 2012 Angel City Brewing was acquired by Boston Beer Company subsidiary Alchemy & Science, run by Magic Hat founders Alan Newman and Stacey Steinmetz, and was rebranded as Angel City Brewery. After a long wait and lots of red tape, the brewery has opened its doors with a new full lineup of beers, a stellar team of beer aficionados including Gordon Biersch brewer Dieter Foerstner and Sam Adams marketing guru Ashley Todd, and a locally focused attitude.

The building is located in the arts district, which is adjacent to Little Tokyo and trendy food stops such as Wurstküche and XLIXE. It's a huge building that used to be a steel cable manufacturing plant; the old cable slide is still visible on the ground floor. The taproom has been decorated in LA-style art deco, and there is generally a small to medium-size crowd. Group tours are available most days and private tours are available upon request, but like so many other breweries in the area, you can see most of the equipment from where you are drinking. There is ample seating and a variety of places to sit, be it at wooden beer-hall picnic tables, on leather stools at the bar, or at tables overlooking local art exhibits. There's definitely enough space at ACB for there to be a kitchen, eventually, but right now there is no food. If you're looking for a bite to eat, either bring food in or try one of the food trucks that are pulled up in front. There's always something different, and it's usually good.

Friendly bartenders will pour you a pint of flagship beers or whatever crazy taproom beer brewmaster Dieter has cooked up. Angel City Brewery focuses both on classic styles like **Eureka! Wit** and **Angeleno IPA,** and also very experimental food beers like the **Avocado Kölsch** and **Pickle Berliner Weisse.** There is an excess of creativity at the brewery, and it makes for a unique and exciting experience. **White Night** is a coffee-infused golden ale, which they cleverly refer to as a golden stout. **The French Sip,** a crowd favorite, is a gruit-inspired beer employing the use of rosemary and other savory spices, which makes it an incredible holiday beer as well as a great food-pairing and cooking beer. Most beer can be taken away in 64-ounce growlers, and there is a good chance that in 2014 bottles will be on their way. Angel City Brewery beer can be found at most local Los Angeles beer bars and gastropubs.

LOS ANGELES ALE WORKS—AT OHANA
Privately listed; losangelesaleworks.com; @LAAleworks
Founded: 2011 **Founder:** Kristofor (Kip) Barnes and John Rockwell **Brewer:** Kristofor (Kip) Barnes and John Rockwell **Flagship Beer:** Gams-Bart Roggenbier **Year-round Beers:** Gams-Bart Roggenbier **Seasonals/Special Releases:** Karma Kölsch, Lievre Saison, Dampfmaschine, Buttress of Windsor, Das Kölsch, Roggenbock, Mugen Kurozake **Tours:** Yes; call for availability **Taproom:** No formal tours offered. Call for private tour availability.

Los Angeles Ale Works is an up-and-coming brewery. Established in 2011, cofounders John Rockwell and Kip Barnes are currently contract-brewing out of Ohana Brewing Company's facility. Using Ohana's 7 BBL system, the team creates ultrasmall batches, which they distribute to local beer-focused bars and gastropubs. Their first beer, Gams-Bart, is a Bavarian-style Roggenbier, a rare style that is seeing a resurgence in today's growing craft beer market. Rockwell and Barnes are incredibly active in the Los Angeles craft beer scene and not only cover LA events on their site Bierkast.com, but also volunteer at and promote other local brewery events. You'll often find them pouring beer and hand-crafted sodas with other home brewers at local festivals and beer-release parties.

PHOTO COURTESY OF GEOFF KOWALCHUCK

Rockwell comes from a commercial real-estate finance background, and Barnes was a film and music major. Both graduated from the University of Southern California and met in the Trojan Marching Band. They launched a Kickstarter crowd-sourcing campaign in early 2013, which was incredibly successful. Exceeding their goal by 150 percent, it allowed them to purchase equipment to be used at the Ohana Brewing facility.

Los Angeles Ale Works focuses on both classic and eclectic styles. Their **Gams-Bart** is a no-frills "to-style" Bavarian Roggenbier, but **Karma Kölsch** is a classic German-style Kölsch with a Thai tea infusion added in secondary. They also have an award-winning **Kumquat Saison** in their lineup, with future plans to brew sake and nonalcoholic soda as well. Their focus is on creativity and supporting LA's home brewers, beer writers, and the growing beer scene. They are currently looking for a location of their own and will be fund-raising for their own manufacturing brewery in 2014.

Gams-Bart
Style: Bavarian Style Roggenbier
ABV: 5.2%
Availability: Limited year-round

Gams-Bart pours a dark-copper cloudy brown and most resembles a German Dunkelweizen, which is appropriate as they are closely related. Rye is the main focus in this beer, along with the outspoken Bavarian Hef yeast. You'll pick up notes of bubblegum, banana, and clove, but because the beer is fermented on the colder side, the clove dominates. Rich caramel and hints of charred brown toast balance out this beer's rye spiciness. All in all, Gams-Bart is like drinking a glass of rye bread, and it's both refreshing and hearty. Perfect for a cold day, but also refreshes in LA's warm weather.

OHANA BREWING COMPANY

1756 E. 23rd St., Los Angeles, CA 90058; (213) 748-2337; ohanabrew.com; @OhanaBrew
Founded: 2012 **Founder:** Andrew Luthi **Brewer:** Eric McLaughlin, Erick "Riggs" Villar, Robert Sanchez **Flagship Beer:** Ohana Pacific Pale **Year-round Beers:** Ohana Pacific Ale (a golden ale), Ohana Pale Ale, Ohana Makin' Moves IPA **Seasonals/Special Releases:** Rhino's Ruin (limited release), Rhino's Redemption (limited release), Grateful Hophead IPA, Surf Shack series (including a 100% Brett beer, Surf Shack Brett), Ohana Das Tart (Berliner Weisse with an authentic sour mash process), The Big Walowski (barrel-aged imperial stout), and a variety of sour beers **Tours:** Yes; call for availability **Taproom:** No

Founded by a 24-year-old craft beer enthusiast, Andrew Luthi, Ohana is the "fresh face in beer." Andrew is currently working two jobs to support himself and the brewery as it expands. They are steadily ramping up production, retrofitting the operation with new equipment, and planning new brews. Ohana Brewing has strong ties to the Long Beach home brew club and has housed local brewers Chip

Rhino's Redemption
Style: Imperial IPA
ABV: 8.5%
Availability: Limited release

Rhino's Redemption is Ohana's limited release sticky dank. It's an imperial IPA, named after a local LA beer celebrity, Alex "Rhino" Rebollo, who is a big, hoppy, craft beer teddy bear. Rhino Redemption has the West Coast hop profile down, but utilizes some lesser-known varietals including Apollo, Bravo, Calypso, and Warrior, which tend to be more popular with

home brewers than commercial giants. Their proximity to the creative home brew community translates very well into this beer, and the result is a well-balanced, medium-bodied, slightly malty DIPA. Letting the brew warm brings out more of the citrus elements, along with tropical fruit and notes of creamy toffee. I especially like that it's not cloying, which adds to the refreshment factor of this beer. It's a limited release in 16-ounce bottles only, so expect to see this beer or iterations of it yearly in small quantities.

Baker, Chris Walowski, Robert Sanchez, and Erick Villar. The brewery also has strong ties to retired BJ's brewers who act as silent mentors helping these brewers expand their brewing chops. The resulting beer is a harmonious combination of both classic and experimental style. Ohana continues to impress drinkers and expand their production capacity, and is even planning to open a tasting room and company store in Alhambra, where Andrew is from.

The brewery location is a heavy industrial warehouse district, and as such their current ABC license does not allow them to have a taproom, but this may change in the future. If you are able to call ahead and get a tour, you'll find a hodgepodge of immaculately clean used equipment, the most exciting of which is the old 7 BBL Craftsman Brewery brewhouse and mash tun. Ohana brews on a major piece of LA-area history, and was able to procure Craftsman's old system when it went on the market a couple years ago. As time goes on, Ohana will upgrade its facility and phase out certain equipment with newer models, but as it stands now, they are making great beer on what they already have.

Hops are the name of the game for Ohana with names like **Rhino's Ruin, Lupulin Shake, Live & Let Rye,** and **Ohana Noir,** but they also toil in styles like saison, Hef, amber, imperial stout, Brett sour, and ESB. They typically brew small 7 BBL experimental one-off batches, but do repeat some of the more popular offerings. Their main goal is to find out what sells well—what people like—and at the end of their first year, they'll assess the most popular style and establish their official flagships. It's an interesting and unconventional approach, but it's working for them and they frequently sell out of their beer a few hours after price posting. Ohana, an LA beer community team player, is also hosting up-and-coming brewery Los Angeles Ale Works and helping them brew their first beers.

Brewpubs

BONAVENTURE BREWING COMPANY

404 S. Figueroa St., Los Angeles, CA 90071; (213) 236-0802; bonaventurebrewing.com
Founded: 1996 **Founder:** David Lott and David Hansen **Brewer:** David Blackwell
Flagship Beer: Marathon **Year-round Beers:** BBC Pale Ale, Marathon, Strawberry
Blonde, Long Beach Crude **Seasonals/Special Releases:** Centennial **Tours:** No formal
tours offered. Call for private tour availability. **Taproom:** Yes

Bonaventure Brewing Company opened in 1996, and they are now the oldest operating brewpub within the city of Los Angeles. The brewpub is actually owned by the same team that runs Belmont Brewing Company, and they also share a brewer, Blackwell, who has been brewing for the two restaurants since April 1999. Bonaventure Brewing offers a full menu with easygoing pub starters like nachos and fries, and more aggressive entrees like the Grand Prix Burger and Chimichurri Steak. They also offer eight guest taps, ranging from domestic to local craft.

Beer Lover's Pick

Marathon
Style: Blonde
ABV: 4.8%
Availability: Year-round
Marathon is an incredibly refreshing light blonde. It resembles a hybrid blonde or Kölsch, which is fermented colder to keep esters down. It has a very light pilsner malt quality to it, with a subdued hop profile. It pours a golden clear, with a nice fluffy white

head. Marathon is dry and is the lightest beer on the menu. That being said, it's one of the more complex beers offered at Bonaventure Brewing. At 4.8% ABV, you can enjoy this crisp dry ale all day or all night long.

The Bonaventure hotel is one of the most iconic locations in Los Angeles. It can easily be seen from the 110 Freeway, with its telltale rounded elevator tubes. The brewery is located on the fourth floor in a sort of old-style hotel pub atmosphere. It seats a fair number of people and is a popular spot for events. There is an impressively large back patio where you can see the 10 BBL brewhouse encapsulated in a glass room. A larger event garden space to the far left is a popular spot for wedding receptions and upscale events. The entire space is open-air, looking out towards the LA city sky while surrounded by skyscrapers. It has a relaxed, classic, and more mature vibe, too.

Bonaventure Brewing Company, like its sister brewpub in Belmont Shore, brews a few straight-ahead classic-style beers, and they share some of the same beers as well. **Strawberry Blonde,** one of their flagship beers, is an intensely strawberry-forward blonde. It's light, sessionable, and has a wide appeal for those new to craft beer. The **BBC Pale Ale** is a light amber beer with a malty backbone. It pours a copper color and is balanced, subdued, and approachable. **Long Beach Crude** is their year-round stout. Like the other BBC beers, it's very approachable and pairs well with food. The best suggestion would be to order a tasting flight. You'll more than likely find one you really like, and then you can order a pint.

Beer Bars & Bottle Shops

BARBARA'S AT THE BREWERY

620 Moulton Ave., Los Angeles, CA 90031; (323) 221-9204; bwestcatering.com;
@BarbarasAtTheBrew
Draft Beers: 15 taps **Bottled/Canned Beers:** 20–30

Barbara's at the Brewery is one of downtown LA's hidden craft beer gems. The restaurant/pub is located at the old Pabst brewery turned artist colony. For the last 13 years, Barbara's has been serving food as an addendum to owner Barbara Huig's Barbara West Catering company. In 2011 Erik Huig took the restaurant over and worked on developing the craft beer portfolio. That being said, bar manager Mike Hane has been ensuring the presence of craft beer during his long tenure at the restaurant. Barbara's offers 15 rotating craft taps and an assortment of 20 to 30 bottles, which change frequently as well. It's one of the few places that consistently carry Craftsman Brewing beer, which says a lot as Craftsman owner Mark Jilg is incredibly particular about where and how his beer is served. Only a finite number of bars have his beers and keep his handles.

Barbara's is tucked deep into the brewery complex, surrounded by tall reconditioned brewery facilities. If you didn't know it was here, you would probably never find it. Parking is limited, but usually open. Walking into the restaurant, you'll notice the mixed seating, reconditioned metal pipe furniture, and art pieces decorating the walls and ceilings. It's an arts colony, and local artists frequent the bar. There really isn't anything within walking distance, so for some, this is *the* place for breakfast, lunch, and dinner. The restaurant portion offers a wide selection of food

Old Pabst Brewery

The artist colony at the old Pabst Blue Ribbon brewery was formed in 1982. Today it's home to one of the largest artist communities in the world. There are over 500 units in the sprawling Brewery Art Colony complex, all of them lofts. They are rented out as live/work spaces and are home to some of LA's most talented artists. There aren't a lot of options around the complex, so many residents frequent the Barbara's at the Brewery pub for sustenance and libation.

from seasonal veggies and hummus to meat loaf and burgers. The meat loaf is delicious, but also try the homemade chips and salsa. Although hidden, Barbara's is a great craft beer bar/pub and worth finding on your beer tour through LA.

BEER BELLY—A CRAFT BEER BAR
532 S. Western Ave., Los Angeles, CA 90020; (213) 387-2337; beerbellyla.com; @beerbelly_LA
Draft Beers: 12 rotating drafts, with an emphasis on hyper-local California craft
Bottled/Canned Beers: 50 assorted craft beer and soda bottles

Beer Belly is honestly named. This artistically graffitied Koreatown-based beer bar opened in 2011 and features regularly rotating California and US craft beer and an incredibly rich assortment of beer-inspired gourmet comfort food. Duck French Dip, house-made sausages, duck fat fries with duck confit, deep-fried Oreos with Nutella, quad-decker grilled cheese smothered in maple syrup, Jidori chicken hot wings—you can't go wrong. I would recommend going with a group, ordering

multiple items, and sharing. Everything on the menu is easily paired with the rotating craft beer offerings, and the menu itself is frequently changing. Most items on the menu incorporate beer as a reduction or basic ingredient. If you are looking for something on the healthier side, you can usually find Brussels sprouts or a spicy Devil's Caesar Salad.

Owner Jimmy Han tirelessly works to promote craft beer and has generated an amazing following of fans. His restaurant was recently featured on *Diners, Drive-Ins and Dives,* which prompted him to expand his small space, adding a front and back patio area outside. Expect large crowds and lines sometimes out the door. Frequent events, single-brewery tap takeovers called "One Night Stands," and charity events are the norm for this LA gem. One of Beer Belly's most popular events was called "Craft for Crap," where they traded pours of good craft beer for cans of crappy macro ones. Come thirsty, come hungry, and come early because this is one of *the* craft spots in LA!

BLUE PALMS BREWHOUSE

6124 Hollywood Blvd., Los Angeles, CA 90028; (323) 464-2337; bluepalmsbrewhouse.com; @BluePalms_Brew
Draft Beers: 24 specialty craft drafts plus 1 cask **Bottled/Canned Beers:** 100–120 assorted craft bottles

Located next to the Henry Fonda/Music Box theater, Blue Palms Brewhouse has been serving craft beer since 2008. With craft advocate Brian Lenzo, who originally worked at the theater, at the helm, the Hollywood gastropub serves a stellar mix of 24 specialty taps. The pub is on Hollywood Boulevard, a stone's throw away from the famous Hollywood strip, which can be seen from the restaurant, and is a block away from the Hollywood/Vine metro station. On the outside is their iconic blue neon sign depicting a oak barrel with palm trees in front. Once you pass through the door, you'll be greeted with warm lighting, a sort of LA art deco tiki vibe, and friendly staff. The bar is directly to the right, and mixed seating from high-top tables to bar stools to more normal dining tables can be found throughout the restaurant. Blue Palms is relatively small, but sees large crowds during its frequent craft beer events and from the concert venue next door.

Blue Palms offers great food. Their burger is very well known, and they also serve eclectic sausages and pub food. Friend and chef Gabe Gordon, who now runs Beachwood BBQ, helped Brian put together the original menu. Beer can be ordered in tasting-size portions or full pours, and with the regularly rotating craft taps, you'll have a lot to choose from. Brian also offers two Blue Palms house beers, a

Bavarian Hef and an IPA, both made by Firestone. Events are held often, from cask tappings to special meet-the-brewer nights to LA Beer Week events. They have an annual anniversary party that showcases some of the rarest beers around, and it always sells out early. If you a lover of hard-to-find beer, make sure you buy tickets. The pub almost shut down a few years ago, but thirsty Angelenos saved it from a premature demise. Now Blue Palms enjoys great crowds, and Brian is even working on plans to open his own brewery, which is slated for a 2014 release. Blue Palms Brewhouse is a great stop for craft beer enthusiasts and is one of LA's original craft beer bars.

BUZZ WINE BEER SHOP
460 S. Spring St., Los Angeles, CA 90013; (213) 622-2222; buzzwinebeershop.com; @BuzzWineBeer
Bottled/Canned Beers: Over 200 bottles
Draft Beers: 6 rotating craft taps

Buzz Wine Beer Shop is a pioneering concept in downtown Los Angeles. Located on S. Spring Street, it is an upscale bottle shop with a tasting room in the back. They have a large refrigerated bottle section towards the front of the space that they keep incredibly well stocked. With over 200 bottles to mull over, including beers from Germany, France, and Belgium along with national and local craft, Buzz a great choice for all your bottle needs.

The tasting area in the back is what makes Buzz shine. There are six rotating beers on tap and on most Friday nights they have a preset tasting flight special where patrons can sample new or classic bottle pours. You can drink bottles you have purchased in the store as well. Along with beer, there is also a wide selection of wines; in fact its about five times as large. Buzz Wine Beer is a great addition to downtown. Its modern, urban, high-end take on a beer and wine store makes it worth a repeat.

FAR BAR
347 E. First St., Los Angeles, CA 90012; (213) 617-9990; farbarla.com; @farbartweets
Draft Beers: 37 regularly rotating California and US craft taps **Bottled/Canned Beers:** 30–40 Japanese beers; 20–30 craft bottles

Deep in the heart of Little Tokyo at the site of the old Chop Suey restaurant and speakeasy is one of LA's best craft beer and sake stops, Far Bar. You can enter one of two ways: through the speakeasy brick alley or through the Chop Suey restaurant, a historic landmark. The restaurant is fairly large, with mixed seating and a long bar that runs the length of the space. Walking back to the speakeasy, you'll find an even smaller bar with more taps and an outside alley patio. The front Chop Suey restaurant still has the old private wooden booths from its original 1935 opening, where people then likely ate and smoked in peace. Today, as with most California establishments, smoking is not permitted. You won't find fedoras or Chop Suey, but you will find an advanced selection of whiskey, sake, and craft beer.

Headed by owner Don Tahara, Far Bar not only serves local craft beer, but is also home to one of the largest selections of imported Japanese craft beer in Southern California. Frequently holding events at both the back and front bars, they have whiskey and sake tastings. What are you waiting for? Order some fusion sushi, munch on garlic-wasabi fries, and then tie one on with a Japanese craft beer.

FLYING PIG CAFE
141 S. Central Ave., Los Angeles, CA 90012; (714) 234-5107; flyingpigcafela.com; @flyingpiginfo
Draft Beers: 6 taps **Bottled/Canned Beers:** 10 assorted import and craft bottles plus sake and soju

Before Flying Pig Cafe found its permanent home hawking pork belly buns on the streets of Little Tokyo, it was a mobile food truck serving the greater Los Angeles area. Chef Brandon Corby, who also ran the food truck, opened the Little Tokyo location in 2011 and opened its newest location in late 2013 at downtown LA's FIGat7th. The restaurant is small, modern, and quaint. It's easily accessible by walking from the Little Tokyo central plaza, and is right in the middle of the hustle and bustle on Central Avenue. You can't miss the giant rusted metal sign.

The Flying Pig offers a very limited and focused draft selection, with local beers as well as Asian imported offerings. You'll also find Vietnamese, Korean, Chinese, and Japanese beers by the bottle. These beers are offered to complement the Asian-fusion food served at the Flying Pig. The main attraction is the Chinese-style fluffy dough buns stuffed with huge pieces of pork belly. This was the most popular item on the food truck, and it translates well in the restaurant. You'll find everything from hoisin duck to lobster mac and cheese to *báhn mì* at the restaurant, and if you are still looking for the food truck experience, you'll find it operating on the streets of Venice on Abbot Kinney.

THE LAZY OX CANTEEN

241 S. San Pedro St., Los Angeles, CA 90012; (213) 626-5299; lazyoxcanteen.com; @lazyoxcanteen

Draft Beers: 12 rotating craft taps **Bottled/Canned Beers:** 12 craft and import bottles

The Lazy Ox Canteen is located in downtown Los Angeles's Little Tokyo district, close to Angel City Brewery, Flying Pig, Far Bar, and a slew of amazing Japanese food. The brainchild of LA restaurateur Michael Cardenas and renowned chefs Hiroyuki Fujita and Josef Centeno, the Lazy Ox offers great craft beer and upscale American gastropub fare with a global influence. Ingredients are local, seasonal, and organic whenever possible, with an added emphasis on craft drink as well. The menu is small and focused, a great sign of a restaurant that takes its food seriously. From Southern fried chicken and Kobe beef tongue to pan-seared mackerel and polenta, there is a wide assortment of meat and veggies to go around.

On tap you'll find an assortment of local California beers like Monkish, Telegraph, and Noble Ale Works, but you'll also find other craft beers like Epic, Avery, and Oskar Blues. The tap list rotates frequently, so check the website before you visit. They also have an assortment of international craft and domestic beers available.

The Lazy Ox Canteen is a boutique space. It's small and dimly lit, with dark reclaimed wood panels, an open kitchen, and a giant red neon ox sign. This is a great after-work hangout space and is perfect for relaxing with a house-made cocktail, craft beer, and some good grub. It's definitely a spot for long-term enjoyment, but would also be a great stopover during a Little Tokyo pub crawl. Everything around it is very walkable, and the Lazy Ox is worth walking to.

LITTLE BEAR

1855 Industrial St., Los Angeles, CA 90021; (213) 622-8100; littlebearla.com; @LittleBearLA

Draft Beers: 17 Belgian-style drafts **Bottled/Canned Beers:** 50–60 assorted Belgian craft bottles

This Belgian beer–only gastropub/beer bar is one of the highlights of the downtown Los Angeles craft beer scene. Little Bear, which was voted Beer Bar of the Year by *Imbibe Magazine,* is located right across the street from the well-known expensive restaurant Church and State. The location is industrial, literally, at the cross street of Mateo and Industrial in an area that has seen recent gentrification. The building houses a posh apartment building/condo complex overhead, and there is a place across the street called Urban Radish that has craft beer bottles.

Before it was converted into Little Bear in 2012 by owners Ryan Sweeney and Chef Andre Guerrero, it was a popular jazz bar called Royal Claytons. The inside space has remained about the same, with a number of aesthetic and cosmetic changes to enhance the overall appeal.

Little Bear is guarded by a bright red door with the Little Bear shield emblem to the right. Walking through the door, you'll find some steps and then a wide-open space. The bar is directly ahead, with mixed seating on the left and right. It's a very relaxed upscale-casual vibe, low lit, with soft music in the background. Little Bear focuses very specifically on Belgian-style beers, and those are the only ones you'll find pouring on the 17 rotating taps. They also have available some 50 Belgian bottled beers, some of them very rare. Ryan Sweeney is well known in the beer world and is able to get his hands on unique beers, some of which cannot be found anywhere else. One such beer is LambicX, a limited reserve beer brewed by Vanberg & Dewulf, which is only available at the most elite bars in the world. It comes with a hefty price tag, but is worth it. Little Bear also offers craft spirits and a full menu. Honestly, though, I would suggest going for one of their eclectic grilled cheese sandwiches or the ale-braised short ribs. Little Bear is an awesome beer bar—one of the best LA has to offer.

LUCKY DEVILS

6613 Hollywood Blvd., Los Angeles, CA 90028; (323) 465-8259; luckydevilsla.com; @luckydevilsinla
Draft Beers: 24 craft beers on tap **Bottled/Canned Beers:** 2 bottles plus 16 wines

Located on Hollywood Boulevard, among the theaters, costume shops, tattoo parlors, and tourist destinations, is this gastropub/craft beer bar destination. You wouldn't know it from its surroundings, but Lucky Devils is a serious contender in the craft beer bar scene. It's hard to miss with the giant smiling devil logo on the front of the building. The vibe is, for lack of a better word, red. With blood-red modern gothic walls, leather, dark wood, and open-air dining, it's a great place to visit before or after a Second City theater performance.

Offering a regular rotating craft lineup of 24 taps, which includes everything from Craftsman Brewing 1903 lager to Brouwerij West Mor Mor to Northcoast Old Rasputin, Lucky Devils has a wide selection of great beers to pair with food. One of their main draws is their Wagyu, American Kobe, 100 percent grass-fed beef burgers, but they also offer grilled cheeses, flatbread pizza, and artisanal salads. They prominently feature wines on Wednesday, burgers on Tuesday, and Randalled or cask beers on Thursday. Worth checking out if you're in Hollywood.

SPRING STREET BAR

626-B S. Spring Street, Los Angeles, CA 90014; (213) 622-5859; springstla.com; @SpringStBarLA
Draft Beers: 26 craft taps

Located between Sixth and Seventh Streets in the downtown Financial District, Spring Street Bar is a small neighborhood craft pub. It was opened in 2010 by founders Michael Leko and Wil Shamlian. They offer 26 craft taps focusing mostly on local beers, but have a number of non-California taps as well. Their selection rotates regularly and can be ordered in tasting flights if you can't decide. One thing to point out: They do not offer a watery adjunct lager. This was actually something they started out with but patrons shunned it, so now each of the 26 taps is all craft all the time. They also offer a small assortment of hot and cold deli-style sandwiches with an old-school "take a number" ticker on the back wall. Try the Cubano sandwich with something hoppy—the bartenders can definitely help you figure out the right pairing. They offer a full bar and excellent wine selection as well.

The space is small and narrow and fills up quickly after the work day, and there is a small outside patio in front. The crowd is mixed young business professionals and craft beer fans. Subway tiles, reclaimed wood, and square metal barstools give it a classic-meets-modern feel. It's a great place to enjoy an after-work happy hour and has a very warm vibe. The entire area is incredibly walkable as well, so if you go on a weekend early evening, you could grab dinner at one of the neighboring cafes or just do a little city touring before or after visiting Spring Street Bar.

SPRING STREET SMOKE HOUSE BBQ

640 N. Spring St., Los Angeles, CA 90012; (213) 626-0535; sssmokehouse.com; @springstreetbarbecue
Draft Beers: 7 mixed American and Euro craft taps **Bottled/Canned Beers:** 40–50 assorted craft bottles and domestics

Located on the edge of LA's Chinatown on Spring Street, Spring Street Smoke House BBQ focuses on meat with a hefty helping of craft beer. They have a small selection of rotating craft taps that includes everything from locally made Eagle Rock Brewery Solidarity to Germany's Weihenstephaner. What's more impressive is their bottled beer selection and its presentation. Behind the wall spanning the entire restaurant are craft beer bottles in 22- and 16-ounce formats, which also rotate. Barrel-Aged Old Rasputin, Bruery Saison Rue, Karl Strauss Mouette a Trois, Saison Dupont—these beers constantly change and offer a very interesting pairing for the smoked BBQ food.

The restaurant is on the smaller side and very kitschy. There is a medium-size bar to the left as you walk in and then long picnic tables, each with bread, barbecue sauce, and rolls of paper towels. The food here is very good, so make sure you order some of the chicken wings or "burnt ends." It's a great stop for lunch and/or dinner, but they close on the earlier side during the week, 10 p.m., so if you are going out late, you may want to plan ahead. Spring Street Smoke House also hosts sporadic beer-pairing dinners where they incorporate local beer in each dish. Definitely worth stopping by for one of these.

THE SURLY GOAT

7929 Santa Monica Blvd., West Hollywood, CA 90046; (323) 650-4628; surlygoat.com; @surlygoatbar
Draft Beers: 27 rotating craft taps plus 1 cask **Bottled/Canned Beers:** 50 bottles; many rare vintage or barrel-aged

The Surly Goat is the West Hollywood craft beer destination. Located on the eastern end of the LGBT West Hollywood scene, it's been pouring craft beer since 2010. Founded by Verdugo Bar and Little Bear craft beer powerhouse Ryan Sweeney, the bar showcases some 27 taps, 1 cask, and a full bar. The atmosphere is dark upper-echelon dive bar and includes two outside drinking patios and a dart

room. You won't find food at the Surly Goat, but you can order from the neighboring restaurant, and a few places will even deliver inside the bar.

The Surly Goat, like Verdugo Bar and Little Bear, showcases some of the best of the best that craft beer has to offer. Rare beer tastings and meet-the-brewer nights, along with other locally themed events, are the norm here. Parking is a bit of an issue with permit parking in the surrounding streets, but the valet accepts cars late into the night and both Fairfax and Santa Monica have many metered spots. Be sure to add this to your must-stop list, as the Surly Goat is one of the top beer bars in LA.

WURSTKÜCHE
800 E. Third St., Los Angeles, CA 90013; (213) 687-4444; wurstkuche.com; @wurstkuche
Draft Beers: 23 German and Belgian drafts plus 2 American **Bottled/Canned Beers:** 25–30 bottled Belgian/German/Euro beers and bottled sodas

Founded and owned by a USC alum, Wurstküche was one of the first new gentrified gastropubs to be added to downtown LA, more specifically Little Tokyo's restaurant repertoire. Specializing in traditional, gourmet, and eclectic sausages, Wurstküche showcases a simple menu, a refined beer tap list and bottle offerings, and a modern take on the German beer hall experience. Get ready to stand in an extremely long line whether you're in the original downtown location or at the new Venice location in West LA, but it's well worth it. Once you get to the front, you'll have the opportunity to order some very tasty German and Belgian draft beers and perhaps even a Rattlesnake & Rabbit sausage. They have one of the best German Berliner Weisses around, 1809, in bottle form, which pairs nicely with their truffle fries and pheasant sausage covered in sweet bell peppers.

The restaurant is located in Little Tokyo's arts district a stone's throw away from Angel City Brewery and across the street from Zip Fusion and Pie Hole. Their iconic cardinal-and-gold-striped warehouse doors are extremely hard to miss, and there is usually a line wrapping around the outside. The front of the restaurant where you order resembles a small upscale deli, while the back resembles a low-lit rustic German beer hall. Food can only be ordered at the front, but beer can be ordered at the seating area in the back. Long wooden tables with communal seating, paper tablecloths, a variety of mustards, and lots of beer make this a very fun and worthwhile stop while in downtown.

Weiland Brewery Restaurant— Now Closed

The streets of Little Tokyo are a little less happy now after the popular dive bar Weiland Brewery Restaurant closed in June of 2013. The restaurant served guests with happy hour from 5 to 7 p.m. and 10 p.m. to 2 a.m., which they referred to as a "reverse happy hour." Comfort foods like french fries, burgers, and fried cheese were the norm here, and the crowds were pretty rowdy. Weiland Brewery Restaurant didn't actually brew its own beer, but it did offer house brews contracted by InBev-purchased Redhook Brewery, which they sold at alarmingly low prices—$2 a pint during happy hour! It's sad to see a fun dive bar like this close, but its closing was forced due to LA Metro train line expansion plans. There are rumors of Weiland reopening in Long Beach; perhaps they will even brew their own beer or have it made locally, which would be an awesome plus.

XLIXE
432 E. Second St., Los Angeles, CA 90012; (213) 620-0513; xlixe.com; @xlixe
Draft Beers: 7 rotating taps **Bottled/Canned Beers:** 10–20 rotating larger-format craft bottles

With pizza by the slice or whole pie and beer by the bottle or draft, XLIXE, located in downtown LA's Little Tokyo, is the perfect place to start a Little Tokyo pub crawl with friends. The space is modest, with a front counter for ordering and a seating area in the back. The walls are adorned with craft beer–inspired idioms in scripted type face, and the whole vibe is neighborhood pizza parlor meets cafe. With a wide variety of pizzas to choose from, including Brazilian-style Portuguesa pizza, oxtail pizza, and even pork belly pizza, you'll be able to find something for everyone. Try the garlic knots, but make sure your significant other has one as well or else it'll be a lonely night.

XLIXE offers local beers on tap as well as a more diverse selection in bottles. Bottles are displayed on the wall with chalkboard descriptions, but nonalcoholic options like Mexican Coke and craft teas are also available for those who want to abstain. It's right across the street from Angel City Brewery, so you'll likely find their beer on draft. If it isn't, you can head over there before or after you grab a slice.

Pub Crawl

Downtown/Little Tokyo

Little Tokyo, aside from being one of the best places to experience Japanese food in LA, is also an incredible hot spot for craft beer. Many places offer fusion food, which pairs very well with the craft beer menu and is truly a unique experience. Little Tokyo is compact and incredibly walkable, with a ton of places a short distance from each other. The best place to park is actually at the city lot on the corner of First and S. San Pedro Streets, with evening parking being a flat $3. What's nice about this area is the sheer number of places that sell import and craft beer. The places suggested below can easily be expanded to include several others.

Far Bar, 347 E. First St., Los Angeles, CA 90012; farbarla.com. Far Bar, one of the most iconic restaurants in Little Tokyo, with it's brilliant neon Chop Suey sign, is a great place to start. Located on first street directly across from the Little Tokyo market plaza, Far Bar showcases two separate bar-type rooms: the restaurant in

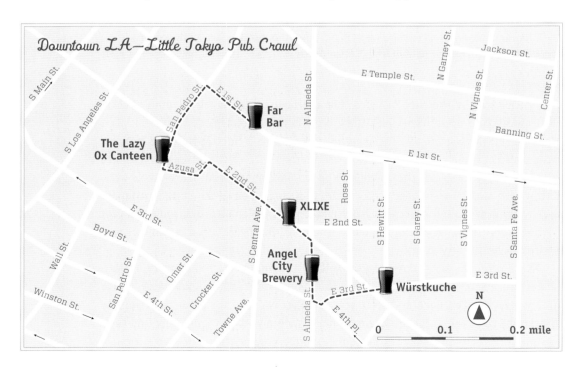

front and the speakeasy in back. The bar in front has plenty of seating including private dining booths, while the bar in the back is a little more compact. There is an outside patio as well, and a full menu of fusion Asian food is available. Far Bar offers 37 taps, about 40 Japanese import and craft beers, and 20 craft bottles.

The Lazy Ox Canteen is 0.2 miles down S. San Pedro Street southwest of Far Bar. Walk out of Far Bar towards S. San Pedro, turn left, and Lazy Ox is on the right side of the just right past Second Street.

The Lazy Ox Canteen, 241 S. San Pedro St., Los Angeles, CA 90012; lazyoxcanteen .com. The walk from Far Bar to Lazy Ox is about 4 minutes. It's located on the bottom floor of a condo building and is hard to miss with its flashy exterior. The gastrobar is a compact and intimate space with a small patio in front. They have a focused selection of 12 craft beers on draft along with a full menu including burgers, fried chicken, mackerel, and polenta. This is a great place to eat dinner or have a snack.

XLIXE is down Second Street about 5 minutes. Walk another 0.2 miles southeast on Second and you'll see XLIXE on the right-side.

XLIXE, 432 E. Second St., Los Angeles, CA 90012; xlixe.com. If your beer crawl group is more in the mood for pizza, make sure to save room for the awesome pies at XLIXE. They have a moderately sized craft beer program, including some large-format 22-ounce bottles displayed behind the counter on the wall, but also feature 7 rotating crafts on draft. Be sure to grab the garlic knots and order the oxtail pizza. Seating is modest in the back of the restaurant and can accommodate medium-size groups.

Luckily for you, Angel City Brewery is right across the street in the big industrial brick building. Take the safe route and use the crosswalk on Alameda. The entrance is on Traction Avenue. Look for a big black gate and an Angel City lighted sign.

Angel City Brewery, S216 S. Alameda St., Los Angeles, CA 90015; angelcitybrewery .com. Luckily for us, Little Tokyo is the location of one of LA's premier breweries, Angel City. It's located right across the street from XLIXE, so walk on over. The brewery has been under new management for the last few years, and because of it has seen tremendous success with rapidly developing beers. The space is absolutely beautiful, showcasing art exhibits, live music, and ample seating for everyone. Angel City has a few regular beers on tap along with lots of experiments. Try their White Nite in addition to their latest experimental beer. The flavored carbonated water is also a fun alternative to beer if you're looking for a break.

Wurstküche, is east of your location, about 3 minutes and 0.2 miles away. Follow Traction Avenue southeast and you'll see it on the corner of Third Street and Traction. You can enter the bar through the big wooden door or through the deli side on Traction through the cardinal-and-gold doors.

LA Craft Beer Crawl

Hosted by 213 and the Craft Beer Chicks, the LA Craft Beer Crawl (213night life.com/lacraftbeercrawl) is a new event happening every August. It's basically a beer fest on foot where guests pay an entrance fee ranging from $55 to $75 per day or $125 for a weekend pass. Patrons get a wristband, a glass, and a map and are able to visit bars throughout downtown Los Angeles. This event features a diverse mix of bars serving both craft and imports. Rare and exclusive beers are served with the $75 early-admission pass, and it's recommended that true purists and enthusiasts choose this option. This also helps keep you one step ahead of the crowd.

Transportation is available via public city methods, and it's easy to navigate when armed with the map. The venues and participants change each year, so there isn't a set guide. Be sure to check the website for an updated list of venues and beers.

Wurstküche, 800 E. Third St., Los Angeles, CA 90013; wurstkuche.com. The last stop on the list doesn't have to be the last stop, but for the purposes of this book, we'll end our crawl at Wurstküche. The line stretches out the front of the place near the cardinal-and-gold barn doors. If you aren't getting food, just go to the back beer hall. From Angel City, it's the first door you approach when you get to the building—the big wooden one on the corner. It leads to communal wooden tables, private booths, and a massive selection of German and Belgian draft beer. They have a large selection of bottles, too. Wait in line to get a sausage or just enjoy the beer.

Closing notes: This is a great crawl list of places that serve gastro fare and craft beer. That being said, Little Tokyo is well known for its amazing Japanese food and izakayas *(Japanese pubs). If you want to do a beer crawl featuring the Japanese side of things, it's incredible easy to do. Far Bar should definitely be on the list, with their massive selection of Japanese bottled beers, and Ebisu is also a great location for a traditional Japanese pub experience. Just walk around—everything, like in Japan, is incredibly close together and convenient.*

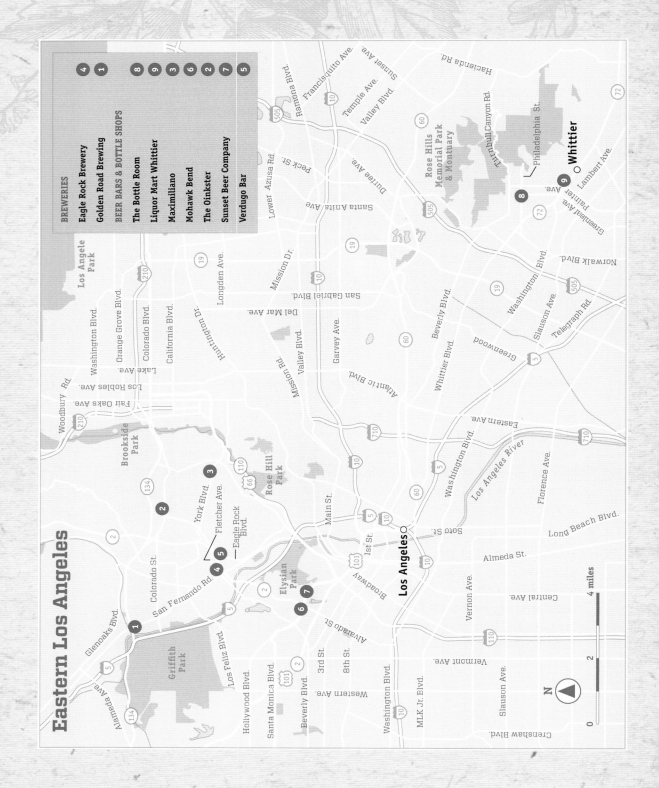

Eastern Los Angeles

BREWERIES

4 Eagle Rock Brewery
1 Golden Road Brewing

BEER BARS & BOTTLE SHOPS

8 The Bottle Room
9 Liquor Mart Whittier
3 Maximiliano
6 Mohawk Bend
2 The Oinkster
7 Sunset Beer Company
5 Verdugo Bar

Eastern Los Angeles

Eastern Los Angeles is home to vibrant hipster communities like Silver Lake, Los Feliz, and Echo Park. The gentrification bug has hit this part of the city hard and people are taking to the streets, expanding both their culinary and imbiber palates to become true epicureans. One of the first breweries to open since Prohibition, Eagle Rock Brewery blazed a path for the LA crowd and now Angelenos can't get enough beer. Culture-rich, dense, and rewarding, this area is also host to a slew of fantastic beer bars and one of the largest breweries in the LA area, Golden Road Brewing Company, which packages their tasty beers in 16-ounce cans.

Breweries

EAGLE ROCK BREWERY

3056 Roswell St., Los Angeles, CA 90065; (323) 257-7866; eaglerockbrewery.com; @EagleRockBrew

Founded: 2010 **Founder:** Jeremy Raub, Ting Su, and Steve Raub **Brewer:** Erick Garcia **Flagship Beer:** Solidarity Black Mild **Year-round Beers:** Solidarity, Manifesto, Revolution, Populist, Unionist **Seasonals/Special Releases:** Equinox, Stimulus, Yearling, Jubilee, Tarte Noir, Ginger Saison **Tours:** Yes; Sun at 1, 2:30, and 4 p.m. **Taproom:** Yes; Wed through Sat 4 to 10 p.m., Sun noon to 6 p.m. (closed Mon and Tues)

Eagle Rock Brewery was the first of the new wave of breweries to open up in LA post-Prohibition. Recently celebrating its third anniversary, co-owners Jeremy Raub, Ting Su, and Steve Raub opened ERB in 2010 to a bustling crowd of thirsty Angelenos, touting their motto "Beer for the People." Located in a small industrial area off the Glendale 2 Freeway, Eagle Rock aims to provide its local community with session-based beers. ERB is small-scale, but the people behind it have made a big impact on the LA beer scene. Jeremy comes from a postproduction sound background; Ting was a physical therapist; and Steve, Jeremy's dad, originally taught the team how to brew. Eagle Rock Brewery is a true brick-and-mortar family operation, and they're known far and wide as one of the most inspirational and supportive craft beer advocates in LA.

Eagle Rock's craft revolution theme can be seen on all their branding along with the signature orange E. The first thing you'll notice in the taproom, other than the orange glow, are the comical portraits on the wall behind the seating area. The taproom is separated from the 15 BBL brewhouse by double doors and etched glass. Seating is moderately limited, and small to medium-size crowds are common. On the third Wednesday of every month, co-owner Ting Su holds the ERB Women's Beer Forum, a beer session open only to women, aimed at creating an inviting, male-free beer-tasting environment. Some of the rarest beers around find their way to Ting's beer forum; it's a must for any interested lady. The brewery also holds educational classes aimed at expanding the public's beer knowledge, as well as regular trivia nights.

The Eagle Rock team works to create a wide array of tasty beers, but they started with the goal of creating session beers. Their most famous is **Solidarity Black Mild.** Once a year they hold a session beer festival, where they serve a wide selection of extremely creative low-ABV beers. This event is highly recommended, so make sure you make it a top priority. They also specialize in a hybrid WIT/saison beer called **Manifesto,** which has a very fruity floral aroma and a dry finish. For

Solidarity
Style: English Black Mild
ABV: 3.8%
Availability: Year-round
Eagle Rock has many beers, but their flagship, Solidarity, is noteworthy. Based on the English mild style, Solidarity is black as night. With a generous amount of roasted grains added, this beer looks like a stout, but drinks very light. Milds are light-bodied and are meant to be sessionable. Solidarity is no different. With notes of roasted coffee and toasted bread, and a slight chalkiness that dries out the tongue, it's frequently given to those who say they don't like dark beers to help them understand that not all "dark beers"

are the same. It's available year-round, is often poured on nitro, and can even be found in cask form with vanilla beans. It is great with ice cream—I prefer cappuccino or bourbon vanilla.

hoppier offerings, try **Populist,** their IPA, or **Revolution,** their XPA; both have big hop character and are packed with citrus flavor. Into the higher ABV styles, their third-anniversary beer, **Threes,** is an American strong ale and has been incredibly popular with the locals. Eagle Rock beers are incredibly creative and always varied. Their lineup of 22-ounce bottles has some of the most impressive labels in craft beer and should definitely be purchased if you see them in a Whole Foods. Growlers can be purchased on-site, and their beer is available in the greater LA area along with most of Southern California.

GOLDEN ROAD BREWING

5410 W. San Fernando Rd., Los Angeles, CA 90039; (213) 373-4677; goldenroad.la; @goldenroadbrew

Founded: 2011 **Founder:** Meg Gill and Tony Yanow **Brewer:** Jesse Houck **Flagship Beer:** Point the Way IPA **Year-round Beers:** Point the Way IPA, Golden Road Hefeweizen, Get Up Offa That Brown, Cabrillo Kölsch, Wolf Among Weeds, **Seasonals/ Special Releases:** Burning Bush IPA, Heal the Bay IPA, Almond Milk Stout, Aunt Sally's Pale Ale, Citrus Bend, Darts Away IPA, El Hefe Anejo, Emil's Special Beer, Golden Road Berliner Weisse, Hudson Porter, It's Not Always Sunny in LA, Schwartz Stout, The Big Le "Brah" Ski Stout, Summer Pale, Mildly Handsome, One Hundred & Two **Tours:** Yes; Fri through Sun at 1:30, 2:30, and 4 p.m., with special tastings for $10 after the 2:30 and 4 p.m. tours **Taproom:** Yes

Founded in 2011 by Tony Yanow and Meg Gill, Golden Road Brewing Company made a huge splash in the burgeoning LA beer scene when they opened their doors near Atwater Village in 2012. Tony, coming from a successful beer restaurant background, and Meg from Oskar Blues and Speakeasy Ales, assembled a dream team of LA beer enthusiasts to help them create a large regional LA-based brewery. With a strong marketing backdrop, distribution into local Whole Foods Markets, and the first 16-ounce cans in LA, Golden Road has been working to expand its young empire through Los Angeles and outward towards San Francisco and San Diego. Taps can be found all through Southern California, along with year-round cans of Point the Way IPA and Golden Road Hef.

Golden Road Brewing started off with a 15 BBL brewhouse but rapidly expanded and added a larger German 50 BBL system, catapulting their annual production to 25,000 BBLs. After installing several large 200–300 BBL fermentation tanks, they will be the largest craft beer manufacturer in the Los Angeles area, and probably will continue to be well into the future.

The location is broken out into three monochromatic buildings. The Blue building houses the brewery and production facility, the Red is cold storage and office space, and the Yellow building holds the pub. Behind the Golden Road pub is the multipurpose event space called Chloe's where industry events and private meetings are held. It's an über-cool spot, and if you can get back there to check it out, it's well worth it. The pub offers fare for vegans, vegetarians, and carnivores alike, sharing some similarities to Tony's other spots, Mohawk Bend and Tony's Darts Away. With a

Beer Lover's Pick

Wolf Among Weeds
Style: Double IPA
ABV: 8.0%
Availability: Year-round
Wolf Among Weeds, named for its featured ingredient hops, started out as a limited release custom IPA but was quickly adopted as a year-round beer due to its popularity. The 80 IBU double IPA clocks in at 8.0%, but drinks like a 6.0% beer. Galena, Warrior, Cascade, Zythos, and Simcoe hops give it an incredibly floral, citrus dankness indicative of West Coast

IPAs. Pouring a crystal-clear gold with a fluffy white head, Wolf has a sweet finish with a subtle nutty maltiness. It has a very impressive hop aroma, which is definitely why this beer is one of the top sellers, rivaled only by Point the Way.

large outdoor seating area, Aunt Sally game court, and ample inner dining room, it's a great place to hang out with hipster friends while enjoying draft and canned beer. It's also one of the only locations to get a formal brewery tour in LA.

Although GRB is large, it's still relatively new. The flagship beers started out with **Point the Way IPA** and **Golden Road Hefeweizen,** but the focus has been slightly shifted towards a new line of custom IPAs. After the resignation of original brewmaster Jon Carpenter and the hiring of Drake's head brewer, Jesse Houck, recipes have been retooled even further. From canned brown ales to tequila-aged Hefeweizens to coffee-infused milds, Golden Road is really coming into its own. The pub also shows its support of other local breweries like Eagle Rock by featuring a nice selection of guest beers on tap. Golden Road produces high-velocity session-based beers, with higher ABV IPAs released seasonally. Their crisp **Cabrillo Kölsch** is a summertime hit perfect for hot days, and their recent **Heal the Bay IPA** is a beautifully floral West Coast beer incorporating Citra, Centennial, and New Zealand hops. All beers are worth trying, so grab a tasting flight and then take a growler and some 16-ounce cans home.

Beer Bars & Bottle Shops

THE BOTTLE ROOM
6741 Greenleaf Ave., Whittier, CA 90601; (562) 696-8000; thebottleroombar.com;
@thebottleroom
Draft Beers: 24 rotating taps **Bottled/Canned Beers:** 80–100 bottles

Located in the heart of historic Whittier on Greenleaf Avenue, the Bottle Room is an East LA treasure. Offering an upscale craft dining experience with everything from local beer and wine to high-class gourmet food, it is a must-stop location. The restaurant was opened in 2009 by active firefighters Patrick Best and Brandon Ibrahim. They partnered with renowned chef Tony Alcazar to bring not only a full lineup of drinks they love, but also a menu that could support them. The restaurant is low-lit, modern, and relatively compact, with a medium noise level and low ambient music. There is a main bar in the center, seating on the side, and a small outdoor

patio. It's located directly across the street from the dive bar 6740 and next door to the Belgian beer bar Rusty Monk. There are other worthwhile landmarks nearby, including a '50s-style diner and craft bottle shop; it's all incredibly walkable.

The Bottle Room offers eclectic burgers and pizza, seasonal starters, and chalkboard specials. Be sure to try the Jidori Chicken Lollipops, generous with the meat, spicy, and very flavorful. The Chorizo Pizza, utilizing hard Spanish chorizo, is a great play on the classic salami pizza. Each item on the Seasonal Starters menu has a "pairs well with . . ." suggestion that will guide you to the perfect pairing. Twenty-four rotating craft brews can be ordered in flights, samplers, and in full glasses. The helpful staff are trained to know their beers, their food, and their pairings, so getting great advice is not a problem. Frequent craft beer events and pairing dinners are held and are a great showcase of both food and beer.

LIQUOR MART WHITTIER
13583 Whittier Blvd., Whittier, CA 90065; (562) 693-7731; liquormartwhittier.com; @Liquor_Mart_Whittier
Draft Beers: 250+ different beers in kegs
Bottled/Canned Beers: 3,500+ and a large selection of kegs for purchase

Liquor Mart Whittier was originally founded in 1976, and current owner Mario Valle Jr. bought the place in 2007. This is one the first locations to actively bring craft beer into East Los Angeles. Mario started carrying craft beer about 14 years ago and since then has amassed a rotating collection of some 3,500 bottles. The spot was actually a lounge and restaurant called XX Michel's before it was converted into a liquor store in 1976. Mario was a craft pioneer, and despite advice from macrobrewery distributors advising against carrying craft beer, Mario carried on and today is one of the largest suppliers of craft bottles in Whittier.

The shop is located off Whittier Boulevard slightly east of Painter Avenue. There's a small parking lot to the side, next to a FedEx Kinko's. Liquor Mart, with its massive retro-looking sign, is very hard to miss. The inside is modest and medium-size. Bottles are artfully displayed and separated by style and location. Mario utilizes the help of young craft beer enthusiast Damien Valdez, who runs the social media and helps order beer for the store. Custom bottle orders are not uncommon and are encouraged.

MAXIMILIANO

5930 York Blvd., Los Angeles, CA 90042; (323) 739-6125; maximilianohp.com; @Maximilianohp
Draft Beers: 7 handles, primarily Craftsman Brewing Company **Bottled/Canned Beers:** 8–10 assorted large- and small-format craft

Opened in 2011 by experienced and esteemed chef Andre Guerrero, Maximiliano is a tribute to traditional and well-made Italian food. In the beer realm it also serves as the unofficial tasting room of Craftsman Brewing Company, housing a full lineup of six or seven specialty Craftsman taps. Through one of those taps flows the famous House Beer, or "Pizza Beer" as many call it. It is an infused version of the Craftsman 1903 Lager spiked with Italian herbs and spices, whose light crispness and herbal bouquet easily lend itself as a pairing for anything on the menu. Chef Andre has an extensive career in the food industry, is the mind behind The Oinkster, and is a partner in the upscale beer bar Little Bear in downtown.

Maximiliano serves dinner starting at 5pm and weekend brunch starting at 10am. Their specialty is hand-crafted pizza made with dough that is fermented for

at least four days and baked in a 500-degree oven. The lower temperature reduces the burnt spots you'll find on other wood-fired pizzas. The Bianca-Verde and Deluxe are a great start. In addition to pies, you'll find an assortment of fresh handmade pastas including spaghetti and meatballs, as well as chicken Marsala and salmon piccata. As with any chef-driven restaurant, the menu changes seasonally and often, but quality is something you'll always find. On Monday nights they do a beer flight of five beers for $12, which is great if you want to try a few of Craftman's unique creations. Staff is knowledgeable about both beer and wine, so they'll be able to point you in the right direction for the perfect pairing—that is, if you didn't already order the "Pizza Beer."

MOHAWK BEND
2141 W. Sunset Blvd., Los Angeles, CA 90026; (213) 483-2337; mohawk.la; @mohawkla
Draft Beers: 72 rotating taps

Enter one of LA's premier vegan- and vegetarian-friendly craft gastropubs, Mohawk Bend. Opened in August of 2011, Mohawk Bend is the second restaurant concept from the mind of vegan craft beer baron Tony Yanow; the first was Tony's Darts Away. Tony is also well known in the City of Angels for his cofounding of the largest brewery in LA, Golden Road Brewing Company. Mohawk is unique in that it houses both vegan and non-vegan food prep areas, which means that if you're vegan, you don't need to worry about food contamination issues. Mohawk also focuses on using only locally sourced California ingredients, beers, wines, and spirits.

Located in Echo Park, it's hard to miss as it's housed in a repurposed theater complete with an outside marquee displaying the latest beer and food events. Mohawk Bend is posh inside, with outside, inside, and back dining room seating areas. It's decently lit, with long bars running on both sides of the restaurant. Speaking of events, Mohawk frequently holds beer-pairing dinners, pint nights, and craft beer educational classes, so if you're looking to increase your craft knowledge, this is a great place to frequent. If you're vegetarian or vegan, you'll love the food; if you aren't, you should definitely give it a whirl anyway. Their buffalo cauliflower is amazing, and their nachos and flatbreads make great companions to the multitude of beers served out of the 72 taps.

German Lions Are Red

Red Lion Tavern—Silver Lake; 2366 Glendale Blvd., Los Angeles, CA 90039; (323) 662-5337; redliontavern.net; @RedLionTavern

If you are in the Silver Lake area and are in the mood for traditional German fare, be sure to check out Red Lion Tavern. It's been a German Gasthaus since 1959, serving traditional German draft beer and amazing sausages and schnitzel. The Red Lion is a great spot with an authentic Old Country vibe. It can get pricey, but it's worth every Deutsche Mark.

THE OINKSTER

2005 Colorado Blvd., Eagle Rock, CA 90041; (323) 255-6465; theoinkster.com; @TheOinkster
Draft Beers: 3 taps

Opening in 2006 to wide acclaim, The Oinkster is Eagle Rock's premier slow-fast-food establishment, offering pulled pork, pastrami, shakes, and other comfort foods prepared in-house with love and care. The Oinkster is Chef Andre Guerrero's first stab at a non-fine-dining restaurant, and it's amazing. The whole concept of the place is to be quality-focused, which is why they only have three rotating taps. Getting on tap at The Oinkster says a lot about the brewery—since there are only a few taps, competition is pretty tough. It was one of the first restaurants to carry Eagle Rock Brewery when they first opened back in 2010. The building, on Colorado Boulevard, is pretty easy to spot, with its triangular roof and red and white paint. It's very retro, harkening back to a different era when hamburgers were served in places like this. The Oinkster has a large outdoor patio and mixed seating inside. Orders are taken at the counter like at a fast-food restaurant, but the interior has many gastropub elements, from polished wood tables to knowledgeable staff.

There are many things on the menu at The Oinkster to order. The house-cured pastrami is excellent, the BBQ pulled pork sandwich is tasty, and the Royale Burger is one of the best in LA. All of these should be paired with Belgian fries or plantains and an ube or taro shake. Even in this slow-fast-food spot, Andre's Filipino ancestry makes its way into the menu. The Oinkster has become well known for its craft focus and is highly respected within the craft beer community. Be sure to order one of the beers on tap; Smog City, Taps Fish House, Eagle Rock Brewery, and El Segundo Brewing are common options. A second location is due to open in Hollywood in early 2014, so stay tuned.

SUNSET BEER COMPANY

1498 W. Sunset Blvd., Los Angeles, CA 90026; (213) 481-2337; sunsetbeerco.com; @sunsetbeerco
Draft Beers: 12 taps **Bottled/Canned Beers:** 700+ bottles

Sunset Beer Company, like Select Beer in Redondo Beach and Bottlecraft in San Diego, is a high-end craft bottle shop with a tasting room attached. Located off Sunset Boulevard less than a mile away from popular craft beer bar and eatery Mohawk Bend, Sunset Beer Company is owned and operated by husband-and-wife team John Nugent and Jennifer Morgan along with Drew and Jenna Von Ah. The spot opened in 2011 in a small strip mall. It's tucked away in the corner and can be easy to miss. It was so popular in its first year that a pizza place opened next door to serve the large crowds. Parking is extremely difficult during peak drinking hours, but if it's early in the day or you are just running in, sometimes double parking is allowed. Many of the patrons of Sunset Beer Company are locals from the neighborhood, and it has a very Echo Park/Silver Lake hipster vibe to it.

The right half is the bottle shop showcasing more than 600 unique, limited, and rare craft beer bottles, while the left half is a tasting room complete with 12 taps. Patrons can either grab bottles and bring them over to the bar side to drink them, or order full pints off their 12 rotating draft lines. Food isn't offered, but it's commonplace to bring your own in and/or order it from LA Pizza Company next door. Mixed seating styles give Sunset Beer Company a fun and young vibe. With high-top tables, a large U-shaped wooden booth area, and an outside patio, there's a lot to choose from. They recently expanded their tap list to feature 12 beers instead of 6, and are also working to increase their in-house bottle count to offer over 1,000 bottles. Sunset Beer Company regularly features rare beers, events, and craft gatherings, so join their Facebook or Twitter to get in the know because you definitely don't want to miss this place.

VERDUGO BAR

3408 Verdugo Rd., Los Angeles, CA 90065; (323) 257-3408; verdugobar.com; @verdugobar
Draft Beers: 27 craft taps **Bottles/Canned Beers:** 60+ bottles

Known throughout Los Angeles as one of the most serious beer bars around, Verdugo Bar sits quietly on the back streets of Eagle Rock. The six-year-old establishment started in 2007 by beer aficionado Ryan Sweeney continues to be one of the most respected beer bars in town. The bar is hidden, having no indication out front other than a light vertical black-and-white sign that says COCKTAILS. Trust your GPS and you'll find it. The inside is dimly lit with an upscale decor. The long bar sits to the right, with a standing area and patent leather booths on the right. On the way to the incredibly large back patio, you'll find another room with euclidean light fixtures and more booths. Events are common, with DJs, craft tap takeovers, and gourmet food trucks. It's also been the site of the Eagle Rock Brewery anniversary party for the last two years (2012 and 2013).

Featuring some 27 craft-only taps, Verdugo also offers a full bar and 60 plus "to-go" bottles. Beers on the list must be approved by Ryan's critical palate. If the beer isn't good, you won't find it on tap. Ryan also owns the popular Surly Goat restaurant/bar in West Hollywood and is part-owner of the popular downtown bar Little Bear. Each establishment has a serious focus on beer and makes no exceptions for mediocrity. Ryan is heavily involved in LA's craft beer scene and is part of the planning committee for LA Beer Week. Verdugo Bar is an original LA craft beer establishment and a great stop for craft purists.

Western Los Angeles

BEER BARS & BOTTLE SHOPS

City Tavern	9
The Daily Pint	2
Father's Office—Santa Monica	1
Father's Office—Los Angeles	11
The Garage	8
Library Alehouse	3
Public School 310	10
Steingarten LA	7
The Tripel	5
Venice Ale House	4
Wally's Wine	6

PACIFIC OCEAN

Santa Monica ○

Culver City ○

Los Angeles ○

N

0   1   2 miles

Western Los Angeles

Western Los Angeles is home to Culver City, Santa Monica, and Beverly Hills. Breaking up LA into districts is the only way to talk about it, and West LA has a lot to talk about, whether it's the laid-back surf and beach vibes near the water or the developing nightlife scenes in cities a bit inland. West LA has plenty of places to enjoy craft beer, although it's currently devoid of breweries, but that is prepped to change, as there is a sizable list of breweries looking to take over the West Side, including Firestone Walker. If you like the beach and craft beer, look no further than Santa Monica. Places like Venice Ale House, Father's Office, and Library Alehouse will take your taste buds for a ride on the craft beer train.

Beer Bars & Bottle Shops

CITY TAVERN

9739 Culver Blvd., Culver City, CA 90232; (310) 838-9739; citytavernculvercity.com;
@CityTavernCC
Draft Beers: 22 California craft tap plus 3 tap tables **Bottled/Canned Beers:** 25–30
cans and bottles plus 4 generic

City Tavern is a premier California craft beer destination on the West Side. Their 22 drafts are devoted to California beers, and their tap tables sport three lines each that regularly feature local breweries, rotated monthly. City Tavern is located right next to Sony Pictures Entertainment in Culver City and has easily become one of the most recognizable craft beer destinations in West LA. Crowds range from moderate during the week to packed on the weekend. Frequent special events such as pint nights, beer-pairing dinners, and craft beer cocktails will keep you coming back. With their most recent addition to the event list, a monthly mystery beer night, they remove half of their tap handles, replace them with numbers, and urge guests to order randomly. It's a great education in tasting. Continued success of this young craft beer location has spawned the opening of a second location in downtown Los Angeles at FIGat7th, which greeted thirsty beer fans with fresh taps in December of 2013.

West Side Beer on the Rise

West Los Angeles is currently brewery-less, but Lynn Weaver of Three Weavers Brewing Co. aims to change that. Look for her brewery in 2014 serving signature "Umami Beer" near Playa del Rey. Firestone Walker is also building a satellite location in Venice, which will house both a pub and a small specialty experimental brewery.

There are also several other breweries looking at West LA's prime drinking real estate, some of which will be opening in 2014 and 2015. Be sure to keep your eyes open for brewery start-ups Pipe Dream Brewery, LA River Brewing Co, Bushido Brewery, and Los Angeles Ale Works to open on the west side within the next few years.

Coupled with an amazing draft list is an equally delicious lineup of upscale gastropub fare. Like the rotating draft lines behind the counter, the menu is also frequently adjusted to showcase seasonal ingredients. Get the short rib poutine if you're a meat lover or even the Brew Burger complete with pub cheese, a pretzel bun, and a beer-battered onion ring. For those who want to shy away from red

Cali Craft Tavern Expansion

The inspired team behind Culver City's City Tavern and Rush Street has opened a second City Tavern location in downtown Los Angeles at FIGat7th, and it includes the same great food options found at the Culver City location along with a few new ones. The restaurant is a California craft beer-centric gastropub featuring world-class beer and delicious food.

The group has also opened a new concept called Roadside Eats in Hollywood, which prominently features Southern flavors in a more casual format. Carolina pulled pork, tri-tip, barbecued chicken, Southern-concept sides, and a rotating list of craft and bottled beers are all available. It's an upscale pitstop dinner feel with a great location next to the Arclight Cinemas.

meat, there are usually plenty of salads to choose from, topped with options like burrata, stone fruit, shrimp, and duck confit. Sides such as bacon Brussels sprouts, Japanese yams, fried grits, and mac and cheese are also available. It's hard to go wrong with the menu, and the knowledgeable servers, who are all Certified Cicerone Beer Servers, can easily steer you in the right direction for a good pairing.

THE DAILY PINT

2310 Pico Blvd., Santa Monica, CA 90405; (310) 450-7631; thedailypint.net; @dailypint
Draft Beers: 33 taps plus 3 casks **Bottles/Canned Beers:** 100 bottles

The Daily Pint, located near the intersection of Pico and Cloverfield in Santa Monica, is celebrating over 25 successful years of flowing beer. Owned and operated by expat Phil McGovern, the Daily Pint serves a wide variety of imported, domestic, and international craft beer. Along with the awesome lineup of 33 rotating taps, they also have at least 3 casks on at all times. From Boddingtons to Stone to Dogfish to Duvel, they have it. The Daily Pint has been touted by many drinking magazines as one of the top 100 bars in the country, and for good reason. Not only does it serve a great assortment of craft beer, but it also includes a full bar and over 700 different whiskeys, which can be seen lined up on the back wall. Some of these whiskeys are incredibly rare and come with very steep price tags.

The Daily Pint is best described as old-style English pub, with the omission of food. Food trucks often pull up out front, but there is no food available to order inside. There's a pool table and standing area in the left-hand section of the pub,

along with more seating in back. The right half is dedicated to the large wooden bar, complete with whiskey bottles, beer signs, and hanging glasses. A large chalkboard displays all the current beers on tap and cask, but you can also find this list online. It gets crowded during peak drinking hours, so be prepared.

FATHER'S OFFICE—SANTA MONICA

1018 Montana Ave., Santa Monica, CA 90403; (310) 736-2224; fathersoffice.com; @fathersoffice
Draft Beers: 36 **Bottled/Canned Beers:** 30–40 rotating craft

The first Father's Office is located in Santa Monica and was originally open in the 1950s before it was reopened in 2000 by Sang Yoon. Sang was previously the chef at Michael's in Santa Monica before he bought the first Father's Office in SoCal to regularly feature beers from Anchor, Bear Republic, and Russian River. He is currently on the TV show *Top Chef Masters*. The Santa Monica location houses 36 hand-selected taps along the narrow bar in the back. The spot is long and narrow with decent lighting, and sees large crowds into the evening. It gets very, very crowded during drinking hours. Seating is rather limited and is first come, first served. Orders for food and beer are taken at the bar and then served at your seat.

Beer is serious here; most taps rotate, but some, like the Russian River taps, are constant when in stock. You'll find a mix of local and regional craft beer along with special featured beers listed on the chalkboard above the bar. The restaurant is well known for its burger, which is probably something you should order, but don't ask for ketchup. Father's Office takes its food very seriously and does not do substitutions or additions. Their motto is "F*** Off" but it's tongue in cheek. This is definitely one of the more classic craft beer destinations in the LA area and is a great destination for craft beer enthusiasts on the West Side.

FATHER'S OFFICE—LOS ANGELES

3229 Helms Ave., Los Angeles, CA 90034; (310) 736-2224; fathersoffice.com; @fathersoffice
Draft Beers: 36 unique mirrored taps to accommodate the extra-long bar (72 total)
Bottled/Canned Beers: 30–40 rotating craft

A few miles away from Santa Monica, adjacent to Culver City, is the second location of Sang Yoon's Father's Office, which opened in 2008 near the old Helms Bakery. The location is about three times the size of the original Santa Monica space and includes a long, narrow, outdoor seating area. The inside is also long and narrow, with small nooks and tables with stools along the entire length of the restaurant/bar. Despite its larger space, crowd size is still an issue, and finding seating Thursday through Saturday nights can be a waiting game, but well worth it. The vibe is upscale club craft with the same focus on the mainstay Russian River, Bear Republic, and Anchor beers. Staff members wear earpieces and dress in black like the Secret Service.

Father's Office has weekly specials that should definitely be considered. From beets to oysters, the food is gastro-eclectic. The signature burger and fries are crowd favorites, but there are many food items on the menu worth trying. The number of taps is 72, but it's actually the same 36 taps mirrored to accommodate the extra-long bar. Water is served from a fire hydrant–shaped tap, and Russian River's Pliny the Elder, for all those that seek it out on draft, is a regular plant. Although it's loud inside, you can get some pretty good pairing and beer advice from the servers and bartenders. They are trained well and are great reference points if you are undecided on what to order. As a brewery, it's considered a great honor to be featured on the Father's Office tap list.

THE GARAGE
3387 Motor Ave., Los Angeles, CA 90034; (310) 559-3400; garagemotorave.com; @garagemotorave
Draft Beers: 12 taps **Bottled/Canned Beers:** 20+ bottles

The Garage Motor Club was established in 2011 by Jamie Lyko and Jim Connors, but didn't open until late 2012. The spot was actually a well-known and notorious dive bar frequented by motorcycle gangs in Palms. Today, it's been revamped and modernized. Jamie was the former GM at South, a gastropub in Santa Monica, and Jim was the 10-year owner of the go-to Boston bar Sunny McLean's on the West Side. Together they've remodeled the restaurant and split it into halves: an upscale pub in the front with big-screen TVs and wooden booths, and a sort of retro '50s garage-style diner bar in the back. The diner area is where most people hang out, as the nicer pub space is frequently used for special events.

As you walk into The Garage, you'll notice a unique water feature displaying giant oil drums and beer taps pouring neon-green oil-colored water. If this doesn't set the scene for you, then maybe the retro-style arcade games and Ping-Pong tables will. They offer a "pretension-free" experience complete with burgers, wings, pizzas, and gourmet salads. The food here is still elevated, but is presented in a looser, more relaxed fashion. The Garage features a full bar and 12 taps. Not all of them are local, but most of them are staples, like Deschutes seasonals, Ballast Point Sculpin, and local favorites like Ohana Brewing Company. Happy hour, featuring select $3 drafts and $5 appetizers, happens every weekday from 4 to 7 p.m. The waitstaff is friendly, and the vibe is laid-back. Definitely a spot to hang out while watching the game or enjoying a trivia night.

LIBRARY ALEHOUSE

2911 Main St., Santa Monica, CA 90405; (310) 314-4855; libraryalehouse.com; @libraryalehouse
Draft Beers: 27 rotating taps, including 2 nitro handles **Bottles/Canned Beer:** 30–35 bottles

Located on Main Street in Santa Monica, not too far from the beach, is one of the West Side's most iconic craft gastropubs, Library Alehouse. Originally opened in 1995 by restaurant veteran Derek Chang and trained chef and culinary teacher Thomas Hugenberger, Library Alehouse has been a solid spot for upscale fare and craft beer for quite some time. It's also the home of Certified Cicerone and local beer celebrity Alex P. Davis, who joined the team in 2010. Today, Alex curates 27 hand-selected craft taps and an impressive lineup of rare rotating bottles to share, and sets up unique pairing events to showcase the wonders of proper beer and food combinations. Library Alehouse also offers a full list of curated wines.

Library Alehouse is made up to look like, well, a library, complete with prop books, librarian ladder, and bookshelves throughout the restaurant. Their front area includes a bar and several high-top bar tables, and there is also a sizable covered back patio area where guests can enjoy a more formal sit-down experience. It gets crowded in the evening hours, but never gets too loud. The restaurant offers fresh seasonal food ranging from oxtail poutine to a variety of salads, including, of course, burgers. The veggie burger is fantastic for anyone who appreciates fresh Cali-vegetarian fare. The beer list showcases local favorites like El Segundo's White Dog as well as craft beer staples like Allagash White. Beers change frequently as a matter of practice and for specific and regular events. The food and drink menus are made to go together, and the learned staff at Library Alehouse will help you choose the perfect pairing.

PUBLIC SCHOOL 310

9411 Culver Blvd., Culver City, CA 90232; (310) 558-0414; publicschool310.com; @PSonTap

Draft Beers: 10 rotating taps **Bottles/Canned Beer:** 8–10 bottles

Officially opened in December 2013, Public School 310 is the second restaurant in the Public School line of gastropubs, the first being Public School 612 downtown. The name, Public School, is a play on the word *pub,* which is short for *public house*. Founded by CEO Bob Spivak, of the Daily Grill and The Grill on the Alley, Public School has something for everyone, focusing on happy hours and upscale pub fare. Public School has an extensive bar offering cocktails and craft beers, along with a diverse selection of gastro and gourmet fare prepared by Executive Chef Phil Kastel. From peanut butter burgers to gourmet deviled eggs, the menu is creative and satisfying, and some of items, like the Dragoons Irish Stout Short Ribs, utilize beer as a main ingredient. The tap list showcases some 10 rotating drafts that focus on regional craft breweries, along with some international selections.

It's well lit inside, and as it occupies the same space as the late Fraiche restaurant, it can easily hold a good-size crowd. True to its namesake, the walls are adorned with microscopes, chalkboards, and school ephemera. Its menus resemble traditional composition-style notebooks, the cocktail napkins look like notebook paper, and happy hour is appropriately referred to as "recess." The theme works well inside and out. It gets very crowded during recess, so plan on getting there early, as this special service is only available in the designated front area. Although Public School 310 has ties to the other Public School locations, 612 and 805, each location has its own unique menu and draft list, which makes each Public School worth seeking out.

Class Started with 612

If you like Public School 310, make sure you check out their original downtown location, Public School 612, right next to the Daily Grill. Same atmosphere, but with a different menu and tap lineup. The third location, Public School 805, opened up in West Lake Village in 2013, and is showcasing a similar experience. Be on the lookout for more locations opening in the greater LA area.

STEINGARTEN LA

10543 W. Pico Blvd., Los Angeles, CA 90064; (310) 441-0441; steingartenla.com; @SteingartenLA
Draft Beers: 20 assorted craft beers **Bottled/Canned Beers:** 50–70 European and US craft bottles

Located on Pico Boulevard a few blocks from Westside Pavilion and Fox Studios, Steingarten LA has billed itself as Los Angeles's featured beer garden. The restaurant offers a mix of fusion gastro and traditional German food. They have a wide selection of sausages ranging from bratwurst to wild game, and also make an impressive lineup of burgers and sandwiches. The restaurant is very nice inside, with a dark wood and copper interior. It can seat medium-size groups in the main area and the full back patio, the Beer Garden, where they host regular beer events. Steingarten LA is a regular hangout for West LA's home brew club, Pacific Gravity.

Steingarten has a very impressive lineup of taps and bottles ranging from traditional Belgian and German beers to modern US and international craft beers. They have weekly events featuring local and regional brewers, special keg/cask tappings, and beer-pairing dinners. Prices are a bit higher at Steingarten LA, but it's definitely worth the visit. The staff is knowledgeable about the beer selection, so you'll be able to order the right beer for you along with the perfect pairing.

THE TRIPEL

333 Culver Blvd., Playa del Rey, CA 90293; (310) 821-0333; thetripel.com; @TheTripelLA
Draft Beers: 14 craft taps **Bottled/Canned Beers:** 30–40 assorted craft bottles and cans

Located in Playa del Rey, near the water and right off Culver Boulevard, is an incredibly hip, trendy gastropub called The Tripel. Opened in 2011, The Tripel is mostly known for "Top Chef" Brooke Williamson and husband, Nick Roberts. This

tiny eatery, seating 25 to 30 people, is host to 14 taps of fresh craft beer and a spread of "elevated" eclectic food. The Tripel does not take reservations, so your best bet is to go early or wait in line. The vibe is hip casual, complete with chalkboards, subway tiles, reclaimed wood walls, and obsidian tap handles. It's like a classy New York deli transplanted into a SoCal beach community.

The tap list is mixed craft with a regular rotation of whatever pairs best with the seasonal menu. One of the most popular menu items, The Tripel Burger, is made with duck confit, pork, and aged beef and topped with an apricot jam, which would pair perfectly with one of the hoppier beers on the menu. If you are feeling more adventurous, you may want to try some of the famous seafood on the menu, like the charred baby octopus. There are usually several light, spritzy Belgians like Allagash White on tap, which makes a perfect sidecar to crispy tentacles. You'll likely find lots to drool over at The Tripel.

Bottle Up Beverly Hills

Vendome Wine & Spirits, 9153 W Olympic Blvd., Beverly Hills, CA 90212, Vendome Wine & Spirits, located in Beverly Hills on Olympic and related to the Toluka Lake spot, is a great space for bottles. They have a huge selection of craft beer along with a full lineup of wine and spirits. Special beers are kept in back so be sure to ask if you are on a hunt for something rare or on seasonal special release.

VENICE ALE HOUSE
2 Rose Ave., Venice, CA 90291; (310) 314-8253; venicealehouse.com; @VeniceAleHouse
Draft Beers: 26 local craft

Venice Ale House is right on the beach. Located on the cross of Rose Avenue and Venice Beach's famous historical boardwalk, it is one of the few places you can enjoy amazing craft beer while watching the waves. Opened in 2010 by friends and Venice locals Tom Elliot and Spoon Singh, Venice Ale House remains a popular craft beer mecca years later. Long-term craft enthusiasts, both Tom and Spoon decided that Venice needed a gastropub that would not only focus on craft beer, but organic

craft food as well. The menu focuses on organics and ultra-local ingredients. Tacos, nachos, mussels, burgers, sandwiches, and brunch, there are hundreds of reasons to come and even more reasons to return.

The vibe is über-beach, modern, relaxed. Surfboard art, subway tiles, and locals, it's always busy and always friendly. Venice Ale House offers 26 constantly rotating local drafts. From Noble Ale Works to Brouwerij West to Venice Beach Ales, you'll have a lot to choose from, and if you can't decide, order a flight or ask for bartender's choice. It comes on a mini skateboard in four-, six-, and eight-taster flights. Venice Ale House also hosts the annual Beer, Art and Music (BAM) Fest in Santa Monica. This is definitely one stop you'll want to make if you are sightseeing, and it's only a stone's throw away from other great stops like Library Alehouse and Venice Beach Wines.

WALLY'S WINE

2107 Westwood Blvd., Los Angeles, CA 90025; (310) 475-0606; wallywine.com; @WallysWine

Bottled/Canned Beers: 600+

Wally's Wine was originally opened in 1968 by Steve Wallace. In 2013 it changed owners, but the high-quality experience remains unchanged. Wally's is located on Westwood Boulevard, not too far from UCLA, and is a mecca on the West Side for fine craft beer, spirits, and great wine. They carry over 10,000 wines, 600 different rotating craft beers, and a whole slew of rare spirits. Bottles are priced individually, allowing customers to mix and match as they please. Wally's is one of the few bottle shops that actively helps their customers pick out the perfect bottle. Don't know what to get? Ask beer manager Stephanie Jensen or manager Kathryn Haslam. They'll walk you through the lineup and help you find the perfect bottle.

Wally's offers monthly in-store tastings featuring beer from local and regional craft breweries and distributor portfolios. This is a great time not only to taste great beer, but also to learn about the people behind it. They also send out e-mail blasts to over 3,500 customers, notifying them of rare beer bottles and the latest inventory. If you're hungry, step into the next-door fromagerie. Wally's has its own cheese shop selling artisanal products and amazing sandwiches. Wally's is a true West Los Angeles gem and is one of the best bottle shops around.

Pub Crawl

West LA

West Los Angeles's Santa Monica/Venice area has a great collection of bars, restaurants, and sights to see. This crawl will take you from Santa Monica's main street to Venice Beach, and then drops you off at the second location of Wurstküche, downtown's famous German sausage restaurant. There are plenty of places not listed on this crawl to stop off at, including cafes, cocktail lounges, and boutique businesses.

Library Alehouse, 2911 Main St., Santa Monica, CA 90405; libraryalehouse.com. One of West LA's premier craft beer bars features elevated food and a curated selection of craft beer hand-selected by Cicerone Alex P. Davis. If you start here, make sure you try the food and utilize Alex's food-pairing suggestions. Library Alehouse features 29 craft taps that frequently rotate and often include many local beers. This is a great place not only to order beer, but also to find the perfect food pairing. Cicerone-trained staff are the perfect people to ask for options if you are unsure.

O'Brien's, the Irish pub, is short walk south down Main Street on the same side of the street.

O'Brien's Irish Pub & Restaurant, 2941 Main St., Santa Monica, CA 90405; obriens pub.com. A classic Irish pub and music venue, O'Brien's serves imports like Guinness and a few classic craft brands like Anchor and Lagunitas. It's not a craft beer bar, but it does showcase local live music, which makes it a great stop on this beer crawl. Depending on how your evening goes, you may want this to be the last place on your list, ending your night with a great band and beer in your hand. O'Brien's offers Irish/American pub fare.

Venice Ale House is about 0.4 mile away, and it'll take about 8 minutes to get there. You'll keep walking south on Main, turning right on Rose, which you'll follow to the beach.

Venice Ale House, 2 Rose Ave., Venice, CA 90291; venicealehouse.com. A short walk southwest towards the beach on Rose Avenue, Venice Ale House features 26 craft taps and a great organic menu. It's one of the few places you'll be able to drink craft beer while looking at the ocean. The Venice Beach boardwalk is a famous point of interest, so if you are sightseeing, you may want to walk around a bit. Seating is limited inside Venice Ale House, but there is a back patio. It's a fun crowd full of friendly locals.

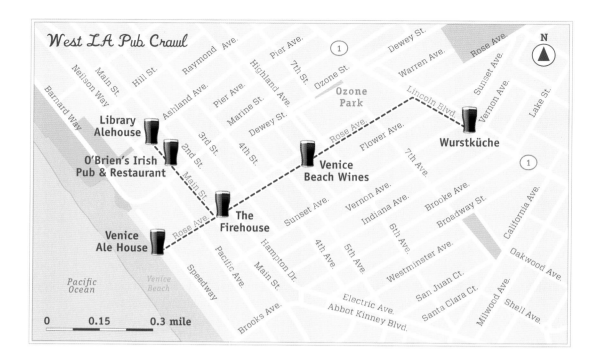

Time for a little backtrack. The Firehouse is on the corner of Rose and Main, and you can't miss its red paint.

The Firehouse, 213 Rose Ave., Venice, CA 90291; firehousevenice.com. The Firehouse is located on the corner of Rose and Main and is hard to miss because it's in a big red building. They have a 16-tap selection of domestic, import, and craft beers and a decent list of craft bottles. The building is broken up into the bar side, the outside patio, and restaurant inside. You'll see a bar and taps right inside from the Rose entrance and that's where you'll want to sit. The Firehouse features breakfast items, burgers, and also Japanese food. A strange combination, but on a pub crawl, this has just the diversity to satisfy everyone.

The route to Venice Beach Wines is a scenic walk through Venice/Santa Monica neighborhoods.

Venice Beach Wines, 529 Rose Ave., Venice, CA 90291; venicebeachwines.com. This place, as the name implies, focuses on wine, but it also has a curated three-handle craft beer menu, which ranges from Allagash to AleSmith. You'll want to come here for the vibe, the melty pots, and the tapas. It's a great place to hang out, and if you like it, you may want to revisit for the great wine selection. Venice Beach Wines enjoys an eclectic mix of people that live in the surrounding area: hipsters, beachgoers, and younger foodies. This is a great place to stop off for a beer and snack before you move on.

Your final destination lies ahead, just 0.6 mile away. It'll take you about 11 minutes to walk to Wurstküche, which will help you build up an appetite for the sausages and German/Belgian beers to come. Follow Rose east until you hit Lincoln and turn right. Wurstküche is a few short blocks away on the right-hand side.

Wurstküche, 625 Lincoln Blvd., Venice, CA 90291; wurstkuche.com. It's about a 10-minute walk to the next place, the modern German sausage kitchen Wurstküche. Wurstküche started in Downtown Los Angeles, and since its opening, its beer and eclectic sausage formula has been repeated all over Los Angeles. The restaurant has two locations: the original in Little Tokyo and the one in Venice Beach. It's hard to miss, with its vibrant cardinal-and-gold barn doors. Inside you'll find a deli-style counter where you can order alligator, buffalo, rattlesnake, and bratwurst sausages as well as a massive selection of Belgian and German draft beer. The communal beer hall seating is in the back along with the bar with draft and bottled beer.

South Bay & Long Beach

BREWERIES

13 Brouwerij West
11 The Dudes' Brewing Company
2 El Segundo Brewing Company
9 Monkish Brewery
10 Phantom Carriage—At Monkish
8 Smog City Brewing Company
6 Strand Brewing Company

BREWPUBS

14 Beachwood BBQ & Brewing
15 Belmont Brewing Company
3 The Brewery at Abigaile
7 Red Car Brewery & Restaurant

BEER BARS & BOTTLE SHOPS

12 The Factory Gastrobar
4 Naja's Place
1 Rock & Brews
5 Select Beer Store

South Bay & Long Beach

The South Bay, including El Segundo through Long Beach, has become a brewery hot spot in the last two years. Whether it's revitalized brewpubs like Abigaile or newly opened ones like Beachwood BBQ & Brewing, food and beer are definitely working together. Not only that, but production brewers Smog City, Monkish, Strand, and The Dudes' Brewing have made a sizable impact, making the South Bay a beer destination. It's possible to visit most locations in two days, but you would be wise to take your time, as these places deserve your attention.

Breweries

BROUWERIJ WEST

110 E. 22nd St., Warehouse No. 9, Port of Los Angeles, San Pedro, CA 90731;(310) 732-1270; brouwerijwest.com; @BrouwerijWest; email@brouwerijwest.com
Founded: 2010 **Founder:** Brian Mercer **Brewer:** Brian Mercer **Flagship Beer:** Dog Ate My Homework, My First Rodeo **Bottled and Draft Beers:** Blond, Saison Extra, Tripel, Mor Mor, Dog Ate My Homework, Dubbel, Brilliant but Lazy **Draft Only:** Invisible Ink, My First Rodeo **Tours:** Yes, by mid-2014 (check website) **Cafe and Taproom:** Yes, by mid-2014 (check website)

Brouwerij West was founded in 2010 by Brian Mercer. Starting his career as a professional photographer, he traveled the world, with significant time in Belgium. Longing to create a classic, true Belgian flavor in his beers, Brian started his own sugar company called Dark Candi, which imported high-end Belgian Candi syrup straight from the source. Brouwerij West is currently a contracted brand brewed in the gypsy style. In 2010 Brian released his first beer, contract-brewed with Bayhawk Ales. He then moved to Sudwerk in the Bay Area in 2011, and in 2012 moved to his most recent contract establishment, Hermitage, which both brews and packages large batches of Brouwerij West beer for distribution across the US and internationally.

By mid-2014 Brouwerij West will make its long-term home in a renovated WWII-era warehouse, located in the new LA Waterfront in San Pedro. The huge 7-acre complex includes an artisan food market and outdoor dining areas as well as Crafted, a marketplace featuring the works of 100 craft artists. Weighing in at approximately 26,000 square feet in this unique space, Brouwerij West will operate a 30 BBL brewhouse with fermentation space for 8,000 BBL and a bottling and canning line. A native son of San Pedro, it's a dream come true to build his brewery back home. Brian is well aware of the pitfalls, perils, and struggles of the traveling brewer, and will offer up some of his new space to enterprising brewers.

Brouwerij West beers have been met with wide acclaim since 2010. Brian is one of the most passionate brewers around, offering a full lineup of inspired Belgian beers. Aesthetic as well as flavor is very important to him: Each brew is packaged in a 500 ml bottle with a label showcasing amazing original artwork from one of his 34 freelance artists. **Mor Mor,** depicting two monsters holding hands, is a Belgian quad; it's simple, dry, slightly bitter, and powerful at 10.0%. Other beers like **Dog Ate My Homework,** a blackberry saison, are a little lighter, but showcase traditional Belgian yeast spiciness with a subtle tart fruitiness. **Brouwerij West** beers can be found widely throughout Southern California at bottle shops and craft beer bars.

Saison Extra
Style: Belgian Farmhouse Saison
ABV: 6.5%
Availability: Year-round

If you don't start with Blond, make sure you start with Saison Extra. This Belgian-style saison is brewed with a proprietary yeast and is not based on the well-known spicy/peppery versions of the style. The beer is slightly funky, pours a hazy golden straw, and is covered by a dense rocky head. The 500 ml

bottle is beautifully red, depicting a cat playing a pinball machine, with art by Jacob Rolfe. The beer clocks in at a sessionable 6.5% and is delightfully effervescent with a citrus hop aroma and notes of bubblegum. Saison Extra can be found in most SoCal bottle shops and Whole Foods, and on draft at beer bars.

When the production facility opens in mid-2014, more draft beers, bottles, and cans will be available.

THE DUDES' BREWING COMPANY

1840 W. 208th St., Torrance, CA 90501; (424) 271-2915; thedudesbrew.com; @thedudesbrew
Founded: 2013 **Founder:** Toby Humes, Jeff Parker, and Mike Holwick **Brewer:** Jeff Parker **Flagship Beer:** Double Trunk (DIPA), Grandma's Pecan (English-style brown ale) **Year-round Beers:** Double Trunk, Grandma's Pecan, Kolschtal Eddy (Kölsch style), Grinning Face Porter (coconut porter) **Seasonals/Special Releases:** Juicebox Series: Blood Orange Ale (spring), Raspberry Wheat, Prickly Pear IPA, Pomegranate Porter, Outsourced IPA, Weisen, XPA **Tours:** No formal tours offered. Call for private tour availability. **Taproom:** Open early 2014

Opened in mid-2013, the Dudes' Brewing Company busted into the South Bay scene with a massive 30 BBL brewhouse. At full capacity, their current system

will output 12,000 BBLs, which they are looking to increase to 50,000 to 60,000 in 2014. A cast of SoCal natives, the Dudes seek not only to create great beer at high capacity, but also to innovate. Their system is, for its size, an incredibly complex mix of pneumatic water mixers and electronics, which allows them to be as consistent as possible. Tours are limited to special circumstances; if you can call ahead and schedule one, the entire system is a sight to behold. If you happen to come on a day their loading dock doors are open, you can't miss their giant conical fermentors, each emblazoned with a different letter spelling D-U-D-E-S.

The Dudes are Toby Humes, Mike Holwick, and Jeff Parker, who was previously the head brewer and co-owner of Strand Brewing Company. The three owners bring expertise in construction, sales, and beer brewing to the table and are focused on bringing unique beer to the South Bay. They aren't packaging beer yet but have ambitious plans to can, so be sure to look for that in 2014. It's too early to call a

Double Trunk
Style: DIPA
ABV: 10.8%
Availability: Limited year-round
Double Trunk is a big West Coast–style double IPA. Clocking in at 10.8% ABV and 101 IBUs, this beer is a starter and finisher. When Jeff and team make this beer, it takes them over two hours to brew, and during fermentation they dry hop it twice and coddle it with corn sugar. It has an intense fruity citrus nose and notes of grapefruit and toffee on the palate. Cascade, Warrior, Columbus, and Chinook hops make it a classic IPA. It has a white head with lots of carbonation and a slightly sweet finish.

South Bay & Long Beach

specific flagship, but the **Double Trunk** double IPA is a hot seller at beer bars. Their **Juicebox Series,** which consists of fruit-centric beers, is also a popular choice. From blood orange vanilla bean ambers to toasted coconut chicory porters, Dudes' beers prominently feature exotic-culinary ingredients. It's also important to note that despite the large size of their operation, they still do things by hand. In the brewery sits a gas range where coconuts, pecans, and other ingredients are hand-toasted before being added them to each batch.

There is no taproom at this time, but Parker and team are looking to expand their cooperage space and open a taproom in the fall of 2013 to early 2014. If you can't make it to their location, you'll likely see their sandy-blue tap handles in South Bay–area beer hot spots. Dudes' Brewing Company beer can also be found in artfully decorated 16-ounce cans around the Southern California area, with Double Trunk and Grandma's Pecan available now and others coming soon.

EL SEGUNDO BREWING COMPANY

140 Main St., El Segundo, CA 90245; (310) 529-3882; elsegundobrewing.com;
@ESBCBrews

Founded: 2011 **Founder:** Rob Croxall and Tom Kelley **Brewer:** Rob Croxall **Flagship Beer:** Citra Pale **Year-round Beers:** Citra Pale, Blue House Pale, White Dog IPA, Blue House IPA, Hyperion's Stout **Seasonals/Special Releases:** Hyperion's Vanilla Stout, Two 5 Left DIPA, Standard Crude, Grand Hill IPA, Casa Azul Dark Mexican Lager **Tours:** No formal tours offered. Call for private tour availability. **Taproom:** Yes

Located directly across the street from the pizza and beer bar Rock & Brews, El Segundo Brewing is home to a cast of extremely fresh hop-centric beers. Proprietor and brewer Rob Croxall, a long-time home brewer and aerospace business manager, opened the brewery with friend, traveler, and Library Alehouse cicerone Tom Kelley in 2011, and today their beers can be found in West Side and South Bay bars and gastropubs. El Segundo Brewing Company also distributes their beers throughout San Francisco and San Diego. Their signature Blue House label is a symbol for small-town America and seeks to raise awareness of supporting small local businesses. It was also, incidentally, Rob's home brew label prior to the pro endeavor, which is very appropriate for the brand in general as Rob is a well-known advocate of local home brewers.

El Segundo sports a 15-barrel brewhouse with four 30 BBL and two 60 BBL fermentors. The popularity of their beer has allowed them to expand, and recently they added a substantial amount of space to their brewery. You can see most of the brewery via the taproom while you are enjoying smooth beers, crunchy pretzels, and good company. They sell growler fills and bottle some of their year-round beers like **White Dog IPA, Citra Pale,** and **Blue House Pale,** but also do special bottle releases for their limited beers, like their **Standard Crude** imperial stout.

ESBC's taproom is small, simple, and quaint. It's always full and peppered with lively locals enjoying the brewery's signature hoppy beers along with seasonal and one-off experiments. **White Dog IPA,** a cloudy and dank wheat ale, is one of their most well-known entrants into the LA beer scene, and it's a unique one at that. Along with the Dog, they have a delicious stout they call **Hyperion's,** which they sometimes infuse with spices. If you're a fan of their beers, you'll definitely want to watch their Twitter and Facebook so you can follow their cask tappings—fresh hop flavor that can't be beat.

Citra Pale
Style: Pale Ale
ABV: 5.5%
Availability: Limited
    year-round

Citra Pale is a great example the ESBC mantra. Their hop-focused beers are what make them special, and Citra Pale, the double-dry-hopped pale ale, is a dank and delicious treat. With an incredibly floral citrus nose and fresh

hoppy doggyness, malt is not the main focus of this beer, but the addition of Vienna malt adds a melanoidin character and slightly sweet complexness. The beer tastes fresh and green (as hops), has a nice lemon-zesty crispness, and at 5.5% is one you can have a few of without tipping over. This beer is a go-to for many of the locals and should be a solid first choice for anyone visiting ESBC.

MONKISH BREWING COMPANY

20311 S. Western Ave., Torrance, CA 90501; (310) 295-2157; monkishbrewing.com; @monkishbrewing
Founded: 2012 **Founder:** Henry Nguyen **Brewer:** Henry Nguyen **Flagship Beer:** Feminist **Year-round Beers:** Oblate, Crux, Red Table, Rosas Hips, Feminist, Anomaly **Seasonals/Special Releases:** Shaolin Fist, Vigil, Dat Moi, Port Tui, Lumin **Tours:** Yes—limited; call for availability **Taproom:** Yes

Henry Nguyen, the owner of Monkish Brewing Company in Torrance, is traveling the true path of the monk. With a PhD in Theology and a modern beer education backing his production, he has set out to create traditional and nontraditional Belgian beers. Henry opened the brewery with his wife in March of 2012 and has since been piloting his 15 BBL Premier Stainless brewhouse to success. Traveling around the southland introducing his unique beers to the masses, Henry has honed

his craft and has created a unique selection of beers that are pure Monkish. In the first year of production, he created 19 unique recipes that he sold in both his modestly sized taproom and at local area bars.

At Monkish you'll find heavily aromatic and refreshing spiced beers like **Lumin** that utilize thyme and a traditional Belgian abbey yeast. These beers not only pair well with food, but are an excellent addition to the cooking process as well. You'll also find infinitely complex high-octane beers like **Anomaly** that you'll want to sip lovingly in front of a wood fire. Newer additions like **Shaolin Fist** incorporate spices such as Szechuan peppercorns, which play well with the herbaceous notes of his house yeast.

Monkish Brewing has several year-round beers with varying alcohol strengths. As with many Belgian-style beers, Henry utilizes the single, dubbel, and tripel philosophy, so you're sure to find something that strikes your fancy. The tasting room is on the smaller side and has a modest, modern feel to it. Stainless easy-pour taps, wooden tables, monastic wood pieces, and a view into the brewery give it a small-town vibe and a warm, inviting atmosphere that you'll want to share with friends. If you're a fan of unique spiced beers and those with a Belgian flair, make sure Monkish is at the top of your list.

Feminist
Style: Tripel with Hibiscus
ABV: 9.4%
Availability: Year-round

Feminist is not only a flagship best seller in the tasting room, it's also a great representation of what Monkish has to offer. Stemming from Henry's focus on feminism and equality on the earth and in beer, Feminist embodies both philosophy and deliciousness. It's a rosy pink color, which comes from the generous addition of 15 pounds of hibiscus petals. At 9.4% it's a beer you'll want to sip and savor, but it also hides the alcohol very well so be careful because you'll want to order more than one. With a floral chardonnay nose, creamy honey-like body, and grapefruit finish, you'll be reminded of Jamaica, the agua fresca, and cool summer nights.

PHANTOM CARRIAGE—AT MONKISH

20311 S. Western Ave., Torrance, CA 90501; (310) 295-2157; phantomcarriage.com; @phantomcarriage

Founded: 2013 **Founder:** Martin Svab **Brewer:** Simon Ford **Flagship Beer:** All Brett Blondes **Year-round Beers:** Muis **Seasonals/Special Releases:** Banning **Tours:** No formal tours offered. Call for private tour availability. **Taproom:** Yes

The carriage approaches at night, in secrecy. The latest creation from longtime beer professional Martin Svab, former Stone & Naja's Place employee and the creator of the widely popular Gentle Scholar Imperial Espresso Stout, Phantom Carriage had been masked in a cloak-and-dagger-style mystery for most of 2011 to 2012. Brewing out of already-established Monkish Brewing Company, Phantom Carriage specializes in small-batch barreled beers and sours. Their Portland Kettleworks system is small, a 3 BBL brewhouse with 7 BBL fermentor, and is accompanied by 27

Muis
Style: 100% Brett Blonde
ABV: 6.5%
Availability: Limited year-round

Funky! This cannot be said enough. When one tastes a 100% Brett beer, one must realize that the standard and familiar flavors of *Saccharomyces cerevisiae* are just not gonna be there. The recent popularity of wilds and sours has allowed beers like this one to prevail and gain popularity. He Who Cannot Be Named is an incredibly deep, earthy blend of palate tingle and refreshment. With notes of forest wood (even though the beer isn't barrel-aged), mushrooms, citrus, and horse blanket, get

ready to take your brain on a trip back to the Belgian countryside. Opaque straw-gold in color, almost saison-like, it lets you know almost immediately what you are getting into. Tart but not sour, this beer will easily pair with fish, poultry, stinky cheese, and fruit.

neutral wine barrels. This allows them to meticulously plan out and QC each one of their small-project beers.

Head brewer and barrel master Simon Ford has been cataloguing his sour homebrewing on his site, Overcarbed.com, for quite some time. Similar to the online sour guru the Mad Fermentationist, Simon's Overcarbed brings with him a wealth of beer bug fermentation knowledge. His focus ranges from sour saisons to blended lambics to cherry browns, which are usually fermented using a diverse collage of bottle dregs and custom blends. Simon brings creativity, method, and determination to the Phantom Carriage project.

The first commercially available beer, the 100% Brett Blonde, is titled **Muis** and sports an earthy complex funk. As they are currently sharing space with Monkish, finding their beers will be focused on following their social media posts directing thirsty Angelenos to those bars that are lucky enough to receive their beer. One of those will most definitely be Beachwood BBQ. With blended lambics and other long-term sour projects to come, expect to keep your eye out for Phantom Carriage in the coming years. Their young beers are fantastic, but the long-term beers are going to be incredible.

SMOG CITY BREWING COMPANY

1901 Del Amo Blvd., Ste. B, Torrance, CA 90501; (310) 320-7664; smogcitybrewing.com; @SmogCityBeer
Founded: 2011 **Founder:** Jonathan Porter and Laurie Porter **Brewer:** Jonathan Porter
Flagship Beer: Groundwork Coffee Porter **Year-round Beers:** Smog City XPA, Sabre-Toothed Squirrel, Hoptonic IPA **Seasonals/Special Releases:** Amarillo Gorilla, Quercus Circus, Barrel Aged O.E., Lil' Bo Pils, Weird Beer, Bourbon Red, Third Nipple Tripel, L.A. Saison, The Tempest **Tours:** Yes—limited; call for availability **Taproom:** Yes

Smog City recently found a new home in Torrance. For the past year and a half, owner Jonathan Porter has been brewing his Smog City beers as a sub-brand under the Tustin Brewing Company roof. In 2012 Porter took home a gold medal at the Great American Beer Festival for his **Groundwork Coffee Porter,** a robust porter infused with locally roasted fair-trade Groundwork coffee, increasing the demand for Smog City beer. After a long wait and plenty of planning, Jonathan and wife Laurie have found their new home right down the street from Monkish Brewing and officially opened to the public in May 2013. Together, the duo is responsible for creating some of the most widely sought-after beer in Los Angeles and South Bay. The team recently expanded when it hired on its first staff members, brewer Chris Walowski, previously of Ohana, and Mike Freeman.

Porter, who developed his brewing chops at BJ's, brews on a German brewing relic where beer is measured in hectoliters. The system size equates to about 15 BBL, and he uses it at capacity to fill up his massive 60 BBL tanks with liquid goodness. Smog City's modest taproom is simple and utilizes recycled pallet furniture handmade by the owners, along with an up-close and personal view into the brew operations. The only thing separating the drinkers from the brewery are a few strategically placed barrels and a metal chain. This atmosphere is perfect for those of us interested less in fabricated ambiance and more in the reality—blood, sweat, and tears—that goes into making each pint.

Groundwork Coffee Porter
Style: Robust Porter Infused with Coffee
ABV: 6.0%
Availability: Year-round

Groundwork Coffee Porter is a perfect example of an expertly executed coffee beer. The coffee is featured but not overpowering to a level that will distract you from the suds beneath. If it were allowed at work, I would replace my morning drink with the Smog City variety every

day. Right off the bat you'll notice the aroma pounding you in the face with that fresh coffee smell. Getting through the creamy head will remind you of a mocha, and when coupled with the chocolate/roasted notes in base beer, it will further affirm. A roasted bite on the back end follows a balanced bittersweet dark cherry along with that dark chocolate flavor. At 6.0% Groundwork isn't quite a session beer, but it's definitely one you can (and will want to) have more than one of.

Smog City has a massive portfolio of beers to put on tap, and they are not afraid to experiment with the classic styles. The session offering **XPA** clocks in at 4.8% and **Amarillo Gorilla** is a bit stronger, but both will satisfy hop heads. **Quercus Circus** is an oak-aged sour saison blended down to 6.0% and is definitely worth a try if you prefer the tart side, but if you are just looking for oak-aged alcohol, make sure to try the **Barrel-Aged OE** or **Bourbon Red,** modestly rated at 9.0% plus. Another beer, **Sabre-Toothed Squirrel,** a hoppy amber ale, has one of the most recognizable and fun names on the market. As time rolls on, you can expect to see more experimental beers, taproom-exclusive offerings, and pint nights at local LA and South Bay beer bars.

STRAND BREWING COMPANY

23520 Telo Ave., Torrance, CA 90505; (310) 517-0900; strandbrewing.com;
@strandbrewing

Founded: 2009 **Founder:** Rich Marcello and Joel Elliott **Brewer:** Joel Elliott **Flagship Beer:** 24th Street Pale **Year-round Beers:** Beach House Amber, 24th Street Pale, Atticus IPA, Musashi Black IPA **Seasonals/Special Releases:** Black Sand Imperial IPA, White Sand Imperial IPA, Second Sleep Imperial Stout, Begheera Spiced Strong Ale **Tours:** Yes—limited; call for availability **Taproom:** Yes

There is no sign for the Strand Brewing taproom, and cofounder Rich likes it that way. Strand Brewing was opened by surfing buddies Rich Marcello and Joel Elliott in 2009 and it had a rocky start, but hard work and determination turned this pipe dream into a fully functioning microbrewery. Rich comes from the wine industry and PR, so he's the main spokesperson for the brewery. Joel's background is in creative photography, and he tends to be on the quiet side behind the scenes. He wasn't a brewer by trade, starting out on the business side of things, and picked up the craft after their original brewer, Jeff Parker, left Strand Brewing to pursue his own project, the Dudes' Brewing Company.

Walking into Strand you'll notice right away, like many of the other breweries located in industrial complexes, that you are drinking at the source. There is an imaginary line dividing the drinkers and the brewery. Next to the bar sit 15 and 60 BBL fermentors, and the copper 15 BBL brewhouse can be seen in the background. Strand produced about 400 BBLs of beer in 2010, but they are projecting a whopping 3,800 BBLs for 2013. There is a nice standing area off to the side with reclaimed wood, which allows for larger crowds to gather. Strand Brewing does not sell food, but encourages patrons to bring their own. Wine and whiskey barrels offer limited makeshift tables.

Strand offers many popular West Coast–style beers of which the most famous and the workhorse is **24th Street Pale.** It's an incredibly executed classic-style, sessionable beer, easily paired with food or the occasional bad day, and it's tasty. Strand has occasional events at the brewery, but you best get on their mailing list or Facebook/Twitter. Rich makes frequent appearances at pint nights at gastropubs and beer bars around town. Both Rich and Joel are old surfing buddies, so you have to remember that when enjoying Strand beer. Strand released its first official bottles in 2013. If you visit the brewery and you're local, you can pick up a 32-ounce growler, but if you want a longer-term option, you can also pick up one of the new, beautifully labeled 16-ounce bottles. Simple, elegant, and effective, these bottles will be easy to see on the shelf and will most likely also attract wine enthusiasts gone beer.

White Sand Imperial IPA
Style: Imperial IPA
ABV: 8.5%
Availability: Limited

It's hard to choose just one. Strand's Black Sand Imperial IPA is great and sports many of the same qualities that the most popular imperial IPAs around have. That being said, I was drawn to White Sand's individuality and complexity. There is so much going on in this beer that you want to put into words, but just can't. Young guava, Sweet Tarts, white wine grapes, citrus, and a slight hop cheesiness

round out the aroma, and coupled with the complex flavors that the Nelson Sauvin hops bring to the table, you have a recipe for "How can I make this DIPA a session beer?" Everyone will likely taste different things in this beer, but I was really drawn to the aroma and seeming lightness of the grain bill. In the back of my mind I know it's an imperial IPA, but it's really a lot more than that. It's probably best just to say, "Try it for yourself."

Brewpubs

BEACHWOOD BBQ & BREWING

210 E. Third St., Long Beach, CA 90802; (562) 436-4020; beachwoodbbq.com;
@beachwoodbarbecue
Founded: 2012 **Founder:** Gabriel Gordon **Brewer:** Julian Shrago **Flagship Beer:**
Melrose IPA **Year-round Beers:** Constantly rotating **Seasonals/Special Releases:**
System of a Stout, Armenian Coffee Imperial Stout, Tovarish Imperial Espresso Stout
Tours: No formal tours offered. Call for private tour availability. **Taproom:** Yes

Beachwood BBQ in Seal Beach was one of the first craft beer bars in LA, and its success and rigorous attention to quality and detail have helped shape additional establishments, including its spin-off location in Long Beach, Beachwood BBQ & Brewing. Owner and chef Gabriel Gordon was a pioneer way back when there were no options at all in LA, and as such opening a brewery seemed like a logical conclusion. He partnered with former engineer, now brewmaster, Julian Shrago to man their 10 BBL brewhouse at the Long Beach location, and together they have been cranking out high-quality brews ever since.

The location is large, with both a spanning bar inside and a large seating area outside, which is nice on hot summer nights. On the wall behind the bar is something that can only be described as looking like the side of a fire engine—a pressure regulator for each individual tap. This is quite a feat, and the result can be tasted. Each tap has its own ideal serving pressure and gas mix, which means no splitting lines, or flat beer that should be lively, or overcarbonated European styles. You can

Foam Top
Style: Cream Ale
ABV: 5.5%
Availability: Limited
   year-round

Ah, the cream ale. A relative of the German Kölsch and the American blonde, typically this is the lightest and most simple, bland, vanilla beer you can order at a brewpub, but in Beachwood's case, it's just the opposite. Crafting complex and layered beers is brewer Julian's specialty, and the cream ale is no exception. It has an extremely creamy light body, and

at 5.5% its quaffability is unparalleled. A complex light-malt graininess will be the first thing you taste, followed by a silky body and effervescent crispness. It's no wonder this beer won a gold medal at the 2012 World Beer Cup and recent 2013 GABF. If you're looking for something light on a hot day and want to be refreshed as well as impressed, make sure you start with this one.

trust the bartenders to give you good suggestions on beers and pairings, and you rest easy knowing that beer you ordered will be tasty.

Unlike traditional brewpub setups, the beer and food are separate focuses. With most brewpubs it's either the food or the beer that gets center stage, but at Beachwood they are mutually exclusive. That all being said, the seasonally rotating beers and amazing barbecued food are a pleasure to pair with each other. Everything at Beachwood is quaffable, their cream ale, **Foam Top,** which has won several medals, especially so. Their Armenian coffee stout infused with cardamom, **System of a Stout,** is also incredibly delicious. They are even distributing bottles with witty titles like **Thrillseeker** and **Full Malted Jacket.** Beachwood isn't your average brewpub, and that's because the team behind the food and beer craft everything very seriously. Make sure you try the exotic meat pies filled with everything from venison to alligator. The ham sandwich is also something of repute—paired with a nice **Hop Vader,** it may put you right to sleep with the promise of very good dreams.

Beachwood isn't your average brewpub, and that's because the team behind the food and beer craft everything very seriously. The team recently picked up 5 medals at the 2013 GABF where the brewpub was named the nation's Mid-Sized Brewpub of the year. Make sure you try the exotic meat pies filled with everything from venison to alligator.

BELMONT BREWING COMPANY
25 39th Pl., Long Beach, CA 90803; (562) 433-3891; belmontbrewing.com; @belmontbrewing
Founded: 1990 **Founder:** David Lott and David Hansen
Brewer: David Blackwell **Flagship Beer:** Strawberry Blonde **Year-round Beers:** Marathon, Strawberry Blonde, BBC Pale Ale, Top Sail, Long Beach Crude **Seasonals/ Special Releases:** Ale of the Month **Tours:** No **Taproom:** Yes

Belmont Brewing is located in Long Beach and is one of the oldest brewpubs operating in LA County. They opened in 1990 and still operate as a traditional '90s-style brewpub with a 7 BBL brewhouse and fermentor lineup behind the bar.

BBC employs the brewing talents of head brewer Blackwell, whose education stems from the American Brewer's Guild at Davis, CA. Blackwell is also the brewmaster for Bonaventure Brewing Company. He travels back and forth between the two spots, making sure they have ample beer in all tanks. Speaking of the beer, Belmont has a very classic lineup of styles: **BBC Pale Ale, Top Sail, Long Beach Crude**, and a constantly changing ale of the month. You can snag a growler for the road as well as several 22-ounce bottle offerings. Belmont brews larger batches at Hermitage Brewing Co in San Jose, and you can often find these bottles at local liquor stores such as BevMo. The **Strawberry Blonde,** with its signature strawberry shortcake flavor, is the most famous and has won several local awards.

Walking into BBC, you'll notice that it's beachfront, literally. The sand is right there, and if you want to take a dip before or after your meal, it's a very real possibility, although make sure you don't do it after a few beers. Be responsible! On most days, Belmont is hopping. The noise is relatively high during peak hours, and you'll probably wait a while if you have a large party. The menu is extensive, with some good vegetarian and seafood options. There's something for everyone, and it's very family-friendly. BBC is definitely a good option after a nice swim.

Top Sail
Style: Amber
ABV: 5.5%
Availability: Year-round
Top Sail is a classic, by-the-book amber. It has a nice, light, toasty note with a moderate hoppiness. The aroma is very subtle, and the body is medium-light. The point of this beer is the session. You can knock them back, and it pairs well with practically any food on the menu. It's a definite crowd pleaser. Nothing too crazy will jump out at you about this beer, but there is certainly something to be said about brewing to classic styles. It's a starter and a finisher.

THE BREWERY AT ABIGAILE

1301 Manhattan Ave., Hermosa Beach, CA 90254; (310) 798-8227; abigailerestaurant
.com; @abigaile
Founded: 2012 **Founder:** Jed Sanford **Brewer:** Brian Brewer **Flagship Beer:** Full
Nelson IPA **Seasonals/Specialty Beers (constantly rotating):** Orange Blossom
Blonde Ale, Half Nelson XPA, Full Nelson IPA, Nihilist DIPA, Black Mass Porter, Polyrhythm
Pale, Cacophony IPA, Sugar Daddy, Not a Wit, Analog Amber **Tours:** No formal tours
offered. Call for private tour availability. **Taproom:** Yes

If you are a beach lover or enjoy dining with the sand and water in sight, make
sure you add Abigaile to your list of breweries. Located in the hip and beautiful
Hermosa Beach, Abigaile is a few blocks away from the actual bikinis and waves.
It offers upscale dining for bros, beer geeks, and families alike. The inside of the
restaurant is posh and modern, with black stone and dark wood. You'll notice the
shiny copper brewhouse right away as it sits quietly sparkling away behind the bar.

If you're lucky, you may even see brewmaster and all-around cool guy Brian Brewer making something new in the brewery or dining with friends in the restaurant.

Abigaile opened in February 2012 in a building with some serious history. From church to hostel to punk rock hangout, the location has a colorful past. The graffiti on the wall pays homage to its South Bay punk history. For a glimpse into the past, check out the movie *The Decline of Western Civilization,* which was filmed in the old church that once occupied this location.

The menu at Abigaile is eclectic and experimental. Executive Chef Tin Vuong has a fondness for fusion, so don't limit yourself by ordering a plain burger. Expand your palate with octopus and quinoa, get some braised oxtail, or refresh yourself on some citrus-kale roughage. The bartenders are extremely knowledgeable and will be able to help you select a suitable pairing.

Abigaile is not your average brewpub. The beers being crafted on Brian's 15 BBL system rival some of the best manufacturing breweries in Southern California.

Full Nelson IPA
Style: IPA
ABV: 7.3%
Availability: Limited year-round

The aroma! Can you *FEEL* the aroma? Full Nelson IPA is light in IBU and intense on flavor. It's not going to wreck your palate completely, but it will expand your mind as you take in the complex signature Nelson aroma. It isn't one-dimensional, and the addition of Maris Otter as part of the grain bill gives Full Nelson a European maltiness that plays nicely with the resin, citrus, and grape from the hop. It'll appeal to hop heads and non–hop heads and should be consumed fresh. At 7.3% it isn't a low-ABV session, but you will be able to have more than one, and you should also grab a growler for the road.

This may have something to do with Brian's extensive brewing history and his formal education at UC Davis. Each beer from the **Black Mass Porter** to the hoppy **Full Nelson IPA** is worth trying regardless of your beer taste preference. Beers are rotated regularly to keep up with the brewmaster's creativity, so you'll likely see some familiar beers along with seasonal and one-off offerings whenever you go. If you are in a beach mood and it's on tap, make sure to try the **Not a Wit;** its wheat, oat, and pils grain profile accompanied by its spicy floral citrus notes will refresh. Abigaile sells growler fills and will be looking at bottling one-offs in early 2014.

RED CAR BREWERY & RESTAURANT

1266 Sartori Ave., Torrance, CA 90501;
(310) 782-0222; redcarbrewery.com;
@redcarbrewery

Founded: 2000 **Founder:** Bob and
Laurie Brandt **Brewer:** Bob Brandt
Flagship Beer: Big Red Ale **Year-
round Beers:** South Bay IPA, Big Red
Ale, South Loop Porter, Mortorman
Reserve, Winsome Wheat, Electra Lite
Seasonals/Special Releases: 2-Rail
Pale **Tours:** No

Co-owner and brewer Bob Brandt developed his love for beer as a home brewer and took it to the commercial scene working for Southern California Brewing Company, Huntington Beach Beer Company, and Tustin Brewing Company. Seeking to run his own establishment, Bob opened Red Car in August of 2000 with his wife, Laurie, and together they have sought to create a family-friendly brewpub environment in downtown Torrance. The result is a traditional brewpub setting featuring brick-oven pizzas, English-style ales, and a spacious parking lot.

Their emblem is easy to spot on the streets of Torrance and harkens back to a simpler time. Red Car gets its name from the famous public transport, which was so cleverly removed from LA by car-manufacturing and oil barons. If you want to learn more about this topic, check out Eddie Valiant's story in *Who Framed Roger Rabbit?* Jokes aside, Red Car cleverly adopts this theme in its beer names, with beers such

Old Town Torrance

After you visit Red Car, check out Tortilla Cantina down the street. They have a decent lineup of craft and domestic beers along with great food. An upscale cigar shop is across the street, so if you like fine tobacco, look no further.

With plenty of quaint storefronts to window shop and puruse, Old Town Torrance is a nice place to spend the afternoon with friends and family.

Motorman Reserve
Style: English-Style Amber/
     Brown Ale
ABV: 4.9%
Availability: Limited year-round

Red Car's focus is English ales that use English ingredients. As such, Motorman Reserve is a great example of Bob's focus on this style of beer. Lower car- bonation, malt forward, fruity ester heavy, and light on hops, this is a classic medium-dark English pub ale that would do well served straight from a cask. Motorman Reserve is primarily Maris Otter malt with a subtle citrus hoppiness. Notes of toffee and up-front banana dominate. It's a slightly toasty session beer that would go well with a pizza for lunch or a scoop of ice cream for dessert.

as **Motorman Reserve** and **Electra Lite** coming from their 7 BBL brewhouse. The restaurant itself is medium-size and well lit, and has a nice outside seating area to the side. A large bar to the right is a great place to start, and tasting flights, served on a paddle, can be ordered right off the bat. The beer list changes regularly, as the system is small, but you'll likely find something tasty.

Red Car has a local feel, so you'll likely see many regulars. As part of Bob and Laurie's mission to support philanthropic causes and give back to Torrance, they often sponsor local events and happenings. They've done a good job at becoming locally active and making sure Torrance knows that they are here to stay and here to contribute. Go for a beer, order a pizza, and see what Red Car has to offer. If you want to take beer home, growlers are available, along with souvenir pint glasses, behind the counter.

Beer Bars & Bottle Shops

THE FACTORY GASTROBAR

4020 Atlantic Ave., Long Beach, CA 90807; (562) 595-4020; thefactorylb.com; @thefactoryLB

Draft Beers: 8 craft taps

The Factory in Long Beach is a quintessential Southern California gastropub. Founded in 2009 by husband-and-wife team Eric and Natalie Gutenkauf, the Factory has become an exciting craft beer destination. Prior to opening the pub, the two restaurateurs owned a beer distribution company, which they later sold. Because craft beer and food was so important to them, they decided the next logical step was to put it on tap.

The Factory is a modern, chic gastropub located in the Bixby Knolls district near the cross of Carson Street and Atlantic Avenue, about 8 miles from the water on Atlantic Avenue. The space is bright, airy, and thoroughly welcoming. They have a spacious outdoor seating area that gets a lot of use year-round but is especially popular on summer nights. The Factory has live music every week, and they have a game corner where patrons can pick up a classic board game to play while enjoying their dinner sourced from local farm ingredients. A big emphasis is placed on local, fresh, and craft beer. From fire-roasted shishito peppers to beet salad to one of their more famous entrees, the Waffle Burger, the Factory has a fresh and inspired menu. The Waffle Burger actually replaces the traditional bun with two soft waffles, topped with 100 percent grass-fed beef, chocolate bacon, and a fried egg.

On Tap at the Factory Gastrobar

The Factory features some eight craft taps, which constantly rotate. They are big on not only pouring craft beer, but also celebrating it. Meet-the-brewer pint nights are frequent, so make sure to join their Facebook and check their website frequently for events. They hold an annual craft beer festival simply called BEERFEST every September, where they invite small local breweries to share their beer and educate the masses. They also hold a home brew competition for local amateur brewers, where the grand prize is getting your beer made on a local beer pro's commercial system.

NAJA'S PLACE

154 International Boardwalk, Redondo Beach, CA 90277; (310) 376-9951; najasplace.com;
@najasplace

Draft Beers: 88 mixed craft, Euro, and macro taps **Bottled/Canned Beers:** 20+ mixed
domestic and craft

Located on the Redondo Beach pier adjacent to boats and fishmongers, Naja's Place is one of the oldest craft bars in LA. As with many water-adjacent establishments, it caters to an incredibly diverse crowd, including nautical enthusiasts, beach bums, college kids, and beer geeks. It's a dive bar through and through, but it has its charm. You'll notice walking in that the wooden Naja's Place sign overhead has seen better days. There is a collection of high bar tables, a side bar to the left of the restaurant, and a music venue that houses local bands and karaoke to the right. The smell of grilled kebabs will punch you in the face, and the tap list will most likely pique your fancy. On the ceiling a tap graveyard shows off some of the more impressive brands they've had on tap.

Naja's is definitely worth a visit, but it's salty and has its own unique vibe. The original owner, Naja, is long gone, and word on the street is that the entire pier will be undergoing a long overdue renovation sometime in the near future. When that happens, it's unclear if Naja's will move or cease to be, but one thing's for certain: It would be a shame to get rid of a place with this much beer history.

ROCK & BREWS

143 Main St., El Segundo, CA 90245; (310) 615-9890; rockandbrews.com; @rockandbrews
Draft Beers: 46 mixed craft and European taps **Bottled/Canned Beers:** 100–200 rotating bottles

Rock & Brews is a modern beer hall with a large outdoor communal seating area. Think Oktoberfest but with pizza and rock paraphernalia surrounding you. Rock & Brews was a 2011 concept restaurant by Michael Zislis, the shrewd businessman behind the Shade Hotel and Rock 'n Fish. He has extensive business and brewery experience, and his Bohemia brand was responsible for setting up many major brewpubs in the '90s including Manhattan Beach Brewing, now a beer bar called Brewco. The restaurant chain is also partly owned by famous Kiss managers Dave and Del Furano, and with the help of Gene Simmons, the team has helped Rock & Brews to expand to greatness in the South Bay area. With the success of the El Segundo location, the restaurant partners have opened a second location on the PCH in Redondo Beach, a third in Cabo, and are primed for opening locations on Maui, in Kansas, and in the LAX Delta Terminal 5.

Walking into the restaurant you'll first notice the large opulent sign, red gateway, and pillars of fire. The restaurant itself is hip and incredibly large, specializing in mixed craft, imports, and some larger domestic brands as well. The Rock & Brews team wants to have something for everyone, so whether you love macro, imports, or local craft, you'll find a brew for you. Pizza is one of the main specialties, but the Bavarian-style pretzel is also a must-order. Those with allergies can order gluten-free pizza, and most everything is customizable.

There is no beer list on the menu; in its place is a QR code and several strategi-cally placed flat-screen monitors, which display the current beer list via slide show. Because the beer list is constantly changing for their 46-plus taps, they update everything online, which they encourage you to view on your smartphones. They also sport an impressive selection of bottles. One of the largest perks to the Rock & Brews El Segundo location is its proximity to El Segundo Brewing Company, which is literally across the street. Definitely a solid option if you arrive early for a reserva-tion, are waiting for a seat, or need a growler fill after a pizza fix.

Rock & Brew Anywhere

Rock & Brews is aiming for world takeover, craft beer and pizza style, with alternate locations in Redondo Beach, Maui, Cabo San Lucas, and Overland Park, Kansas. The formula works and the atmosphere, food, and beer are great. Be on the lookout for more locations opening for this beer and pizza chain worldwide

Brewpub to Beer Bar

Redondo Brewery, *1814 S. Catalina Ave., Redondo Beach, CA 90277; (310) 316-8477; redondobeachbrewery.com*

Redondo Beach Brewing Co, now Redondo Brewery, used to be a fully functioning '90s-style brewpub owned and operated by John Waters, whose team also ran Manhattan Beach Brewing Co, now Brewco Manhattan Beach, and Stadium Brewery in Alesa Viejo. When the beer climate changed, Redondo Beach Brewing closed down its brewing operation, but kept the pub part open. It went through a massive remodel in 2013 as well as a branding change, which makes it a hot new craft beer bar rather than a brewpub. This shift and rebranding is very similar to the Brewco Manhattan Beach change. Redondo Brewery reopened with a full lineup of taps while still retaining some of its old brewpub beers. It's a great location just a stone's throw away from Select Beer Store, Rock & Brews, and the actual beach.

SELECT BEER STORE

1613 S. Pacific Coast Hwy., Redondo Beach, CA
90277; selectbeerstore.com; @selectbeerstore
Draft Beers: 12 taps, mostly local **Bottled/
Canned Beers:** 500+ bottles, constantly changing

Walking into Select Beer Store, you'll instantly feel a sense of community and warmth. Large beverage coolers inset into the walls take up the left side of the store, a bar sits in the center, room-temp bottles are stored at the back right, and a large seating and standing area takes up the front right portion of the store. Although the shop has an extensive selection of amazing bottled beer, it also boasts a full lineup of taps, including many locals. Owners Wes and Heather opened in 2012 and have done a great job promoting local craft. They are also very knowledgeable about the bottles they sell and the beer they serve. You can either pull up for a pint, crack open a bottle, or pick something up for takeaway.

Select Beer Store has regular beer-tasting events and food guests, so be sure to check their schedule out online on their website, Facebook, or Twitter. There is limited parking in the front and more parking in the back. The surrounding area is very walkable, and it's just a few blocks to the beach. If you're hungry, there are many local restaurants nearby—get something to go and then head over to Select for the perfect pairing.

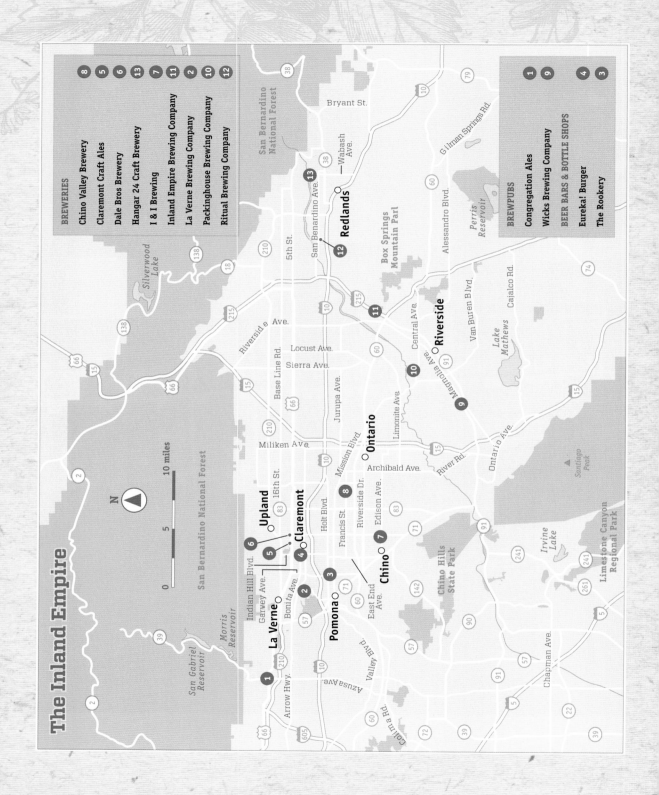

The Inland Empire

BREWERIES

8 Chino Valley Brewery
5 Claremont Craft Ales
6 Dale Bros Brewery
13 Hangar 24 Craft Brewery
7 I & I Brewing
11 Inland Empire Brewing Company
2 La Verne Brewing Company
10 Packinghouse Brewing Company
12 Ritual Brewing Company

BREWPUBS

1 Congregation Ales
9 Wicks Brewing Company

BEER BARS & BOTTLE SHOPS

4 Eureka! Burger
3 The Rookery

N

0 5 10 miles

The Inland Empire

Vast, expansive, dry, hot, and teeming with beer life, the Inland Empire is home to many great breweries. From LA you're looking at at least 90 minutes before you hit the beer scene, but turn on the Brewing Network and set the cruise control and you'll be there in no time. The IE is home to classics like Hangar 24 and TAPS Fish House and Brewery, but it is also the location of a few worthwhile nanobreweries and production houses. If you like music and food, downtown Pomona is a great stop, and if you are a fan of air shows, make sure you visit Redlands or Riverside during one of the many beer fests that take place on the airstrips. The IE is the place to be.

Breweries

CHINO VALLEY BREWERY

1630 E. Francis St., Ste. J, Ontario, CA 91761; (951) 291-7117; chinovalleybrewery.com; @chinovalleybrew

Founded: 2012 **Founder:** Matt Maldonado and Ray Duran **Brewer:** Matt Maldonado **Flagship Beer:** Route 83 Red Ale **Year-round Beers:** Prado Porter, West End Pale, Butterfield Blonde, Route 83 Red Ale, Foggy Morning Stout, Mule Car IPA **Seasonals/ Special Releases:** N/A **Tours:** No formal tours offered. Call for private tour availability. **Taproom:** Yes

Chino Valley Brewery is a 1.5 BBL nanobrewery located in an industrial park off E. Francis Street in Ontario. It's not too far away from the 60 and is pretty easy to get to. The taproom is on the smaller side, but it fits the local nano style. The first thing you'll notice is Chino's logo, a dairy cow, paying homage to the historical dairy industry of Chino Valley, artfully composed on a chalkboard outside. Inside the tasting room is a petite bar, some high-top tables, and a Blichmann nano system in back. The ambience is sparse but warm, with dairy signs, ephemera, and even hammered tin plates displaying the China Valley Brewery logo. There are no tours, but if you want to look at the brew system, it's in the back of the room and owner/brewer Matt Maldonado will be happy to show you.

Matt owns and operates the brewery with his business partner Ray Duran, a retired East LA cop. They have strong ties to the local fire and police departments and make a point to support them with liquid libations whenever possible. Matt himself has an interesting past in brewing, learning the craft in England in 1986 at the Wellington in Cambridgeshire. He learned how to brew British styles, which he loves, so most of the Chino beers have a European focus. They currently self-distribute their beers while trying to keep up with demand. Chino Valley Brewery is fairly new, but they get pretty busy on Saturday nights, when they have local food trucks stop by. They are planning to double both their brew and fermentation capacity in early 2014.

Chino Valley beers are mostly focused on classic styles. Their most popular beer, **Route 83 Red Ale,** is their flagship beer. This is also the beer they make a lot of for Dave & Busters, which is a big supporter. It has a nice, assertive hoppiness and is balanced nicely with British malts. Their **Butterfield Blonde,** named after the Butterfield Ranch, is also a popular offering, with its pilsner-forward graininess and Willamette hops. Chino Valley has plans to vary their beers quite a bit, but for now they are sticking to the core offerings that they make for their local accounts. Fliptop growlers are offered, complete with their screen-printed cow, and can be filled with any of the beers on tap for take home.

Foggy Morning Stout
Style: Milk Stout
ABV: 5.6%
Availability: Year-round

It's only appropriate that a dairy-themed brewery would have a milk stout on tap, and in this, Chino Valley Brewery delivers. Foggy Morning Milk Stout is an incredibly sessionable sweeter stout that utilizes nitro to give it that dense, creamy head. It has slight notes of coffee and darker milk chocolate, and a slightly toasted smoky flavor towards the tail end. Because of the strong ties to

British history that this style has, it's only appropriate that it has a balanced British maltiness that pairs well with pub fare. It's definitely a beer that will go well alongside or in food including, but not limited to, dessert.

CLAREMONT CRAFT ALES

1420 N. Claremont Blvd., #204C, Claremont, CA 91711; (909) 625-5350; claremontcraftales.com; @ClaremontBeer
Founded: 2012 **Founder:** Simon Brown and Emily Moultrie **Brewer:** Simon Brown and Brian Seffer **Flagship Beer:** Jacaranda Rye IPA **Year-round Beers:** Jacaranda Rye IPA, Willow Blonde, Carlisle Pale Ale, Double Dude Double IPA **Seasonals/Special Releases:** Royal, Roblé'd Oaked Red Ale, Buddy Imperial Black Rye IPA, Padua Porter **Tours:** Ask No formal tours offered. Call for private tour availability. **Taproom:** Yes

Claremont Craft Ales is a microbrewery located in an industrial park in Claremont. Founded in 2012 by the husband-and-wife team of Simon and Emily, they've piloted their 6 BBL system into success with their flagship beer, **Jacaranda,** named for the iconic purple flowering trees found throughout California. The brew team recently expanded their operation and doubled their brewing capacity. They are

planning on increasing their fermentation capacity in the coming year, and then upgrading their brewhouse soon after.

CCA's focus is on the local scene. They want to feature Claremont and California in each of their beers, and have partnered with a local coffee roaster, Klatch, to brew some tasty coffee-infused special releases. They also have a small, unique barrel-aging program that produces several impressive beers, such as **Royal,** an imperial oatmeal stout aged for four months in a Buffalo Trace Bourbon barrel. **Roblé'd,** an oak-aged red ale, is another customer favorite.

Claremont Craft Ales has a beautifully warm and inviting taproom, featuring a table seating area, a plush couch, and a nice wooden bar that runs in front of the taps. The decor is dominated by a unique installation of two-tone painted canvases featuring clever sayings, creating a colorful and lively setting. Oranges, purples, blues, and pastel colors abound, imparting a lovely summery feel to the taproom. They currently supply growlers and growlettes for taking beer home. They will also be adding cans to this lineup soon, when they begin utilizing a local mobile canning service to package Jacaranda.

Jacaranda
Style: Rye IPA
ABV: 6.7%
Availability: Year-round

Jacaranda, a spicy rye IPA, started out as one of Simon's home brew recipes six years ago. It's now their flagship beer and just recently won a gold medal at the Los Angeles International Beer Competition. Centennial and Columbus hops give it a classic West Coast floral aroma, and the addition of wheat and rye makes the beer both creamy and peppery. The body in this beer is very nice and not too heavy. It's a 6.7% easy-drinking beer, and it's obvious why it's so popular. Balance is king in this beer, so although the hops are up front, they don't blow away the maltiness in the beer, and it ends dry, not sweet. It pours a lovely copper color with a white head and, as mentioned earlier, it'll likely be in cans sometime in late 2013.

DALE BROS BREWERY

2120 Porterfield Way, Upland, CA 91786; (909) 579-0032; dalebrosbrewery.com; @dalebrosbrewery
Founded: 2007 **Founder:** Curt and Andy Dale **Brewer:** Curt Dale **Flagship Beer:** Pomona Queen **Year-round Beers:** Pomona Queen, Runway IPA, California Black Beer **Seasonals/Special Releases:** Oktober Fiesta, Winter Haze, Shameless McDale, The Dude of York, Pacific Daylight **Tours:** Yes; free tours Sat at 4 p.m.; personal tours with tastings Thurs at 6 p.m. and Sun at 2 and 4 p.m. for $10 per person **Taproom:** Yes

In Upland, CA, two cool dudes decided they wanted to make beer professionally. Curt opened Dale Bros Brewery 2003, and Andy joined to build the business in 2007. They take brewing their beer very seriously, but they make sure to have fun in the process. They consider themselves black sheep, which is why they've newly

Pomona Queen
Style: California Amber Lager
ABV: 4.9%
Availability: Year-round

Pomona Queen is the beer that started it all. It's brewed with a San Francisco lager yeast, which may actually place this beer in the California common "steam" beer category, but it takes on more of the lager characteristics than its hybrid brethren. The beer pours a crystal-clear amber with a light white head. It's effervescent with a light body. Spicy biscuit notes and a mellow malt profile make this an incredibly easy drinking beer. It has a long, persistent, citrus hop finish that pairs well with a hot day or post-surf rest on the beach. Pomona Queen is a great example of what Dale Bros has to offer; after this one, go straight to California Black Beer.

rebranded themselves with these wooly mammals as their mascots. Curt comes from a computer programming background and left his practice to pursue an education in brewing science, while Andy studied finance and business strategy, getting his MBA from the University of Chicago. Together they make up the management team for Dale Bros and, yes, these guys built the brewery from the ground up. They take pride in being at the brewery, meeting the people that visit, and being as cool and approachable as possible.

Dale Bros Brewery recently moved from their cramped warehouse in Upland to a new, bright and shiny gigantic one a few blocks away. The old location had little room for people to congregate, but the new one is a high-ceilinged warehouse with not only enough space for their rapidly expanding brewing operation, but also a full taproom, seating area, and live music. The locale is perfect for enjoying beers with friends and is amazing for the frequent events the Dale bros plan. Their anniversary party is something you definitely don't want to miss, as it takes over most of the industrial park as a full-scale beer fest—and there is plenty of parking! Free tours are given on Saturday, and personal tours with tasting are conducted on Sunday and Thursday with online sign-up available.

Dale Bros Brewery focuses primarily on lager beers, using a hybrid lager yeast harkening back to the old West Coast–style steam beers. They use the term *hybrid* to the fullest extent of their ability, utilizing ale-style grain bills and brewing process, with slightly colder lager fermentation temperatures and yeast, which give their beers a signature crisp finish. Their year-round beers **Pomona Queen** and **California Black Beer** come out crystal clear, crisp, and tasty. To keep up with the hoppy demand, they produce an IPA called **Runway,** and they also create seasonal ales from barleywines to English-style bitters. Dale Bros is currently working on their barrel program, so expect to see some higher ABV experiments in the near future. Beer is available in 22-ounce bottles as well as 64-ounce and 32-ounce growlers for take home.

HANGAR 24 CRAFT BREWERY

1710 Sessums Dr., Redlands, CA 92374; (909) 389-1400; hangar24brewery.com; @hangar24brewery
Founded: 2008 **Founder:** Ben Cook **Brewer:** Ben Cook **Flagship Beer:** Orange Wheat
Year-round Beers: Orange Wheat, Amarillo Pale Ale, Alt-Bier Ale, Helles Lager, Columbus IPA, Chocolate Porter, Double IPA **Seasonals/Special Releases:** Belgian Summer Ale, California Spring Beer, Oktoberfest, Hullabaloo, Local Fields Series, Barrel Roll Series
Tours: Yes; call for availability **Taproom:** Yes

Hangar 24 Craft Brewery is located on an airfield, literally. It's a polished brand that has seen major success in the last few years as craft beer grows in popularity. Owner and brewmaster Ben Cook runs his 15 BBL brewhouse 24/7, which allows the company to crank out an impressive 40,000 BBLs a year. They recently expanded, adding even more fermentation space, which allows them, with the distribution company they own, to get the beer out to more areas.

Hangar 24 beers focus on being palatable and approachable. Many of them introduce local ingredients from neighboring farms such as citrus, dates, grapes, apricots, pumpkins, cherries, and spruce. Their most famous beer, **Orange Wheat,** is an American wheat beer with 100 percent locally grown oranges added. If you are a fan of citrus or beer or the combination of the two, make sure you try it. They also release an incredible barrel-aged beer each year in their Barrel Roll Series, so if you're a beer geek, get a bottle.

The taproom is beautiful and fully utilizes the airplane hangar feel. It's a wide-open building, but gets crowded quickly. The outside patio overlooks the beautiful San Bernardino Mountains, which, depending on the time of year you go, may be covered in snow. The brewery conducts tours at specific times, so make sure you call ahead. You can get bottles in 12-ounce, 22-ounce, and in the case of the Barrel Roll Series, 750 ml sizes. Cans and growlers are also available. Hangar 24 may be a serious drive for most Angelenos, but it's well worth the trip for the beer and view.

Belgian Summer Ale
Style: Belgian Spiced Ale
ABV: 5.8%
Availability: Seasonal

There are many awesome beers at Hangar 24 Brewery, but Belgian Summer Ale sticks out in the lineup. The brewery often focuses on employing the use of fruit, especially citrus, in their beers, so it's fascinating when you taste a beer that has all the citrus notes without the citrus addition. Belgian Summer Ale utilizes a sour mash to create a lightly tart, almost Berliner Weisse–like beer. Based on the 3rd Anniversary Ale, Belgian Summer Ale has a spicy, citrus quality, and it's dangerously easy to drink. A complex light grain profile shows through after the spicy Belgian yeast notes, and it's finished off with a tropical fruit tartness that is perfect for a hot summer day. It's a seasonal release (April–August) so you won't find it year-round, but if you do see it, the four-pack is worth a purchase.

Put Beer in Your Food

Brewcakes Dessert Gastropub, *1150 Brookside Ave., Redlands, CA 92373; (909) 792-1399; brewcake.com.*
While in Redlands, make sure you stop by the crazy cool gastropub Brewcakes. They make everything on the menu with some form of alcohol as an ingredient. Beer, wine, and spirits all find their way into their tasty collection of savory sandwiches and desserts. Definitely a must-stop. Brewcakes also makes regular appearances at beer festivals, so chances are you'll at least be able to try their desserts when you're at a fest.

The Inland Empire

I & I BREWING

14175 Telephone Ave., Chino, CA 91710; (909) 591-3915; iandibrewing.com; @iandibrewing

Founded: 2012 **Founder:** Eric Millspaugh, Chris Miller, and Chuck Foster **Brewer:** Chuck Foster and Johnny Foster **Flagship Beer:** Session IPA **Year-round Beers:** Coconut Porter, Session IPA, Irish Red Ale **Seasonals/Special Releases:** Raspberry Stout, Black Rye IPA, Honey Cream Ale, California Common, Orange Flower Amber, Molasses Brown Ale, Pekoe Tea Pale Ale, Fairly Regular, Strawberry Wheat, Berliner Weisse, Blonde Coffee Ale **Tours:** Yes **Taproom:** Yes

In beer brewing, there is no limit to culinary or chemical creativity, and there is no other nanobrewery that is as creative as I & I. The facility and taproom is located in Chino off Edison Avenue, not too far from the 71 Freeway. Owners Eric Millspaugh, Chris Miller, and Chuck Foster see the brewery project as a labor of love. All but Chuck, the full-time brewer, have day jobs and work the taproom on nights and weekends. Chuck, a chemist by trade, and his son Johnny man the brewery 24/7. The team's main goal is to make unique experimental beers that they want to drink themselves and share with others. Because the size of the system is so small, their tie to home brew and home brewers is incredibly strong.

The tasting room is tiny, but they've expanded the seating area to encompass the brewery as well, so even though there are always crowds, you'll be able to get some beer. "I & I" is a reggae reference, so you'll see the telltale red, yellow, green, and black colors all around the brewery and taproom. In the back by the brewhouse they have a massive wall of stickers covering the fermentation room, a reconditioned florist refrigerator. Currently I & I does not distribute their beer; their entire business model is geared towards tasters, pints, and growler fills. Because of this, they are able to brew small amounts, 1.5 BBLs, of unique beer daily, which they use to fill their 18 taps. Their capacity is currently about 100 BBLs a year, but that will increase when they move into their new 4,400-square-foot space. The brew system will stay the same size, but the fermentation capacity will become more substantial.

Chuck and the I & I team make incredibly unique beers along with more standard, but equally tasty, classic styles. Their **California Common** and **Coconut Porter** are very tasty and as such fill many growlers. The point at this nanobrewery, though, is to taste new things every time you come in. The website always has the current tap list, so you'll know before you go that there is a **Dill Tzatziki Saison** or **Sorachi Pale Ale,** made with sorachi ace hops, on tap. From hard lemonade to cherry Berliner Weisse, I & I does it, and if they haven't made it, they probably will. You'll definitely find something on tap that you like, and the creativity will be something you want to share with friends, so buy a growler and bring it to the weekend barbecue.

Session IPA
Style: IPA
ABV: 4.7%
Availability: Limited year-round

I & I's entire business model is built around never having the same beers on tap, constantly experimenting, and being as creative as possible. That being said, while their beers are always different when you visit the taproom, they do have a few beers that are more regular. The Session IPA is one of those beers, and it's a very tasty West Coast take on the style. Cascade, Columbus, Centennial, and Chinook can all be found in this beer, with a flavor/aroma blast of Citra and Magnum dry-hopped at the end. The first thing you'll notice is the dark citrus characterized by an incredibly light malt profile. The floral resin zestiness of the hops are the main feature here, and with a 4.7% ABV, this beer definitely lives up to its namesake.

INLAND EMPIRE BREWING COMPANY

1710 Palmyrita Ave., #11, Riverside, CA 92507; (951) 643-7687; iebrew.com; @ieBrew
Founded: 2009 **Founder:** David Hiebert and Paul Murphy **Brewer:** Paul Murphy
Flagship Beer: Habsburg Hefeweizen **Year-round Beers:** Habsburg Hefeweizen, Pale Ale, Brown Ale, India Pale Ale, Victoria, Pepin "The Short" Porter **Seasonals/Special Releases:** Scotch Ale, Barrel-Aged Berliner Weisse, Rivertucky 2013 Reserve Barleywine, Imperial Stout **Tours:** Yes—upon request **Taproom:** Yes

Inland Empire Brewing Company opened in February of 2009 and is located in the city of Riverside, right off the 215. Founded and operated by bootstrapping home brew friends David Hiebert and Paul Murphy, IEBC showcases a unique assortment of classic styles along with some very strong barrel-aged ones. The team runs a Frankensteined 7 BBL brewhouse fashioned from old dairy equipment. The boil

Victoria

Style: American Strong Ale

ABV: 11.0%

Availability: Year-round

Victoria is the tastiest beer in Inland Empire Brewing's repertoire. It incorporates local honey, local oranges, and a generous helping of Columbus, Cascade, and Chinook hops. Clocking in at 11.0%, it's anything but session, but it's definitely a beer you can appreciate drinking down to the last drop. The honey shines through, with a citrus acidity and hop bite following through. Caramel and toffee flavors dominate. It pours deep-brown amber with a creamy head. This would be a great beer with which to create a syrup reduction for pancakes.

kettle is actually square with electric heating elements on the bottom, which gives IEBC's beers a very distinct flavor and caramelization. There are plans to expand down the line and upgrade the reconditioned dairy equipment, replacing it with modern brewing pieces and a bottling line, which should happen in early 2014.

Inland Empire Brewing's taproom is small and modest. They have an L-shaped bar kegerator setup with about 9 to 12 taps flowing at a time. Their year-round beers are always on tap, although their Hefeweizen goes fast in the summer months, and they usually have some high-ABV seasonals on tap as well. IEBC recently acquired a distribution partner which is placing their beers at local bars, liquor stores, and even Costco. They're currently reaching as far as San Francisco, but are found mostly in the Inland Empire and Orange Country. IEBC holds several beer festivals during the year, their biggest being their anniversary party, which invites local breweries to pour in their large industrial-district parking lot. It draws quite a crowd and is definitely worth looking into. Paul and David also like to help aspiring brewers, so they frequently contract-brew small batches and are currently the brew space for the Off the Grid Brewing Company.

IEBC makes some pretty good classic styles, but they truly shine in their high-ABV offerings. Their third-anniversary barleywine, playfully named **Rivertucky,** clocks in at 16.0% and comes in a burlap sack. They also make an imperial stout barrel-aged in bourbon barrels, which is pretty solid. **Habsburg Hefeweizen** is a summer go-to beer and is a clove-forward Bavarian-style variety. They currently bottle their Hefeweizen, **Pepin "The Short" Porter,** and **Victoria** beers and plan to bottle more in 2014. You can purchase 22-ounce bottles directly from them at the tasting room, or look for them in the local liquor stores; 32-ounce growlers are also available for take home.

LA VERNE BREWING COMPANY

2125 Wright Ave., La Verne, CA 91750; (626) 733-1380; lavernebrewingco.com; @lavernebrewing

Founded: 2013 **Founder:** Tony, Richard, and Jordan Feole **Brewer:** Tony Feole and Amy Heller **Flagship Beer:** N/A **Year-round Beers:** LVBC Cream Ale, Golden Hills Wheat, LVBC American Strong, Palomares Pale Ale, 32 Highboy Double IPA, Old Flathead Oatmeal Stout **Seasonals/Special Releases:** B Street Pineapple Blonde **Tours:** No formal tours offered. Call for private tour availability. **Taproom:** Yes

La Verne Brewing Company, one of the newest breweries to establish itself in the Inland Empire, opened in April of 2013. The brewery is owned and operated by the Feole family. Tony, his wife Jordan, and dad Richard run the business and taproom together, while Tony handles the brewhouse portion himself. Tony has been brewing beer since 2005, with a side hobby of fixing up hot rods. He has fond memories of brewing with his dad under an old oak tree. His day job is in IT, so opening a brewery is a big jump, but an exciting one. La Verne Brewing is small, operating a 7 BBL brewhouse with a total of 30 BBLs worth of fermentation space. They are projecting a 1,500 BBL capacity in a full year, which will be partially met by catering to the local race car–focused crowd.

La Verne Brewing is located off Arrow Highway, smack dab in the middle between the 10 and 210. They're tucked back in a modern industrial park a stone's throw from the NHRA racing track, which no doubt drives a high demand for La Verne beer. Patrons can easily walk to and visit the brewery before and/or after a race. The taproom is moderately small, with six taps on the wall. There is an expanded seating area in the back where the brewhouse lives, along with some souped-up hot rods and funny car frames. The focus here is definitely on the race and car culture with an emphasis on old hot rods, hence the car on the label. If you are a fan of the countryside, you'll definitely feel at home here, and the staff is incredibly friendly. The brewhouse is amid the museum of cars, so no formal tours are needed. Still, if you want more information, you can easily ask Tony, Jordan, or Richard, who are usually behind the counter and will be happy to talk to you about their story.

The brewery is still developing its beers, so there isn't a specific flagship as of yet. That being said, both the **32 Highboy Double IPA** and **B Street Pineapple Blonde** are top sellers. Tony likes to focus on easy-drinking beers, with most beers

Beer Lover's Pick

B Street Pineapple Blonde
Style: Blonde Ale with Fruit
ABV: 5.2%
Availability: Seasonal
La Verne Brewing uses farmers' market fresh pineapples to infuse B Street Pineapple Blonde with intense tropical fruitiness. The base blonde beer is light and bready, with a moderate cloudiness. The pineapple is added during secondary and aged for a short time to infuse the beer. The result is a very fruit-forward light beer with subtle hop character. B Street is slightly sweet with an acidic bite to it, which makes a very pleasant beer to enjoy on a hot afternoon. At 5.2% it's easy drinking and definitely a beer you can have a few of. This beer is only available seasonally and goes fast in the hot months.

averaging between 5.0% and 7.0%; the highest, the **LVBC American Strong,** is 8.1%. You won't find anything too crazy or wild here, but you'll definitely find beers that you can enjoy with friends in high quantities. The **Old Flathead Oatmeal Stout** is silky smooth, with a very mellow roastiness. It's a great start to get a tasting flight so you can narrow in on the beers you want to get full pours of. La Verne is still small, so you'll likely only find their beer at the taproom and a few local bars. Growlers will be available early 2014 for take-home beer.

PACKINGHOUSE BREWING COMPANY
6421 Central Ave., Riverside, CA 92504; (951) 688-2337; pbbeer.com; @phousebeer
Founded: 2010 **Founder:** Tim Worthington and Sam Stager **Brewer:** Matt Becker
Flagship Beer: Riley's Irish Red **Year-round Beers:** Black Beauty Cream Stout, Heritage Pale Ale, Riley's Irish Red, Sunburst Blonde **Seasonals/Special Releases:** Greek Series, Tipsy Tibits, Coup de Main **Tours:** Yes; call for availability **Taproom:** Yes

Packinghouse Brewing Company derives its name from Riverside's long history in the citrus industry. The California citrus market was quite literally built in Riverside, and hundreds of warehouses in the city were responsible for packing and moving the fruit to the open market. The brewery itself doesn't focus as much on citrus as much as, say, Hangar 24, but they do prominently feature the fruit in one of their seasonal brews, **Tipsy Tibbets,** an orange Belgian strong whose name is inspired by Eliza Tibbets, a founder of Riverside and the woman responsible for bringing navel oranges to SoCal. Packinghouse owners Tim Worthington and Sam Stager love their town and have been brewing beer in Riverside since October 2010.

They drive a 5 BBL brewhouse, originally from Oggi's, with a number of 10 BBL fermentors, which gives them an average of 400 BBLs a year. Like most breweries their size, expansion is in the near future, and Tim hopes to be at 800 BBLs by the end of 2013. The Packinghouse taproom is quaint and narrow. They recently expanded their sitting area by 100 percent,

Riley's Irish Red
Style: Irish Red Ale
ABV: 5.3%
Availability: Year-round

In this day and age, with high-octane barrel-aged beers, enamel-peeling triple IPAs, and mouth-puckering sours, it's sometimes nice to see a classic style done right. Riley's Irish Red is just that, a classic Irish red ale done to perfection. It's quaffable, creamy, and ruby red, and pours with a nice, frothy white head. The malt profile is very well balanced with subtle notes of caramel, toffee, and warm Irish brown bread. The Magnum hops are subdued, but still lend a nice crispness to the finish of the beer. Riley's would be an awesome cask beer, and as such it's good to let it warm a bit so you can taste the full grain profile; it'll also give you that traditional Euro experience. Make sure you start with this one, and if you're a fan of Riley's, you'll probably dig the Black Beauty Cream Stout, too.

and the room is sparsely decorated with red brick and dark wood. It's a friendly place that gets very busy on the weekends and during their frequent events. Their annual Brewgrass Beer and Music Festival is a local favorite and pulls large crowds from miles around; it's held at the neighboring Riverside airstrip.

Packinghouse beers are very clean, very quaffable, and classic. Their flagship and most popular beer is **Riley's Irish Red,** a traditional Irish red ale. In close second is their Greek Series, which produces one IPA every month, each with a different hop profile and a different letter of the Greek alphabet. **Epsilon Centennial, Gamma Rye, Zeta Black,** and **Alpha IPA** are all worth looking for if they are still on tap when you go. Another highlight is their **Black Beauty Cream Stout,** a very light, slightly sweet, and refreshing milk stout, and their beer-geek favorite, **Coup de Main,** a double IPA that is brewed quarterly. Coup de Main sells out quickly, but since it's brewed quarterly, it's a beer you can taste if you plan your brewery hopping well. Packinghouse provides growlers for take home and carries 22-ounce bottles of their core year-round beers. If you like classic styles, make sure you visit Packinghouse Brewing Company.

RITUAL BREWING COMPANY
1315 Research Dr., Redlands, CA 92374; (909) 478-7800; ritualbrewing.com; @ritualbrewing
Founded: 2012 **Founder:** Steve Dunkerken and Owen Williams **Brewer:** Steve Dunkerken and Owen Williams **Flagship Beer:** Extra Red **Year-round Beers:** Extra Red, Tafelbier, Wit's End, Hop-O-Matic **Seasonals/Special Releases:** Hellion, Big Deluxe, Little Oat, Fat Hog **Tours:** Yes **Taproom:** Yes

Located in Redlands, a few minutes from the freeway off-ramp, Ritual Brewing is creating classic and new-age styles their way. The production facility is beautiful, open, and massive—large enough for the present and the future. Steve has a background as a financial executive in manufacturing, and Owen has 20 years in commercial brewing, having trained several brewers who now have their own breweries or are head brewers at well-respected breweries in the region. They met when Steve was a home brewer, and as their friendship evolved, so did their plans to open a brewery. They operate a new 30 BBL Specific Mechanical brewhouse built to their specifications and hope to produce close to 2,000 BBLs in their first year, 45,000 BBLs at full building capacity. It's clear that their goal is to make unique high-quality beer, and a lot at that. With the help of their sales guy, former *Celebrator Beer News* writer Ed Heethuis, the team is spreading their beer across Southern California with further expansion in the works.

Ritual Brewing creates a focused set of beers, each having entertaining stories and impressive labels behind them. One of the most unique traits of their beer is the focus on small beers. **Hellion,** a Belgian-style golden, clocks in at 8.4% alcohol and is one of their staple beers. Hellion's little sister **Tafelbier,** literally translated "Table Bier," is a Belgian-style single. This is one of the abbey styles rarely brewed outside of Belgium, where it is commonly reserved for the monks. One of the unique beers

Tafelbier
Style: Belgian Table Beer
ABV: 4.5%
Availability: Taproom only

Ritual's Tafelbier is a delight, and the idea behind this Belgian table beer is right on point. A beautifully complex grainy aroma will be the first thing you notice. Classic Belgian pilsner flavors meet a layered earthy yeast profile, which is finished off by tropical fruit. The beer is incredible quaffable and rewarding with each sip. The only drawback is that it can't be found in bottles, but that can be easily rectified by asking for a growler fill. If you want to do a fun comparison, drink Hellion and Tafelbier side by side—they are related after all.

is **Little Oat,** a small beer made from the second running of their imperial oat stout **Big Deluxe.** All four of these beers are worth trying and appreciating.

At Ritual, nothing goes to waste. If it's in season, be sure to try the **Fat Hog Barleywine** as well. Despite its hard-hitting 12.0% ABV, it drinks smooth without the cloying attribute that most beers of the same style share. Ritual Brewing has a beautiful, large taproom adjacent to the brewery. The tables are made from reconditioned '60s vintage bowling lanes, and the table legs are fabricated from the steel cradles used to ship the brewery equipment. **Extra Red, Wit's End,** and **Hop-O-Matic** can be found regularly in bottles, while bottles of Hellion, Big Deluxe, and Fat Hog are special-release bottles only. Be sure to grab a growler for the road.

The Inland Empire

Brewpubs

CONGREGATION ALES

619 N. Azusa Ave., Azusa, CA 91702; (626) 334-BEER; congregationalehouse.com;
@congregationale
Founded: Pub 2011/Brewhouse 2013 **Founder:** Travis Ensling **Brewer:** Caleb McLaughlin
Flagship Beer: N/A **Year-round Beers:** Congregation 3 Chords & The Truth, Congregation
Praise On! Saison, Congregation Ales Dark of the Covenant **Seasonals/Special Releases:**
Congregation Dunkelweiss, Congregation Wit & Wisdom, Congregation Summer Pale **Tours:**
No formal tours offered. Call for private tour availability. **Taproom:** yes

Congregation Ale House was originally founded in 2010 by Travis Ensling, the first location being in Long Beach near Beachwood BBQ & Brewing. Travis has since opened up two other locations: the second in Azusa and the third in Pasadena. The newest addition to the Congregation family is the brewery, dubbed Congregation

Ales. Congregation Ales officially opened in late 2013 in the Azusa location, which prominently showcases the shiny stainless 10 BBL brewhouse in the front window. They secured distribution early, which will make them a fully distributed beer vendor serving product to not only their other locations, but also the greater Los Angeles area.

The brewpub, like other Congregation Ale House locations, includes a large stained-glass window, pew-style seating, and collection box–style tip jars. Servers and staff are titled "Sisters" or "Brothers," happy hour is referred to as "Mass," and the leather-bound menus resemble religious reading material. The new brewhouse and brewery are also adorned with religious icons, the fermentors being the most prominent, with a giant etched angel and demon graphic. The entire experience is very surreal, but very fun. The food served at Congregation is fantastic, ranging from breakfast sandwiches to rib eye burgers to exotic sausages. The pub pretzel with beer fondue is incredibly tasty and comes highly recommended, especially when paired

Congregation Dark of the Covenant

Style: Dark Ale/Old Ale

ABV: 7.7%

Availability: Year-round

Covenant pours a dark black-brown with a fleeting head. The beer incorporates some darker abbey beer flavors with a light, sweet maltiness followed up by roast. The beer is actually an old ale, but is not currently aged. It has an intense full-bodied mouth-feel and English malt caramel notes. The flavor combination reminds one of toasted marshmallows, so it's clear that it would be a good pairing with a dessert course. The chocolate tart would

definitely amplify the roasted notes. At only 7.7% the beer drinks bigger than it actually is. You might not session this one, but you could if you wanted to.

with some of the great craft beer on tap. Congregation pours some 27 drafts, including a cask, and has around 100 bottles to choose from.

Congregations Ales is new and as such their tap list and beer production line may change frequently. Brewmaster Caleb makes three beers regularly: a saison, a pale, and a dark ale. The **Congregation Praise On! Saison** has a nice citrus-forward nose with a slightly funkiness to it. It pours a hazy straw color and is very effervescent. The **Congregation Summer Pale** has bitter finish with a light, hoppy aroma. With a nice, balanced grain profile, it would go well with spicier menu items like the Hot Atomics sausage. The **Congregation Dark of the Covenant** is big, roasty, and satisfying. The beers are well made and pair easily with the great menu. Growlers are available for takeaway, and plans to bottle are in the distant future.

Congregation Ale House Locations

If you're in Southern California near Long Beach or Pasadena, make sure you stop at one of the other Congregation locations. Each serves the same food menu but has a unique draft and bottle list. Both Pasadena and Long Beach feature 32 taps plus one cask along with about 100 different bottles. Congregation Ale House features a monthly beer week at all locations where they have a featured tap list or a focus on a specific brewery. They also do a local beer fest in April at the Pasadena location, as it has a large parking lot out in front.

Long Beach Chapter, 201 E. Broadway Ave., Long Beach, CA 90802; (562) 432-BEER. Opened: 2010; Drafts: 32 taps plus 1 cask; Bottled/Canned Beers: 100+

Pasadena Chapter, 300 S. Raymond Ave., Pasadena, CA 91105; (626) 403-BEER. Opened: 2011; Drafts: 32 taps plus 1 cask; Bottled/Canned Beers: 100+

WICKS BREWING COMPANY

11620 Sterling Ave., Riverside, CA 92503; (951) 689-2739; wicksbrewing.com; @wicksbrewingco

Founded: 2013 **Founder:** Brad Wicks and Ryan Wicks **Brewer:** Brian Herbertson
Flagship Beer: Black Knight Imperial Porter **Year-round Beers:** Belgian Blonde, Black Knight Imperial Porter, Belgian Dubbel, Rais'n Hell, Sir Gordon's Pale **Seasonals/Special Releases:** Wicktoberfest, Barbaric IPA, Freight Crain Stout, Red Monk Belgian Red
Tours: Yes; hourly **Taproom:** Yes

Wicks Brewing Company is a jack-of-all-trades. Opening in April of 2013, founders Brad and Ryan Wicks wanted to do more than just open a brewery, brewpub, or home brew store, so decided to do all three. In addition to these, they are also one of the few places in SoCal that offer a brew-on-premises service, which allows locals the opportunity to brew on one of their six 1 BBL systems. The beer is then cared for, fermented out, and bottled for the customer, which is perfect for hobbyists and home brewers looking to make more than the standard 5 to 10 gallons at a time. Wicks Brewing started out in the first two months as a nanobrewery, but in June 2013 they purchased a 7 BBL copper pub system, which allows them to put out more volume than their original 1.5 BBL Blichmann setup. The team has also enlisted the help of head brewer Brian Herbertson, aka Herbie Homebrew, a local home brewing celeb, to bring Wicks beers into greater Riverside.

Wicks not only serves its own beer, but also has an impressive lineup of rotating craft guest taps. They have 12 taps total for both house and non-house. The menu is smaller and focused mainly on high-end sandwiches. They get their bread from a local bakery, and Cole Wicks is the head chef. They encourage innovation in the kitchen, so expect the food menu to change regularly and to incorporate whatever house beer is on tap at the moment.

Wicks beers are varied and combine traditional brewpub ideology along with home brew. Their **Belgian Blonde** is a straight-ahead shooter, and the **Imperial Porter** is nice, alcoholic, and roasty. The unique **Rais'n Hell** is a polarizing Helles with the addition of raisins and anise; its up-front aroma is interesting and bound to get a reaction.

Beer Lover's Pick

Imperial Porter
Style: Strong Porter
ABV: 8.5%
Availability: Limited
The standout beer at Wicks is their Imperial Porter. A fruit-forward, roasty, dark beer with charred bread and molasses, it embraces fruity esters and a thick body. It has a slight tartness that makes this 8.5% beer seem crisper and less alcoholic than it is. Imperial Porter utilizes six different grains in its grain bill and is hopped with traditional English hops. It's not available in bottles, but you can take it away in growlers.

Beer Bars & Bottle Shops

EUREKA! BURGER

580 W. First St., Claremont, CA 91711; (909) 445-8875; eurekaburger.com; @EurekaBurger
Draft Beers: 30 **Bottled/Canned Beers:** 30–40

The original location opened in 2009 and met with great success. Now with eight locations in Central/Southern California and another four coming, including a spot in Seattle, Eureka! Burger restaurants are poised to be the next hip chain capitalizing on America's "craft movement." Their signature orange exclamation point can be seen from afar, illuminating your way to satisfaction. The restaurants are big on the reclaimed dark wood and low-lit modern interior, with a target demographic of craft beeries and foodies. They get incredibly busy during the dinner hours, so be sure to make reservations or arrive early if you have a group. They serve breakfast, lunch, and dinner. The Claremont location is placed on a nice street next to a mall and plenty of parking. It would make a great stop for lunch or dinner.

Eureka! Burger—like California Pizza Kitchen or, more appropriately, Umami Burger—focuses primarily on eclectic "craft" hamburgers, sandwiches, salads, and drinks. Eureka! uses high-quality meats and ingredients and if you are a vegetarian, look no further than the San Joaquin Veggie Burger—it's fantastic. Portions are large and each location has a slightly different menu, so be sure to check prior

Other SoCal Eureka! Burger Locations

Hawthorne Airport, Eureka! Tasting Kitchen, 12101 S. Crenshaw Blvd., Hawthorne, CA 90250; (310) 331-8233

Indian Wells, 74985 Hwy. 111, Indian Wells, CA 92210; (760) 834-7700

La Jolla—San Diego, 4353 La Jolla Village Dr., San Diego, CA 92122; (858) 210-3444

Redlands, 345 W. Pearl Ave., Ste. 130, Redlands, CA 92374; (909) 335-5700

Santa Barbara, 601 Paseo Nuevo, Santa Barbara, CA 93101; (805) 618-3388

to going. Unfortunately, a tap list detailing the 30 drafts in-house is not available online; however, specials and events are frequently posted on each location's Facebook page. Each restaurant has its own tap list with local rotating beers as well as some standards. If you are looking to get an eagle's eye view of the local scene, this is a great place to start.

THE ROOKERY

117 W. Second St., Pomona, CA 91766; (909) 815-5215; rookeryalehouse.com; @RookeryAleHouse

Draft Beers: 16 rotating taps **Bottled/Canned Beers:** 16–20 specialty rotating bottles

Located in downtown Pomona, the Rookery is a solid gastropub with a great beer menu and tasty comfort food. Their logo, a wooden tankard with a raven burned into it, does a great job preparing you for the vibe. Dark wood, low lighting, Queens of the Stone Age playing in the background, and 16 fresh taps pouring local craft beers, the Rookery is a great place to hang out with friends while grabbing dinner. Their custom hot wings are unique and spicy, and their IPA-battered pickle chips, asparagus, and onion rings should be ordered right away.

The Rookery is a family-owned-and-operated business. If you get there early enough, you can pull up a chair and talk to owner Raymond or the friendly serving staff. It's clear that craft beer and gourmet comfort food are top priorities. Their menu features salads, sandwiches, burgers, and unique fried foods that are all excellently paired with the rotating tap list. The restaurant itself is located within walking distance of a music venue and several other restaurants and nightlife spots, so the Rookery is the perfect location to start and/or end your evening. Make sure to check the bottle list for any local rarities.

Lancaster

Farther to the north is the Antelope Valley, also part of Los Angeles County. This region is known for its rich aerospace history. It's about 70 miles north of downtown LA, but has two very worthwhile beer spots, a brewpub called Kinetic and a microbrewery called Bravery. Both of these beer manufacturers supply the rocket-propelled region with craft beer and should be a definite stopover when you are on your way to and from Kern River Brewing.

Breweries

BRAVERY BREWING COMPANY

42705 Eighth St. West, Lancaster, CA 93534; (661) 951-4677; braverybrewing.com; @BraveryBrewing

Founded: 2011 **Founder:** Brian Avery, R. Lee Emery, and Dave Conett **Brewer:** Brian Avery and Roger Morrisey **Flagship Beer:** Brighton ESB, Allegiance IPA **Year-round Beers:** Brighton ESB, Blackberry IPA, Allegiance IPA, Old Rat, Nitro Korova Sweet Stout **Seasonals/Special Releases:** Mr. Quality, La Fleur, Kobi, A Bitter, Hopped Up Half Wit XPA, RPA, Buster's Brown **Tours:** Yes; call for availability **Taproom:** Yes

Bravery Brewing Company has established itself as a brewery dedicated to the men and women of the armed forces. Founded by Brian Avery, R. Lee Emery (of *Full Metal Jacket* fame), and Dave Conett, Bravery Brewing creates craft beer on the nano scale using a 3 BBL brewhouse. With about 40 BBLs of current fermentation space, beers are mostly limited, but several of their beers are brewed regularly and

Allegiance IPA
Style: IPA
ABV: 7.1%
Availability: Year-round (but check online prior to going)

Bravery Brewing Company's Allegiance IPA is one of their most popular beers on tap and rightly so. Not only does the name speak to the general theme of supporting the armed forces, but the beer itself is a well-made IPA with a high level of complexity. A small dose of Munich adds a melanoidin maltiness to the base beer, but the hops are definitely center stage. Allegiance is a dry IPA with light, fruity esters and a refreshing

citrus crispness. The highlight hoppiness comes from the addition of Centennial, Cascade, and Zythos hops, which gives it a very classic West Coast IPA feel with minimal dankness.

there are plans to expand to a larger 20 BBL system in 2014. Brian started out as a home brewer and went on to work at Bootlegger's Brewery and Kinetic prior to opening his own space. He's the workhorse and has piloted his company to success with both the high-quality beers and support for the local military presence in Lancaster.

Bravery has a huge taproom for a brewery of its size and youth. The room expands into a beer hall with large communal tables propped up by oak barrels. There is an outdoor seating area in the back that can easily house large groups as well. If you want to be close to where the beer is poured, there is also a sitting area at the bar. The most prominent feature of the brewery is the massive American flag on the wall surrounded by the photos of servicemen and women. If you are a fan of the brewery and have served in the military, you can get your picture up on the wall. Along with the flag is R. Lee Emery's drill sergeant uniform from *Full Metal Jacket* displayed in a glass case. The brewery itself is right next to the taproom. It's an open warehouse, so there really isn't any separation other than a dividing line made of shirts, hats, and other merchandise.

The 3 BBL setup allows Brian to control creativity and keep experimentation going. He has several eclectic styles on tap along with a number of classic styles. Beer can be ordered in tasters, pints, or growlers, and tasting everything is highly recommended. **Old Rat** is an 8.5% English-style old ale, which is a style you don't see too often at a taproom in tasting format. The beer is traditional European style with a British graininess, residual sweetness, and notes of umami from the classic British yeast. Another worthwhile try is the **Blackberry IPA,** a solid IPA base with pureed fresh blackberries added into the secondary. Beers are rotated often, so check online before you go so you'll know what to expect from the tap list.

Brewpubs

KINETIC BREWING COMPANY

735 W. Lancaster Blvd., Lancaster, CA 93534; (661) 942-2337; kineticbrewing.com; @kineticbrewing
Founded: 2011 **Founder:** Steve Kinsey **Brewer:** Alexandra Nowell and Steve Kinsey
Flagship Beer: Potential Blonde, Rusted Gear **Year-round Beers:** Potential Blonde, Rusted Gear, Ignition, Propulsion, Fusion **Seasonals/Special Releases:** White Thai, Slingshot, El Dorado Mexican Lager, Kranken Festbier, Red Line, Citrafuge, McLennons, Afterburner, Paradox, Conundrum, Pendulum, Velocity Stout **Tours:** No formal tours offered. Call for private tour availability. **Taproom:** Yes

Kinetic Brewing Company is a new-age brewpub that pays serious attention to its beer. Founded in December 2011 by Steve Kinsey, an audio engineer from Lucasfilm and Technicolor and experienced home brewer, Kinetic is an upscale gastropub that houses a 10 BBL Premier Stainless brewhouse. The name is a play on both Steve's last name and Lancaster's vibrant history as a leader in aviation, aerospace, and now alternative energy.

Steve has been home brewing for the last 15 years and has developed most of the recipes himself, including the award-winning blonde and porter recipes. Recently he made the jump to hire a head brewer, Alex Nowell of Drake's fame, and together they are working on readjusting the recipes to prep for expansion.

The steampunk-like theme has been woven into every fiber of the space with shiny metal, airplane parts, cog sampler trays, spinning-gear tap handles, and dark wood. The flying gear logo can be found on everything from the menus to the brewhouse door. The result is a very classy, upscale gastropub feel that is both family-friendly and conducive to an older crowd as the drinking hour approaches. Kinetic also takes its food very seriously, offering lobster mac and cheese, house-made spent-grain garden burgers, Bavarian pretzels, and cottage pies. It's Euro

Fusion
Style: Porter
ABV: 6.0%
Availability: Year-round

Fusion is an incredibly drinkable porter. It focuses on body and malt depth rather than overly roasty characters. With notes of Belgian milk chocolate, pumpernickel bread, Ovaltine, and toast, Fusion is extraordinarily balanced. The hop character is subdued, which is to style but also makes this a beer that can be cooked with without bittering the food too much. This is a porter that will go equally well with ice cream, a burger,

or spicy Mexican food—versatile. Fusion won a silver at the 2012 LA County International Beer Festival. It should be ordered in a pint glass and then taken home in a growler.

fusion and pure tasty. In addition to the 6 rotating house beers they have on tap, they also have 22 guest taps, 40 assorted craft bottles, and 10-plus rare beers that range from $75 to $700.

Kinetic beers are solid. Beer is a serious focus and passion, so it takes center stage here. You'll find the beers quaffable, but not bland or lifeless. The **White Thai Witbier** is an incredible example of creativity and culinary experimentation, as it incorporates not only coconut, but also Kaffir lime and lemongrass—a perfect pairing for seafood. The **Propulsion,** a complex West Coast–style IPA, is also a solid option and would go well with the burger. The current version is incredibly tasty,

but with Alex and Steve working together now, the hop presence will likely be even more pronounced on future iterations. Kinetic is a solid option for anyone looking to marry food and beer for lunch and/or dinner. It's a bit of a drive from LA, but it's well worth it.

Desert City Day Trip

Babe's Bar-B-Que and Brewhouse, *71800 Hwy. 111, Rancho Mirage, CA 92270; (760) 346-8738; babesbbque.com*

If you're out near Palm Springs, be sure to check out Babe's Bar-B-Que and Brewhouse in Rancho Mirage. It's locally owned and operated, and serves great food and tasty craft beer. Bottles and growlers are available at and they frequently hold events. Check their website for tap listings, food specials, and events. They were recently named "Best of the Best" in *Palm Springs Life*. Keep an eye out for local beer celeb Erin Peters of TheBeerGoddess.com and founder of International Stout Day (November 8). Babe's is one of her favorite hangouts and you'll likely find her perusing the tap list and helping to educate the crowd on the best local beer.

Orange County

BREWERIES

7 Anaheim Brewery
3 Bootlegger's Brewery
6 The Bruery
16 Cismontane Brewing Company
8 Noble Ale Works
10 Old Orange Brewing Company
9 Valiant Brewing

BREWPUBS

14 Newport Beach Brewing Company
15 Stadium Brewing Company
5 TAPS Fish House & Brewery
13 Tustin Brewing Company

BEER BARS & BOTTLE SHOPS

1 Beachwood BBQ
12 Haven Gastropub
4 Hopscotch
11 Provisions Market
2 Schooner at Sunset

N

0   3   6 miles

Orange County

Orange County has exploded with craft beer in the last few years. It's teeming with amazing beer bars, a few fantastic brewpubs, and some of the greatest breweries in SoCal. From the bombastic and creative large-format bottles coming out of The Bruery to the calculated classic styles made at TAPS Fish House to the Naughty Sauce made by Noble Ale Works, the OC's beer culture is flourishing. After you take in the scene at Old Towne Orange, drive down the coast into Seal and Sunset Beaches for some craft beer and water time.

Note: Beware of toll roads. Several highways in Orange County have been converted to toll roads, which makes traveling with cash a good idea. Pay attention to signs, especially when approaching Rancho Santa Margarita and the beach cities.

Breweries

ANAHEIM BREWERY

336 S. Anaheim Blvd., Anaheim, CA 92805; (714) 780-1888; anaheimbrew.com;
@AnaheimBrewery

Founded: 2010 **Founder:** Barbara and Greg Gerovac **Brewer:** Barbara and Greg Gerovac
Flagship Beer: Anaheim 1888 **Year-round Beers:** Anaheim 1888, Anaheim Gold,
Anaheim Red, Anaheim Hefeweizen, Coast to Coast IPA **Seasonals/Special Releases:**
Schwarz Beer, Oktoberfest, Winter Wheat **Tours:** No formal tours offered. Call for private
tour availability. **Taproom:** Yes

Located in the heart of Anaheim, approximately 1.5 miles from the north end of
Disneyland, Anaheim Brewery is revitalizing an old brand. Founded and reopened
by beer-loving couple Barbara and Greg Gerovac, Anaheim Brewery reopened its new
tasting room in 2011. The original brewery closed in 1920 during Prohibition, but
the new team decided they wanted to bring not only the name back into recognition,

but also some of the old styles. Both Barbara and Greg are no strangers to beer and spent a seven-year spread in Bavaria, immersing themselves in the local brewery beer culture. It's this influence, along with a family tie to Milwaukee's Pabst Brewery, that led them to open up and revamp the old Anaheim name.

Anaheim Brewery is located right off Anaheim Boulevard in a decent-size building next door to an Umami Burger. The neighboring park has been set to receive a farmers' market and fresh packinghouse produce vendors, so the community's open-air vibe is sure to please beer lovers from all over. The tasting room is a long, narrow room with an equally long old-style wooden bar. Each beer tap is crowned with a classic monochromatic wooden lathed handle proudly displaying the brewery's name. Several large glass windows sit behind the bar, with a great view into brewing operations. Everything is out in the open, including the 20 BBL brewhouse. There is

Beer Lover's Pick

Anaheim 1888
Style: California Common—
    Steam Beer
ABV: 5.5%
Availability: Year-round

Anaheim 1888 is based on one of the original Anaheim Brewery recipes and is a classic-style steam beer updated with a modern hop profile. 1888 was actually the year that the original owner of Anaheim Brewery, Friedrich Conrad, started construction on the facility. The gold medal winner is amber-colored, includes Centennial and Columbus hops, and has a small portion of wheat added to increase body. It has a nice toffee finish along with a citrus-zesty hop bite. Beers like this go down well all year, and this one is no different. You'll be able to find Anaheim 1888 at Disneyland, in bottles locally, and at the taproom.

a large outside patio area along with an open food policy that allows people to bring in whatever food they want. Make sure to visit on Taco Tuesday and Fiesta Friday to get your beer and Mexican food fix.

Anaheim Brewery beer focuses primarily on German classic styles along with revitalizing old styles from the original brewery. Most offerings are made to style à la Reinheitsgebot guidelines and are in the 4.0 to 5.5% range. Their flagship **Anaheim 1888** is based on a recipe from the original Anaheim Brewery, with an upgraded hop profile. The **Anaheim Gold** is a standard blonde ale, and the **Anaheim Hefeweizen** is a Bavarian-style offering. **Anaheim Red** is a full-bodied, malty ale with a noticeable caramel character. **Coast to Coast IPA** is made with 100 percent California-grown barley and a generous amount of Columbus hops. There are a few seasonal taproom-only offerings as well, such as the **Schwarz Beer, Chocolate Porter,** and **Oktoberfest Lager.** Beer can be purchased in 12-ounce bottles and taken home in large German-style flip-top growlers.

BOOTLEGGER'S BREWERY

130 S. Highland Ave., Fullerton, CA 92832; (714) 871-2337; bootleggersbrewery.com; @bootleggersbrew
Founded: 2008 **Founder:** Aaron and Patricia Barkenhagen **Brewer:** Aaron Barkenhagen **Flagship Beer:** Old World Hefeweizen **Year-round Beers:** Old World Hefeweizen, Palomino Pale Ale, Rustic Rye IPA, Black Phoenix, Golden Chaos **Seasonals/Special Releases:** Milk Chocolate Porter, Mountain Meadow, Herbed Blonde Ale, Pumpkin Ale, Knuckle Sandwich, Eliminator IPA, Dr. Tongue, Doggery Brown Ale, Lupulin Thrill, Amber Alt Ale **Tours:** No **Taproom:** Yes

When Bootlegger's Brewery originally opened in 2008, it placed itself next to the Fullerton train tracks, a stone's throw away from where their new facility and taproom is. Owner and brewer Aaron Barkenhagen recently expanded the Orange County–based brewery and has since separated the facility and serving room aspects. The brewhouse and taproom live in two completely separate buildings. Tours of the brewing facility are currently not being offered, but you can enjoy the large-format tasting room, complete with outdoor courtyard.

Bootlegger's stays true to its namesake and serves all beers out of mixed mason jars. It's a fun and unique presentation. The taproom is decently sized and can accommodate large groups with the addition of the courtyard, which comes complete with Cornhole and giant Jenga. For fans of retro arcade games, there's an antique Joust cabinet between the restrooms. The pilot system can easily be seen through a viewing window to the left of the bar and may even be running when you visit. The bar itself is a laminated countertop of pennies. If you're planning to visit

and it happens to be the second Saturday of the month, bring a stein because it's Stein Night. Patrons can bring in their favorite German mugs and get fills of any beer under 7.0% for a quarter an ounce.

Bootlegger's beers are making their way around SoCal and can be found in most gastropubs from Ventura through San Diego, if they're on rotation. The 22-ounce bottles are available for their core brands and some special releases like **Knuckle Sandwich,** but the most eclectic experiments are saved for taproom only. If you like classic styles, you'll definitely find some great examples here, but you'll also find twists like **Black Phoenix,** a chipotle coffee stout. There are also one-offs like lemongrass Witbiers, cherry sours, and beers brewed with dark molasses. The brewery prides itself in being creative and experimental, having a good time, and sharing everything with the local community.

Knuckle Sandwich
Style: Double IPA
ABV: 10.0%
Availability: Brewed four times a
year

Every brewery has their amazing,
popular seasonal release, and for
Bootlegger's it's Knuckle Sandwich.
In the craze of double IPAs and
super-hoppiness, beer can get lost in
the fray, but Knuckle is one of OC's
original big hoppy beers. Clocking in
at about 10.0% ABV, it's a big beer,
but it doesn't drink that way. With
forward notes of fresh tropical pineapple and an overall tropical aroma,
the alcohol is expertly (dangerously)
masked. It's not cloying and has a level of refreshment to it that most DIPAs lack.
The malt profile is low and there is a subdued, but present, dankness to the beer.
You'll definitely want to try this floral, citrus bomb of tropical goodness.

Bayhawk Ales

Bayhawk Ales, *2000 Main St. Irvine, CA 92614; (949) 442-7565; bayhawk
ales.com.*
Located in the Irvine McCormick & Schmick's Seafood Restaurant is one of
the oldest contract breweries in Southern California, Bayhawk Ales. Owner
and brewer Karl Zappa has been making beer in Orange County since 1994
and continues to be one of the only production and contract breweries in
the area.

THE BRUERY

715 Dunn Way, Placentia, CA 92870; (714) 996-6258; thebruery.com; @thebruery
Founded: 2008 **Founder:** Patrick Rue **Brewer:** Tyler King **Flagship Beer:** Saison Rue and Mischief **Year-round Beers:** Saison Rue, Mischief, Loakal Red, Humulus Lager, Rugbrod, Hottenroth Berliner Weisse **Seasonals/Special Releases:** Saison De Lente, Trade Winds, Autumn Maple, Partridge in a Pear Tree, 2 Turtle Doves, 3 French Hens, 4 Calling Bird, 5 Golding Rings, Batch 1 Levud's, Batch 50 GFAR, Batch 300 Tripel, Papier, Coton, Cuir, Fruet, Black Tuesday, Oude Tart, White Oak, Smoking Wood, Pinolambicus, Oui Oui, Melange, Sour in the Rye, Filmishmish, Trois Poules Francais, Otiose, Reueuze, San Pagaie, Tart of Darkness, Collaboration Series beers, Humulus Bruin, Humulus Gold, Humulus Blonde, Humulus XPA, Humulus Rice, Snicklefritz **Tours:** Yes; free tours Sat, every hour on the hour from noon to 7 p.m. **Taproom:** Yes

Few breweries in Southern California have developed as large a cult following as Orange County–based The Bruery. Cleverly named after brewery owner Patrick Rue, The Bruery could be said to be the Dogfish Head of the West Coast. Their bottles are all large-format 750 ml champagne style and are usually higher on the ABV scale as well, though they do have some very low-alcohol options like their **Hottenroth Berliner Weisse,** a personal favorite of mine. Patrick started the operation about three years ago with lead brewer Tyler King on a 15 BBL stainless system purchased from Escondido-based supplier Premier Stainless. It has since grown into one of the most respected and popular breweries in the greater LA area.

Bruery beers are unique, all of them. They use a house yeast that is of Belgian origin and typically blend it with other strains to get their desired flavors. No ingredients are off-limits, and as such they've put everything in from yams to *shichimi* ("seven spices" in Japanese), and more recently Thai tea and coconut milk. Barrel aging at The Bruery is a serious focus, and that includes oak-aged bourbon monsters like **Black Tuesday** as well as blended lambics such as **Ruezue** and **Sour in the Rye.**

The Bruery recently expanded their facility to accommodate their cooperage as well as build an entirely new tasting room, and, boy, is it beautiful. Dark wood, stainless, chalkboards, and windows that look into the brewery—what more could you ask for? Tours are available at selected times; you can also check their website and/or call ahead. The tap list is constantly changing as specialty projects continue, and now that the brewery has a small-scale, fully functioning 3 BBL pilot system, you'll see even more cool one-offs. The Bruery is a destination, and if you are in Orange County or LA for a weekend, it should definitely be added to your must-see list. If you are a local, you can even join the ranks of their highly coveted and pricey mug club, the Bruery Reserve Society and Hoarders Society.

Orange County

Beer Lover's Pick

Hottenroth Berliner Weisse
Style: Berlin-Style Tart Wheat Ale (Berliner Weiss)
ABV: 2.5%–3.1% (batch range)
Availability: Year-round

Hottenroth indoctrinated me into the sour world. It also taught me that beers can be below 3.0% ABV. It's a great gateway sour beer, as it is light-bodied, modest in alcohol, spritzy, and has a very pleasant citrus tartness. One could even liken it to champagne, and they often do when they make mimosas with Hottenroth on the weekends. Hottenroth is opaque and funky, and if you're in the taproom, can be altered with traditional woodruff and raspberry syrups. This Berliner Weisse is unfiltered, bottle-conditioned, and sometimes comes in a kumquat-infused version called Nottenroth. It was named in memory of Fred and Sarah Hottenroth, friends of the Rue family. It's a perfect summer beer and is easy to take home and share in a signature Bruery 750 ml bottle.

CISMONTANE BREWING COMPANY

29851 Aventura, Ste. D, Rancho Santa Margarita, CA 92688; (949) 888-2739; cismontanebrewing.com; @CisbrewCo
Founded: 2009 **Founder:** Evan Weinberg and Ross Stuart **Brewer:** Evan Weinberg
Flagship Beer: The Citizen **Year-round Beers:** The Citizen, Holy Jim Falls, Black's Dawn, Coulter IPA **Seasonals/Special Releases:** 1st Anniversary Black Lager, 2nd Anniversary Belgian IPA, 3rd Anniversary Belgian Strong, Belgian Dubbel, Black's Nocturne, Brut Du Sauvin, California Buckwheat Oktoberfest, Cali IPA Easy as ABZ,

Chardonnay Barrel-Aged Brut du Sauvin, Classified Doppelsticke, Dos Cone Es, 2011 Dead Santa, 2012 Dead Santa, Double Rainbow IPA All the Way, Deciduous XPA, The Mesa, El Modena Mild, Oso, Pandion Pale, Smokin' Santiago Scotch Ale, Session Saison, Southern Hemi, Small Beer, TJ Slough, El Corazon Rojo, La Crema, Nopalito de Trigo, Salto Vivo, collaboration brews **Tours:** Yes—upon request; dependant on availability **Taproom:** Yes

Cismontane Brewing Company is nestled in an unassuming strip mall in the quaint hamlet of Rancho Santa Margarita. Founded by down-to-earth artisan Evan Weinberg and his compadre Ross Stuart, Cismontane has made a name for itself with its über-creative beer styles and laid-back demeanor. Evan actually comes from an engineering and geography background, so beer wasn't his first career path. In fact, his road to beer has included oceanography, commercial real estate, organic heirloom tomato farming, Napa winery work, and business analysis software. The engineering analytics, attention to quality ingredients, and wine influence have definitely remained and are the basis for Cismontane's brand, which focuses on local ingredients and small batches. Evan is very easygoing and is a pleasure to talk with, so if you see him in the brewery, make sure to say hello.

The 3,500-square-foot facility officially opened in 2010 in the old Saddleback Brewery location, which was originally one unit (1,500 square feet). Since then it has expanded to two units operated by Cismontane. The 15 BBL Bohemian brewhouse pumps out four to six batches a week, which brought them up to 2,000 BBL in 2013. They are projecting to double that in 2014. The brewery portion of the facility lives in the back and wraps around the sides of the tasting room, where most people gather. The tasting room is modestly sized, with a sort of light-wood cedar look to it—it's very rustic, borrowing from Evan's Napa past. Tables to the left and right of the door overlook the fermentation tanks, and there is limited seating at the 6-foot-wide bar. The entire establishment is synergic with Evan's basic life philosophy. They pour anywhere from six to eight beers at a time and frequently have casks. Bottles and growlers of their limited-release and year-round beers are also available for purchase.

Cismontane beers run the gamut from classic styles to barrel-aged sours. Evan and head brewer James Classick brew what they want, the way they want to, and when they want to. The flagship beer, **The Citizen,** is a California common, aka "steam," beer, and although it's the most popular, putting them on the map, it's Evan's least favorite to brew. Lately he's been experimenting with a lot of oak, creating American strongs, barrel-aged sours, and offerings that blend the world of wine and beer. The limited release **Mesa** is an incredibly complex blend of 25 percent Santa Lucia highland Riesling and 75 percent pilsner and is a local favorite. Bottles

Dos Cone Es

Style: Rye IPA—Strong Ale Hybrid

ABV: 11.5%

Availability: Limited year-round

This hard-hitting strong rye ale blends the strength of traditional American strong ale with the hoppy maltiness of a rye IPA. Intense caramel and fruity esters dominate the beer, with both bright and dark citrus and prune notes. It pours a brilliant orange-amber color with a persistent head. Dos Cone Es is a hybrid style, which Evan refers to as "a Hoppy Strong Double IPA." He made this 130 IBU beer on a bet and oak ages it for

four to five weeks. Brewing it is taxing, as it yields half the volume of a regular brew and requires four brews to fill up a single fermentor. It was a beer he hoped nobody would like, yet it's now being bottled and added to the regular rotation due to its overwhelming popularity.

were sold in 750 ml format and flew off the shelves. Other beers like **Dos Cone Es** and **Dead Santa** kick up the ABV and experiment with nontraditional brewing methods and or fruit/spice additions. If you are looking for a straight-ahead dank IPA, check out **Coulter IPA.** It delivers high-velocity resin and an intense floral hoppiness. It's definitely recommended to get a tasting flight here, as the Cismontane crew experiments regularly with different beers and you don't want to miss your new favorite beer that you didn't know existed.

NOBLE ALE WORKS

1621 S. Sinclair St., Anaheim, CA 92806; (714) 634-2739; noblealeworks.com;
@noblealeworks

Founded: 2011 **Founder:** Jerry Kolbly **Brewer:** Evan Price **Flagship Beer:** Breakaway
Pale **Year-round Beers:** Good Ship ESB, Big Whig IPA, Breakaway Pale, Pistol Whip'd
Seasonals/Special Releases: Picnic Bubbly, Early's Grey Dinghy, Rosalita Lager,
Naughty Sauce, Until the Night Man, Black Sass **Tours:** Yes—upon request **Taproom:** Yes

Opening in January of 2011, Noble Ale Works actually started out as a contract
brewery manufacturing out of the Upland-based Dale Bros facility. They secured
a nice location in Anaheim near the Anaheim Angels stadium and went through a
major beer-brand revamp in 2012. Founder Jerry Kolbly wanted to take the fledgling

Beer Lover's Pick

Pistol Whip'd
Style: Pilsner
ABV: 4.2%
Availability: Year-round
These days, traditional style pilsners
tend to get passed over for bigger, bolder beers. Pistol Whip'd is
definitely not one you should pass
up. Evan spent serious time at BJ's,
Hangar 24, and TAPS learning how to
make classic styles and how to make
them well. Pistol Whip'd is a beautifully done Czech-style pils with a crisp
citrus hop finish. Instead of the classic Saaz, Noble uses the New Zealand
Motueka hop, which imparts a lime
zestiness. When paired with the light,

creamy-bread malt profile, it is a real treat. At 4.2% this is a quaffable yet complex
baseball beer, perfect for pregame, postgame, and during the game. Get a growler or
a 22-ounce bottle to take home.

brewery to new heights and made an executive decision to woo the hotshot head brewer from TAPS Fish House & Brewery, Evan Price. Evan, who had worked at three BJ's locations and Hangar 24 before moving to TAPS, was looking to move up and take on his own beer program. Together, Jerry and Evan have created one of the best up-and-coming breweries in the Orange County.

Noble Ale Works, like many other breweries, is located in an industrial park off the freeway. It is pretty simple to get to and easy to find, as it's the only building with a grain silo on the outside. Noble's taproom is modestly sized and sports an average of 7 to 10 beers on tap, which usually includes a cask ale. The facility is in two parts, the main taproom and the brewhouse next door. They both have seating and standing areas. If you're on the brewery side, you'll be able to gaze at the 15 BBL brewhouse and large conicals, which just recently were expanded. Noble currently does about 1,300 BBLs a year, but with the new tanks plans on more than doubling that to 3,000 BBLs. All in all the taproom has a pleasant vibe, is very sports-friendly, and features some cool hand-carved wooden signs.

Noble beers can be ordered in flights or growlers, and they also have four of their flagships, **Breakaway, Good Ship**, **Big Whig**, and **Pistol Whip'd,** available in 22-ounce bottles. The beers are top-notch and clean, with a few style variations. One of the most sought-after beers on the Noble roster is a seasonal coffee-infused stout called **Naughty Sauce,** which pours golden clear, not dark and opaque. Other worthy mentions are **Earl's Grey Dinghy,** which is an Earl Grey tea–infused small beer made off of the Good Ship; **Rosalita,** a hibiscus-infused lager; and **Picnic Bubbly,** a tasty saison-style ale. The beers at Noble are very well crafted, and you'll definitely find something that fits your tastes.

OLD ORANGE BREWING COMPANY

1444 N. Batavia St., Orange, CA 92867; (714) 744-8410; oldorangebrewing.com; @OldOrangeBrewCo
Founded: 2011 **Founder:** Tony Foster, Jerry Nine, Brian Lambrose, and Mark Villa
Brewer: Brian Lambrose **Flagship Beer:** Smudge Pot Imperial Stout **Year-round Beers:** Street Fair Summer Ale, Old Dummy American Strong Ale, Thumb Master Double IPA, Backseat Blonde Ale, Cannonball IPA, OOBerweizen Hefeweizen, Statesman Porter, Smudge Pot Russian Imperial Stout **Seasonals/Special Releases:** Apple Wheat, Blonde with Agave, Cussin' Jim **Tours:** No formal tours offered. Call for private tour availability.
Taproom: Yes

What do you get when you combine four local Orange County friends who wanted nothing more than to open a business together? Old Orange Brewing Company. Old Orange opened its doors in July of 2011 with the mission to make

Smudge Pot
Style: Russian Imperial Stout
ABV: 11.2%
Availability: Year-round

Other than having a supercool name, Smudge Pot is a heavy-hitting Russian imperial stout that hides its high octane content very well. It is very smooth, with balanced roasted barley, burnt toast, plum, and coffee notes. The beer is served on nitro, which brings out a sort of vanilla quality that rounds out the overall flavor. What's unusual about the production of

Smudge Pot is the generous amount of brown sugar added during the brew. The result is a slightly sweeter stout with some molasses notes. You won't be able to session this, so if you want more, bring a growler home and enjoy it with friends.

small-production beers using traditional manual brewing methods. Friends Tony Foster, Jerry Nine, Mark Villa, and brewer Brian Lambrose had been home brewing for over five years. When Brian completed his second tour in Iraq, they decided it was time to make their dreams come true. Together they pilot an 8 BBL brewhouse with 42 BBL of fermentation space.

Old Orange Brewing is a small operation, but has a decent-size taproom. The first thing you'll notice walking in is a tall metal contraption to the left of the door that looks like a steampunk stove. It's a smudge pot, which was used in the orange orchards to prevent frost from harming the trees, and it's only fitting that a brewery celebrating SoCal's citrus industry would have one. The taproom has mixed seating, including small-format tables and about 15 seats at the bar. It also has a standing area in the back that overlooks the brewhouse. On the walls you'll find local art, including the original pieces used for their label artwork. The labels are fun and have a bit of a carnival beach art look to them. Old Orange holds frequent events with military veterans celebrating the city of Orange and the men and women who fight to protect it.

The brewery focuses on classic styles, but does deviate a bit with a few of their specials. Because they are small production only, beer is very limited and runs out frequently, which gives them the opportunity to experiment with a wide array of recipes. You'll find their year-round beers like **Backseat Blonde** and then iterations of it like **Blonde with Agave.** Their **Cussin' Jim** is a crowd-favorite IPA with an incredibly light body and balanced malt profile. You may also find experiments like the **Apple Wheat,** a Bavarian wheat-style beer spiked with sour apple concentrate, which tastes like a caramelized apple pie. You can order the Beer Lover's Pick first, but I would recommend grabbing a sampler flight so you can check out the unique one-offs they have available. Old Orange Brewing Company recently got distribution within San Diego and LA and bottles a few of their year-round beers like **Street Fair.** You can also take home beer in growlers.

VALIANT BREWING

2294 N. Batavia St., Orange, CA 92865; (714) 408-2825; valiantbrewing.com; @valiantbrewing

Founded: 2013 **Founder:** Brian Shroepfer and Kelly Schroepfer **Brewer:** Brian Schroepfer **Flagship Beer:** Fields Ablaze **Year-round Beers:** First Flight, Jericho, Axiom, Fields Ablaze, 31 Kings, Hotspur, Veranda, Mighty Maximus **Seasonals/Special Releases:** Octave, Crescendo, Mounds of Grounds, Pathos, Stentorian, The Bruce **Tours:** Yes **Taproom:** Yes

Brian and Kelly Schroepfer opened Valiant Brewing's doors in 2013 and set out not only to make a plethora of styles, but also to focus on the largest of them. Both coming from mechanical engineering backgrounds, the couple picked up their love for beer from home brewing. Brian is always in the taproom making sure his guests are happy, and is happy to giving brewing advice. Coming from a Catholic background, Valiant has decided to identify itself and its beer names with scripture-related or equivalent titles. Both Brian and Kelly believe very strongly in the passion of brewing, community, and supporting those around them.

The Valiant tasting room is set inside a large, open industrial warehouse. High-top and repurposed barrel tables are set up around the floor space, and a medium-size bar sits in the back. The main feature of this space is the beautiful 15 BBL Premier Stainless brewhouse with matching fermentors. Everything is new, shiny, and built to make large quantities of the bubbly stuff. There is plenty of room to

Fields Ablaze
Style: Saison
ABV: 7.2%
Availability: Year-round

While not as strong as some of their other beers, the Fields Ablaze saison is still a modest 7.2%. It's a very quaffable farmhouse ale with notes of lemon, vanilla, and almond. Fields Ablaze is not heavily spiced and has very high carbonation. It's a beer that refreshes with its dry finish and citrus overtones. The inspiration behind the beer is actually more of a historical reference. Brian named it after the blazing fields that farmhands work in during hot days in Belgium. Recently this beer took a silver medal at the Los Angeles Commercial Beer Competition, which is a great honor and even more of a reason to make this the first beer you try when you visit.

stand, barrels in the back corner, and even a chess board. Brian keeps a large bucket of pretzels by the bar as well to help people stay well nourished. Tours aren't officially given, as the brewery is right next to you, but Brian is proud to talk about the brewhouse provided there isn't a large line waiting for refills.

Although still very new, Valiant Brewing has been making a name for itself among local OC patrons by serving high-octane strong ales, barleywines, and Belgians. One of their most popular beers is a 13.7% giant called **First Flight**, part of their Pillars of Strength series. It's a strong ale with an incredibly strong aromatic component. Their other go-to is a double IPA called **Jericho,** which is sufficiently dank with heavy citrus notes and a 10.0% rating. If you're looking for descriptions of beers while you sample your flight, they have takeaway tasting sheets with descriptions and QR codes, which direct right to their location on the website. Beers can be taken home in 32- and 64-ounce growlers, and bottles are slated for 2014.

Brewpubs

NEWPORT BEACH BREWING COMPANY

2920 Newport Blvd., Newport Beach, CA 92663; (949) 675-8449;
newportbeachbrewingcompany.com; @NBBrewingCo
Founded: 1995 **Founder:** Mike Madlock **Brewer:** Derek Bouchet **Flagship Beer:**
Newport Beach Blonde **Year-round Beers:** Newport Beach Blonde, Hoppy Ending IPA,
Pelican Pale Ale, Bisbees ESB, Funky Monkey, I Got Wood, Newport Coast Steam, Lil
Cowboy **Seasonals/Special Releases:** Double Dry Hop IPA, Rip Tide Red, JD Stout,
Newport Beach Sour **Tours:** No formal tours offered. Call for private tour availability.

Newport Beach Brewing Company is a traditional brewpub and is the only brewery on Balboa Island. Mike Madlock opened the brewery, which used to be an old-style gourmet fish market, in 1995. Coming from a real estate and construction background, studying at Cal State Fullerton, Mike wanted to own a "Cheers bar" and decided that Newport Beach was the perfect home for it. The result is a family-friendly Euro pub/beach bar that serves American fare and a wide selection of house

Newport Beach Sour Ale
Style: Sour Blonde
ABV: 3.5%
Availability: Seasonal summer

It's not often you find tasty sour beers at a brewpub, but Newport Beach Brewing Company has definitely proved that statement wrong. Rather than making an enamel-peeling sour beer, they've created a barrel-aged Berliner Weisse with a relatively low ABV and smooth tartness. It's beers like these that help educate those new to sours about the potential of the style. The blonde is very spritzy with

notes of cherry and a light oakiness. It has an incredible fruity aroma along with a lactic bite. It's not a regularly available beer, but it should be, as it's the perfect companion to a long stroll on the beach.

beers. Since its 1995 opening, Newport Beach Brewing has become a fixture on the island and enjoys crowds young and old, locals and travelers.

Mike's entire philosophy is to provide a smart location, good value, and great beer to the people of Newport Beach. Prices are very reasonable and portions are large. You'll notice it right away when you drive onto the island over the bridge— the sign in front is big and orange. Coming from the back, you'll see an intensely colorful grain silo and playful beach artwork. The vibe, with its diner tables, beach umbrellas, and stained glass windows, is very friendly. Parking in back is definitely recommended if there is space. Newport Beach Brewing has regular events and an annual beer fest in the fall. They have late-night drink specials Friday and Saturday, Taco Tuesday, and all-day happy hour on Monday. Be sure to check the website or call before visiting to see if there is anything special going on.

Award-winning brewer Derek Bouchet brews on a 14 BBL steam-fired specific mechanical system and offers a wide variety of classic styles. From IPAs to stouts, you'll find them here. The **Lil Cowboy** stout is an incredibly refreshing version of the style with a complex roastiness and smooth aftertaste. It also comes in a Jack Daniels barrel-aged version, which is perfect for dessert pairings. Their flagship **Newport Beach Blonde** ale is a hit with the beachgoers and pairs nicely with any of the seafood on the menu—try the BrewCo Ceviche. If you're into spicy, order the **Double Dry Hopped IPA** and pair it with their tasty chicken wings. Order a colorful flight and share it with a friend. You'll definitely find something you like. Beer can be taken home in growlers, and there are even limited 22-ounce bottles of brewmaster reserve one-offs available for purchase.

STADIUM BREWING COMPANY

26731 Aliso Creek Rd., Aliso Viejo, CA 92656; (949) 448-9611; stadiumbrewingco.com
Founded: 2002 **Founder:** John Waters **Brewer:** Greg Schneider **Flagship Beer:** Blueberry Lager **Year-round Beers:** Blonde Lager, Blueberry Lager, Stadium Hefeweizen, Amber **Seasonals/Special Releases:** Southern Hemi Pale Ale **Tours:** No formal tours offered. Call for private tour availability.

Stadium Brewing Company is located in a shopping and restaurant complex in Aliso Viejo. It's right next to a Buffalo Wild Wings and the Stadium Theater. Founded by beer professional and restaurateur John Waters, of Stadium Tavern, Redondo Beach Brewing, and Manhattan Beach Brewing fame, Stadium opened in 2002. John was joined by renowned brewer Greg Schneider and highly respected chef Octavio Montoya. Together the team brings forth a classic upscale brewpub and sports bar that is family-friendly and beer drinker approved.

Stadium Brewing Company is tucked away in the back corner behind all the shops and next to a park. The classic 15 BBL copper brewhouse is right in the front of the restaurant behind a glass atrium. If you are lucky, and early, you'll get to see head brewer Schneider working his magic as he brews the Stadium beer lineup. The inside of the pub is large and open, with a huge dining area to the right and the sports bar to the left. There is an extremely large outdoor seating area, which on hot summer Sundays is host to reggae bands and other live music. They do beer events seasonally, with a World Beer festival featuring international bottled beer every couple of months. Leftover beer is put in the mystery beer bin, and patrons at the bar can order 12-ounce bottles for $3 or anything bigger for $5. The restaurant offers a full lineup of food, including pizza, burgers, chophouse entrees, and pub food.

Blueberry Lager
Style: Pre-Prohibition Lager
    with Fruit
ABV: 4.8%
Availability: Year-round

Craft beer drinkers and purists may scoff, but Blueberry Lager is not only a fruit-infused beer, but an impressively well made one at that. The base beer recipe is a traditional German Lagerbier with a heavy focus on light German pilsner malts. An up-front melanoidin breadiness dominates the palate, which is then blasted with notes of fresh blueberry. This beer tastes like fresh blueberries, not artificial flavoring, and is not sweet. It pours a slightly purple straw color with a persistent and creamy head. Blueberry Lager is served with or without whole blueberries added. Get the blueberries—they're fun to watch.

The beer lineup at Stadium Brewing Company is pretty focused and traditional. Many people that come in ordering a Stella, Coors, or other macro draft will be swayed by knowledgeable staff to try one of the house brews. The lightest offering is the **Blonde Lager,** a crisp hybrid pilsner. Stadium also offers a traditional **Bavarian Hefeweizen** and **Amber Ale.** The **Southern Hemi Pale Ale** is offered in the summer and uses 100 percent New Zealand hops, a fact they are proud of. It has a wonderful lime-citrus aroma, a medium body, and a touch of caramel. Flights are available and are a great start if you are undecided. Aside from the house beers, Stadium Brewing offers 21 rotating guest taps, including both craft and macro brands. They do not offer growlers.

TAPS FISH HOUSE & BREWERY

101 E. Imperial Hwy., Brea, CA 92821; (714) 257-0101; tapsfishhouse.com; @TapsFishHouse

Founded: 1999 **Founder:** Joe Manzella **Brewer:** Victor Novak **Flagship Beer:** Cream Ale **Year-round Beers:** Cream Ale, Crystal Pils, Cali Gold XPA, Irish Red, Vienna Lager, 90-Shilling Scotch Ale, American Pale Ale, Bohemian Pils **Seasonals/Special Releases:** Belgian White, Kellerpils, Helles, Schwarzbier, Mocha Stout, Imperial Balinese Coffee Stout, Pumpkin Ale, Doppelbock, Oktoberfest, Rye Kooder, Bière de Garde, Roggenbier, Crystal Pils, Seaward Pale Ale—Single Hop Series, Saison, Barleywine, Thomas Jefferson Ale, Oaked Thomas Jefferson, India Pale Ale, Freyr White IPA, Toasted Santa, Alt, Belgian Tripel, Biere de Luxe, Blanche de Conundrum, Dunkel, Vienna Country Lager, German Pilsner, Hefeweizen, Kölsch, Neo-Colonial Stout, Oatmeal Stout, Porter, Poseidon, Imperial Russian Stout, Remy, Trace of Remy, Pappy Remy, Hillbilly **Tours:** No formal tours offered. Call for private tour availability. **Taproom:** Yes

In Orange County's Brea lives one of the most awesome traditional and serious brewpubs around. TAPS Fish House & Brewery is more like a full-production brewery with a phenomenal restaurant attached. Here you'll find an exceptional focus on world-class beer and food with reason to celebrate both together or separately. TAPS originally opened its doors in 1999 under the direction of talented restaurateur Joe Manzella. Joe needed an exceptional brewer to make his vision come true, so he hired classic-style brewmaster Victor Novak, who continues to brew for TAPS today. Victor brews over 50 different styles of traditional/neo-traditional ales and lagers, which change regularly. Many of these beers can be found around Southern California, as TAPS is a fully distributed brewery with a second location in Corona, CA. In the summer months, they hold their annual TAPS Craft Beer Festival, and in April and October they have a special beer-pairing dinner that is not to be missed.

TAPS Fish House & Brewery is a beautiful location. The building is huge, and you can easily find it off Imperial Highway by looking for the large red-and-orange TAPS logo and grain silo. Inside you'll find an incredibly upscale restaurant that resembles a very fancy European-style pub crossed with a fine-dining establishment. They specialize in excellent seafood and chops, which includes amazing, fresh market catches and oysters. They have a wonderful brunch on Sunday that should not be missed; it includes not only an oyster bar and full buffet, but also two beers of your choice. Quality is taken very seriously at TAPS, so you won't find anything on the mediocre side. The 15-barrel brewery is located on the right of the restaurant as you walk in and is responsible for some 1,800 barrels of award-winning beer annually. Speaking of awards, Victor's beers are some of the best examples of classic styles around, and he remains one of the most decorated brewers in Southern California.

Orange County

Thomas Jefferson Ale
Style: American Strong Ale
ABV: 9.5%
Availability: Seasonal
summer—July Fourth

Thomas Jefferson Ale draws from Victor's obsession with history and education in political geography. The recipe is based on what the famous politician may have been brewing and drinking in Monticello 200 years ago. East Kent Goldings pair nicely with the base Maris Otter malt and gives it a spicy dark toffee nose. It's fruit forward with a ripened strawberry character.

With an assertive caramel breadiness, the beer warms as it goes down and is satisfyingly hearty. It's a complex beer that sort of reminds one of the German beer Aventinus, and is a great way to celebrate the Fourth of July, when it is released every year. The oaked version spends one year aging on American oak chips and has a richer caramel and toffee character.

The brewery focuses on classic styles like German pilsners and Vienna lagers, but then interesting and exciting deviations like the **Imperial Balinese Coffee Stout, Oscura,** and **Biere de Luxe,** a Bière de Garde aged in Cabernet barrels. The **Cream Ale** is one of their lightest beers and is definitely a great start. Victor is one of the few brewers in the area that makes actual traditional lagers regularly, and it's something he takes very seriously. The full beer lineup changes regularly and seasonally, but you are bound to find a German-style lager on the menu, which you should immediately order. The **Kellerbier,** a Dortmunder-style lager, has the body of a Helles and the hoppiness of a German pils. **Cali Gold IPA** is a worthwhile selection if you are in the mood for something more American-themed. Victor barrel-ages an imperial Russian stout series called **Remy** that is bottle-released annually. If you can get your hands on some on tap or in bottle, it should not be missed. TAPS sells growlers, and they will be bottling and canning more of their beers in 2014, which, like their kegged beer, can be found throughout Southern California.

TUSTIN BREWING COMPANY

13011 Newport Ave., #100, Tustin, CA 92780; (714) 665-2337; tustinbrewery.com; tustinbrewery@gmail.com
Founded: 1996 **Founder:** Jason Jeralds **Brewer:** Jerrod Larsen **Flagship Beers:** Lemon Heights Hefeweizen, Old Town IPA **Year-round Beers:** Golden Spike Light Ale, Lemon Heights Hefeweizen, American Pale Ale, Old Town IPA, Red Hill Red, Blimp Hangar Porter **Seasonals/Special Releases:** Jackson's Double IPA, Bogey's Dry Irish Stout, Honey Badger Blonde, Stay All Day India Session Ale, Oktoberfest **Tours:** No formal tours offered. Call for private tour availability.

Tustin Brewing Company is located off Newport Avenue in an upscale strip mall in Tustin. The classic brewpub was originally opened in 1996 by proprietor Jason Jeralds. Up until recently the brewing program was headed by none other than Jonathan Porter, now at Smog City, but is currently being overseen by head brewer Jerrod Larsen. Together the team aims to create a classic brewpub experience with a rainbow of beer and great food.

Tustin Brewing Company is located in what looks like a white castle or windmill. The quaint strip mall it's located in has a sort of European look about it and houses boutique clothing, food, and craft stores. Inside the brewery, the bar is to the left along with the brew system. There is a dividing line made up of a narrow bar and barstools between the main dining area and the drinking area. It's a family establishment, so these two areas are appropriately separated. Tustin Brewing has a medium-size outdoor patio area as well for those who enjoy drinking in the sun. The entire thing has a neighborhood vibe to it—it's more of a restaurant and less of a pub. A wood-burning pizza oven sits in the back kitchen, filling the entire space up with a lovely campfire aroma. Tustin has a full lineup of great guest taps, including Russian River, to complement their house-brewed beers and is one of the few places in Orange County to get kegs of Pliny the Younger. They have frequent events, from beer dinners to annual beer fests.

Tustin Brewing Company beers are brewed to style, and there are usually about eight house beers on tap at any time, with a couple seasonal and experimental releases. Your best bet is to order a tasting flight to see which one you like the most. The **Lemon Heights Hefeweizen** is a locals' favorite, while the **Old Town IPA** is a

Old Town IPA
Style: West Coast IPA
ABV: 7.4%
Availability: Year-round

There is definitely something to be said about a traditionally brewed West Coast IPA. Old Town IPA is just that. It is effervescent and medium-bodied, and pours a delightfully orange-amber color. Notes of tropical fruit, spring flowers, and pine resin dominate the nose on this beer. It is nicely aromatic but not overpowering, with a tasty dank hoppiness. Old Town IPA has a robust bitterness that will please IPA hop heads, and it represents the West Coast style very well. It's best paired with spicier items on the menu.

favorite of hop heads. The **Golden Spike Light Ale** is the lightest beer available on tap. The **American Pale Ale** is hoppy and bitter, yet balanced, and the **Red Hill Red** has a malty, biscuity flavor. All of these beers are made to be paired with food, and they are all very tasty. Speaking of food, make sure to try their famous chili. It's spicy and smoky, and is served in a bread bowl. They also offer pizzas, burgers, and standard brewpub fare. Make sure to check out the specials on the chalkboard, and don't forget a 64-ounce growler to take home.

Orange County

Beer Bars & Bottle Shops

BEACHWOOD BBQ

131 Main St., Seal Beach, CA 90740; (562) 493-4500; beachwoodbbq.com;
@beachwoodbarbecue
Draft Beers: 22 taps plus 1 cask, craft only **Bottled/Canned Beers:** 200 bottles, all
vintage

Beachwood BBQ in Seal Beach is one of SoCal's original craft beer bars and does
not sport an adjoining brewery like its Long Beach counterpart. Owner and chef
Gabriel Gordon started Beachwood BBQ in 2006 and designed one of the most iconic
draft systems in Southern California, which he calls the "Flux Capacitor." The Flux

Capacitor allows for each draft line to have a unique gas mix and be served correctly, rather than splitting CO^2/nitrogen lines and serving beers that are too flat or too carbonated. The Hop Cam, another Beachwood BBQ original, gives online beer lovers the opportunity to see the tap list before a visit to the restaurant. Chalkboards listing the current beers are changed out as kegs are changed in real time.

The location is tiny and almost always has a line out the door, but waiting is worth it. Limited seating is available at the bar on the right side of the restaurant, and a small, narrow table area can be found on the left. The food menu at both locations is the same and sports some of the best barbecue SoCal has to offer. The staff is well trained, and many are Certified Cicerone Beer Servers, so you'll definitely be able to find the right barbecue-plus-beer combination.

HAVEN GASTROPUB

190 S. Glassell St., Orange, CA 92866; (714) 221-0680; havengastropub.com; @HavenGastropub
Draft Beers: 14 craft taps **Bottled/Canned Beers:** 70–80 rotating bottles

Haven Gastropub opened its original Old Towne Orange location in 2009. Old Towne Orange resembles a place trapped in time, with quaint storefronts, a family-friendly environment, and a true city square. Haven is right off S. Glassell Street and serves as a craft beer bastion, just a few minutes walk from Plaza Square Park. The place is easily identifiable with its large shield emblem logo and massive wooden front door. Owners Wil Dee, Ace Patel, and Chef Greg Daniels wanted to create a restaurant that was truly craft, free of the drudgery of both mediocre drinks and food. What you'll find is a well thought-out menu, impressive craft draft and bottle selection, quality wines and cocktails, and an elevated dining experience.

Chef Daniels presents diners with a multitude of meat, specifically pork-centered options. If you've never had pig ears before, make sure you try them—they're like pork rinds, only better, and go incredibly well with a lighter, spritzier beer or IPA. The Haven Burger is a local favorite and is an easy choice for newbies. If you want something more interesting, try the lamb neck poutine or lobster flatbread, or get a group together and order the whole roasted suckling pig. Wait and bar staff are well trained in the ways of craft and will be able to point you to the correct pairing, although I might recommend trying a Haven beer, brewed at the Pasadena location, and pairing it with either the burger or spring mix salad. Haven has frequent events celebrating craft beer, food, wine, and spirits, so head over to their website and check out the blog before visiting—they are well worth attending.

HOPSCOTCH
136 E. Commonwealth Ave., Fullerton, CA 92832; (714) 871-2222; hopscotchtavern.com; @hopscotchtavern
Draft Beers: 24 rotating craft taps **Bottled/Canned Beers:** 50+ bottles

Hopscotch is a relatively new craft beer and whiskey–centered gastropub, opening in Fullerton in November of 2012. Including both drafts and bottles, the restaurant showcases over 75 craft beers along with over 105 specialty whiskeys. The place has a unique vibe that blends modern-day lodge with the 1890s. Their logo is the iconic penny-farthing, a high-wheeled bike with a smaller wheel in back that was popular in the late 1800s. If you can picture this bike and an upscale gastropub, you'll have a good idea what to expect from Hopscotch. The restaurant is located in historic Fullerton's original Pacific Electric Railway Station. Dark reclaimed-wood floors along with tables and iron lantern lights seal the deal.

Hopscotch's focus is on food and drink, though, not just atmosphere. You'll find an eclectic assortment of house-made sides like pickles, unique meat dishes like braised rabbit, and an awesome fried chicken dish. Their hot wings are anything but traditional Americana, drawing from Southeast Asian flavors that incorporate a sweet-spicy sauce with cucumber and cilantro. Lots of great choices, most of them incredibly rich and flavorful, but there are some lighter options, too. The beer selection includes everything from local breweries like Bootlegger's and Noble Ale Works to Euro classics like Young's Double Chocolate Stout. With over 50 bottles to choose from, you'll also have some nice rarities to share with friends. They also offer tasting sizes for $3 if you can't decide. Hopscotch has frequent food pairing and craft events, so join their mailing list and plan ahead.

PROVISIONS MARKET

143 N. Glassell St., Orange, CA 92866; (714) 997-2337; provisionsmarkets.com; @provisionsmrkts
Draft Beers: 30 craft taps **Bottled/Canned Beers:** 600+ bottles

Provisions Market, originally The Bruery Provisions, was purchased and rebranded by the Haven Collective in 2013, with an aim to retain as much of its original appeal as possible. Located in Old Towne Orange, a few minutes from Haven Gastropub at the north end of the city center, Provisions Market offers an incredibly unique bottle shop experience. Not only does it house a tremendous selection of craft bottles—over 600 to choose from—but it also offers a craft deli and grocery and houses a Portola coffee roaster. To make it even more appealing, there is a total of 30 local and regional craft taps to choose from if you want to taste beers while having lunch.

The Haven Collective

The Haven Collective has seen great success in 2013 with their gastropubs in Orange and Pasadena. With the addition of their new brewery and acquisition of Provisions Market, in combination with a new distribution deal, more Haven beer is making its way into gastropubs and craft taverns. The collective also owns the popular taco spot Taco Asylum, which showcases canned beer only—40 to 50 craft cans, that is. With demand at an all-time high, there is a rumor that a larger-scale brewery is in planning, so stay tuned—2014 may be an even bigger year for the Haven Collective.

Wil Dee fell in love with the idea of having a bottle shop in Orange after opening the original Haven location. When The Bruery owner Patrick Rue opened the original Bruery Provisions, Wil opted out of opening his own shop. As luck would have it, The Bruery decided to focus on other areas, and the Haven Collective jumped at the opportunity to keep the unique craft grocer alive. It fits incredibly well into the vibe of Old Towne Orange, which resembles the streets of Pleasantville or *Back to the Future*'s Hill Valley. The market itself is old-school modern, with subway tile walls and barbershop-style glass windows complete with gold leaf. Come to Provisions Market to grab a bottle, have lunch, taste local craft, or just to see how cool it is. It's worth the drive, and the surrounding area is beautiful.

SCHOONER AT SUNSET
16821 Pacific Coast Hwy., Sunset Beach, CA 90742; (562) 592-2121; schooneratsunset.com; @sunsetschooner
Draft Beers: 21 rotating craft taps **Bottled/Canned Beers:** 12 craft bottles and 12 craft cans

Schooner at Sunset, previously the divey beach bar Harpoon Harry's, reopened as a craft-beer beach gastropub in early 2013. Its extremely close proximity to Sunset Beach makes it a popular stop before or after water activities in the afternoon and evening. Sunset at Schooner features live music and a very large space that accommodates groups of every size. The labyrinthine recesses of the restaurant mix a bar atmosphere with intimate fireside dining, along with a private dining room in the back. It has a warm, inviting atmosphere with a heavy nautical beach theme throughout, complete with a sailor statue near the front entrance.

Owner Curtis Fullerton was looking to create a beer bar that not only served world-class food, but also boasted an incredible tap lineup. It was for that reason alone that he hired local LA beer celebrity and freelance beer writer Daniel Drennon, who personally curates the tap list. Beers served at Schooner must be good, and each one is tasted by Drennon, who proctors the 21-draft lineup making sure each beer is fresh and pouring correctly. Schooner is a popular location for local brewery pint nights and beer industry meetings, and serves as a craft-beer beer education center for beach folk. They are even working on an overnight package deal with several local hotels that'll get you a discount on a room, beach activities, and a local beer-bar hop.

Pub Crawl

Old Towne Orange

Old Towne Orange is an incredible place to walk around. Streets are populated with boutique shops, family-owned restaurants, and retro storefronts, and everything converges into a circular park in the middle. As you would imagine, this spot is also host to some great eateries and craft hot spots. You can do this crawl as fast or as slow as you want, but I suggest taking your time to enjoy the scenery. The tour starts at the Hollingshead, which is followed up by a short cab ride or long walk to Old Towne Orange city center.

Hollingshead's Deli, 368 S. Main St., Orange, CA 92868; hollingsheadsdeli.com. The Hollingshead's Deli is one of Orange's oldest fixtures, having opened in 1963. They regularly feature awesome craft beer on their 22 rotating taps and showcase over 500 types of bottled beer, specializing in the rarest of them. The restaurant was founded by the Kenneth family and has since enjoyed three generations of ownership. Due to the large amount of taps and bottles, they regularly host tastings

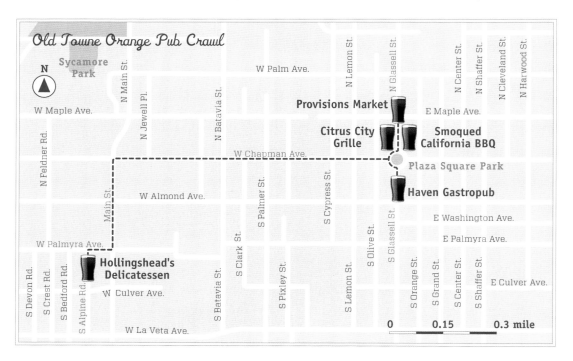

and beer events. The only drawback is that they close on the earlier side, 8 p.m. This should likely be your first stop. If you're hungry, they have a full deli offering classic sandwiches, salads, and sides.

Plan to drive or cab to the next spot, Provisions Market. It's northeast about 1.4 miles.

Provisions Market, 143 N. Glassell St., Orange, CA 92866; provisionsmarkets.com. A combination deli, craft bottle shop, and beer bar, Provisions Market is an amazing mix of classic look and feel with modern options. If you end here, you can pore through over 600 bottles to take home, or you can enjoy custom sandwiches and artisanal cheeses. Provisions has over 30 taps to choose from, which makes it a great beer destination. Beers are rotated frequently and the staff is incredibly knowledgeable, so please ask questions.

Head across the street to the next spot, Smoqued BBQ. It's about 118 feet away.

Smoqued California BBQ, 128 N. Glassell St., Orange, CA 92866; smoquedbbq.com. Smoqued BBQ is another great spot in Orange. The location was originally occupied by local restaurant Beach Pit Barbeque, but switched over to Smoqued in 2012. They feature 12 rotating taps of incredible focused, local, *California* craft beer. It's a barbecue joint, so they also offer a full assortment of barbecued meats, comfort food, and sides. Try their smoked chicken wings, the 420 Mac, or a pulled pork sandwich.

Citrus City is right next door, so just walk on over.

Citrus City Grille, 122 N. Glassell St., Orange, CA 92866; citruscitygrille.com. Citrus City Grille is a popular destination for those looking for some upscale food in Orange. They prominently feature a wide menu that includes seafood, pasta, and tapas, and are reputed to have one of the best happy hours in Orange (Sun through Thurs from 3 p.m. to close; and Fri and Sat from 3 to 7 p.m.). Their main focus is on the food, wine, and cocktails, although they do have craft beer as well. This would be a great side stop for some grub accompanied by Lost Coast Brewing's Great White or Downtown Brown. Citrus City has 12 taps of mixed craft and domestic beer.

The final stop is Haven Gastropub. It's about 0.2 mile south of your current location on the right-hand side of the street. It'll take about 4 minutes.

Haven Gastropub, 190 S. Glassell St., Orange, CA 92866; havengastropub.com. A great place to start or end your crawl, Haven has some incredibly tasty food and a great selection of craft beer. With 14 taps and about 80 rotating bottles, Haven is 100 percent craft. The menu focuses on meat dishes and pork, but you can find lighter veggie-friendly options as well. The restaurant is spacious and has plenty of room for groups to sit inside, with limited seating outside as well.

Temecula

To Craft Brewing Company
See Inset

2

Prielipp Rd.

Wildomar

Inset

74

74

15

Central Ave.

Pasadena St.

Crane St.

Collier Ave.

3rd St.

Minthorn St.

Birch St.

Chaney St.

1

Lake Elsinore

0   0.1   0.2 mile

Clinton Keith Rd.

Los Alamos Rd.

215

Whitewood Rd.

N

0   4   8 miles

Pond Park

79

Murrieta Hot Springs Rd.

Palomar St.

Clinton Keith Rd.

Nutmeg St.

Jackson Ave.

California Oaks Rd.

Calle Del Oso Oro

Washington Ave.

Jefferson Ave.

Los Alamos Rd.

215

Ivy St.

Adams Ave.

15

Murrieta

Date St.

Nicolas Rd.

Guava St.

Washington Ave.

Jefferson Ave.

Date St.

Cherry St.

Winchester Rd.

79

3

Temecula

Rancho California Rd.

Enterprise Cir.

Zevo Dr.

4

5

Diaz Rd.

15

79

6

7

Rancho California Rd.

Ynez Rd.

Pauba Rd.

Ave Del Oro

8

9

Pujol St.

10

11

Old Town Front Rd.

Santiago Rd.

Via Santa Rosa

Santa Creek Dr.

Via Vaquero Rd.

Cam Estribo

79

15

BREWERIES

Aftershock Brewing Co.	11
Black Market Brewing Company	4
Craft Brewing Company	1
Ironfire Brewing Company	5
Refuge Brewery	7
Wiens Brewing Company	6

BREWPUBS

| Bulldog Brewery | 3 |
| Stadium Pizza Wildomar | 2 |

BEER BARS & BOTTLE SHOPS

Crush & Brew	8
Old Town Liquor	10
Public House	9

Temecula

Temecula is well known for its wine culture. It's a frequent vacation spot for young 20- to 30-somethings looking for a vineyard getaway. Temecula is also where Vinnie Cilurzo from Russian River started out before he became the beer baron of the north. In terms of craft beer, Temecula's scene exploded in 2009, bringing forth a plethora of great packaging breweries and some smaller boutique ones as well. Temecula has a unique vibe and beer culture that is all its own. It's definitely worth making a trip out here and staying a few days in the quaint and walkable Old Town district.

Breweries

AFTERSHOCK BREWING CO.

28822 Old Town Front St., Temecula, CA 92590; (951) 972-2256; aftershockbrewingco
.com; @Aftershockbrew

Founded: 2012 **Founder:** Marvin Nigh **Brewer:** Marvin Nigh **Flagship Beer:** Jess y
James Imperial Stout **Year-round Beers:** Tremor Pale Ale, Espresso Stout, Third Degree,
Faultline, Dubbel Vision, Pinacate, Magnitude **Seasonals/Special Releases:** Richter
Rauch, Amerifest, Jess y James **Tours:** No formal tours offered. Call for private tour
availability. **Taproom:** Yes

Aftershock Brewing Co., located right off the 15 Freeway in an industrial park,
focuses on eclectic styles and stouts. Owner and brewer Marvin Nigh had been
home-brewing for 28 years and before opening the brewery ran a successful furniture repair business. He opened the brewery, fulfilling a lifelong dream, and makes a
point to do everything by hand, from brewing to bottling. Aftershock takes pride in
the fact that all beer is conditioned and carbonated in kegs using natural conditioning. Marvin operates a 15 BBL system with two 7 BBL fermentors and is able to do
about 500 BBL per year. With the local success of his beers, he has plans to expand
in 2014, which will increase his capacity to 3,000 BBLs a year.

Jess y James
Style: American Imperial Stout
ABV: 9.9%
Availability: Seasonal

At 9.9% Jess y James has the highest ABV of any beer at Aftershock, with Dubbel Vision following close behind at 8.8%. It's not only an award winner, but it's also their flagship beer. Bottles of Jess y James are sold with Aftershock's signature yellow-and-green labels and are wax-sealed in gold. The beer itself is a complex roast bomb. No coffee is used, but there are definitely lingering notes of coffee beans and bitter cacao pres-

ent. The hop character is subdued and lends just enough to give the beer balance. Jess y James pours with a thick, dark brown head and is not only a great sipping beer, but would be a great addition to a spicy chili.

The Aftershock taproom is humble, small, and completely separated from the brewhouse, which lives in the back of the building. They have a main bar that wraps around half of the room and a seating area on the other side. It gets crowded into the night and is decently populated in the afternoon. If you want to do a tasting, get a seat at the bar so you can talk to the tasting room staff. A local sandwich shop is right next door, so if you're in need of good local fuel to accompany your tasting, it's a recommended option. Limited-release bottles are available for purchase, along with growler fills.

The motto "Hand Crafted Stouts and Other Fine Ales" sums up Marvin's focus, but in all honesty, he has something for everyone at the taproom. His **Richter Rauch** recently won a gold medal at the San Diego International Beer Festival, so if

Temecula

you are a fan of the ancient Bamberg smoked style, make sure you try it. There's a traditional pale on tap, **Tremor,** that is a great all-around beer, and **Third Degree IPA** is a crowd favorite. The flagship and best seller is the **Jess y James Imperial Stout.** Temecula's water is really good for brewing all styles, so you'll likely see something different each time you go. Make sure to check their website to get the most up-to-date tap list so you aren't surprised to find something tapped out.

BLACK MARKET BREWING COMPANY

41740 Enterprise Cir. North, #109, Temecula, CA 92590; (951) 296-5039; blackmarketbrew .com; @blackmarketbrew

Founded: 2009 **Brewmaster:** Shaun McBride **Brewer:** Aaron Heyden **Flagship Beer:** Black Market Hefeweizen **Year-round Beers:** Hefeweizen, Invasion Imperial IPA, Aftermath, Brown, Rye IPA, Scottish Eighty, Liberation DIPA, Revolution, Quadrophenia **Seasonals/Special Releases:** Black Hole Sun, 1945 Berliner Weisse, Irish Red, Barrel-Aged Imperial Brown Ale, Pumpkin Ale, Oktoberfest **Tours:** Yes, with tour bus **Taproom:** Yes

Black Market Brewing Company opened in 2009 and is one of Temecula's first breweries. The brewery itself is owned by Kevin Dyer, but the brewery is managed and operated by Shaun McBride, who directs production of the 15 BBL, two-kettle brewhouse. Having two kettles puts them closer to 30 BBLs, and they are looking to expand even more. They ship over 700 kegs every month to retailers and have a full line of bottles that are available throughout the southland, and their beers are synonymous with quality. Look for even more expansion, increased production capacity, and wider distribution in 2014.

The taproom is clean, outfitted with reclaimed wood, and expands into a large beer-hall seating area that sits alongside the brewery, with only a line of spirit barrels separating patrons and operations. Black Market pulls its name from the prominent bootlegging history in the area, and they have employed the talents of graphic designer, teacher, and home brew paragon (and personal idol) Randy Mosher, which gives their brand a classic feel. The labels are slick, and their bottles easily catch the eye on store shelves. The brewery itself is spotless, and it's clear that, even at its large size, their focus is on quality beer and sanitation.

Black Market has a full lineup of bottled beers, drafts, and taproom-only offerings. From Hefeweizen and Berliner Weisse to DIPA and barrel-aged imperial stout, Black Market does it all. Their imperial stout, **Black Hole Sun,** is one of the most sought-after beers in Southern California. Their most popular beer right now is the **Hefeweizen,** and it's also their flagship. Temecula gets hot, and this super-refreshing Bavarian-style beer hits the spot on a sunny day. At Black Market you'll

Invasion
Style: Imperial Red
ABV: 9.9%
Availability: Seasonal—limited

The only thing cooler than this beer's awesome Randy Mosher label, depicting bootleggers moving crates of BMB, is the taste. It's a favorite at the brewery and available year-round. Using El Dorado hops and both Euro and bold roasted grains, the beer takes on a chocolate flavor up front. The second flavor to hit your mouth and your nose is orange sherbet. It's a unique and complex flavor combination stemming from the marriage of malt and hops. The beer pours a deep red amber with a very light white head. Invasion has a citrus finish, and at a 9.9% it takes after barleywine, making it a perfect dessert beer.

find classic styles, experimental ones, and seasonal limited-bottle releases. This is definitely one brewery you want to put on your tour agenda.

CRAFT BREWERY COMPANY

530 Crane St., Ste. C, Lake Elsinore, CA 92530; (951) 226-0149; craftbrewingcompany.com
Founded: 2010 **Founder:** Kurt Carroll, Kirk Medeiros, Tim Reagan, and Bob Thompson
Brewer: Kurt Carroll, Kirk Medeiros, Tim Reagan, and Bob Thompson **Flagship Beer:**
Friar Bob's Raspberry Wheat, Fallen Angel Blonde **Year-round Beers:** Friar Bob's
Raspberry Wheat, Fallen Angel Blonde, Raven Stout, Four Headed Hef, Warlock IPA
Seasonals/Special Releases: Twelfth Night Spiced Ale, Stout No Vanilla, Anniversary
Barrel-Aged Barleywine **Tours:** Yes; call for availability **Taproom:** Yes

Craft Brewing Company is located north of Temecula in Lake Elsinore. It's relatively easy to get to—just a few turns off the freeway in a business industrial park. You'll know you are close when you see the giant dragon on the special-effects building across the street. The brewery is a team-effort project by career home brew hobbyists Kurt Carroll, Kirk Medeiros, Tim Reagan, and Bob Thompson. Each of the

Warlock IPA
Style: IPA
ABV: 6.7%
Availability: Year-round

The Raven stout is a great classic style, but the Warlock IPA is a top pick. It's a solid West Coast–style IPA showcasing classic Chinook and dry-hopped Cascade hops. Extreme pine and resin notes dominate the bouquet of this beer, with the malt profile playing a very minor role in the overall flavor. The body is medium-light, which makes it a solid go-to session beer slightly under the ABV of some of the bigger IPAs out there. Complex earthy bitterness follows through till the end, leaving a lingering pine quality. Warlock is one of Craft Brewing's best sellers, and it's also one the brewing team's favorite beers. It's available in bottle form with a slick black and neon green label and would be a perfect addition to a summer barbecue.

four brings something different to the table, and each of them has a decorated home brew history. At the time of their soft opening in April of 2010, they were operating a 3 BBL modified home brew system to craft their beers, but they have since graduated to a 25-hectoliter brewhouse and commercial-size equipment to keep up with demand. They chose to name their brewery after the craft they loved so dearly and built a brand highlighting witchcraft and alchemy around it.

The tasting room at Craft Brewing Company is on the smaller side, but it was recently expanded to include more space when they took over the building next door. Plans are currently under way to increase their space even more, which could happen as soon as early 2014. The taproom sits amid the brewing equipment and fermentation tanks, like most breweries of its size, which gives it an industrial feel.

There are several large tables created from reconditioned barrels, with the signature warlock mascot emblazoned on them. This is where the beer is made.

Craft Brewing comes from home-brewing roots, so they want to make sure they pay homage to creativity and the craft they came from. The beers are all based on classic styles, with small twists that give them character. Their current best seller is an American wheat-style ale infused with raspberries called **Friar Bob's Raspberry Wheat.** It has a big nose, but it's not overly sweet and goes great mixed with the **Raven Stout,** which makes it taste like a chocolate truffle. They recently released a big barleywine ale for their third anniversary and do specialty releases seasonally. Growlers and bottles are available for take home of some but not all styles. The bottles look great and sport high-contrast bichromatic labels with the signature Craft Warlock.

IRONFIRE BREWING COMPANY

42095 Zevo Dr., Temecula, CA 92590; (951) 296-1397; ironfirebrewing.com; @Ironfirebrew
Founded: 2012 **Founder:** John Maino and Greg Webb **Brewer:** John Maino and Greg Webb **Flagship Beer:** 51/50 **Year-round Beers:** Gunslinger Gold, Synner Pale, 51/50 IPA, 6 Killer Stout, Vicious Disposition **Seasonals/Special Releases:** One-offs and collaborations **Tours:** No formal tours offered. Call for private tour availability. **Taproom:** Yes

Ironfire brings a San Diego flair to Temecula. The brewery is owned and operated by two guys, John Maino and Greg Webb, who previously worked as brewers at Ballast Point. John and Greg wanted to open a brewery together, but felt that San Diego was too saturated. They turned their eyes to Temecula, seeing it as a great opportunity to bring their beers to a developing beer town. Together they run a small 15 BBL Premier Stainless brewhouse and produce a full lineup of their flagship bottles.

Ironfire has a beautiful but small Western-themed tasting room complete with rebar and reconditioned barrel furniture. It has a very rustic feel when the daylight pours in through the windows. Their signature mascot is a sort of undead cowboy who is the centerpiece of both their logo and each of their labels. They're doing something unique with their screen-printed bottles: telling a story. Each one of their bottles has a different moment in the dead cowboy's life, and putting them all together you get a sense of what and who he is. It's a bit abstract, but has a very cool comic book feel to it. The name Ironfire comes from the term "iron in the fire," as the brewery was a long-term project that the duo hoped to complete.

Ironfire beers are very good. One can easily see where the Ballast Point history comes into play, as West Coast hoppiness plays a big role in most of their beers, but

each has its own uniqueness. Their flagship IPA, **51/50,** with its signature dank overtones and minimal malt profile, is as West Coast as it gets. If you want something with a bit more kick, they also brew beers that incorporate hot peppers like habanero. Their **6 Killer Stout** is a very robust coffee stout that incorporates a local San Diego coffee roaster's hazelnut coffee—a definite must for fans of the darker beers. All Ironfire beers are incredibly clean, well executed, and worth trying, so get a flight and then take some bottles and/or a growler home.

Viscous Disposition
Style: Imperial Porter
ABV: 9.0%
Availability: Year-round

Vicious Disposition is an intense, robust imperial porter that utilizes a unique local ingredient, avocado honey. The beer does not taste like avocado, but the honey addition smooths out the entire beer and gives a residual sweetness and a thick body without being cloying. The roasted notes are layered and complex, and the bitter hop profile is definitely a feature without it being overdone—it complements the roasted malt notes very well. It's suggested that you enjoy Viscous Disposition at a warmer temperature, and I definitely recommend this as well. Drinking this beer too cold will hide the complexity and will not do it justice. There is a seasonally available barrel-aged version in the fall. The label has the iconic undead cowboy, very Dia del los Muertos, holding a shotgun. Tasty.

REFUGE BREWERY

43040 Rancho Way, Temecula, CA 92590; (951) 506-0609; refugebrew.com; @refugebrewery
Founded: 2012 **Founder:** Curt Kucera, Glenn Wichert, and Jake Kucera **Brewer:** Curt Kucera **Flagship Beer:** Refugee Tripel **Year-round Beers:** Abbey Road, Illusion IPA, Refugee Tripel, Asylum IPA, Entropy Porter, Rampart Red, Oracle, Exile Pale Ale, Blood Orange Wit **Seasonals/Special Releases:** Oak-Aged Refugee Tripel, Mystique Rose, Kentucky Red **Tours:** Yes **Taproom:** Yes

Refuge Brewery focuses largely on traditional Belgian styles. Cofounders Curt, Glenn, and Jake have created a high-class modern tasting room, which acts as a haven from life outside the brewery. Their goal was to create a production brewery in the burgeoning Temecula beer scene, but their main focus when they opened in December 2012 was the beer, of course, and the tasting room aesthetic. Curt has been a home brewer for over 20 years. He and his brewing buddy, Glenn, outgrew the garage brew system and decided it was time to upgrade. Refuge houses a highly efficient 10 BBL brewhouse with 80 BBLs worth of fermentation capacity, 80 percent of which is devoted to Belgian styles.

The taproom is very modern, with a hint of modern industrial. Dark shaped stone, dark wood, and beautifully shiny stainless fermentors give the tasting room a metal-meets-rustic feel. Jake Kucera, Curt's son and cofounder of Refuge, is largely responsible for the aesthetic. His graphic arts background has shaped the taproom, polished "Flight to Freedom" logo, website, and the brand as a whole. Curt also owns the 801 Brewing Company, which custom designed the brewhouse and tanks for Refuge. Manufacturing and selling the tanks may prove to be a side business at a later date, but until then the focus is on getting the beer out in Temecula and

Refugee Tripel Aged in Virgin Oak
Style: Belgian Tripel
ABV: 9.0%
Availability: Limited

The backbone of this beer is the super-solid Refugee Tripel. The Tripel itself is a wonderful beer with slight sweet notes that are complemented by a biscuity maltiness. It's effervescent, aromatic, and strong. The barrel-aged version of this beer adds an incredible complexity that is wonderful. Refuge uses medium-toasted virgin oak for a very short aging cycle. The beer spends enough time in the barrel to pick up wooden oak notes

with no vanillin or extra alcohol. What you get is a rustic, spritzy sipping beer with a subtle citrus and light warming quality that will leave you trying to convince Refuge to fill a growler of it for you. Unfortunately, like most limited releases, it's tasting room only, but you can definitely take the base Tripel home, and it'll give you a reason to come back. I suspect there will be bottles of this beer in Refuge's future.

serving patrons at the tasting room. They currently fill growlers and are working on bottling their first beers in 2014.

The beer at Refuge is very polished, and for a super-young brewery, this is a major accomplishment. The entire lineup is solid, from Belgians to IPAs, and they even have a custom nonalcoholic root beer. The IPA is a necessity in the current craft beer scene, but the real stars of the brewery are the Belgians. **Abbey Road** is a solid, easygoing Witbier and **Illusion IPA** combines the citrusy hops with a classic Belgian yeast. If you want to try something truly different and inspired, order the **Oracle**

Temecula

Abbey Ale. It has an aromatic addition of juniper berries that also gives the beer a slight bitter citrus-pine character. **Mystique Rose,** a bourbon-barrel-aged dark Belgian-style strong ale, clocks in at 10.4% and is wildly complex and warm. You can't go wrong with any of the beer choices and a tasting flight at Refuge Brewing is always a great way to start.

WIENS BREWING COMPANY

27941 Diaz Rd., Temecula, CA 92590; (951) 553-7111; wiensbrewing.com; @Wiensbrewing

Founded: 2012 **Founder:** Pete Wiens and Ben Wiens **Brewer:** Pete Wiens and Ben Wiens **Flagship Beer:** Insomnia IPA **Year-round Beers:** Front Street Lager, Far Post Brown, Plateau Pale, Old Town Lager, Insomnia IPA, Descend **Seasonals/Special Releases:** Single Hop Series, Dead Pan Pilsner, Honey Wheat, Big Cog Double IPA, Red **Tours:** Yes; call for availability **Taproom:** Yes

The Wiens family has been in the alcohol business for some time, but not as beer brewers—as winemakers. They moved down from the Northern California wine scene to establish themselves in Temecula in 2001. The family owns Wiens Cellars, a local Temecula winery that is known for their beautiful rustic location and, as their motto says, is "famous for big reds." Pete and Ben Wiens love beer and saw an opportunity to involve themselves in the up-and-coming beer scene in Temecula, so in November of 2012 they opened Wiens Brewing. Located just a stone's throw from Refuge Brewery and adjacent to a massive home-brewed wine and beer shop, Vintner's Vault, Wiens Brewing specializes in IPAs and lagers. Pete, a UC Davis grad and ex–AB guy, started their operation with a 1 BBL pilot system, upgraded to a Prospero 7 BBL brewhouse, and just recently upgraded again to a new 15 BBL system. The demand for their beer is driving the expansion, and they're pouring at over 60 locations locally.

The taproom is large and could easily host small parties and medium-size groups. It gets crowded during the evening drinking hours, but the massive tap list will more than likely satisfy everyone. It draws from traditional rustic winery ambience, showcasing reclaimed wood and barrels. The bar spans almost the entire length of the narrow tasting room, and there are also large high-seated tables.

Wiens is one of the only breweries in the area doing actual lagering, and their offerings are excellent. They have over 16 beers on tap, most of which are taproom only or seasonal beers. It's not uncommon for them to have over eight different IPAs on tap, as this is Pete's favorite beer to brew. Each one showcases a different hop, blend, or malt balance. Their 1 BBL pilot system is a home brewer's dream, and they

Insomnia IPA
Style: IPA
ABV: 7.5%
Availability: Year-round

Insomnia IPA was inspired by the actual insomnia that both Pete and Ben suffer from. Starting a new business can be taxing and stressful, so they decided to name this flagship beer after the sleep they were losing. This is also where the Wiens logo, a bloodshot eye, comes from. Wiens is obsessed with hops, so this IPA employs some big ones: Falconer's Flight, Centennial, and Columbus. The

result is an incredibly floral, dank IPA that is heavier on aroma and flavor than IBUs. It's not palate obliterating and gets most of its character from dry hopping. The malt profile is clean and subdued, and the beer isn't overly sweet. Insomnia IPA is superfresh and demands to be consumed on a hot day or after a hard day's work.

have several dedicated small temperature-controlled refrigerators that they ferment their batches in. This is why you'll likely see different beers each time you go. They are well known in the area for their IPAs, but are also known for their **Honey Wheat**, an American-style wheat beer with local honey added. They don't want this beer to be their focus, so they only put it on seasonally.

Brewpubs

BULLDOG BREWERY

41379 Date St., Murrieta, CA 92562; (951) 461-6200; bulldog-brewery.com; @BulldogBrewery

Founded: 2013 **Founder:** Tom and Sandy Caso **Flagship Beer:** Shih-Tzu Saison **Year-round Beers:** American Bully Amber, Pug's Porter, Rotty's Red Ale, Weiner Dog Wheat, Boxer (Nut) Brown Ale, Beagle Blond **Seasonals/Special Releases:** Shih-Tzu Saison, Weimaraner Weizen Bock **Tours:** No formal tours offered. Call for private tour availability.

Bulldog Brewery is a brand-new brewpub in the Murrieta area, north of Temecula. Like other breweries in the area, it's located in an industrial park, but it's not too far off the 15 and it's relatively easy to find. The first thing you'll notice pulling up are the large, frosted, double glass doors showcasing the bulldog logo. The taproom inside is spacious, spread out, and very well constructed. It's the perfect size for late-evening drinking, beer tours, and large groups. The bar is in the back along with the 8 BBL brewhouse, which is behind glass. Guests will have an easy time finding a seat at the speckled black stone bar, as it spans the whole width of the restaurant.

Owner and founder Tom Caso opened the brewpub with his wife, Sandy, in mid-May of 2013, and together they have employed the help of family and friends to evolve their beers and grow clientele. They opened the brewery as part of a lifelong dream to start a business together and have, in Bulldog, been able to make that dream come true. The taproom offers a full menu of pub fare including sausages, flatbread, and even Polish pierogi. The goal is, simply, to have something for everyone. They have seasonal rotating appetizers as well; if you visit in the summer, try the fried avocado slices.

Bulldog is currently an all-extract brewery and is in transition to incorporate more whole grains into their lineup. They have rotating house beers along with a full lineup of 10 guest craft taps. Beer enthusiasts can order growlers to go or enjoy pints and snacks in the restaurant. Each beer is cleverly named after a dog breed that best fits: **Weiner Dog Wheat, Pug's Porter, Shih-Tzu Saison, American Bully Amber** (named after the resident bulldog, Lola, of course), and **Boxer (Nut) Brown Ale,** to name a few. They even have a root beer for kids or those who just need a break from the booze. It's a family establishment and is aimed at pleasing all types of groups.

Shih-Tzu Saison
Style: Saison
ABV: 6.0%
Availability: Seasonal

Despite the funny name, Shih-Tzu Saison is a unique beer. It's not like a traditional saison, as it is relatively low in the funky horse-blanket department, but it is pleasantly tart. The body is incredibly light and hides the 6.0% ABV very well. It pours a glassy golden straw with a quickly fleeting white head. Immediate notes include cherry, citrus fruits, and biscuit. As the beer warms, the cherry character picks up noticeably along with light maltiness. Shih-Tzu is meant to be a session beer and does a great job of being just that. It's not super-complex, but it's very drinkable and is the perfect companion for a hot day in the Temecula sun.

STADIUM PIZZA WILDOMAR

32278 Clinton Keith Rd., Wildomar, CA 92595; (956) 678-7826; stadiumpizza.com; @stadiumpizzaspw
Founded: 2012 **Founder:** Sandy Kordick **Brewer:** Rick Kordick **Flagship Beer:** Gridiron IPA, Brushback Pale Ale, Southpaw Blonde **Year-round Beers:** Gridiron IPA, Brushback Pale Ale, Southpaw Blonde **Seasonals/Special Releases:** Pumpkin Ale, Dunkelweizen, Double IPA **Tours:** No formal tours offered. Call for private tour availability.

Stadium Pizza Wildomar has been a family-friendly pizza mecca in the Temecula area for over two decades, but in the last few years it has become more craft beer focused. You can visit any of the franchise locations to get a good pizza, but if you want a more interesting and exciting beer experience, head to the Wildomar location and check out the Locker Room. There you'll find 21 craft beer taps and a 2 BBL nanobrewery. The restaurant is decked out in sports gear, video games, and

communal tables—everything you want from a pizza joint. The Locker Room is for adults only and showcases a bar with baseball bats under glass. It's very pro sports.

The brewery arm of Stadium Pizza Wildomar opened in May of 2012 and supplies the Locker Room with four house taps of rotating beer. As with most small nanos, beers change regularly. Nanobrewing has an extremely close relationship to home brewing, and so it allows these brewers to create multiple small batches while focusing on creativity. Brewer and owner Rick Kordick is currently focused

Brushback Pale
Style: Pale Ale
ABV: 5.9%
Availability: Year-round

Pale ales often get overlooked when their big cousins, IPAs, are on tap. In the case of Stadium Pizza Wildomar, the Brushback Pale steals the show. Brushback is an incredibly drinkable and complex pale ale that is wonderfully paired with any pizza on the menu. The initial aroma blend of citrus and pine can only be described as Sweet Tarts, and the follow-through flavor is crisp and refreshing. Slight notes of caramel, toast, and citrus round out and balance this beer. It's not overly sweet and finishes dry. A citrusy pale ale like this is pretty hard to find these days and makes a perfect counterpart to mild and/or spicy Mexican food.

on classic styles with his 2 BBL system, but has plans to do more. Along with their regular beers like **Gridiron IPA** and **Southpaw Blonde,** Rick makes a **Pumpkin Ale, Dunkelweizen,** and **Double IPA** seasonally.

The pizza at Stadium is very good. It's a cross between gourmet and classic-style pizza, so you'll be able to get traditional pies like pepperoni along with eclectic ones like Mexican or *Carnitas*. Getting a half-and-half pizza, Mexican and Carnitas, is highly recommended along with ordering a pint of the pale.

Beer Bars & Bottle Shops

CRUSH & BREW

28544 Old Town Front St., #103, Temecula, CA 92590; (951) 693-4567; crushnbrew.com; Facebook.com/CrushNBrew

Draft Beers: 30 beers on tap

Crush & Brew seeks to celebrate Temecula's most vibrant offerings: its wonderful wine heritage and its up-and-coming craft beer scene. The restaurant is split down the center, with a large wine bar on the left-hand side and a smaller craft beer bar on the right. The vibe of the establishment is upscale, but it's friendly to all those of drinking age. If it's a hot day, Crush & Brew offers the perfect refuge from the sun and heat, and its large space also makes it conducive for big groups. It's smack dab in the middle of Old Town Temecula, so it'll be very hard to miss.

Wine is broken out by winery and includes local varieties as well as other California offerings. The beer menu sports 30 craft taps with mostly local Temecula/Inland Empire beers, but incorporates some San Diego varieties as well. As with most

upscale beer bars, the menu, food, beer, and wine are constantly rotating. Crush & Brew offers a full menu with lighter fare such as cheese platters and roughage to more eclectic sandwiches, flatbreads, and surf and turf. Come here for lunch or after beer touring. It's the perfect place to start and/or end your day.

OLD TOWN LIQUOR

28780 Old Town Front St., Ste. A1, Temecula, CA 92590; (951) 676-6909
Bottled/Canned Beers: 75–100

Old Town Liquor looks like an ordinary liquor store from the outside, and when you walk in, it's pretty much got the vibe of one at first glance. Complete with a scuffed linoleum floor, a telltale bell when you enter, and the pleasant hum of fridge compressors, Old Town Liquor has been supplying thirsty Temecula natives well for the past 10 years. In addition to cigarettes, processed snacks, and ice, it also houses a massive selection of refrigerated craft beer. The main plus here is that everything is cold-stored. From Stone Enjoy By to Aftershock to Dogfish Head, Old Town Liquor has a great selection of local and regional brews. It's a hodgepodge of big bottles, but you are bound to find something good and maybe even something rare.

PUBLIC HOUSE

41971 Main St., Temecula, CA 92590; (951) 676-7305; publichouse.tv; facebook.com/
thepublichouse
Draft Beers: 31 taps **Bottled/Canned Beers:** 10, rotating selection

Public House is an upscale eatery right off the main drag in Old Town Temecula. The five-year-old restaurant is rustic modern with a wooden facade and open back patio. The building was originally constructed in the 1800s and accompanies the history vibe of Old Town Temecula well. Inside seating is limited, and you should expect longer waits during the dinner hours. Public House boasts an impressive lineup of local and regional craft options on their 31 taps, and if you're traveling with a wine enthusiast, there is a healthy assortment, about 20 wines, that they can choose from as well. The restaurant has a very warm vibe, perfect for young and older couples alike. The back patio is perfect for a sunny-day lunch.

Public House food includes your standard upscale gastropub fare, with seasonal ingredients like heirloom tomatoes and savory options like goat cheese sandwiches. All ingredients are locally sourced whenever possible from neighboring Temecula farmlands, and the menu is constantly changing to meet the time of year. Expect to find crisp salads, charcuterie, grass-fed burgers, and delicate desserts.

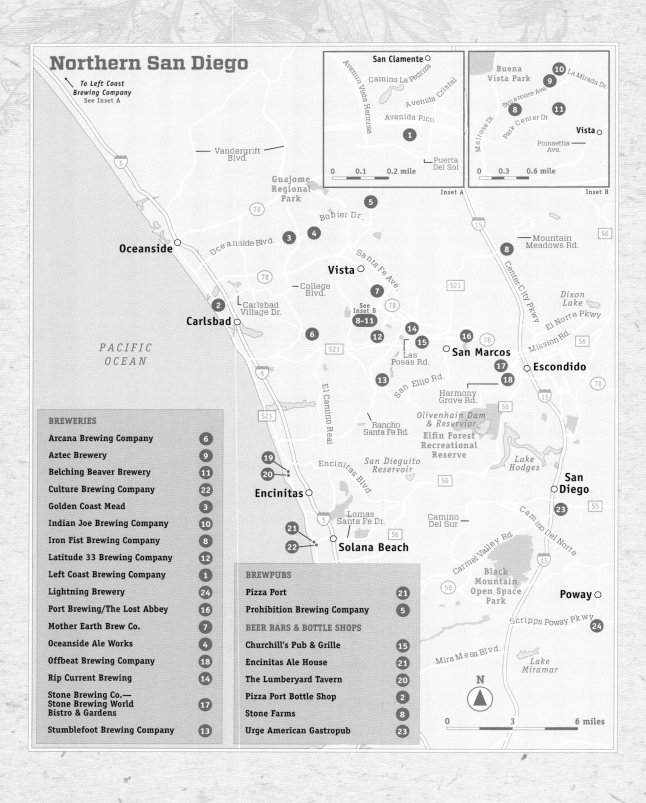

Northern San Diego

To Left Coast
Brewing Company
See Inset A

Inset A

San Clamente

Avenida Vista Hermosa
Camino La Pedriza
Avenida Cristal
Avenida Pico
Puerta Del Sol

1

0   0.1   0.2 mile

Inset B

Buena Vista Park
10
9
Melrose Dr.
Sycamore Ave.
8
Park Center Dr.
11
Vista
Poinsettia Ave.
La Mirada Dr.

0   0.3   0.6 mile

Vandergrift Blvd.

Guajome Regional Park

Bobier Dr.

5

Mountain Meadows Rd.

Oceanside Blvd.
3   4

Oceanside

Santa Fe Ave.
Vista

College Blvd.

Dixon Lake

El Norte Pkwy

Center City Pkwy

Carlsbad Village Dr.
2

Carlsbad

See Inset B

7

8-11

PACIFIC OCEAN

6

12

14

15

16

San Marcos

17

Escondido

18

Las Posas Rd.

13

San Elijo Rd.

Harmony Grove Rd.

Rancho Santa Fe Rd.

El Camino Real

Olivenhain Dam & Reservoir

Elfin Forest Recreational Reserve

Lake Hodges

San Dieguito Reservoir

19

20

Encinitas Blvd.

Encinitas

San Diego

23

Lomas Santa Fe Dr.

21

22

Solana Beach

Camino Del Sur

Camino Del Norte

Carmel Valley Rd.

Black Mountain Open Space Park

Poway

Scripps Poway Pkwy

24

Mira Mesa Blvd.

Lake Miramar

N

0   3   6 miles

BREWERIES

Arcana Brewing Company	6
Aztec Brewery	9
Belching Beaver Brewery	11
Culture Brewing Company	22
Golden Coast Mead	3
Indian Joe Brewing Company	10
Iron Fist Brewing Company	8
Latitude 33 Brewing Company	12
Left Coast Brewing Company	1
Lightning Brewery	24
Port Brewing/The Lost Abbey	16
Mother Earth Brew Co.	7
Oceanside Ale Works	4
Offbeat Brewing Company	18
Rip Current Brewing	14
Stone Brewing Co.— Stone Brewing World Bistro & Gardens	17
Stumblefoot Brewing Company	13

BREWPUBS

Pizza Port	21
Prohibition Brewing Company	5

BEER BARS & BOTTLE SHOPS

Churchill's Pub & Grille	15
Encinitas Ale House	21
The Lumberyard Tavern	20
Pizza Port Bottle Shop	2
Stone Farms	8
Urge American Gastropub	23

Northern
San Diego

And here we are—San Diego. As we travel farther south, the beer scene gets more and more developed. Northern San Diego is host to several incredible microcosms of beer. The Vista region showcases some wonderful craft spots, large and small. The beach areas showcase brewpubs, upscale beer bars, and plenty of pizza. And then there's Escondido, home to the 10th-largest brewery in the US, Stone Brewing Co. Northern San Diego is a place you'll want to spend serious time in. Take it slow, book a hotel by the beach, and find a designated driver because you'll be enjoying yourself way too much—you can't help it.

Breweries

ARCANA BREWING COMPANY

5621 Palmer Way, Ste. C, Carlsbad, CA 92010; (909) 529-2337; arcanabrewing.com; @ArcanaBrewing

Founded: 2012 **Founder:** Daniel Guy **Brewer:** Daniel Guy **Flagship Beer:** Marley's Ghost **Year-round Beers:** Tiny Tim Cream Ale, Voyager English IPA, Bitter Brown Ale, Annabelle's Umber Ale, Darby Porter Ale, Infinity Stout, Marley's Ghost **Seasonals/Special Releases:** Belle's Boysenberry Ale, Dark Xmas Ale, Curmudgeony Barleywine, Newton's Graph, Passionate Monkey, Collaborator Doppelbock—Breakwater Brewing collaboration **Tours:** Yes—upon request **Taproom:** Yes

Arcana Brewing Company, formerly Fezziwig's Brewing Co., is located in Carlsbad a short jaunt off I-5 near El Camino Real and Faraday. The location is tucked back in an industrial complex, but there is plenty of parking, which is definitely a perk. Founder and brewer Daniel Guy opened the brewery in September of 2012 and does everything, with help from some passionate friends. Daniel had been home brewing for 10 years and started when he was undergrad studying neuroscience and English. After graduation he worked an environmental consulting job and decided he wanted to do something more fulfilling—thus Fezziwig's was born. In May of 2013 he was forced to change his brewery name due to a dispute with Sam Adams, but that definitely didn't discourage him. Daniel is a driven individual who loves craft beer and loves sharing his passion with others.

Daniel loves steampunk, a fact you'll immediately notice when you step foot inside his brewery's tasting room. All along the narrow space you'll see old speakers, cogs, skulls, candelabras, a corgi with a jetpack, and Victorian ephemera. The mead hall–style bar is to the right as you walk in, and a standing area runs half the length of the building. An assortment of hand-turned clay mugs, for the mug club, are displayed next to the taps and are made by art potter Jesse Martin. The 3.5 BBL brewhouse is tucked away in the back to the right with all the fermentation equipment. Formal tours aren't offered, but Daniel will definitely show you the system if you ask, provided it isn't too busy. Arcana Brewing is looking at producing 240 BBLs in 2013, with plans to expand to a 15 BBL system in the coming years.

Arcana Brewing produces a full lineup of inspired and experimental ales. The best-selling of his lineup include **Voyager English IPA, Tiny Tim Cream Ale,** and **Marley's Ghost,** an 8.3% strong ale or brown porter. **Marley's Ghost** has a really nice, toasty malt profile with a ruby-brown body. This is more than likely what

Voyager English IPA
Style: English-Style IPA
ABV: 7.1%
Availability: Limited year-round

In a town where the West Coast IPA is king, it's nice to find more creative versions of the style. Voyager focuses on the dark, malty side of the IPA category and delivers with a roasty caramel flavor profile. Notes of cherry, ripe strawberry, and fruity English ale esters are also present. The beer pours a deep caramel with a fluffy head. It tastes exactly as it looks. Hops are definitely present, but they are more balanced in this variation rather than being overly forward.

Voyager is brewed year-round, but due to the small production capacity, it may not be available every day. It's definitely a great place to start on your tasting journey.

porters used to look like before they approached and eventually defined the stout style. **Passionate Monkey** is an 11.5% ABV braggot, or beer/mead hybrid. The fruit is very forward on the nose with light spritzy body. Like other nano-style breweries, Arcana's beers are creative, inspired, and unique. It's definitely recommended to grab an entire flight to see what you like. Beer is available for take home in 32- and 64-ounce growler form.

AZTEC BREWERY

2330 La Mirada Dr., #300, Vista, CA 92081; (760) 598-7720; aztecbrewery.com; @AztecBrewery
Founded: 2011 **Founder:** John Webster, Claudia Faulk, and Rob Esposito **Brewer:** Rob Esposito and Paul Naylor **Flagship Beer:** Sacrifice Red IPA **Year-round Beers:** El Dorado (Aztec Blonde), Coffee Blonde, Hibiscus Wheat Beer, Aztec Amber, Aztec Agave

Northern San Diego

Wheat, Chipotle IPA, Sacrifice, Cacao Chocolate Porter, Noche de Los Muertos, Poco Gigante IPA **Seasonals/Special Releases:** ABC Retro Lager, ABC Habanero Barrel-Aged Noche with Cinnamon, Chipotle IPA, Chocolate Porter, Doomsday Barleywine **Tours:** Yes—upon advance request **Taproom:** Yes

Located in the growing Vista brewery empire, Aztec Brewery is reviving a dead brand. The original Aztec Brewery opened in Mexico during Prohibition and was in operation from 1921 to 1953. Post prohibition the Aztec was moved to San Diego where it later retired.The brand, with its Aztec sundial pictogram, was long since extinct—that is, until John Webster and Claudia Faulk revitalized it and adopted the classic title as the name of their new brewery in August of 2011. Together they partnered with local North County Home Brewers Association president and Siebel grad Rob Esposito. John comes from a design and freelance art background, and Claudia has experience in website design and social media. With John and Claudia's branding background and Rob's brewing experience, they were able to take their fascination with the old Aztec label to the next level.

Aztec Brewery has a true taproom, which is completely separate from the brewery. Adorned with skulls, adobe-colored walls, piñatas, and other Latin flair, the theme and feel is evident immediately when you walk into the room. It's reminiscent of a Southwestern tavern and comes complete with an upright piano in the corner. The main bar is located to the left as you walk in, and various high- and low-seated tables are peppered around the tasting room to give guests a place to enjoy their beers. Behind the bar you'll notice both draft lines and a beverage cooler filled with 22-ounce versions of some of their mainstays and special releases. A door leading into the production portion of the operation is to the right of the bar. Behind it is a 15 BBL brewhouse, which pumps out 180 BBLs a month.

Aztec Brewery takes its theme pretty seriously, and along with revitalizing the brand as a whole they are even bringing back some of the older beer names like the **ABC Retro Lager,** which is based on the original old brewery's canned beer. **Noche de los Muertos** sports a festive skull on the label and their flagship **Sacrifice** showcases an Aztec dagger cutting through a heart. They are pulling from a pretty colorful, and arguably violent, history here, and they use details like these to help them solidify their brand. Other beers like the **Chipotle IPA** and **Hibiscus Wheat** utilize Latin culinary spices to increase heat and simulate some of the famous *agua frescas*. Grab a flight to figure out which one is for you, and then buy a growler or purchase a 22-ounce bottle. Aztec doesn't make it too far outside San Diego and Vista, but their distribution circle is growing.

Aztec Sacrifice
Style: Red IPA
ABV: 7.6%
Availability: Year-round
Aztec Sacrifice, the brewery's flagship beer, is a West Coast–style red ale. Incorporating both an impressive malty background and a forward hop profile, this beer is rich, medium-bodied, and satisfying. Heavy notes of caramel and toffee pair nicely with an up-front punch from West Coast Citra hops. The beer is less balanced and more layered, which makes it a nice food-pairing beer. Spicy Latin dishes bring out the caramel malt notes and accentuate the floral citrus bitterness, which will also kick up the heat if you are eating something hot. The beer pours deep amber red with a fleeting head.

BELCHING BEAVER BREWERY

980 Park Center Dr., Vista, CA 92081; (760) 599-5832; belchinbeaver.com; @belchingbeaver
Founded: 2012 **Founder:** Tom Vogel, Dave Mobley, and Troy Smith **Brewer:** Troy Smith and Mike Callahan **Flagship Beer:** Beaver's Milk and Dammed! Double IPA **Year-round Beers:** Me So Honey—Honey Wheat Ale, Beaver's Milk—Milk Stout, Rabid Beaver Bite—Rye IPA, Dammed! Double IPA, Saison De Beaver—Saison, Blushing Beaver—India Red Ale, Ol' Dirty—Russian Imperial Stout **Seasonals/Special Releases:** Hop Highway IPA, Tail Slap'd XPA **Tours:** Yes—upon request **Taproom:** Yes

Founded by professional friends Tom Vogel, Dave Mobley, and Troy Smith, Belching Beaver Brewery, located in Vista, opened in October of 2012. With Tom coming from a real estate development background and Dave architecture, they were missing one piece of the puzzle: a brewer. Tom immediately called his friend Troy Smith, a brewer with years of experience and Coronado Brewing Company lineage. The team

Beaver's Milk
Style: Milk Stout
ABV: 5.3%
Availability: Year-round

Beaver's Milk, despite its funny name, is a serious milk stout. Utilizing lactose in the recipe, this beer is roasty on the nose and has a pleasant residual sweetness. Sweet stouts, when made right, can be very satisfying and are great accompaniments to spice-forward desserts. The body of this beer is very creamy and when served on nitro becomes even more so. You'll definitely detect forward notes of coffee and milk chocolate. Beaver's Milk pours dark black with an off-white head.

now creates solid classic styles on their 15 BBL brew system as well as some more unique offerings. Belching Beaver is a completely self-financed brewery and is also promoted as being a family-friendly establishment. Due to the great success of their Vista location, Belching Beaver opened a secondary tasting room in San Diego's North Park district.

The Belching Beaver taproom is industrial modern, with plenty of concrete and stainless to go around. It's not a lavish establishment, but it is decently sized. The first thing you'll notice is the hand-painted beaver logo on the left and behind that, the bar. The brewhouse sits in the back right, waiting for Troy and Mike's magic touch. The tasting room can easily hold large groups and is definitely well equipped for events. Summer, winter, and other seasonal beer fests are a common occurrence, so check their event schedule online before plotting a trip. The brand and logo are designed to be comical and fun, and there is talk of it becoming a clothing line as well in the near future.

Belching Beaver North Park

Along with the full-scale production brewery, Belching Beaver Brewery has opened a satellite tasting room in North Park. Nestled in amid an already hopping high-density craft beer scene, the North Park tasting location goes through a significant amount of beer. It's now one of the major features on the SD DrinkAbout, which is an ongoing beer/bar hop. If you're in San Diego and you can't make it up to Vista to try these wonderful beers at the brewery, this tasting room is a great alternative. Heck, you can even get a bar hop in. Win Win.

Belching Beaver beers are well made and have entertaining names. **Dammed! Double IPA** is a rich fruity and citrus-zesty IPA. Other beers like **Rabid Beaver Bite** utilize rye in their grain bill along with Simcoe hops. **Me So Honey**, their honey wheat ale, is a popular option among light-beer drinkers. The team is also working on a small barrel-aged program, which will produce barrel-aged versions of **Dammed!** and their **Ol' Dirty** Russian imperial stout. Look for these special releases as well as taproom-only offers when you visit. Sixty-four-ounce growlers are available for take home, and Belching Beaver beer is widely available at local beer bars.

CULTURE BREWING COMPANY

111 S. Cedros Ave., Solana Beach, CA 92075; (858) 345-1144; culturebrewingco.com; @CultureBrewCo
Founded: 2012 **Founder:** John Niedernhofer, Steve Ragan, and Dennis Williams
Brewer: Steve Ragan **Flagship Beer:** Black IPA **Year-round Beers:** Amber Ale, American Strong Ale, American Brown, Belgian Saison, Black IPA, Black Lager, Blonde Ale, Double IPA, Hefeweizen, Imperial Stout, IPA, Pale Ale **Seasonals/Special Releases:** N/A **Tours:** Yes **Taproom:** Yes

Culture Brewing Company opened in February of 2013, and although it's still relatively young, it's drawing large crowds as it makes a name for itself. Located across the street from the beach, it's one of the few production-only breweries around located in a high-rent beach zone. The three owners, Steve, Dennis, and John, were longtime home-brewing buddies before they decided to open their own place. The trio brought with them skills from their day professions—architecture,

Black IPA
Style: Black IPA
ABV: 7.2%
Availability: Limited year-round

Culture Brewing Company names their brews by style, so it's easy to know what you are getting when you order it. The Black IPA is one of their most popular offerings, and it's easy to see why. This San Diego–style IPA is made with Simcoe and Cascade hops, which are then balanced out effectively with the generous portion of roasted malts added. There is a big hop presence, but the coffee and roast is also there. It has a light body with crisp afternotes of citrus, which makes it wonderful on a cool beach day. Culture Brewing's Black IPA pours a jet black with a light white head, and at 7.2% you can probably enjoy more than one.

marketing, and branding—which allowed them to open not only a brewery, but also a hip tasting room aimed at elevating the craft of beer.

Culture Brewing is located near the intersection of N. Cedros Avenue and Lomas Santa Fe Drive. The building is well lit during the day, with a large open-air front, which allows the ocean breeze to cool the space. N. Cedros Avenue is a classic beach community strip overflowing with boutique stores, cafes, and eccentric small businesses. Culture Brewing, with its reclaimed wood exterior, chalkboard interior, and modern minimalist approach, fits right in. The brewhouse is tucked away on the back patio that overlooks the beach, and three of the five fermentors are located directly behind the bar. The bar/serving area is small, usually with two bartenders, but they manage to control the crowds with quick and efficient service. It's an upscale beach vibe, so you'll see plenty of flip-flops, flat brimmed hats, tank tops, and swimwear.

Culture Brewing Company considers itself a boutique microbrewery. They brew a wide array of styles, but the most popular tend to be of the hoppier variety. Just check the chalkboard or the website prior to visiting if you're looking for a specific beer. Their **Blonde Ale** is worth noting, as it's actually a traditional German Kölsch and not the American variety. It's incredibly complex, light, and effervescent, with a very tasty light-grain complexity. The **Russian Imperial Stout,** served on nitrogen, is also very tasty. It pours with a thick tan head and is super creamy, with heavy notes of milk chocolate and roasted coffee beans. Culture brews their classic styles very well. Beer is available for takeaway in a 64-ounce growlers, and draft varieties can be found throughout North County.

GOLDEN COAST MEAD

4089 Oceanside Blvd., Oceanside, CA 92056; (619) 796-1774; goldencoastmead.com; @GoldenCoastMead
Founded: 2010 **Founder:** Frank Golbeck, Praveen Ramineni, and Joe Colangelo **Head Mead Maker:** Frank Golbeck **Flagship Mead:** Mirth in a Bottle **Special Limited Releases:** Mirth in a Bottle, Farm House Batch, Orange Blossom, California Oak **Tours:** No formal tours offered. Call for private tour availability. **Taproom:** Not yet

Let's start out with the obvious here: Mead is not beer, but it is a craft-fermented beverage and this is one brand you don't want to miss. Founded by head mead maker Frank Golbeck, CFO Praveen Ramineni, and head of sales Joe Colangelo, Golden Coast Mead started out as a home-brewing project among college friends. Frank first tasted mead made by his grandfather, who used local honey off of the family's apple ranch. It was this tasting that set in motion the events that would spawn Golden Coast Mead.

The team of friends made their first batch of mead in 2010, renting space under a custom-crush arrangement that boutique wineries use. The honey was locally sourced, and extra care was used to ensure that this batch not only lived up to their high expectations, but also promoted the idea of local craft mead. In 2012 they launched a successful Kickstarter campaign that led to the purchase of their own tanks, increased local investment through Slow Money, and gave them the ability to lease a small space in Oceanside. The team makes mead but is also actively involved in sustainable beekeeping, honey production, and environmental advocacy groups aiming to help bees survive.

Golden Coast Mead is located in Oceanside in an industrial building off Oceanside Boulevard. It's not currently open to the public and there isn't a tasting room yet, but that will all come in time. The facility is small, with a tiny office in front, and the equipment sits in back near the loading dock. They have two 300-gallon tanks, which will allow them to produce 2,400 gallons per year. They are working on securing three more tanks, which will bump up their production to 7,000 per year. Until then, product is limited and will always be time-intensive. Their first release, **Mirth in a Bottle,** which can be found throughout San Diego in bottle shops, took over six months to make. Their second release, **Farm House Batch,** literally made in a farmhouse, had a similar lead time. Their next two releases utilize a slightly faster yeast, which will allow them to package more product in a shorter time, but care is still taken to ensure the mead is ready.

Mead, especially craft mead, is a relatively difficult drink to get. There isn't much representation within Southern California, and that's a shame. Golden Coast

Beer Lover's Pick

Farm House Batch
Style: Semisweet Still Mead
ABV: 12.5%
Availability: Limited year-round

On a personal note, I'm not much of a mead connoisseur, as I simply haven't had much in my lifetime. That being said, Golden Coast meads are amazing and people sing praises about the quality. Farm House Batch is the meadery's second offering. First made using a custom-crush arrangement in a literal farmhouse, Farm House Batch presents drinkers with a complex bouquet of citrus, tropical fruit, and honey. There is a pleasant and light effervescence to it, and it pours a crystal-clear gold.

It's easy to see why early people wrote about mead as being a drink of the gods. A glass of Farm House Batch, like other meads, is the combined essence of 200,000 flowers—think about that while you enjoy it.

meads are nothing short of amazing. The drink can be enjoyed cold or cellar temperature, flat or carbonated, and has an incredibly complex range of flavors. Golden Coast mead is never boiled, and that is intentional to preserve the honey's natural aromatics. Mirth in a Bottle has an incredibly floral spicy bouquet with notes of citrus and pepper. It pours clear like a white wine, and the aroma is intense and intoxicating. Farm House Batch is very different, with more of an earthy complexity. The two new variations being offered will be unlike Mirth and Farm House, but will be equally delicious. Bottles can be found in all San Diego Whole Foods and in high-end bottle shops. Availability will increase in 2014.

INDIAN JOE BREWING COMPANY

2379 La Mirada Dr., Vista, CA 92081; (760) 295-3945; indianjoebrewing.com; @IndianJoeBeer

Founded: 2012 **Founder:** Max Moran **Brewer:** Max Moran **Flagship Beer:** Premium Red **Limited-Release Nano Styles:** Premium Red, Chocolate Hazelnut Porter, Dandelion IPA, Apricot/Peach Hefeweizen, American Indian IPA, Black IPA **Tours:** Yes—upon request **Taproom:** Yes

Brewer Max Moran has been making beer for the last 25 years, and in December of 2012 decided to take his hobby to the next level and open up Indian Joe Brewing Company. Max brews on a 55-gallon nano system which fuels some 20-plus taps ranging from elderberry red ales to dandelion IPAs. Being the only Native American in California to own a brewery, Max takes his Luiseno Indian heritage very seriously and infuses it into everything he does. He first learned about brewing from his dad, who frequently made beer with his German brewer friend. You'd be hard-pressed to find someone as passionate about beer and the culture surrounding it as Max, and it's a difference you can taste.

Indian Joe Brewing Company's tasting room has been made to look like a back-woods country saloon, complete with corrugated roofing, country music, and neon signs. It's a unique look, and it gives the tasting room a laid-back feel. Max has frequent food-service guests, from gastro-trucks to German sausage grillers, so be sure to check the website and Twitter before you go. Guests can sit at the long, wooden L-shaped bar or at any one of the many circular stone tables. The space is designed to pack in a good amount of people. Max has events often, from new beer releases to chili cook-offs to cultural festivals. The brewhouse is set a bit back from the tasting room behind a small gate. If you ask Max nicely, he may take you back to show you where the magic happens. He brews frequently and has to in order to keep up with demand.

American Indian IPA
Style: Sage-Infused IPA
ABV: 7.0%
Availability: Regular

Max tries to keep the American Indian IPA on tap most of the time, as it's both one of his best sellers and one of his favorites. The beer is brewed with white sage, tangerine, and apricot, which give it a wonderful fruity spiciness. The hop profile is both piney and citrusy, and when coupled with the other additions in the beer, it's very reminiscent of being out in the desert during the springtime. When Max brews this beer, he conducts a Native American purifying ritual with the white sage, which rids his beer and those who drink it of negative energy. Not only is this beer great on the palate, but it turns out it's good for the soul as well. American Indian IPA is a pleasure to drink.

Like many nanobrewers, Max serves a plethora of styles and they are constantly changing. Flagships are hard to pinpoint with a brewery of this size, but Max knows what sells well, so it's likely that if you can't find the Premium Red, there is something similar and equally delicious on the menu. Speaking of **Premium Red,** it's a nice malty and hoppy amber spiked with notes of honey and elderberry. Other solid go-tos are his infused IPAs. **Dandelion IPA** is a medium-ABV offering with an assertive dandelion bitterness at the tail end of the tasting. The **Chocolate Hazelnut Porter** is a crowd favorite and is often paired or topped with a dollop of whipped cream, so it can be treated as a dessert. Flights are offered and should definitely be considered because there are so many creative small-batch beers on tap—you'll definitely find something you like. If you want to take beer home, Max offers 32-ounce branded growlers.

IRON FIST BREWING COMPANY

1305 Hot Spring Way, Vista, CA 92081; (760) 216-6500; ironfistbrewing.com;
@ironfistbrewing

Founded: 2010 **Founder:** Eve and Greg Sieminski **Brewer:** Brandon Sieminski **Flagship Beer:** Renegade Blonde **Year-round Beers:** Renegade Blonde, Nelson the ImpALEr, Hired Hand, Dubbel Fisted, Golden Age, The Gauntlet, Uprising, Velvet Glove **Seasonals/ Special Releases:** Imperial Rebellion, Spice of Life **Tours:** Yes **Taproom:** Yes

Iron Fist is creating an uprising in Vista! The family-run brewery is owned and operated by the Sieminski family, with Eve and Greg the founders and their son Brandon the brewer. The family started their brewing adventures on a home brew scale with Greg and Brandon. In October of 2010 they opened the commercial brewery with the goal to focus primarily on big Belgian beers. Iron Fist employs a 20 BBL brewhouse and seeks to expand beyond this. Growlers and 750 ml bottles are available at the bar, with some beers clocking in at 12.0%.

The taproom was expanded in 2012. Originally there was a giant community mural complete with pencil, crayon, and marker drawings that included an image of a giant squid. This was removed when the taproom was expanded to twice its size. The brewery took over the space next door and increased not only their drinking space, but also their barrel program and storage capacity. Bottles are now packaged

using a slick state-of-the art bottling line, and thirsty patrons can find a place to sit comfortably in amid barrels, Iron Fist–branded surfboards, and brewery paraphernalia. The brewery is somewhat separated from the dog-friendly taproom and sits in the back of the building, but tours are available upon special request and private parties are also an option.

Iron Fist focuses mainly on Belgian-style beers, but has a few German offerings as well. Their **Renegade Blonde** is actually a German-style Kölsch and is the current flagship beer, selling over most others. Their saison, **Hired Hand,** is also a popular option, as is their **Dubbel Fisted Belgian Dubbel.** Most Iron Fist beers are above the 6.5% mark, some employ local fruits and spices, and many are made to be cellared. Still, there are some lower-ABV options, including the **Nelson the ImpALEr,**

Beer Lover's Pick

Uprising
Style: Belgian Tripel
ABV: 12.0%
Availability: Year-round
Uprising is made in small batches but is available year-round. Bottles are pricey but well worth it. If you are a collector of beer whales, this is probably one you'll want to have in your cellar. Uprising is a dry-hopped Belgian tripel that clocks in at 12.0% ABV. It has rich notes of apricot, apple, plum, and citrus, which are accompanied by a fresh tartness. Substantial alcohol heat accom-

panies the telltale Belgian yeast fruitiness, and the hops—Nelson, Motueka, and EK Goldings, among others—only deepen the complexity of this beer. Uprising makes a great food pairing with spicy holiday dishes and/or rich desserts. It's best shared in a large group and is available in the Iron Fist taproom on draft and in bottle only.

an appropriate San Diego West Coast IPA. If you are a fan of Belgian-style beers and like breweries with larger-format tasting rooms, Iron Fist is a great option. They frequently have food trucks and food vendors set up in the loading dock, so it's a great way to spend an afternoon or evening when you are brewery hopping.

LATITUDE 33 BREWING COMPANY

1430 Vantage Ct., #104, Vista, CA 92081; (760) 913-7333; lat33brew.com; @Lat33Brew
Founded: 2012 **Founder:** Kevin Buckley **Brewer:** Kevin Buckley **Flagship Beer:** Camel Corps IPA and Vanilla's Porter **Year-round Beers:** Camel Corps IPA, GB's Pale Ale, Straw Horse Wheat Ale, The Pasha's Rye Brown, Vanilla's Porter **Seasonals/Special Releases:** Carolina Honey Hips, First Fleet Wheatwine, Breakfast With Wilford, Camel Corps Double Hump, Germans in the Desert Lager, Biere de Mars **Tours:** Yes—upon request **Taproom:** Yes

Latitude 33 Brewing Company opened its doors in March of 2012 with brewmaster Kevin Buckley at the helm. Kevin, whose brew history includes stints at Alberta's Grizzly Paw Brewery, Alpine's Alpine Beer Company, and Vista's Backstreet Brewing, took over the original Green Flash Brewing location and uses the 20 BBL brewhouse to create traditional beer styles with modern-day twists. Accompanying Kevin on his Latitude 33 journey are Sage Osterfeld and Jim Comstock from the Lost Abbey. The name is based on the 33rd parallel and the many military and occult

references related to it. As such, the beers take colorful names poking fun at both of these subjects with a sort of pseudo old-school/Pan-American art style. The labels are really fun and have a sort of colonial comic look to them.

The brewery is modestly sized with a large-format tasting room, which sits right next to the brewery production line. As you walk in through the loading gate or the front glass doors, you'll immediately notice the massive Latitude 33 mural in the back, which ties the whole taproom together. The bar runs along the length of the building, and from it are served five year-round beers along with a slew of seasonal and experimental one-offs. The brewhouse sits to the left of the tasting area in all its brilliant copper glory. Brewing equipment and its history is always something I find fascinating, and knowing that the now-massive Green Flash started on this system is a fun factoid. Tours are available upon request, although they aren't really needed, as everything is out in the open.

Beer Lover's Pick

Vanilla's Porter
Style: Vanilla-Infused English Porter
ABV: 6.5%
Availability: Year round

Vanilla's Porter is based on an English-style porter, but incorporates a healthy dose of Mexican and Madagascar vanilla beans. It pours a dark amber/coffee black with a beige head. Vanilla's measures in at 6.5%, so it's easy to session, and with rich Munich malt notes accompanied by English pale and crystal toffee flavors, it's a beer you'll want to come back to. The mouthfeel is broadened by the addition of wheat and a medium level of carbonation. It's roasty, refreshing, and satisfying. The vanilla shines through, making it an easy pick for dessert. The 22-ounce bottle label depicts a colonial officer proposing to Vanilla in that signature Pan-American comic style.

Kevin likes brewing beers based on classic styles with small twists. Their flagship **Camel Corps IPA** blends West Coast hops and English malts to create a nonstandard West Coast IPA experience. The **Vanilla's Porter** is also a very nice beer, with strong English malty notes and a pleasant dose of Mexican vanilla beans. The **Biere de Mars** is a seasonal release, but definitely worth trying if it's available. Heavy bread notes from the Munich and Belgian malts and a nice touch of coriander bring the spicy beer together. It has a sweet aroma and is amber in color. All Latitude 33 beers are worth trying, and it's always strongly recommended to grab a flight. Kevin's primary focus is on style diversity, but many patrons stick to the IPA. Growlers can be filled, and 22-ounce bottles of their year-round beers are readily available.

LEFT COAST BREWING COMPANY

1245 Puerta Del Sol, San Clemente, CA 92673; (949) 218-3964; leftcoastbrewing.com; @LeftCoastBrewCo
Founded: 2004 **Founder:** George, Dora, and John Hadjis **Brewer:** Randal Dilibero
Flagship Beer: Hop Juice **Year-round Beers:** Hop Juice, Trestles, Una Mas, Asylum, Voo Doo **Seasonals/Special Releases:** The Wedge, Ale Epeteios, Board Walk, Red Tide, Barrel-Aged Voo Doo **Tours:** Yes—limited; call ahead for availability **Taproom:** Yes

Left Coast Brewing Company was founded in 2004 by George, Dora, and John Hadjis, the same founders as SoCal's famous Oggi's Pizza. Oggi's Pizza has been a successful brewpub chain, and up until recently brewed all their own beer in-house on their brewpub systems. Today Left Coast does all the brewing for the Oggi's brand as well as a number of their own specialty beers. Brewer Randal Dilibero, formerly of Lagunitas Brewing Company, drives the 30 BBL brewhouse, which produces over 9,000 BBLs a year. The brewing facility is located in San Clemente in an industrial district, not too far from the nearby military base.

The brewery opened a tasting room to the public in February of 2013, where guests can enjoy 12 taps of delicious beer. The taproom itself is moderately small, but has a large bar and a number of small wooden tables. You'll immediately notice the big Left Coast logo behind the bar and the large thematic tap handles in all their colorful glory. If you're lucky, you may also see Tommy or John Hadjis behind the bar, so feel free to strike up a conversation. The brewhouse and fermentors are in a different building, along with the keg cold box and bottling line. Tours must be arranged ahead of time and are limited in availability.

Left Coast Brewing produces a large selection of classic styles and experimental beers. You'll be able to find beers like Hop Juice, Voo Doo, Una Mas, Asylum, and Trestles on tap all the time, but there are also a number of seasonals worth a try.

Hop Juice
Style: Double IPA
ABV: 9.7%
Availability: Year-round

Not only is Hop Juice their best-selling beer, but it's also a multiple medal winner. It recently picked up a bronze at the 2013 Los Angeles County Fair and was awarded medals at the Great American Beer Festival. Hop Juice is a big beer, and at 82 IBUs it's also going to work your palate. The base beer is medium-bodied and malty, made primarily with American two-row. Added to that are CTZ, Cascade, Mount Hood, and a West Coast dry hop blast of Simcoe, Amarillo, and Centennial. This

beer has West Coast IPA written all over it, and is intensely flavorful and juicy with a powerful bitterness.

Tasters are served in small plastic cups, but you are also welcome to order full pints. **Una Mas** is a great one to try if you are looking for a light, refreshing lager with forward bread notes, as it recently was awarded Best of Show at the 2013 California State Fair. **Voo Doo** is also a great choice if you prefer roastier beers. They are working on expanding their barrel-aging program so look forward to some interesting beers like **Rye Whiskey Barrel-Aged Voo Doo,** which will be released in 22-ounce bottles only and available in the taproom. Growlers are available for takeaway, along with 12- and 22-ounce bottles of the year-round beers. Left Coast beer is distributed to 17 (soon to be 25) states, and can be found in many local beer bars and all the Oggi's Pizzas in SoCal.

LIGHTNING BREWERY

13200 Kirkham Way, Poway, CA 92064; (858) 513-8070; lightningbrewery.com;
@lightningbrew

Founded: 2006 **Founder:** Jim Crute **Brewer:** Jim Crute and Bruce McSurdy **Flagship Beer:** Thunderweizen Ale **Year-round Beers:** Amber Ale, Black Lightning Porter, Double Strike IPA, Electrostatic Ale, Elemental Pilsner, Fair Weather, Ionizer Lager, Old Tempestuous, Sauerstrom Ale, Thunderweizen Ale **Seasonals/Special Releases:** N/A **Tours:** No formal tours offered. Call for private tour availability. **Taproom:** Yes

Founded in 2006 by head brewer Jim Crute, Lightning Brewery focuses on the science of making beer. Jim was a PhD biochemist by trade before he made the jump to brewing, so it's no surprise that Lightning Brewery employs a heavy science theme in both beer-naming conventions and label artwork. Whether it's the periodic table shorthand labels or the tagline "better beer through science," Jim takes brewing very seriously, with the philosophy of keeping things simple. Lightning is the only brewery in the area that employs 100 percent bottle conditioning for each offering packaged in a bottle. The brewery also prides itself in its German-style decoction system with lagering tanks.

Lightning Brewery is located in Poway, about 20 minutes outside of Mira Mesa in an industrial park. The building is on the smaller side, with the brewhouse and equipment jam-packed into every nook and cranny. The 50 BBL kettle allows them to do an average of 30 BBLs at a time, and they bottle everything with their fully automated bottling line. The tasting room is currently being run out of their cold box, so patrons get to drink amid the tanks and equipment, but an expansion into the building next door will allow them to open up a more traditional tasting room, slated for completion in early 2014. There are currently no formal tours available but in the current brewhouse you'll get the self-guided tour as you enjoy beers amid the machinery.

Jim and team do not use chemical additives in their beer and employ a strictly yeast/water/hops Reinheitsgebot mentality. Lightning beers run the gamut from traditional German ales to amped-up lagers and imperial farmhouse ales. **Thunderweizen,** a Bavarian-style wheat ale, is their best seller and comes complete with a shiny silver-and-gold metallic label. **Old Tempestuous,** the 9.0% winter warmer, is a actually an English-style old ale suitable for cellaring and has claimed quite a few awards in local California beer competitions. Lightning beers benefit from the decoction brewhouse and as such take on a deeper, more melanoidin character. They have strong ties to German traditional beers not just in their method and yeast profile, but also in their other ingredients. All beers are available for purchase in 22-ounce bottles but are subject to availability. You can also find Lightning beers in most beer establishments in San Diego.

Thunderweizen Ale
Style: Bavarian Hefeweizen
ABV: 5.5%
Availability: Year-round

Thunderweizen is the current flagship and is also the beer that put Lightning on the map. Jim named the beer after a very impressive lightning storm he witnessed prior to opening the brewery. This rich bottle-conditioned wheat beer is intensely clove-forward with banana overtones. It has a creamy, thick mouth-feel that harkens back to the heartier German-style ales. It pours an opaque goldenrod with a thick, pillowy head and should be enjoyed in a traditional German wheat beer glass. It's a multi-award

winner in several local competitions and was named one of the top 10 Hefeweizens in the country by the New York Times. It's definitely a solid go-to beer on both hot summer days and cold winter nights. It can easily be found on tap at local San Diego beer bars and at bottle shops.

PORT BREWING/THE LOST ABBEY

155 Mata Way, #104, San Marcos, CA 92069; (800) 918-6816, ext. 107; lostabbey.com; @lostabbey

Founded: 2006 **Founder:** Tomme Arthur, Jim Comstock, Gina Marsaglia, and Vince Marsaglia **Brewer:** Tomme Arthur and Matt Webster (Lead Brewer) **Flagship Beer:** Red Barn and Devotion for the Lost Abbey, Wipeout and Mongo for Port Brewing **The Lost Abbey Year-round Beers:** Avant Garde, Devotion, Inferno, Judgment Day, Lost and Found Abbey Ale, Red Barn Ale **Port Brewing Year-round Beers:** Mongo Double IPA, Old Viscosity, Shark Attack, Wipeout, Board Meeting **The Lost Abbey Seasonals/ Special Releases:** Carnevale, Gift of the Magi, Serpent's Stout, The Ten Commandments, Witch's Wit, Cuvee de Tomme, Deliverance, Duck Duck Gooze, Red Poppy Ale, The Angel's Share **Port Brewing Seasonals/Special Releases:** Anniversary, High Tide, Hop 15, Hot

Rocks, Midnight Expression, Panzer Pils, Santa's Little Helper, SPA, Older Viscosity **Tours:** Yes; free tours Sat every 20 to 25 minutes from noon to 5 p.m.; call ahead for private tours **Taproom:** Yes

Port Brewing and the Lost Abbey is one brewery producing two brands in a single location. The story is semi-complicated, but the gist of it is that Tomme Arthur opened up the Lost Abbey in 2006 with Jim Comstock and Pizza Port founders Gina and Vince Marsaglia. Before opening the brewery, Tomme was the head brewer at Pizza Port in Solana Beach, where he worked since 1997, working his way up to director of brewery operations. Jim is in charge of the financial side of Port Brewing, and both Vince and Gina have built a successful beer empire with their Pizza Port brewpub locations.

The brewery is located near the 78 off Rancheros Drive in an industrial district. You'll know you've arrived when you see the giant grain silo. You can enter through the front glass doors, prominently featuring both Port Brewing and the Lost Abbey logos, or you can go through the loading gate door. The monastic tasting room is a wide open space with a large L-shaped bar serving both Port Brewing and Lost Abbey beers. This space is actually the location of Stone Brewing's first facility. A chalkboard above the taps displays the current list. It's easy to tell the beer brands apart: flip-flops for Port Brewing and crucifixes for the Lost Abbey. Merchandise and bottles are located to the left of the bar, along with barrels and plenty of standing room. The 30 BBL brewhouse is tucked away in the back portion of the space and manufactures upwards of 16,000 BBLs of beer each year, much of which is packaged on their nearby bottling line. Informal tours are offered on the weekends upon demand every 20 minutes or so.

It's important to note that there are essentially two brands being produced in this location. Port Brewing consists of the more American styles like IPAs, stouts, and hoppy beers, while the Lost Abbey is focused on Belgian-inspired and barrel-aged beers. Depending on your preference, you may want to focus on one or the other, but the fact is that both are worth trying. Port Brewing beers are similar to but not exactly the same as the ones you'll find in the Pizza Port locations. The Lost Abbey beers include some upper-alcohol offerings and bottle-aged rarities. Try the **Red Barn Ale;** it's a crisp, funky saison. The **Red Poppy Ale,** a sour cherry–infused Flanders, is also highly recommended. **Old Viscosity** and **Older Viscosity** are motor oil–thick imperial stouts, with rich roasty notes. **Older Viscosity** is the barrel-aged version. Most beers are available for takeaway in bottle format, although growlers are also available.

Northern San Diego

Judgment Day
Style: Belgian Dark Strong Ale
ABV: 10.5%
Availability: Year-round
This 10.5% Belgian dark strong ale is made with over 180 pounds of raisins per batch, which coupled with the overall maltiness of the beer, gives it an incredible deep and rich body. It's thick. Judgment Day has up-front notes of dark fruit, prune, and, of course, raisin. It's chewy with a very spicy nose. The beer

pours dark ruby-brown with a thick, persistent tan head. This is not a session ale, but it is a perfect one for food pairing and fine dining. This style of beer is also frequently used in cooking due to its richness. If you want a sour version, try Cuvee de Tomme, the barrel-aged sour that uses Judgment Day as its base.

Mongo Double IPA
Style: Double IPA
ABV: 8.5%
Availability: Year-round
Mongo Double IPA is Port Brewing's signature West Coast–style IPA. It's exploding with citrus notes, focusing on orange and also apricot. The malt definitely plays second fiddle to the overall hoppiness, but it is slightly sweet on the tail end of the taste. Hop flavor lingers and the

main hop, Columbus, dominates everything about this beer. It's a dry beer that pours a golden yellow with a white head. Mongo Double IPA isn't a session beer, but at 8.5% it's not overly alcoholic, so you may be able to enjoy more than one.

MOTHER EARTH BREW CO.

2055 Thibodo Road Suite H, Vista, CA 92081 (760) 599-4225; www.motherearthbrewco .com; @motherearthbrco
Founded: 2008 **Founder:** Daniel Love, Jon Love, and Kamron Khannakhjavani
Brewer: Daniel Love, Kamron Khannakhjavani, Jon Love, Mike Rodriguez, and Johnny Johur **Flagship Beer:** Kismet IPA **Year-round Beers:** Cali Creamin', Siren, Kismet IPA, St. Elmo, Sin Tax, Thibodo, Local First, Hop Diggity DIPA, Pin Up, 63 Red Dog Rye **Seasonals/Special Releases:** Barely Legal Blonde, Big Mother, Righteously Hopped Red, Primordial Double Decker, El Hefe, I.R.A., New Girl, Pipe Dreams, Por Que No?, rEvolution, Roundabout, Rysing Tide, Wet Hop Dreams **Tours:** Yes **Taproom:** Yes

Mother Earth Brew Co. is located off Thibodo Road in Vista. It's important to note that there is actually a taproom and retail store as well located on Main Street, but the Thibodo Road location is the brewery. Both locations are worth a visit and are open to the public. Started in 2008 by Daniel Love, Mother Earth focuses on an intense lineup of classic styles and hoppy IPAs. Daniel hired master brewing consultant Lee Chase from Stone Brewing Co. fame to help with setting up the brewery and finalizing the recipes. Together with his stepson, Kamron, and brother Jon, they built Mother Earth Brew Co. In 2010 the group opened up a brewing supply store, and in 2012 they moved the store to a new location and paired it with a tasting room. During that time the original brewery's tasting room was

Mother Earth Brew Co. Tap House and Home Brew Shop

Tap House, 206 Main Street, Vista, CA 92084; (760) 726-2273
Retail Store, 204 Main Street, Vista, CA 92084; (760) 726-2273
Mother Earth Brew Co. is not only an amazing boutique brewery, but it also runs a home brew shop located on Main Street in Vista. Home brewers can pick up ingredients for their next batch and then enjoy a pint of extremely fresh Mother Earth beer. The home brew shop originally opened in 2010 but was moved to a new location in 2012, which also houses a tap house right next door. They are separated by address for regulation purposes. It's a wide open space, 4,000 square feet, which makes for a less cramped shopping and drinking experience. The team at Mother Earth, staying true to their roots, does it right and is eager to not only make great beer, but also help home brewers make great beer.

Cali Creamin'
Style: Cream Ale with Vanilla
ABV: 5.2%
Availability: Year-round

While Mother Earth Brew Co. is known for its amazingly fresh and creative IPAs, Cali Creamin' must be highlighted because of its uniqueness. This beer pairs a solid, original cream ale backbone with fresh vanilla, and the combination is wonderful. True, it's one of their lightest beers and is their second-best seller, but it's also one of the most incredibly complex. It has a nice, smooth, creamy body and a pleasant malt graininess. Suddenly the

dry infused vanilla kicks in, and the resulting balanced flavor is heaven. This is a beer that non-craft-beer drinkers and seasoned vets can both appreciate. It pours a crystal-clear gold with a frothy white head and is available in 22-ounce bottles.

closed, but it reopened in late 2013. Now beer fans can drink Mother Earth beer in either location.

Mother Earth is a small operation. The team operates a newly installed 20 BBL brewhouse and manages to output a tremendous amount of beer. Walking into the Thibodo brewery facility, you'll notice it's split into two adjoining buildings. The right half is the brewery, with a chain-link fence barring access to the production facility, and the left half is the tasting room. The entire brewery is decorated with old rock albums, rainbows, blankets, and music paraphernalia. It has a very hippie "one-love" air about it. The tasting room is modest, with a stainless bar and a dry-erase board displaying what's on tap. Mother Earth is a family-run operation, so you'll likely see the guys making the beer and working the taproom at the same time. Their hard work shows.

Mother Earth makes beers of all styles, but they tend to focus more on the floral, hoppy ones. Their flagship **Kismet IPA** is a beautiful IPA utilizing the wonderful Nelson hop. On the opposite end of the scale, they have a popular vanilla-infused cream ale called **Cali Creamin',** which marries the breadiness perfectly with light effervescence and fresh vanilla. **Sin Tax,** their imperial stout, is a sweet peanut butter stout, which tastes exactly the way it sounds—smooth and nutty. **Thibodo** is their taproom namesake IPA incorporating Mosaic and Belma hops, which adds a strawberry flavor. All these beers are wonderful, and you can't really go wrong with anything on tap. If you are a hop head and you like good people, look no further than Mother Earth Brew Co. Flip-top growlers are available for fills, and some of their year-round beers like Kismet and Cali Creamin' are available in 22-ounce bottles.

OCEANSIDE ALE WORKS

1800 Ord Way, Oceanside, CA 92056; (760) 721-4253; oceansidealeworks.net; @OAW_Brewery

Founded: 2005 **Founder:** Mark Purciel and Scott Thomas **Brewer:** Mark Purciel and Scott Thomas **Flagship Beer:** Orange Agave Wheat **Year-round Beers:** Pier View Pale Ale, San Luis Rey Red Ale, Buccaneer Blonde, American Strong Ale **Seasonals/Special Releases:** Orange Agave Wheat, Pirate Cove IPA, Dude Double IPA, Duck Dive Dunkel, Elevation 83 **Tours:** No formal tours offered. Call for private tour availability. **Taproom:** Yes

Founded in 2005 by local teacher Mark Purciel and firefighter Scott Thomas, Oceanside Ale Works is a brewery with a focus on surfing. Mark and Scott wanted to go into business together and focus on not only brewing beer, but also being a locally focused business. They believe very strongly in supporting their local community. Mark's background is in woodworking and math; he was a woodshop teacher for years before the brewery opened. He is currently the most present of the two while Scott literally puts out fires as an active firefighter. That being said, the duo has won a number of awards for their beers and continues to promote a local, friendly vibe in their brewery.

The brewery is about 7 miles from the beach, but you would probably guess by walking in, feeling the vibe, and seeing the beer names that you were there already. It's located off Ord Way, an industrial street, in a series of tall warehouse buildings. The brewery name is clearly labeled on the building, so it's relatively easy to find.

Orange Agave Wheat
Style: American Wheat
ABV: 5.2%
Availability: Limited year-round

Orange Agave Wheat is a low-ABV American wheat beer aimed at those wanting to enjoy a few beers after a long day's work. It's a nice, easy-drinking summer beer with pleasant citrus notes and a bit of residual sweetness from the agave. The wheat gives this otherwise light beer a bit of body and breadiness, making it satisfying but not filling. It recently took a third place at the San Diego International Beer Competition. There is a small tartness on the back end followed by a slight hoppy bitterness. The beer pours a golden clear and is highly effervescent. It's a great version of an American wheat, a style that you don't see too often these days.

Once you walk into the taproom, you'll immediately notice barrels to the right and the bar and tasting room to the left. The tasting room comes complete with vintage Dairy Queen booths, a long wooden bar made from reclaimed dock wood, and an outdoor patio. It's open and inviting with an industrial feel. The 20 BBL brewhouse lives next door with its cool graffitied fermentation tanks. It's a not a conventional system and was actually put together by the crew by hand. Oceanside Ale Works produces about 1,700 BBLs of beer a year, and they recently won the opportunity to shadow Jim Koch from Sam Adams in a professional development contest.

Oceanside Ale Works makes smooth-drinking beach beers along with some heavy-hitting hoppy ones as well. They take their theme pretty seriously and as such name their beers with nautical titles like Buccaneer Blonde and Pirate Cove. They recently won first place in the San Diego International Beer Competition for their **Dude Double IPA.** This beer clocks in at 9.4% with over 100 IBUs. Beers like **Pirate Cove,** the citrus resiny IPA, are more straightforward. **Buccaneer Blonde,** their lightest beer, has a biscuit and breadiness to it and is one of their top sellers. Oceanside Ale Works recently set up a bottling line, so their beers will become more available in the near future. Until then they are available locally in San Diego only or via a filled growler takeaway.

OFFBEAT BREWING COMPANY

1223 Pacific Oaks Pl., Ste. #101, Escondido, CA 92029; (760) 294-4045; offbeatbrewing .com; @offbeatbrewing
Founded: 2011 **Founder:** Tom Garcia and Sarah Garcia **Brewer:** Tom Garcia **Flagship Beer:** Caticorn IPA **Year-round Beers:** Giraffcopter Session Pale Ale, Caticorn IPA, Bear Arms Brown, Bitter Robot Red, Deer Grandpa Abbey Ale **Seasonals/Special Releases:** Caticorn IPA with Sage, Barefoot Harem Theft Scotch Ale, Grain-Fed Dog American Strong, CinnaBear Brown, Sporkupine Pale Ale **Tours:** Yes; call for availability **Taproom:** Yes

Offbeat Brewing Company was founded in 2011 by former Stone Brewing Co. cellar supervisor Tom Garcia and his wife, Sarah. Tom, who trained under Lee Chase, went off to do freelance brewery consulting after his tenure at Stone. In August 2012 his dreams came true when he opened the doors to his new art and community outreach–focused brewery. Offbeat Brewing Company is located in Escondido roughly 1 mile away from Stone Brewing World Bistro & Gardens, which is about a three-minute drive. Tom and Sarah know Escondido well and have lived in the area for a while; that was the reason why they decided to call Escondido the home of Offbeat Brewing.

Offbeat Brewing is located in a small modern industrial complex near the cross streets of Harmony Grove Road and Pacific Oaks Place. The first thing you'll notice as you walk through the large loading dock gate entrance to the taproom is a massive

Caticorn IPA with Sage
Style: San Diego–Style IPA
ABV: 7.7%
Availability: Limited

The normal Caticorn IPA is available year-round and is definitely a great example of the San Diego–style IPA. The sage-infused version of Caticorn is available at limited times throughout the year and adds another level to an already great beer. This citrus, resin, and tropical fruit–forward beer is bright, effervescent, and has a nice grainy backbone. When the spicy sage is introduced, it plays very nicely with the orange zestiness and brings out earthy hop undertones. The resulting flavor is pleasant and complex.

It's easy to overdo sage, but this one is balanced and would make an incredible food pairing with Asian dishes and anything spicy.

mural on the left wall. This piece by three local artists, with its Sasquatch beasts, hollow deer, weird birds, ice crystal mountains, and psychedelic forests, is a modern marvel. They also feature other local artists underneath the mural in a rotating gallery. The taproom is relatively open, with an L-shaped bar that wraps around the back right corner of the space. It's animal friendly, and one of their main focuses is to raise money for charity and Humane Society–related efforts. Animal portraits, jazzy metal tap handles, and bright paint make Offbeat a real trip. The art colony vibe is super-warm, relaxed, and hip.

Offbeat operates a 10 BBL brewhouse to make their creatively named beers. The animal focus carries through with beers like **Bear Arms Brown** and **Caticorn IPA.** The **Girafficopter Session Pale Ale** is really nice, with a light straw color and pleasant melanoidin graininess. **Grain-Fed Dog American Strong** is a larger beer at 8.0%, with nice dark fruit notes and a sweet finish. Offbeat makes a wide range of styles, but focuses on relatively small production. They have a focused tap list that rotates relatively frequently, but rest assured, all beers are made very well. They have a near-term plan to bottle, so look for that in late 2014, but for now you can take home their tasty beer in growlers.

RIP CURRENT BREWING

1325 Grand Ave., #100, San Marcos, CA 92078; 92078; (760) 481-3141; ripcurrentbrewing .com; @RipCurrentBeer

Founded: 2011 **Founder:** Paul Sangster and Guy Shobe **Brewer:** Paul Sangster and Guy Shobe **Flagship Beer:** Lupulin Lust IPA **Year-round Beers:** Lupulin Lust IPA, Red Flag IIPA, Barrier Reef Nut Brown, Marine Layer San Diego–Style Hefeweizen, Rescue Buoy Russian Imperial Stout, Vanilla Storm (Kona Coffee, Vanilla, Imperial Porter), Palomar Porter, Hazardous Hazelnut Porter **Seasonals/Special Releases:** Palomar Chocolate Porter, Black Lagoon Scottish Strong, Stringer Scottish 80, sURGing Current Session IPA, Rail Grab German Rye, Marine Layer German-Style Hefeweizen, Raked Over Red, Rotating Double Overhead (pilot batches) **Tours:** Yes; call for availability **Taproom:** Yes

Rip Current Brewing, located in San Marcos, is relatively new to the scene. Opening its doors officially in December of 2012, Rip Current is founded and powered by two amazing award-winning home brewers, Paul Sangster and Guy Shobe, turned pro. Paul has won over 150 medals, three Amateur Brewing Championships, a California Home Brewer of the Year award, and the Coveted Ninkasi Award, and is one of the very few home brewers that have won a medal in every single beer style category. Paul started his home brewing in the early '90s, while Guy got into it a little later, in 2006. They are both active members of the QUAFF home-brewing club, and they've successfully taken their home-brewing creativity to new heights on the commercial scale.

The facility is located off the 78 on Grand Avenue. There is a large tasting room in the front, with the brewing equipment and storage living in the back. The tasting room only takes up about 25 percent of the entire facility, so there is definitely room for the team to grow. The theme is beach-focused, with beers adopting clever names like **Rail Grab German Rye.** Painted concrete floors, shiny bar taps, and vintage cans make the taproom pop. Rip Current Brewing operates a midsize 15 BBL brewhouse with room and plans to expand. Their goal is to produce around 6,000

Lupulin Lust IPA

Style: San Diego–Style IPA

ABV: 8.3%

Availability: Year-round

San Diego is known for its epic, bitter, dank, fruity IPAs, and Rip Current has a really good one on tap. Lupulin Lust IPA has an incredibly intense and beautiful floral nose. Citra, Simcoe, and Centennial round out the hops for this offering and give it that signature SD flavor. The beer is dry on the palate and clocks in at 8.3%. It's not technically a session beer, but the alcohol

is hidden very well, so you could easily get carried away with this one. The flavor in this beer follows through nicely from first sip to aftertaste. Definitely a must-try.

to 7,000 BBLs a year. Tours are given but aren't officially offered, so call ahead to check their availability.

Paul's and Guy's home-brewing backgrounds have made their beers incredibly creative and varied. They brew everything from double IPAs to Roggenbiers, and each one of them is extremely well made. The goal is to have something for everyone, so they brew a huge selection of styles using their custom reverse-osmosis water. Their **Palomar Porter,** a robust-style porter, is a superrich and beefy roast bomb, while their **Rail Grab German Rye** is a classic clove-forward Bavarian Roggenbier. They also do frequent pilot test batches, which they sell under their Rotating Double Overhead menu. These beers are limited-release one-offs that are fun to try and are unique. Rip Current Brewing doesn't bottle yet, but it plans to in the near future. For now you can take their amazing beer home in their stainless steel growlers.

STONE BREWING CO.—STONE BREWING WORLD BISTRO & GARDENS

1999 Citracado Pkwy., Escondido, CA 92029; (760) 294-7866; stonebrewing.com; @stonebrewingco

Founded: 1996 **Founder:** Greg Koch and Steve Wagner **Brewer:** Mitch Steele **Flagship Beer:** Stone IPA **Year-round Beers:** Stone Pale Ale, Stone Smoked Porter, Stone IPA, Stone Ruination IPA, Stone Levitation Ale, Stone Cali-Belgique IPA, Stone Sublimely Self-Righteous Ale, Arrogant Bastard Ale, OAKED Arrogant Bastard Ale **Seasonals/Special Releases:** Double Bastard Ale, Lukcy Basartd Ale, Stone RuinTen IPA, Stone Enjoy By IPA, Stone Old Guardian Barley Wine, Stone Imperial Russian Stout, Stone Anniversary Ale **Tours:** Mon through Fri at noon, 2, 4, and 6 p.m.; Sat and Sun every hour on the hour from noon to 6 p.m. ($3 for adults 21 and up with valid ID; ticket includes souvenir tasting glass and four 4-ounce samples; $1 for youths and adults not wishing to drink) **Taproom:** Yes

If you are planning to do a brewery tour of San Diego—or of Southern California, for that matter—make sure Stone Brewing Co. is on your list. Co-founders Greg Koch, CEO, and Steve Wagner, president, founded the brewery in 1996. Their original brewhouse was in San Marcos, where the Lost Abbey is currently located. After seeing colossal success as one of the fastest-growing breweries in America, Stone Brewing Co. moved to its current location in Escondido in 2005. One year later they opened the adjacent farm-to-table restaurant Stone Brewing World Bistro & Garden. In 2011 the company announced plans to expand with another brewery-restaurant

Arrogant Bastard Ale
Style: American Strong Ale
ABV: 7.2%
Availability: Year-round

Arrogant Bastard Ale is one of the most notorious beers available. The label cleverly challenges the drinker with the signature statement "You're Not Worthy." The beer itself is an intense, caramelly malt bomb generously accented with bitter hops. Up-front biscuit notes and a toasted toffee aroma make Arrogant Bastard a delight. The beer is changed up a bit in an oaked version cleverly named OAKED Arrogant Bastard Ale, which adds vanilla notes to the beer. Double Bastard Ale and Lukcy Basartd Ale are also special-release versions worth a try.

location in San Diego. Add the purchase of a local organic-methods farm, Stone Farms, and the opening of additional Stone Company Stores throughout Southern California, and the Stone story is a tale of success, quality production, and expertly executed marketing. Spokesman Greg Koch is an incredibly passionate craft beer advocate and is not afraid to fight for what he believes in.

The current brewing location in Escondido is massive. The main building is split into two parts, the restaurant Stone Brewing World Bistro & Gardens and the brewery. Walking into the facility is like passing through the gates of Jurassic Park. Huge green plants hang overhead, massive wooden doors mark the threshold, and colossal stone gargoyles decorate the rock walls. Both the brewery and restaurant are beautiful. In the brewery you'll see two 120 BBL brewhouses, which will pump out a total of 210,200 BBLs in 2013. To put that in perspective, in 1996 their production was 400 BBLs. Massive fermenters, stainless pipes, immaculately clean floors, and a mini pilot system are some of the things you'll see. The bottling and packaging facility,

where bottles fly down a conveyor belt into cardboard boxes that are then wrapped up and loaded onto trucks, is housed in an adjacent building. Brewery tours are available but fill up fast, so make sure you get a space as soon as you arrive. Outside of the brewery, Stone Brewing World Bistro & Gardens is where you'll be treated to world-class food and beers. Quail knots, farm-to-table salads, decadent desserts, and cask ales are some of the things you'll find. Many of the foods incorporate beer, and you can buy Arrogant Bastard Ale BBQ sauce at the on-site Stone Company Store.

Stone Brewing Co. beers are hop-centric. The brewery has made a name for itself by selling bitter hop-forward beers, which in the time of macro fizzy yellow stuff was just what the doctor ordered. Since the release of Stone IPA, Arrogant Bastard Ale, and Stone Smoked Porter, which goes incredibly well with barbecued meat, they've expanded their creativity quite a bit. Stone now prominently features incredible collaboration beers that feature everything from pecans to mint to coconut. A 2013 collaboration beer Drew Curtis/Wil Wheaton/Greg Koch Stone Farking Wheaton w00tstout joined the forces of Stone's Greg Koch, actor Wil Wheaton, and Fark.com creator Drew Curtis to create an imperial stout brewed with pecans, wheat, and rye then partially barrel-aged in bourbon barrels. Other very noteworthy beers include the newest hop craze Stone Enjoy By IPA, a dank West Coast IPA with an "enjoy by" date printed on the front of the label, which is systematically ripped from the shelves if it's not fresh enough. As hop-centric as they are, Stone's beers are also varied—those that aren't hop fans will, no doubt, still find something they like. Growlers, kegs, and bottles are available in the Stone Company Store for takeaway.

STUMBLEFOOT BREWING COMPANY

1784 La Costa Meadows Dr., #103, San Marcos, CA 92078; (760) 208-1012; stumblefoot
.com; @StumbleFootBrew

Founded: 2012 **Founder:** Bill Randolph and Pat Horton **Brewer:** Bill Randolph and
Pat Horton **Flagship Beer:** Otay Chipotle Stout **Year-round Beers:** GrassYass IPA,
Vixen Dunkel **Seasonals/Special Releases:** Apollo Double IPA, Schwarz be with you...
Black Lager, Mojo American Stout, Otay Chipotle Stout, Tommeknocker Belgian Style
Dubbel, Back to Blacken IPA, Vixen Dunkelweizen, Muchas GrassYass Double IPA, Carli's
Honey Blonde Lager, Creekside Honey Blond Ale, Flakey Robin Belgian Sour, Red Dress
Robust Porter, Head Slap Barleywine **Tours:** No formal tours offered. Call for private tour
availability. **Taproom:** Yes

Stumblefoot Brewing Company, located in beautiful San Marcos, is the defini-
tion of grassroots. Founded by home brewers Bill Randolph and Pat Horton,
who before opening commercially, home-brewed for 10 years, Stumblefoot is all
about being local. They were both incredibly active in their local home-brewing club,
QUAFF, one of San Diego's largest and most well-known home-brewing clubs, where
they met judges, brewers, and friends that helped them on their way. In February of
2012 the planning, research, and connections paid off when they opened their doors
to the thirsty public. Together with cellarman Zack Horton and home brewer Steve
Mayer, Stumblefoot is seeing great success in the local scene.

The brewery is located in an industrial park off La Costa Meadows near Melrose
Drive and Rancho Santa Fe Road. It's a smaller space with a modest-size taproom.
When you walk in through the pull-up loading door, you'll immediately see the taps
in the back. Several barrels and tables are strategically set so you'll have somewhere
to rest your drink while you converse with the locals. The oranges are painted
orange with hand-painted designs all around the perimeter. Everything you see
in the brewery is done by hand by the Stumblefoot team. They are not only great
brewers, but also incredibly handy. The 7 BBL brewhouse is in the back, tucked away
behind the bar, and there are plans in motion to upgrade to a 15 BBL system. They
are also looking at adding a bottling line and doubling the space by expanding into
the next-door unit.

Stumblefoot has a full lineup of beers, 11 taps, which range from hoppy IPAs to
decadent Dunkelweizens. Strangely their most famous beer, flagship **Otay Chipotle,**
is a stout, and not only that, it's infused with peppers. Peppers also appear in their
Dragon Kissed Porter, which is pretty spicy. Other fan favorites include the **Vixen
Dunkel,** which is a gold medal–winning dark Hefeweizen. It's relatively sweet and

Otay Chipotle Stout
Style: American Stout with
     Chilis
ABV: 7.75%
Availability: Year-round
Otay is Stumblefoot's flagship
bear. It's the Mojo American
Stout with the addition of chipotle peppers. What's nice about
this beer is the balance. Most
chili beers achieve the novelty
of the heat, but rarely do they
offer anything other than a
mouth-burning sensation. Otay
has an assertive roastiness,
which coupled with the chocolate notes and the chipotle
flavor, is reminiscent of a spicy
mole. It pairs extremely well

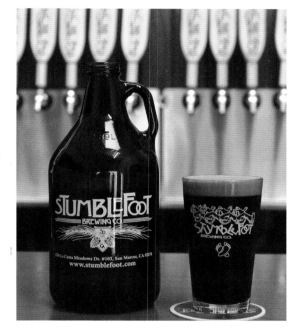

with red meat and Mexican food and would make a good addition as a braise. It pours
a jet black with a light tan head and clocks in at a sessionable 7.75%. If you like
spice, order this, and if you don't, still order it—you may be surprised.

clocks in at 6.0%, with a nice roasted wheat character accompanied by assertive
banana and clove notes. The **GrassYass IPA** series encompasses both a normal and
double IPA, so if you are a hop head, this should be the first one you order. A
64-ounce screw-top growler is available for to-go beer.

Brewpubs

PIZZA PORT

135 N. Hwy. 101, Solana Beach, CA 92075; (858) 481-7332; pizzaport.com/locations/
pizza-port-solana-beach; @pizzaportSB

Founded: 1987 **Founder:** Gina and Vince Marsaglia **Brewer:** Devon Randall **Flagship
Beer:** Swamis IPA **Year-round Beers:** Swamis IPA, Ponto Pale Ale, Grandview Golden
Ale, Dawn Patrol Dark, California Honey Ale, Shark Attack Imperial Red, Whale's Tails Pale
Ale, Kook IPA, Aggie's IPA, Cardiff Chronic **Seasonals/Special Releases:** 1 Down Brown,
Toronado Hi Fives Session IPA, May The Port Be With You Imperial Porter, Oats Oatmeal
Stout, Silky Heads Lemongrass Wheat, MichelTangelo Tangelo Wheat Beer, Follow Your
Passion Pale Ale, Brown Bag Malt Liquor, Cowabunga Cream Stout, Hot Spots Hefeweizen,
Old Boneyards Barleywine, Solana Peach Ale, Santa's Little Helper Imperial Stout, Seaside
Stout, Trippel Overhead Golden Ale **Tours:** No formal tours offered. Call for private tour
availability. **Taproom:** Yes

Founded in 1987 by Gina and Vince Marsaglia, Pizza Port has become much more
than a standard brewpub—it's a San Diego pizza and beer empire. Since 1987
the brand has opened four other locations (Carlsbad, Bressi Ranch, Ocean Beach,
San Clemente) and a bottle shop, and
were key players in the opening of Port
Brewing/The Lost Abbey. It's important to note, though, that the Solana
Beach Pizza Port is the original location, starting its beer brewing in 1992.
It still enjoys a heavy crowd of thirsty
beachgoers. Solana Beach head brewer
Devon Randall, previously lead cellarman in charge of the barrel program
of the Lost Abbey, joined the team in
2013 and brews a combination of the
Pizza Port mainstay beers along with
plenty of innovative custom beers from
her own arsenal.

Pizza Port is easy to spot off N. Highway 101. Look for a giant blue awning,
thatched roof facade, and beer drinkers out front. The brewpub is best described
as a quick-serve pizza joint, although lines and wait times are usually very long,
with a brewhouse in the back. Solana Beach, like the other locations, is enjoyed by

Other Pizza Port Locations

The Pizza Port brewpub chain is one of the most well-known beer spots in San Diego and enjoys fans of all ages. The beer portion of the operation is unique in that each location has a different head brewer. While each spot brews a set of mainstay styles, they are also given free rein to experiment with their own styles and offerings. Food is generally the same at each location, but the locations themselves each have their own signature pizza.

From the thatched roofs at Solana Beach, to the bottle shop at Carlsbad, to the surfboard sign at Ocean Beach, to the massive facility at Bressi Ranch, they all have their own charm. The newest location, Bressi Ranch, will actually double as a massive production facility that will eventually bottle the Pizza Port beers and increase distribution coverage. It's also the location of the conical fermentor turned aquarium that was featured on the Animal Planet reality show *Tanked*. If you are going on a beer tour, be sure to stop by at least one of these spots for lunch or dinner and enjoy a classic San Diego brewpub experience. This makes each individual Pizza Port spot worth going to. Up-to-date beer lists are shown on webcam on the Pizza Port website.

Year-round beers for all locations: LightSwitch Lager, Brewhouse Blonde, Harvest Hefeweizen, Piranha Pale Ale, Hopstorm IPA, Jeremiah Red, Nutty Brewnette, P.M. Porter, Tatonka Stout

Bressi Ranch, 2730 Gateway Rd., Carlsbad, CA 92009; (760) 707-1655; pizza port.com/locations/pizza-port-bressi-ranch; @pizzaportBressi. Brewer: Sean Farrell

Carlsbad & Bottle Shop, 571 Carlsbad Village, Carlsbad, CA 92008; (760) 720-7007; pizzaport.com/locations/pizza-port-carlsbad; @pizzaportCbad. Brewer: Mike Aubuchon; Assistant Brewer: James Hodges

Ocean Beach, 1956 Bacon St., Ocean Beach, CA 92107; (619) 224-4700; pizzaport.com/locations/pizza-port-ocean-beach; @pizzaportOB. Brewer: Ignacio Cervantes

San Clemente, 301 N. El Camino Real, San Clemente, CA 92672; (949) 940-0005; pizzaport.com/locations/pizza-port-san-clemente; @pizzaportSC. Brewer: Ryan Fields

patrons of all ages, so you'll usually see a mix of beach bums, skateboarders, older guys in Tommy Bahama shorts, and little-league teams. There are two counters to order from, one food and one beer, and seating is communal-style with giant wooden picnic tables. Like all Pizza Port locations, there is a video game arcade in the back. Pizza can be ordered with any topping, but there are specials on the board. Each location has its own classic: The Solana Beach one has clams, shrimp, onions, olives, bell peppers, and mushrooms—worth a try if you've never had a seafood pie.

Pizza Port beers run the gamut from blondes to IPAs to imperial stouts. Each location has a different brewery team, but they all brew their versions of the flagships and usually share beers with each other, so you can find some overlap. All the beers are listed above the beer counter in their classic hand-drawn-meets-crazy-collage

Beer Lover's Pick

Swamis IPA
Style: West Coast–Style IPA
ABV: 7.5%
Availability: Year-round
Swamis IPA is one of the original Pizza Port beers and is touted as the "The Original San Diego IPA," having been brewed since 1992. It's similar to the Wipeout IPA, which is a big, hoppy citrus bomb with a dry finish. Swamis is a straight-ahead IPA. The body is incredibly light with heavy orange, grapefruit, and tropical citrus notes. It's probably one of the most well-known of Pizza Port's

beers, and as such they go through a lot of it. It pours a clear golden color with a frothy white head. There are plans to can the beer in the near future when the Bressi Ranch production facility is up and running.

style. Devon's brewery is sunk into the floor in the back, and she focuses on beers of all styles, from barrel-aged varieties to those with fruit added. One of her latest, the **MichelTangelo,** a 5.0% ABV tangelo-infused wheat ale, is a perfect pairing for the Solana Beach Pizza. You'll always find something different, so order a pint or a taster set. Growlers are also available to go.

PROHIBITION BREWING COMPANY

2004 E. Vista Way, Vista, CA 92084; (760) 295-3525; prohibitionbrewingcompany.com; @prohibitionbc
Founded: 2011 **Founder:** Ron Adams & Kathy Adams **Brewer:** Matthew Adams and Jonathan Riley **Flagship Beer:** Hef-U-Up **Year-round Beers:** Hef-U-Up, Chocolate Oatmeal Stout, Ruby Red Ale, Sweet Biscuit Amber Ale (SBA), Dirty Blonde, Cali IPA, Extra Pale Ale, Saison **Seasonals/Special Releases:** N/A **Tours:** No formal tours offered. Call for private tour availability. **Taproom:** Yes

Prohibition Brewing Company was opened on November 11, 2011, by husband-and-wife team Ron and Kathy Adams. Ron comes from an electrical contracting background and had always wanted to open a business. He still has his contracting business, but the main focus is the brewpub. The brewery portion is handled by their

Sweet Biscuit Amber Ale (SBA)
Style: Amber Ale
ABV: 6.1%
Availability: Year-round
Sweet Biscuit Amber, abbreviated as SBA, is one of Ron's personal favorites. It's a medium-bodied beer that pairs with pretty much any item on the menu. Sweet Biscuit, as the name implies, finishes slightly sweet with an up-front malty grayness reminiscent of fresh cereal. The biscuit character is familiar to anyone that is used to biscuit malt—it's very bready.

It pours a crystal-clear amber red with a soft pillowy head. SBA is a great session beer and goes very nicely with the fries and the ProCo. Burger, but would also be great alongside the Street Tacos.

son Matthew and his friend Jonathan Riley, who owns a hop farm with over 500 hop plants. Matthew home-brewed and spent some time in Austria studying beer, returning to drive the 10 BBL brewhouse. Prohibition Brewing is family-operated, a fact that the team is proud of.

Prohibition Brewing is located in Vista off Vista Way. The place is hard to miss with the large Prohibition sign in front and murals on the side of the building. Walking inside, you'll immediately notice the bootlegging-era inspiration. There is a long narrow bar to the left and a large beer hall directly in front. The beer hall is furnished with circular wooden tables, 1920s paraphernalia, and locally built replica tommy guns. It has a pretty cool vibe, and despite the beer focus here, it's very family-friendly. They serve a full menu of beer-friendly foods and are well known for their ProCo. Burger. The menu changes seasonally, they frequently have specials, and they offer Sunday brunch.

Prohibition Brewing Company brews a range of beers, so it's best to start off with a sampler unless you know exactly what you are in the mood for. Their most popular beer is **Hef-U-Up,** a Bavarian-style Hef, which is followed closely by their **Sweet Biscuit Amber Ale, Ruby Red Ale,** and **Dirty Blonde.** These are all brewed to style, so you'll know exactly what you are getting when you order them. The **Cali IPA** is a traditional West Coast–style IPA offering an intense floral nose and dank notes on the palate, and is definitely what the hop heads will want to order. If you're looking for something a little less hoppy, order the **Extra Pale Ale** or **Ruby Red;** both have great malt character. Growlers of the 64-ounce variety are available for take home.

Beer Bars & Bottle Shops

CHURCHILL'S PUB & GRILLE

887 W. San Marcos Blvd., San Marcos, CA 92069; (760) 471-8773; churchillspub.us;
@churchills
Draft Beers: 50 taps plus 2 casks **Bottled/Canned Beers:** 200+ bottles, some
extremely rare

Churchill's, ranked as one of America's top 100 beer bars by *Draft Magazine,* is a must-stop if you are in the San Diego/San Marcos area. Located on San Marcos Boulevard right off the 78, Churchill's is an old English–style pub, with elevated beer and food. The pub as it's known today was opened in December of 2002. It was converted from a mediocre pub to an upscale beer bar by current owner Ivan Derezin. Everything in the kitchen at Churchill's is made from scratch, and many of the seasonal items on the menu are made with beer. Try any of the items listed under "Craft Entrees" for a great craft food experience. The Beer Blanc Grilled Salmon is incredibly savory and tasty, and pairs nicely with a lighter Belgian ale. You'll also want to pay attention to the Scotch eggs, chicken wings, and hand-breaded mozzarella sticks.

Drinking beer at Churchill's is a wonderful experience. There are 50 craft taps along with 2 casks to choose from and over 200 bottles, including some incredibly rare offerings, to share with friends. "Meet the Brewer" nights are common, along with brewery-specific tap takeovers. The staff is knowledgeable and friendly and can easily help you with drink suggestions or food pairings. The vibe is elevated English pub, and it gets very busy around peak drinking hours. If you just want to hang out, there are pool and foosball tables to enjoy along with a back patio away from the main dining area. Churchill's is one of the top destination beer bars and gastropubs in the San Diego area and should not be missed.

ENCINITAS ALE HOUSE

1044 S. Coast Hwy. 101, Encinitas, CA 92024; (760) 943-7180; encinitasalehouse.com;
@encialehouse
Draft Beers: 32 taps plus 1 cask **Bottled/Canned Beers:** 350+ bottles

Encinitas Ale House, founded by Tommaso Maggiore, opened its doors in November of 2009. Tommaso, who also owns and operates Acoustic Ales Brewing Experiment and the Public House in La Jolla, opened the bar to pay homage to and share his favorite beers. The pub offers over 350 constantly changes bottles ranging from rare

The Public House

The Public House, located in La Jolla, shares a similar menu and the same friendly vibe as Encinitas Ale House. Also opened by craft beer advocate Tommaso Maggiore, the Public House serves La Jolla crowds great craft beer and eclectic pub food ranging from kangaroo burgers to mac and cheese. They are known for their local Angus and Kobe Wagyu burgers. The Public House, like Encinitas Ale House, showcases some 300-plus rare bottles and 45 taps. Acoustic Ales Brewing Experiment is always on tap. Be sure to check this place out if you are in the area and in need of great beer and sustenance.

Belgians to local favorites. There are also 32 taps of local craft along with a cask, which changes weekly. The space is moderately sized and is located right off S. Coast Highway 101, surrounded by restaurants, eateries, and boutiques. Walking in, the bar is to the right, with a limited seating and standing area on the left. Get there early to avoid crowds and/or put your name on the waiting list. It's a popular spot.

Encinitas Ale House also offers some incredibly good food. Some of the menu items are crazy, and they have a host of frequently rotating special burgers with meats ranging from kangaroo to buffalo. There are always Acoustic Ales beers on tap. If you are up for a challenge and you're local, you might want to join their 80 Beers in 80 Days Club. Patrons that successfully finish this challenge get entered into a raffle for a custom tour of some of the world's greatest beer spots. Munich, Belgium, Colorado, and Portland, Oregon have been past focuses. This is just another way that owner Tommaso shows his appreciation for his beloved patrons. You'll likely see him sharing a pint and lively conversation, so go over and say hello.

THE LUMBERYARD TAVERN

967 S. Coast Hwy. 101, Encinitas, CA 92024; (760) 479-1657; lumberyard101.com; @Lumberyard101

Draft Beers: 20 taps, mixed domestic and craft **Bottled/Canned Beers:** 18 bottles, mixed domestic and craft

The Lumberyard Tavern is an American-style pub located off S. Coast Highway 101 almost directly across the street from Encinitas Ale House. It sits in a large strip mall next to boutique clothing, spice, and olive oil stores. The inside of Lumberyard is

100 Beers in 30 Days

Laurie Delk is a popular San Diego food, beer, and craft blogger best known for her "100 Beers in 30 Days" and promiscuouspalate.com online persona (@100beers30days). Her online blog, the Promiscuous Palate, covers everything from beer and wine to food and spirits. She has an ongoing video series where she explains how to make cocktails and appreciate beer, which is shot at the Lumberyard Tavern in Encinitas. Laurie is an outspoken craft beer advocate and is definitely someone you should follow if you're interested in San Diego's so-called craft culture.

super-rustic and looks like an old log lodge. Wide open seating, an outside patio, and a large U-shaped bar make it extremely easy to find a seat. Red Hot Chili Peppers plays quietly in the background, mingled with the medium hum of pub-goers. The tavern is family-friendly and has a wide appeal for all ages. The Lumberyard opened in its current form in 2009, founded by husband-and-wife team Lisa and Pete Belasco. Today it features craft beers, spirits, and pub food. It is also the current home of local San Diego craft beer personality Laurie Delk, who acts as the beverage director.

The Lumberyard Tavern offers about 20 taps to choose from, with beer coming from locals like Green Flash, Ballast Point, Stone, and Lost Abbey and national favorites like Allagash, Firestone, and Sierra Nevada. Patrons can order tasting flights, and if you really don't know what to order, ask the knowledgeable staff. The menu changes seasonally but offers breakfast, lunch, and dinner options. Buffalo wings, chili, salads, pizza, pastas, burgers—you name it, the menu is huge. They specialize in grill and barbecue, so that is definitely a good start. Every Tuesday is "Tasting Tuesdays," which features 20 percent off all items all night. There is also a 4x4 Burger Challenge which, if you succeed, gets you a mention on their website, a T-shirt, and engraved plaque. The Lumberyard Tavern is a classic American pub with great food and tasty beer.

PIZZA PORT BOTTLE SHOP

571 Carlsbad Village, Carlsbad, CA 92008; (760) 720-7007; pizzaport.com/locations/pizza-port-bottle-shop; @pizzaportbeer
Bottles/Canned Beer: 600+ bottles

The Pizza Port Bottle Shop in Carlsbad is a great place to go to grab great craft beer, both vintage and current. With over 600 bottles to choose from, the store maintains an incredibly rare assortment of local, regional, and international craft offerings. The shop is located right next door to the Pizza Port Carlsbad brewpub and hosts tastings in the back alley behind the shop. Walking in, it's small, narrow, and is even accompanied by some spillover fermentation tanks from the brewhouse next door. Shop manager Brad Vint is well versed in everything he carries, so make sure you ask for help if you need it. If you're in Carlsbad for pizza or in the market for some bottles to add to your growing collection, make sure to stop by.

STONE FARMS

9928 Protea Gardens Rd., Escondido, CA 92026; stonebrewing.com/farm
Draft Beers: 6 Stone taps

What's something that most breweries don't have? A farm! Located about 15 minutes north of Stone Brewing World Bistro & Gardens—Escondido, is the hidden Stone Farms. The modest 19 acre farm has an eclectic array of organic

produce and small livestock. That's right—not only will you find greens, but you'll also find an assortment of rescued chickens, ducks, quails, and peacocks, who will follow you around from behind their cages expecting food. The farm is a great place to kick back and unwind after a brewery tour.

Located in a little shack off the dirt road is a mini store that offers six draft beers ranging from Stone Brewing Co. year-round releases to special beers brewed exclusively for Stone Farms using ingredients grown on-site. When I was there they had an impressively bitter Stone Farms Dandelion IPA. This sort of organic beer experimentation is something to be appreciated. Visitors can order a beer, buy a trucker hat, and then waltz through the farm grounds until they find a suitable place to sit down, relax, and enjoy their liquid refreshments. This is definitely an unexpected destination, but one that is truly worthy of seeking out for its uniqueness.

URGE AMERICAN GASTROPUB
816761 Bernardo Center Dr., San Diego, CA 92128; (858) 673-8743; urgegastropub.com; @UrgeGastroPub
Draft Beers: 50 taps plus 1 cask **Bottled/Canned Beers:** 120+ bottles

Urge American Gastropub opened its doors in July of 2010 in the Rancho Bernardo area right off Bernardo Center Drive in an outdoor strip mall called The Plaza. Urge, like Haven or City Tavern, is a upscale, gastropub-style restaurant serving elevated pub fare, craft beer, and wine. The founders, Grant Tondro, Zak Higson, and Nate Higson, come from a mix of restaurant and wine backgrounds. The result is a warm, modern dining experience with menu options that change seasonally. Walking into Urge, you'll notice a massive outdoor patio perfect for lunch and warm nights. Inside the restaurant you'll find dining to the left and the large bar to the right. Behind the bar are some 50 rotating local craft taps, a cask, and a host of fine wines. You'll more than likely want to make a reservation if you have a group, but if it's a party of one, the bar usually has no wait.

Urge offers high-end reimagined pub food. Poutine, beer cheese soup, goat cheese salad, burgers, meat loaf—you're bound to find something tasty. A big focus is put on meat here, but there are some vegetarian options as well. They have a house vegan burger that gets high praise. If you want meat, the Garbage Burger, incorporating both wild boar and beef, is pretty awesome. Frequent craft-themed events happen at Urge, so be on the lookout and check their Facebook and website. Like other successful Cali gastropubs, they have plans to open a brewery of their own sometime soon, so keep your eyes peeled for that.

Beer Hops & Bus Tours

In some cases, the best beer can only be acquired by use of motor vehicle. If this is the case, why not take advantage of a beer tour bus? There are some great beer tours offered that include all-you-can-drink beer, food, and transportation for small and large groups. This is the perfect option for birthday parties and celebrating friendship.

LA Beer Hop, labeerhop.com

The LA Beer Hop is a popular LA-centric beer bus that offers local tours in both public and private formats. Run by craft beer aficionado Hal Mooney, LA Beer Hop has several packages that each focus on different areas, the most popular being the Beach Cities and East & Central LA tours. The LA Beer Hop picks up guests from designated areas in a hotel shuttle converted to beer wagon. Tastings are included with each three-brewery tour along with fantastic music and your personal tour guide, typically Hal himself. The LA Beer Hop is a fantastic option for birthday parties and special events. Hal also offers a shuttling service. LA Beer Hop features frequent, changing beer circuits through some of LA's most entertaining beer spots. The bus has designated drop-off/pickup times and shuttles guests from bar to bar at their own pace for a reasonable fee, usually $15 for a wristband.

Brewery Tours of San Diego, brewerytoursofsandiego.com

There are so many breweries in San Diego that you may want to think about taking a bus tour of some of the bigger ones. Brewery Tours of San Diego offers several daily public tours, which include tastings, lunch, and a souvenir glass. They have many tours to choose from, each on different days and featuring different breweries. Prices range from $65 to $90 per person. Group rates are available provided you can get enough people. Popular stops for Brewery Tours of San Diego include Stone Brewing, Green Flash Brewing, Mission Brewery, Pizza Port, Ballast Point, San Marcos Brewery & Grill, Ale-Smith, San Diego Brewing, and the Lost Abbey. There are more options for larger groups seeking private tours. This is definitely a great option, though, and is perfect for celebrating birthdays and bachelor parties.

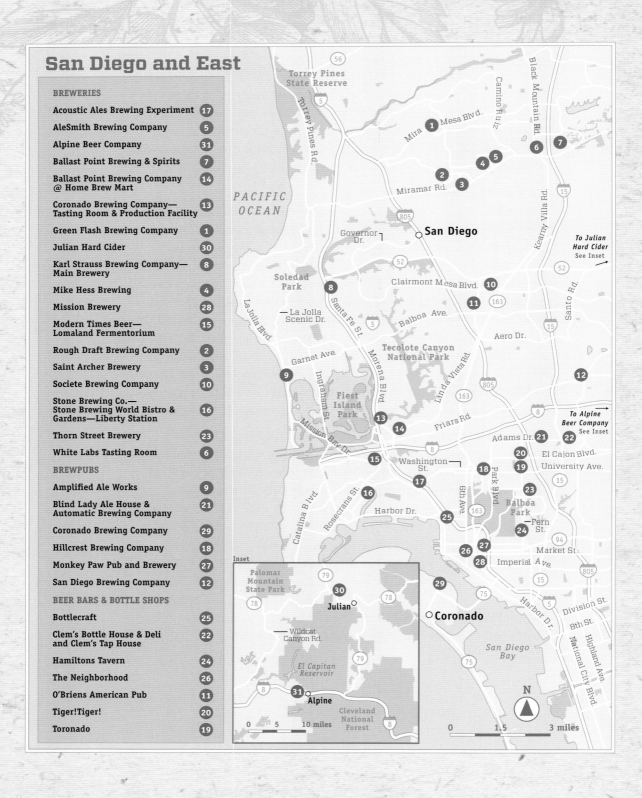

San Diego and East

BREWERIES

Brewery	No.
Acoustic Ales Brewing Experiment	17
AleSmith Brewing Company	5
Alpine Beer Company	31
Ballast Point Brewing & Spirits	7
Ballast Point Brewing Company @ Home Brew Mart	14
Coronado Brewing Company—Tasting Room & Production Facility	13
Green Flash Brewing Company	1
Julian Hard Cider	30
Karl Strauss Brewing Company—Main Brewery	8
Mike Hess Brewing	4
Mission Brewery	28
Modern Times Beer—Lomaland Fermentorium	15
Rough Draft Brewing Company	2
Saint Archer Brewery	3
Societe Brewing Company	10
Stone Brewing Co.—Stone Brewing World Bistro & Gardens—Liberty Station	16
Thorn Street Brewery	23
White Labs Tasting Room	6

BREWPUBS

Brewpub	No.
Amplified Ale Works	9
Blind Lady Ale House & Automatic Brewing Company	21
Coronado Brewing Company	29
Hillcrest Brewing Company	18
Monkey Paw Pub and Brewery	27
San Diego Brewing Company	12

BEER BARS & BOTTLE SHOPS

Bar / Shop	No.
Bottlecraft	25
Clem's Bottle House & Deli and Clem's Tap House	22
Hamiltons Tavern	24
The Neighborhood	26
O'Briens American Pub	11
Tiger!Tiger!	20
Toronado	19

San Diego and East

Like the previous chapter, this one covers several amazing microcosms of San Diego craft beer. The Miramar/Mira Mesa area is home to a few of the most well-known breweries in Southern California, and most of them are a short distance from each other, which means they can be visited in succession. As you go farther south, you'll encounter some truly inspired boutique brewpubs, amazing beer bars and bottle shops, and an intoxicatingly evolving craft beer scene. San Diego has been at this since the early '90s and so is one of the most amazing craft beer destinations in the world—showcasing some 80-plus breweries with even more in planning. San Diego is Southern California's most craft-beer-dense region. Have fun—it's impossible not to.

Breweries

ACOUSTIC ALES BREWING EXPERIMENT

1795 Hancock St., San Diego, CA 92110; (619) 299-2537; acousticales.com
Founded: 2013 **Founder:** Tommaso Maggiore **Brewer:** Tommaso Maggiore **Flagship Beer:** N/A **Year-round Beers:** Greatest Hits, Tush, Run for the Hills, Mosh Pit, You'll Hop Your Rye Out, Unplugged **Seasonals/Special Releases:** The Groupie, Mad Dub, Shake Your Monkey Maker, What the Hop, Passion Pils, Witte Snake **Tours:** No formal tours offered. Call for private tour availability. **Taproom:** Yes

Acoustic Ales Brewing Experiment is located in the old Mission Brewery building right off the 5 Freeway near midtown San Diego. The building, a historic landmark and oldest brewery building in San Diego, was used by Mission Brewery beginning in 1912 and was closed during Prohibition in 1919. The old landmark was also used as a quarantine for influenza in the early 1900s and was later home to a kelp manufacturing plant. Acoustic Ales, founded by successful bar-and-restaurateur Tommaso Maggiore, began using the facility for beer production in early 2013 and opened the doors to its taproom the following October. Tommaso is no stranger to the beer business and has an extensive background in both the restaurant industry

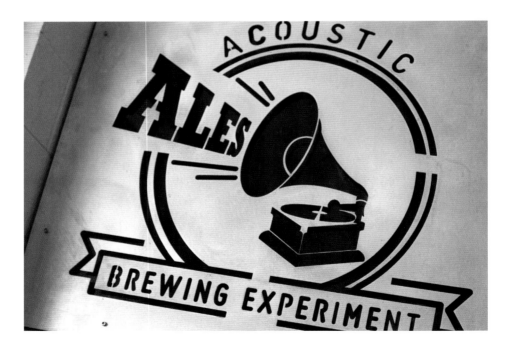

The Groupie
Style: Belgian Blonde
ABV: 8.0%
Availability: Year-round

Tommaso takes frequent trips to Europe for research and has developed a love for Belgian beers. The Groupie is an 8.0% Belgian blonde ale utilizing a Trappist yeast. It has a classic spicy bread aroma with hints of tropical fruit. The Groupie is medium-bodied with high carbonation, giving it a delightful creaminess. The flavors in the beer are entirely from Belgian malts and yeast, so there really isn't anything to hide behind. It's very complex, dry, and a great representation of the classic Belgian beer style.

San Diego and East

and the craft beer bar scene. He is currently the owner of the popular craft pub Encinitas Ale House and the Public House in La Jolla.

Mission Brewery's original brew kettle is now a fountain in the courtyard for the current multiunit complex. The complex is littered with history and old artifacts. Acoustic occupies two spaces: The brewery is located in a glass-front atrium on the right side of the central plaza, and the taproom is on the opposite side at the south end. The brewhouse, a stainless 15 BBL system, is surrounded by fermentors in a narrow industrial work area. Keg storage is currently downstairs, directly below the brewing facility. For the tasting room, Tommaso has created a modern space that borrows historical elements from beer's past. From antique cash registers to wooden Belgian beer boxes to an old-style wooden bar, the tasting room is very cool. It showcases 15 unique taps, has the capacity for 3 casks, and there is even a private tasting room in the back.

Acoustic Ales Brewing Experiment focuses on all styles, but Belgians are some of Tommaso's favorites. The **Witte Snake,** a Belgian-style Witbier, is brewed with kaffir lime, fresh ginger, and orange peel. It's a spicy beer with a very nice refreshing balance. Another popular beer is the **Mosh Pit Red Ale,** clocking in at 6.66% ABV. It's a great food-pairing beer with a malty balance of caramel, chocolate, and dark fruit notes. Acoustic Ales names beers with music inspiration in mind. The labels are retro illustrations, while the tap handles are gramophones. Tommaso's beer can be found around San Diego in beer-centric pubs.

ALESMITH BREWING COMPANY

9368 Cabot Dr., San Diego, CA 92126; (858) 549-9888; alesmith.com
Founded: 1995 **Owner/Brewmaster:** Peter Zien **Brewer:** AleSmith Brewing Team
Flagship Beer: Anvil ESB, X, IPA **Year-round Beers:** AleSmith X , AleSmith IPA,
Anvil ESB, Nut Brown Ale, Lil' Devil, Horny Devil, Grand Cru, Wee Heavy, Old Numbskull,
Speedway Stout **Seasonals/Special Releases:** Decadence, AleSmith Old Ale, Evil Dead
Red, My Bloody Valentine, Yule Smith—Winter, Yule Smith—Summer, Barrel-Aged Old
Numbskull, Barrel-Aged Speedway Stout, Barrel-Aged Wee Heavy **Tours:** Yes; Sat at 2 p.m.
(limited to 35 spots) **Taproom:** Yes

AleSmith Brewing Company is one of San Diego's original and most well-known breweries. AleSmith opened in 1995 and is run by Peter Zien, former home brewer and current BJCP Grand Master judge. Since then he has expanded his brand, showcasing decadent styles while staying true to his home-brewing roots. AleSmith brews an eclectic mix of classic styles and heavy-hitting high-ABV specialty beers. The brewery broke 1,000 production barrels in 2005, and Peter expanded operations in 2008, bringing in a 30 BBL brewhouse. In 2011 the brewery expanded again, and 2013's projected output is upwards of 12,000 BBLs.

AleSmith is located in the Miramar area of San Diego close to Ballast Point, White Labs, Green Flash, and other breweries. Their complex started off small, but after a few expansions, they have not only taken over the neighboring units, but completely remodeled their taproom as well. Pulling up to the brewery, you'll notice their signature anvil with a beer logo. The taproom is beautiful and showcases an impressively large bar and a picturesque barrel-aging lineup. The brewhouse is in the back as well as the bottling line, which pumps out both 22-ounce bottles and champagne-style 750 ml. The main barrel-aging facility, along with offices, is next door, and you can see all of this on Saturdays at 2 p.m. during their free tours. It's

a great vibe, a fun place to drink, and is frequently the meeting place of local home brewers.

AleSmith flagship beers include the **Anvil ESB, "X"** extra-pale ale, and **IPA.** These come in 22-ounce bottles with white silk screen and are easy to find in most bottle shops in SoCal. The larger 750s, like **Grand Cru, Old Numbskull,** and **Horny Devil,** are also fairly easy to find. Each beer is made very well, and the larger-format bottles are intended to be shared as elevated craft, like wine. **Decadence,** their yearly anniversary ale, is a highly sought-after bottle, and the beer inside changes every year. From **Old Ale** to **Dunkel Weizenbock,** this beer is always a treat and disappears fast. **Speedway Stout** is a high-octane imperial stout, which they also make into a mustard. If you like Belgian beers, look no further than **Horny Devil.** This spicy strong ale pours golden straw and clocks in at 11.0%. There is a lighter version called **Lil' Devil** available, too. Bottles are available at the taproom as well as growlers fills and merchandise.

Old Numbskull
Style: American Barleywine
ABV: 11.0%
Availability: Year-round

Old Numbskull is perhaps one of AleSmith's most notoriously delicious beers. It also happens to be the favorite beer of Vicky Zien, Peter's wife. This multi-award winner is a well-attenuated barleywine-style ale that succeeds in being incredibly complex without being cloying. Dark fruits, toasted caramel, and an up-front hoppiness make this beer a great one to bring to a bottle share. Old Numbskull pours a deep amber brown with a thick head and heavy glass lacing as you finish your glass. It comes in a 750 ml bottle with silver foil wrapping at the top. It also comes in a barrel-aged variety that should not be passed up.

AleSmith and Home Brew

AleSmith is a well-known supporter of home brewers, and this is mainly due to Peter Zien's and fellow brewers Tod Fitzsimmons's and Bill Batten's long histories as home brewers themselves. All three are past presidents of the QUAFF home brewers' club, and Vicky Zien currently heads up the San Diego Home Brewers Alliance. Vicky is also the president of the Mash Heads, a younger home brew club, which started in 2011. AleSmith believes firmly in giving back to the home-brewing community, and the brewery is a frequent location for home brewers. Peter also maintains his BJCP Grand Master ranking by frequently judging at home brew competitions.

ALPINE BEER COMPANY

2351 Alpine Blvd., Alpine, CA 91901; (619) 445-2337; alpinebeerco.com
Founded: 1999 **Founder:** Patrick McIlhenney **Brewer:** Patrick McIlhenney and
Shawn McIlhenney **Flagship Beer:** Pure Hoppiness **Year-round Beers:** Alpine Ale,
McIlhenney's Irish Red, Pure Hoppiness, Mandarin Nectar, Captain Stout, Duet, Willy,
Nelson **Seasonals/Special Releases:** Pure Hoppiness Triple IPA, Ichabod Ale, Great,
Briscoe, Chez Monieux, Odin's Raven, Hoppy Birthday **Tours:** No **Taproom:** Yes—pub

Alpine Beer Company was founded by Pat McIlhenney in 1999, starting out as a contract brewery with San Diego's AleSmith Brewing Company. AleSmith made McIlhenney's Irish Red first, followed by Mandarin Nectar and Pure Hoppiness. In 2002 Pat opened his own production brewery in Alpine and expanded his operations in 2008. In 2010 Alpine Beer Company added a pub adjacent to the brewery, and there are plans for even further expansion, including an additional contracted beer coming out of Minnesota in the near future. Pat and his team try to balance production capacity with the high demand for their product. Alpine Beer started its brewing operations long before (eight years) opening a pub on the side, so calling it a brewpub would not be accurate—it's more of a brewery plus pub. The city of Alpine is far from San Diego and the drive is considerable, which definitely adds to the allure of this brewery.

Alpine Beer Company is a tiny operation with a small-town feel. The pub opens a full hour before the brewery starts pouring growlers. It's located right off Alpine Boulevard in a tiny white building complete with carved wooden signs displaying the local businesses. The pub, to the right, is a local diner serving the full lineup of available Alpine beers along with fantastic barbecue. The smoked wings are terrific and can be ordered in three flavors—BBQ, Buffalo, or Dry Rub. Other barbecue items, sandwiches, salads, and pub fare can also be had. You can order a flight of four or eight, which is the best way to get a feel for their beer, for $8 to $10. The brewery opens to the public at noon, but really it's more of a small alcove where people can stand while they wait for growler fills. The line grows quickly and moves very slowly, so be prepared to wait a long time. Everything about the brewery is old school, from its copper kettle to its cramped space to its general vibe—it feels more like an old town garage than a modern brewery, which is very quaint.

It's important to understand that all Alpine beers are considered limited due to high demand and a smaller-size brewhouse. They frequently sell out of all of their beers—Duet, Nelson, and Pure Hoppiness especially. Small production, high demand, and limited availability equals beer geek heaven. Alpine Beer Company is well known for their hoppier beers like the pale **Alpine Ale,** the simcoed West Coast

Pure Hoppiness
Style: Double IPA
ABV: 8.0%
Availability: Limited year-round

Although it's a flagship and produced year-round, Pure Hoppiness is still limited release. This 8.0% double IPA has a complex floral citrus bouquet, so make sure you get your nose over the glass as soon as it exits the bottle or draft. It pours a crystal-clear gold with a thick, frothy white head, and notes of perfumey lavender are immediately perceptible. As the beer warms, you'll notice more of the alcohol warmth followed by the rich caramel overtones. This is a strong ale and drinks like one. It's made for hop heads that like big, hard-hitting beers and it definitely delivers.

IPA **Duet,** the golden Nelson rye IPA **Nelson,** and their flagship double IPA, **Pure Hoppiness.** However, Alpine also offers a full lineup of other styles. They make an American wheat beer, **Willy,** which is light and quaffable, along with a vanilla-infused variety, **Willy Vanilly,** that is a unique spin. Their slightly sweet **Irish Red** is based on their first-ever beer and is the easiest to pair with the food on the menu. For darker beer enthusiasts, **Odin's Raven** is a thick, black molasses imperial stout, and **Captain Stout** is a dry, mild oatmeal variety. If you don't live in Alpine and you see Alpine beer, it'll more than likely be Duet, Nelson, or Pure Hoppiness; hop heads go wild for these beers. Beers are available in 22-ounce bottles and growlers, and can be found sporadically around Southern California.

BALLAST POINT BREWING & SPIRITS

10051 Old Grove Rd., San Diego, CA 92131; (858) 695-2739; ballastpoint.com;
@BPBrewing
Founded: 1996 **Founder:** Jack White and Yuseff Cherney **Brewer:** Yuseff Cherney
Flagship Beer: Pale Ale, Sculpin IPA **Year-round Beers:** Pale Ale, Big Eye IPA, Sculpin
IPA, Black Marlin Porter, Calico Amber Ale, Wahoo Wheat Beer, Longfin Lager **Seasonals/
Special Releases:** Indra Kunindra, Victory at Sea, Habanero Sculpin, Fathom IPL, Longfin
Lager, Piper Down Scottish Ale, Dorado Double IPA, Sea Monster, Steamboat, Abandon
Ship, Pescadero Pilsner, Even Keel, Schooner Dried Hop, Sextant Oatmeal Stout, Tongue
Buckler, East to West IPA, 3 Sheets Barley Wine **Tours:** Yes; every day at noon, 2, 4, and
6 p.m. **Taproom:** Yes

Ballast Point Brewing & Spirits had humble beginnings, starting out as a home brew store called Home Brew Mart in 1992. In 1996 founder Jack White and fellow home brewer Yuseff Cherney decided to go pro, thus Ballast Point was born. The nautical theme was inspired by Yuseff's love of fishing, and the brewery has a fishing team that is still active today. In 2004 the demand for Jack and Yuseff's beer was so great that they expanded, moving to their current production facility off Old Grove Road. The original Home Brew Mart is still used for experimental R&D brewing, and they have a third location in Little Italy that rocks a 5 BBL system. Ballast Point's newest addition is a micro craft distillery that they opened in 2008.

The main production brewery is located in an industrial district near Miramar. There is a long, narrow tasting room on the right side of the building that serves all core beers as well as seasonals. The taproom is decked out in a sort of light wood reminiscent of a Chris-Craft boat deck—again very nautical. Current beers are listed on a chalkboard, and large bottle coolers provide patrons with bottled and canned options for takeaway. Growlers can also be filled. Unfortunately, due to California state law, distilled spirits can neither be tasted nor sold at the brewery's tasting room. If you are visiting the brewery, make sure you plan for a tour. They start at noon, run until 6 p.m., and are incredibly educational. Yuseff runs a 50

Beer Lover's Pick

Victory at Sea
Style: Coffee-Vanilla Imperial Porter
ABV: 10.0%
Availability: Seasonal

Label artist Paul Elder's visualization of this vanilla-coffee-infused imperial porter is a skeletal pirate steering through a violent storm. The beer pours dark black with a thick, persistent head. The beer itself is smooth and roasty, with an up-front vanilla and coffee flavor. Ballast Point employs a cold-brewing method to extract a smoother coffee flavor (coffee sourced from local roasting plant Caffe Calabria Coffee), which works very nicely with this beer. It's a big one at 10.0% ABV, but it doesn't taste particularly boozy. I can see this beer going really well with a decadent chocolate dessert or locally made vanilla ice cream. Victory at Sea is seasonally available in 22-ounce bottles.

BBL brewhouse, originally from Red Nectar, which does five turns a day, producing around 80,000 BBLs annually. Current plans in motion include securing an even larger brew system from Germany, which clocks in at a whopping 150 BBLs! The brewery is clean, methodical, and a pleasure to see.

Ballast Point is one of the original San Diego breweries and so their beers do a great job of representing the area. Their flagship **Pale Ale** is incredibly smooth and balanced. It's actually closer to a Kölsch than a traditional pale ale, using all-German hops and malts. **Sculpin,** a personal favorite of mine, is their signature IPA. Not only can you find Sculpin at most California beer bars, but you'll also find unique casked renditions of it employing spices like habanero or dry hops. You've also got beers like the **Calico Amber, Wahoo Wheat,** and **Black Marlin Porter,** which are more classically focused but great nonetheless. All beers coming out of Ballast Point are solid, and Yuseff, Jack, and the Ballast Point team have done a great job building their brewery into a world-class brand. Slick new cans are also now available. When you are done with the beer, make sure you find a local liquor store and pick up the spirits. Their single-malt whiskey was just released in August 2013.

BALLAST POINT BREWING COMPANY @ HOME BREW MART

5401 Linda Vista Rd., San Diego, CA 92110; (619) 295-2337; homebrewmart.com; @BPBrewing

Founded: 1992 **Founder:** Jack White and Yuseff Cherney **Brewer:** Yuseff Cherney **Director of R&D/Specialty Brewer:** Colby Chandler **Flagship Beer:** Ballast Point Pale Ale, Sculpin IPA **Year-round Beers:** Pale Ale, Big Eye IPA, Sculpin IPA, Black Marlin Porter, Calico Amber Ale, Wahoo Wheat Beer, Longfin Lager **Seasonals/Special Releases:** Indra Kunindra, Victory at Sea, Habanero Sculpin, Fathom IPL, Longfin Lager, Piper Down Scottish Ale, Dorado Double IPA, Sea Monster, Steamboat, Abandon Ship, Pescadero Pilsner, Even Keel, Schooner Dried Hop, Sextant Oatmeal Stout, Tongue Buckler, East to West IPA, 3 Sheets Barley Wine, Copper Ale (Only available at Home Brew Mart) **Tours:** Yes—upon request; contact for availability **Taproom:** Yes

Before Ballast Point was the widely successful brewery and distillery it is today, it was a home brew supply place called Home Brew Mart. Home Brew Mart, originally founded by Jack White in 1992, is still a fully functioning home brew store today. The benefit to this store is that it also has a full-scale 15 BBL brewery in it. This location, off Linda Vista Road, has a lot of history. Before Ballast Point moved to its new facilities near Miramar in 2004, all brewing was done at this location. Today the spot is run by director of R&D and specialty brewer Colby Chandler, who is in charge of brewing experimental beers.

Ballast Point @ Home Brew Mart is located in a small, narrow strip mall with limited parking. Walking into the location, you'll immediately notice all the home brew paraphernalia taking up the right half of the store along with the front region. In the back left, you'll see a plethora of Ballast Point gear along with the actual tasting room. A chalkboard above the taps shows what's on tap, and because this is technically an R&D facility, this list changes frequently. The brewhouse and fermentation space are in the back behind a swinging door. Tours aren't normally offered, but if you call ahead or ask nicely, you may be able to get a brief walk-through. Ballast Point is seeing massive success, and because of that it's still expanding. The Home Brew Mart recently went through an expansion and upgraded its brewhouse.

In order to be served, you need to relinquish your driver's license, which gets clipped to your tab. You can get any number of tasters, but only one of each. If you

Copper Ale
Style: Amber Ale
ABV: 5.5%
Availability: Limited seasonal

This is the original beer that started it all and the precursor to the Calico Amber Ale. Copper Ale is served on nitro at Ballast Point's Home Brew Mart location and should definitely not be missed. Somewhat less crazy than their hopped-up pepper beers, Copper Ale is rich, chocolatey, silky smooth, and slightly sweet. It's very Euro pub–inspired with herbaceous hop notes and an earthy backbone. Copper Ale utilizes European malts and hops to give it an old-school vibe, and that coupled with the

nitro gives it a very creamy caramel mouthfeel. For a great historical comparison, try Copper Ale side by side with its distant cousin, Calico Amber.

want to know before you go, you can check out the Ballast Point website to see an updated webcam picture of the tap list. Most core offerings like **Wahoo Wheat, Ballast Point Pale Ale, Calico Amber,** and **Sculpin IPA** are regularly on tap. Tasters will run you $1 to $3, so try a few. If you are adventurous and it's available, try the spicy **Habanero Sculpin;** its mix of floral hops and tongue-blistering heat will definitely wake you up. If you are lucky enough to see Colby walking around, you may even be able to snag a taste of whatever he's got brewing in the back. I tasted a pretty crazy **Ghost Pepper IPA** when I visited, which coincidentally also put my mouth to sleep. The home brew level of creativity at Ballast Point is very refreshing and fun. Bottles and cans are available for takeaway and can be found in easy-to-see beverage coolers.

CORONADO BREWING COMPANY—
TASTING ROOM & PRODUCTION FACILITY

1205 Knoxville St., San Diego, CA 92110; (619) 275-2215; coronadobrewingcompany.com; @CoronadoBrewing

Founded: 2012 **Founder:** Rick Chapman and Ron Chapman **Brewer:** Ryan Brooks **Flagship Beer:** Islander IPA **Year-round Beers:** Coronado Golden, Orange Ave Wit, Islander IPA, Mermaid's Red, Blue Bridge Coffee Stout **Special Releases:** Idiot IPA, Hoppy Daze, Red Devil, Frog's Breath IPA, Stupid Stout, Coronado Collection—Barrel-Aged Beers **Tours:** Yes; Sat and Sun at 12:30, 2, and 3:30 p.m. (first come, first served; $5 per person; four 5-ounce tasters and 10% off retail purchases); private tours also available **Taproom:** Yes

Coronado Brewing Company originally opened in 1996 on Coronado Island. Founders Rick and Ron Chapman grew up on the island. The family has roots in Italy, which is the inspiration behind one of their beers, Uncle Al's Amber. Rick and Ron set their sights on opening a grand brewpub after a successful coffee shop venture called Cafe 1134. They were ultimately so successful at brewing beer that they needed to expand to meet demand. In 2012, nearly 16 years later, the brothers decided to open the tasting room and production facility in a huge warehouse off Knoxville Street. Not only did this help them meet customer demand, but it also reduced the serious strain on the old 10 BBL brewhouse on Coronado Island. The talented duo can often be seen at both the Coronado brewpub and the production facility and are incredibly friendly—definitely say hello if you see them.

The location is beautiful and is split into two parts: the tasting room and the production facility. The production facility can be seen from the tasting room and the entire space is wide open, with the tasting room portion covered by a rustic wood trellis. The brewhouse is an impressive 30 BBL system, which in 2012 produced over 8,000 BBLs. In 2014 they are projecting 18,000 BBLs, and upon reaching full capacity, the facility is capable of 70,000. Coronado takes its beer seriously, and today demand is so high that they are distributed in 13 states and 6 countries. Beer can be purchased in tasters and pints and can be taken away in growlers as well as 12- and 22-ounce bottles. Their 22-ounce bottled beers are their flagships, although some special releases are also available.

Coronado Brewing Company started as a brewpub, and as such their flagship beers are takes on various classic styles. They are expertly made, and although they deviate slightly from style norms, they are pretty straightforward. With the addition of the new production facility, Coronado is now free to experiment with new beers both at the tasting room and the original brewpub, so expect to see new beers regularly. **Mermaid's Red** is the original beer and is definitely popular with

Islander IPA
Style: West Coast IPA
ABV: 7.0%
Availability: Year-round

Islander IPA is a traditional West Coast IPA. The grain bill is relatively simple, utilizing two-row and Munich, and the hop profile incorporates traditional resin varietals Columbus, Centennial, and Chinook. The beer is dank, sticky, and super-flavorful. It pours a golden amber with a thick white head. The aroma is intense with pine, and flavor notes of citrus, apricot, mango, and tropical fruit become dominant as the beer warms. Islander IPA, named after Coronado Islanders, is the flagship beer of Coronado, and it's easy to see why. It's incredibly fresh and consistent, and is a solid go-to if you are in need of a local IPA.

the locals. Its biscuity amberness is hard to beat. That being said, both Orange Wit and Islander IPA take up a majority of the sales. **Orange Wit** incorporates a solid, creamy Belgian background with up-front citrus, while **Islander IPA** is piney, dank, and super-floral. The **Blue Bridge Coffee Stout** is also worth noting, as its overall roasty balance is smooth and refreshing. All flagship beers can easily be found in local beer bars and bottle shops.

GREEN FLASH BREWING COMPANY

6550 Mira Mesa Blvd., San Diego, CA 92121; (858) 622-0085; greenflashbrew.com; @GreenFlashBeer
Founded: 2002 **Founder:** Mike Hinkley and Lisa Hinkley **Brewer:** Chuck Silva **Flagship Beer:** Green Flash West Coast IPA **Year-round Beers:** West Coast IPA, Hop Head Red,

Imperial IPA, Double Stout Black Ale, Saison Diego, Rayon Vert, Trippel, Barleywine, Le Freak, Palate Wrecker, Grand Cru **Seasonals/Special Releases:** Hop Odyssey Series: Citra Session IPA, Imperial Red Rye, Black IPA, Symposium IPA, Cedar Plank Pale, Double Columbus IPA **Tours:** Yes; Wed through Fri at 5 p.m.; Sat at 1, 3, and 5 p.m.; Sunday at 2 and 4 p.m.; private tours also available **Taproom:** Yes

In 2002 husband-and-wife team Mike and Lisa Hinkley founded and opened what is today one of the most well-known breweries of the new craft beer movement, Green Flash Brewing Company. Before operating one of the most successful breweries on the West Coast, Mike was the owner of a pub, the Board Room Bar, which was located in North County. With this experience along with his extreme love for bottle shops, rare beers, and the craft beer movement, opening a brewery with his wife was a slam-dunk decision. In 2004 Mike and Lisa welcomed brewmaster Chuck Silva to the team, and together they set out to brew world-class greatness in a glass. Green Flash Brewing has since expanded its operation considerably, moving from its original home in Vista to a larger location in Miramar, and is opening a satellite production facility in Virginia Beach, VA, to keep up with demand.

The first thing you'll notice about Green Flash Brewing is how truly massive it is. The 50 BBL brewhouse, which runs an average of eight turns a day, is tucked deep behind the giant 250 BBL fermentors. Tours are available at mixed times Wednesday through Sunday and are definitely worth it, as the facility is impressive. The tasting room is large and also includes an outside patio area, the Beer Garden, that can easily handle large groups. The whole experience is very modern and achieves a sort of warmth. The signature high-contrast Green Flash labels and branding dominate the view in every direction, and there is a gift shop to the right of the taps. As Green Flash is a highly efficient production brewery, patrons can enjoy seeing the magic happen from the comfort of the bar tables. The entire operation is easily viewable from any location in the tasting room.

On tap you'll find all the year-round beers plus an array of special releases and experiments. The Genius Lab series includes one-off taproom-only exclusives that can be anything from chili beers to sours. There is an incredibly wide selection of beers to drink, each with the telltale hoppiness that people have come to know and love about Green Flash. The 95 IBU **West Coast IPA** is a definite must, as this is the flagship beer. It's super-floral with a giant grapefruit-zest presence, which screams San Diego. For those who appreciate saisons or stouts, **Saison Diego** is a hoppy, bready farmhouse ale, and **Double Stout Black Ale** is an oat-filled blast of roasted goodness. **Hop Head Red, Rayon Vert, Grand Cru**—you really can't go wrong, and if you are in the mood for a hop overload, try the **Palate Wrecker,** their DIPA, which was originally

Le Freak
Style: Hybrid Belgian Tripel—Imperial IPA
ABV: 7.0%
Availability: Year-round

Green Flash Brewing bottles are beautiful. Le Freak's label pops with high-contrast red and white, and the bottle is etched with the signature sunburst. Le Freak is essentially a hybridized Belgian imperial IPA, which borrows some of the finer abbey notes from the tripel category. You'll immediately notice the telltale fruity Belgian yeast aroma, which is complemented by a zesty citrus hoppiness. Le Freak is effervescent and bottle-conditioned with a rich mouthfeel. It finishes on the sweet side with a bitter bite on the back of the tongue. This is definitely one of the most well known of Green Flash's lineup, and it's also a multi-award winner. Be sure to check it out.

brewed for San Diego staple Hamiltons Tavern. Growlers are available for filling, and most year-round beers can be purchased in bottle format as well. Green Flash is widely available in San Diego and throughout most of Southern California.

JULIAN HARD CIDER

4468 Julian Rd., Julian, CA 92036; (760) 765-2500; julianhardcider.biz; @JulianHardCider
Founded: 2009 **Founder:** Paul Thomas **Brewer:** Paul Thomas **Flagship Cider:** Harvest Apple **Year-round Ciders:** Harvest Apple, Cherry-Bomb, Black and Blue, Rasmataz **Seasonals/Special Releases:** N/A **Tours:** No formal tours offered. Call for private tour availability. **Tasting Room:** Yes

Cider is not beer, but it is closely related and you would be remiss to pass up an opportunity to try Julian Hard Cider if you are in the area. Located in Julian, which is only 45 minutes away if you made the trek to Alpine Beer Company, is the

Julian Hard Cider tasting room. The brand was founded in May of 2009 by entrepreneur and passionate cider brewer Paul Thomas. In February 2010 he launched his first cider, Harvest Apple, and has since released three others with plans of even more. Due to the sheer number of apples needed, his cider production is actually contracted out at a location in Oregon, but plans are in motion to open a full-scale Julian-based facility in 2014, which will make this even more of a destination. Paul is a relaxed guy with strong surfing roots and is a Desert Storm veteran. Before cider brewing he was a chef, so coincidentally during my interview he was brining a turkey. His passion and drive to make a quality product is easy to see, and it makes Paul an easy man to believe in and support.

Julian Hard Cider has a tasting room called the Miners' Saloon, which is located off the Old Julian Road, Highway 78/79. Before it was known for apples and baked pies, Julian was a mining town, and much of the town still embraces this past. You'll find rusty mining equipment, wooden miner buildings, and vintage photos all over Julian and in the JHC tasting room as well. Julian Hard Cider's tasting room sits

Black and Blue
Style: Hard Cider with Blackberries and
    Blueberries
ABV: 6.99%
Availability: Year-round

You should definitely start off with their Harvest Apple cider before you get into the infused fruit versions. It's important to understand the base cider blend. After that you'll want to try Black and Blue, which is an incredibly tart and dry mix of fruit and carbonation. You'll immediately notice the fresh dark berry nose on this one—it's intoxicating. The fruit balance is exquisite and not overly sweet. It pours a beautiful dark purple-blue with a small purple head. Notes of fresh tart apple, blueberry, and blackberry will punch you in the face lovingly, followed up by a dry tart finish. It's a drink that most anyone will be able to appreciate and would make a wonderful addition to a reduction or glaze in cooking.

inside a barn turned craft marketplace, among antique dealers, a small cafe, and an Orfila wine tasting room. The facade is made from reclaimed Julian wood, and tasters are served out of wooden casks with taps installed. The general store, the left half of the tasting room, is where you can buy cider to go as well as merchandise. The whole experience has a small-town vibe to it, and you'll likely run into Brad Hill, the friendly manager of the JHC store. After visiting the tasting room, head into town and pick up a fresh apple pie from Apple Alley.

JHC's motto, "Show Us Your Apples," is a quality-based challenge, as Paul is one of the few cider producers that uses fresh tree-picked apples rather than the oxidized overripe ones that macro cider producers commonly use. This is a difference you can see. The flagship **Harvest Apple** pours clear white, which is how fresh cider looks, versus a darker orange, which signifies old second-grade apples. Julian

Julian Brewing Company

In Old Town Julian there is a pretty awesome barbecue joint called the Bailey Wood Pit Barbecue. It's hard to miss—just look for the massive line of motorcycles and choppers outside. The restaurant is split into two parts: a quaint, rustic dining area on the left, and a large open bar on the right. The barbecue and spicy chili are must-order items. It's also the home of Julian Brewing Company, touted to be "the first commercial brewery in historic downtown Julian in over 120 years." Owned by Pizza Port chain owners Vince and Gina Marsaglia, the brewery offers a small lineup of beers in the bar portion of the restaurant.

Hard Cider currently offers four varieties and is working on more. Aside from Harvest Apple, they have **Cherry-Bomb**, a cherry-infused cider; **Black and Blue**, made with blackberries and blueberries; and **Rasmataz**, a raspberry-infused version. The juice used is fresh-pressed and so the ciders do not taste flavored. They are tart, crisp, and wonderful. If you've never tried cider before, this a great one to start and end with. Currently only one tasting of each cider is offered at a time, but when the production facility opens in 2014, that will likely change.

KARL STRAUSS BREWING COMPANY—MAIN BREWERY

5985 Santa Fe St., San Diego, CA 92109; (858) 273-2739; karlstrauss.com; @Karl_Strauss
Founded: 1989 **Founder:** Chris Cramer and Matt Rattner **Brewer:** Paul Segura **Flagship
Beer:** Red Trolley Ale, Tower 10 IPA **Year-round Beers:** Tower 10 IPA, Red Trolley Ale,
Karl Strauss Amber, Pintail Pale Ale **Seasonals/Special Releases:** Big Barrel Double IPA,
Blackball Belgian IPA, Boardwalk Black Rye IPA, Off the Rails, Tower 20 IIPA, Wreck Alley
Imperial Stout, Barrel-Aged Wreck Alley, SDBW Peanut Butter Cup Porter, Imperial Maltball
Stout, Oktoberfest, Windansea Wheat, Fullsuit Belgian Brown Ale, 20th Anniversary
Bourbon-Aged Trippel, 21st Anniversary Ale, 22nd Anniversary Vanilla Imperial Stout,
23rd Anniversary Old Ale, 24th Anniversary Flanders-Style Ale, Parrot in a Palm Tree
Holiday Baltic Porter, Two Tortugas Belgian Quad, Mouette a Trois Holiday Fruitcake Ale
Tours: No formal tours offered. Call for private tour availability. **Taproom:** Yes

Karl Strauss Brewing Company opened in 1989 in its original downtown San Diego
location off Columbia Street. It still stands as one of the original and most
iconic brewpubs in San Diego. Founded by Chris Cramer and Matt Rattner, the brewpub's namesake came from their brewing consultant, master brewer Karl M. Strauss,
nicknamed "Uncle Karl." Together the trio set out to create something incredibly
special, and with the help of Uncle Karl, they were able to create classically focused

Red Trolley Ale
Style: American Red Ale
ABV: 5.8%
Availability: Year-round

Red Trolley Ale is classic Karl Strauss. It pairs extremely well with a wide variety of foods, it's sessionable, and it's astonishingly complex. It's the most award-winning beer in the Karl Strauss portfolio, having won a gold in its category at the 2010 and 2012 World Beer Cup as well as 2010 Great American Beer Festival. The beer pours a deep ruby amber with a persistent white head. Notes of raisin, toffee, and caramel go nicely with

the crackery malty finish. Its a beer you don't have to think too deeply about, but if you do, you'll be rewarded. It's medium body and low ABV make it perfect for repeat orders. Red Trolley Ale is readily available at most beer retailers in SoCal and easy to spot with its iconic red streetcar.

and technically accurate beer. Karl Strauss passed away in 2006, the same year the brewing company opened up their main production facility off of Santa Fe Road. Luckily, Karl, Chris, and Matt were collectively able to enjoy the company's success as they opened six brewpubs across Southern California.

The production facility has been closed to the public, save private tours, until just recently. In July of 2013 a modern tasting room was added to the facility as a front-facing congregation area for thirsty fans. The facility is located a stone's throw from several macro beer distribution centers, so if you see them, you'll know you're close. Walking into the tasting room, you'll immediately notice the bar to the right. Set up to pour year-round beers, special releases, and some pub-only varieties, you'll most definitely be able to find something you like. Merchandise is set up to the left, and there is a beautifully large and rustic back patio complete with sand floor, barrel tables, and light-decorated trees. Several large glass windows offer views into the brewing facility, but currently official tours are not offered.

Karl Strauss Brewing Company is a classic-style American brewpub. The beers they have become known for fall along classic-style guidelines and fly somewhat beneath the craft-brewing radar. That being said, the beers are fantastic, and extra effort, including the tasting room opening, has been put forth to educate more drinkers on the Karl Strauss portfolio. **Tower 10 IPA** is one of their most well-known beers, along with **Red Trolley Ale.** Another solid option and slightly lesser known is the tasty **Boardwalk Black Rye IPA** and **Wreck Alley Imperial Stout.** If you are looking for something a little more festive, their **Mouette a Trois Holiday Fruitcake Ale** is incredibly unique and makes a great pairing with rich dessert. Various bottles are available in 12- and 22-ounce formats, and there are 64-ounce growler fills as well.

MIKE HESS BREWING

7955 Silverton Ave., #1201, San Diego, CA 92126; (619) 786-4377; hessbrewing.com; @HessBrewing

Founded: 2010 **Founder:** Mike Hess and Greg Hess **Brewer:** Mike Hess and Nate Sanson **Flagship Beer:** Habitus **Year-round Beers:** Claritas, Grazias, Habitus, Intrepidus, Ex Umbris, Amplus Acerba **Seasonals/Special Releases:** Aurum, Brunus Robustus, Deceptio, Fors Hibernaie, Magnus Aeunus, Venator, Jucundus, Villain **Tours:** No formal tours offered. Call for private tour availability. **Taproom:** Yes

Mike Hess Brewing, known by the locals simply as Hess, is one of the original new wave nanobreweries in San Diego. Starting in July of 2010, the Hess team has piloted their 1.6 BBL system to greatness with many year-round and seasonal offerings. Mike, who has been brewing for over 18 years, pilots the company with his brother Greg, who mans the sales arm of the operation. Together they built the brewery from the ground up in their tiny tasting room. Recently Mike and Greg went to work on a second location in North Park, which drastically increased the size of their operation to a 30 BBL brewhouse.

Hess focuses on community and high-quality experimental beers. The taproom is small and intimate, and usually showcases a local food vendor. Coming from outside, it looks like you're walking into a large self-storage locker. It's not uncommon to see sushi being made inside the brewery, and it should be ordered immediately alongside a Jucundus, if it's in season. Tasting hours get busy and there is usually a line for a pint, but it moves quickly. Merchandise can be found on the right-hand

Claritas
Style: German Kölsch-Style Ale
ABV: 5.8%
Availability: Year-round

Claritas pours very clear, with a dense creamy white head. At 5.8% it's a bit stronger than many of its Kölsch brethren, but the alcohol is balanced nicely. Notes of white malt, light citrus, and crisp hoppy bite at the tail end of the taste make this beer very refreshing. The German malt is very pronounced and adds a nice melanoidin graininess to the overall beer. The beer is bready and hearty, while also being very light in body. Kölsch is making a resurgence as of late, and it's nice to see breweries making good ones. Hess's variation is very tasty and would be a great regular summer beer if you can get a ready supply.

side of the small bar, and chilled stainless growlers are available for take-home purchase. The original tasting room is the epitome of local small-craft passion.

Hess beers are varied and creative. Because the system is so small, offerings are rotated regularly. As a habit, you wouldn't find the same beer twice, but with the recent production location opening in North Park, it'll now be easier to get a full lineup of tasters. Beers are named using Latin, which fits the Hess crest very nicely. The beers themselves are not Latin-inspired, but rather a varied mix of traditional and nontraditional styles peppered with nanobrewery creativity. **Jucundus,** for example, is a popular American wheat beer made with orange blossom honey and citrus peel. Another strong offering is the **Villain,** a Belgian saison with strong notes of cantaloupe, coriander, and black pepper. Hess is a fun tasting room to visit and is a great place to start if you have the new North Park location on your bucket list.

Hess North Park Location

Mike Hess Brewing recently opened a massive facility in North Park San Diego, which showcases an impressive 30 BBL brewhouse. The location officially opening in August 2013 and is a massive step up from the previous nanobrewing location in Miramar. While they will still continue operating the Miramar tasting room, the production facility in North Park will carry out the brewing and packaging of all canned beer. The original nano system will be for special pilots only. The new North Park brewery has an incredible entrance. Guests walk through the front door over a long catwalk bookended by fermentors, bright tanks, corrugated metal, and the brewhouse itself. It's a beautiful layout in terms of aesthetics. The tasting room is in the back and will be pouring a full line of classic and new Hess brews!

MISSION BREWERY

1441 L St., San Diego, CA 92101; (619) 544-0555; missionbrewery.com; @missionbrewery
Founded: 2007 **Founder:** Dan Selis **Brewer:** John Egan **Flagship Beer:** Mission Blonde
Year-round Beers: Mission Amber, Mission Blonde, Mission Hefeweizen, Mission IPA, Shipwrecked Double IPA, Dark Seas, El Conquistador Extra Pale Ale, Carrack **Seasonals/Special Releases:** Armada Collaboration Saison, Falconers IPA, Stigmata Grand Cru, Mission Pils, Mission Dunkelweizen, Mission Light Lager, Mission Coconut Brown Ale
Tours: Yes; every hour on the hour Fri and Sat 1 to 7 p.m., Sun 1 to 4 p.m. ($12 per person, including seven 3-ounce tasters) **Taproom:** Yes

Located in the historic Wonder Bread building in downtown San Diego, Mission Brewery was a lost brand that has been recently revitalized. Founded by home and pro brewer Dan Selis, Mission Brewery was reopened in 2007. The original brewery opened near the airport in 1913 and was shut down by Prohibition in 1919. The newly rebranded brewery opened in the historic 14,000-square-foot Wonder Bread factory building off of L Street. In 2012 beer production was at 4,500 BBLs annually, but Mission is projecting that they will more than double that number to 10,000 BBLs in 2013.

Mission is hard to miss, as it's near the center of downtown San Diego in a giant brick building complete with a Mission-branded grain silo. The tasting room is large, open, and able to accommodate upwards of about 400 people. It resembles the inside of a ship, with wooden struts and ribs lining the ceilings. There is a shuffleboard table that spans half the length of the tasting room, and you'll most definitely see a small crowd huddled around it. The 30 BBL brewhouse is separated by a long wooden bar where patrons can enjoy beers in comfort while watching the brewers do their thing. Formal tours are offered for $12 and include seven 3-ounce tasters. The tours impart a very high level of beer knowledge while guiding guests through the inner workings of the brewery, the bottling line, and cold storage. Events are frequent at Mission, so checking the website is definitely suggested.

Mission offers a wide selection of classic styles, including their celebrated flagship **Mission Blonde,** a Kölsch-style ale. Mission Blonde is one of the lightest beers offered in the taproom and has won multiple awards at California-based competitions. Other beers offered include the **Mission Amber,** which is actually an Altbier, and the Bavarian-style **Mission Hefeweizen.** German-style beers are taken pretty seriously at Mission, but they deviate a bit for their IPAs. They have both the

Beer Lover's Pick

Dark Seas
Style: Imperial Stout
ABV: 9.8%
Availability: Year-round

Mission's Dark Seas Imperial Stout was recently voted the number one stout in America by *USA Today*. It's a dark black, velvety, roasty beer with a subtle layered flavor. At 9.8% it's a beer you want to sip and savor or share with friends. It has a very heavy roasted nose and pours jet black with a thick, dark head. The beer tastes slightly of toasted marshmallows and will immediately make you want to go beach camping. It has a thick body with a bitter finish and would do wonders paired

with vanilla ice cream. Dark Seas comes in both 22-ounce and 12-ounce formats, making it easier to enjoy a smaller portion at a time.

American-style **Mission IPA,** with Cascade and Centennial hops, and **Shipwrecked Double IPA,** a San Diego hop bomb clocking in at 9.25%. Mission also offers one-offs, seasonals, and taproom-only beers, which can be sampled by the pint or by 3-ounce taster. Local chocolate truffles, made with the darker Mission beers, are offered at the bar and make fantastic pairings with the beers they are made with. Bottles are available in both 22-ounce and 12-ounce four-packs, and growlers are always available for takeaway.

MODERN TIMES BEER—LOMALAND FERMENTORIUM

3725 Greenwood St., San Diego, CA 92110; (323) 620-1136; moderntimesbeer.com; @ModernTimesBeer

Founded: 2013 **Founder:** Jacob McKean **Brewer:** Matt Walsh, Derek Freese, Alex Tweet, and Mike Tonsmeire **Flagship Beer:** TBD **Year-round Beers:** Blazing World Amber IPA, Fortunate Island Wheat IPA, Black House Coffee Stout, Lomaland Saison **Seasonals/ Special Releases:** Neverwhere Brett IPA, Oneida American Pale Ale, **Tours:** Limited on weekends; call for availability **Taproom:** Yes

Founded in 2013 by social media guru and beer advocate Jacob McKean, Modern Times Beer seeks to create unique and inspired beer for San Diego's saturated market. Jacob's previous job was working social media for world-famous brewery Stone Brewing Co., and he decided to open his own place in January of 2012. After an aggressive private offering, Jacob's success became even more pronounced when he launched the most successful brewery Kickstarter to date, raising over $65,000. Jacob's team includes brewers from well-known fixtures such as Ballast Point, Karl Strauss, Monkey Paw, and the Internet-famous Mad Fermentationist. While still an incredibly young brewery, the beers being produced at Modern Times have all the makings of being world-class.

Modern Times Beer—Lomaland Fermentorium is located off Greenwood Street on Point Loma. It's right next to a Denny's, some strip clubs, and a sprawling factory district. The brewery itself is in an impressive medium-size industrial complex with 30-foot ceilings and room to grow. The brew team operates a 30 BBL, two-vessel system from Premier Stainless and has the capacity to produce 5,000 BBLs a year. The main point of the Kickstarter was to pimp out the tasting room, which is where most people will be enjoying the beer. It's industrial "modern" with lots of hip flair, like a Post-it note mural of Michael Jackson and Bubbles. Logo-emblazoned oil drums, reclaimed wood, bookcases full of ephemera and books, Christmas lights, and giant tumbleweeds pretty much sum up the experience. It's a fun place to drink, and it definitely has its own feel to it. Tours of the facility are given upon request, so be sure to call ahead.

Fortunate Islands
Style: Session Wheat IPA
ABV: 4.7%
Availability: Year-round

Fortunate Islands, the hoppy, citrusy wheat beer, is not specifically categorized as an IPA, but it's basically a session variety of the classic style. Incorporating Amarillo and Citra, the beer is sticky, dank, and zesty. The carbonation in this beer is super-effervescent, which adds to its quaffability, and with a relatively low ABV, it's a beer you can enjoy a few of. Fortunate Islands is light-medium bodied, the wheat adding a little more to the mouthfeel, and it's crystal clear with a nice, fluffy white head. You'll likely find variations of this beer, including a cask version at the taproom, so be on the lookout. The name itself is derived from Jacob's fascination with historical whimsy and mythology.

Modern Times seeks beer for people with "devastatingly good taste." Their flagship beers may change, but for the time being there are four to choose from, with two extra seasonal releases. **Blazing World** is a sticky, dank amber IPA; **Fortunate Islands** is a citrusy session IPA; **Black House** is a coffee stout utilizing house-roasted coffee, which they also plan to brew and serve on the side; and **Lomaland** is a saison with a proprietary yeast blend. They also have the only 100 percent Brett IPA I've encountered, **Neverwhere,** which is definitely a trip if you like hints of funk. Modern Times also plans to adopt open-source brewing, which means their recipes will be public so local home brewers can brew up their own versions. Colorful language and amazing branding will definitely draw you to the 16-ounce cans the brewery will be producing. Until then, you'll be able to find Modern Times beer at most beer-centric gastropubs and craft bars like Toronado, Tiger!Tiger!, Encinitas Ale House, Sublime Ale House, and Hamiltons.

San Diego and East

ROUGH DRAFT BREWING COMPANY

8830 Rehco Rd., San Diego, CA 92121; (858) 453-7238; roughdraftbrew.com;
@RoughDraftBrew
Founded: 2012 **Founder:** Jeff Silver **Brewer:** Alex Rabe, Keith Shaw, and Pedro
Carvalho **Flagship Beer:** Hop Therapy Double IPA **Year-round Beers:** Eraser IPA, Amber
Ale, Belgian Vanilla Stout, Freudian Sip Strong Ale, Weekday IPA, Hop Therapy Double
IPA **Seasonals/Special Releases:** Southern Triangle IPA, Emboozlement **Tours:** Yes
Taproom: Yes

Jeff Silver opened Rough Draft Brewing Company in March of 2012 after a nine-month setup period. The name comes mostly from his approach to things—"don't take life too seriously"—and so the theme used incorporates plays on words and a lot of tongue in cheek. Jeff comes from a financial services background, but has been home brewing since the age of 22. Opening a brewery had always been a dream, but it wasn't possible right out of college, so he had to be patient. After running the marketing department at a large insurance company, Jeff seized a new opportunity, hired a commercial brewer from out of state, and the rest is history. Jeff and the brew team collaborate on everything, and together they run a 15 BBL brewing system which produces about 3,000 BBLs a year.

Rough Draft Brewing Company follows a typical format for its tasting room, having the tasting room and brewery adjacent to each other. This gives the whole vibe a very modern industrial feel, and it's very effective. Jeff's wife built some really cool wheeled tables that have succulent plants growing out of a trough in the center, giving it an urban garden look. The taproom is decently sized to handle large groups, and there is a lobby-type sitting area as well as plenty of standing room. Patrons can enjoy an intimate view of the brewery, fermentation space, and barrels, as everything is in the same room. Tours are self-guided, but if Jeff is around, he'll be happy to talk about the space provided he isn't pouring beers for everyone.

One thing you'll notice right off the bat is the quirky names of Rough Draft beers. **Freudian Sip** is a wildly popular strong ale with heavy English malt characters; **Hop Therapy** is their top-selling DIPA with a super floral nose; **Eraser IPA** is citrus-pine-forward medium ABV offering; and **Emboozlement Tripel** is a hot, bready, abbey-style Belgian tripel. The beer styles here are mixed and showcase North County San Diego as well as world classics. Jeff's go-to beer is the **Amber Ale,** and it's on tap because it's one of his favorite styles. It's light in IBUs and is an easygoing classic. Bottled varieties of their year-round beers can be found in the taproom, at Whole Foods, and in various bottle shops. You can also take home 32- and 64-ounce growlers full of anything on tap.

Hop Therapy
Style: Double IPA
ABV: 9.0%
Availability: Year-round
Hop Therapy is a great example of what
Rough Draft is all about. The name itself
is thematic and definitely implies that
you'll be getting a blast of up-front hops.
At 95 IBUs and 9.0%, Hop Therapy packs
a punch, but where it really shines is its
aroma. Galaxy and Summer hops give this
beer an incredibly complex tropical nose
and notes of passion fruit and pineapple,
which play nicely with the toffee toast
malt notes. The beer pours a caramel
amber with a light head and the carbon-
atiom is medium-high, giving it a nice car-
bonic bite. This beer is their flagship and can easily be found on tap and in 22-ounce
bottle form at many local beer bars and bottle shops in SoCal.

SAINT ARCHER BREWERY

9550 Distribution Ave., San Diego, CA 92121; (858) 225-2337; saintarcherbrewery.com;
@SaintArcherBrew
Founded: 2013 **Founder:** Josh Landan **Ambassadors:** Mikey Taylor, Paul Rodriguez,
Taylor Knox, Dusty Payne, Sean Malto, Bryan Herman, Josh Kerr, Omar Salazar, Chase
Wilson, Chris Miller, Dane Zaun, Derek Dunfee, Todd Richards, Jeff Johnson, Brian "Slash"
Hansen, Atiba Jefferson, Shane O'Neill, Chris Christenson, Laura Enever, and Eric Koston
Brewer: Yiga Miyashiro and Kim Lutz **Flagship Beer:** Pale Ale **Year-round Beers:**
Saint Archer Blonde Ale, Saint Archer Pale Ale, Saint Archer IPA **Seasonals/Special
Releases:** Scotch Ale, Cask IPA **Tours:** Call for availability **Taproom:** Yes

Saint Archer Brewery entered the San Diego brewing scene in April of 2013
with a unique business model. Unlike any other brewery in the market, Saint
Archer is part-owned by celebrities, pro sport celebrities to be exact. The project was

conceived by visionary documentary filmmaker Josh Landan, who has made a career photographing and filming pro alternative sports like skateboarding, snowboarding, and surfing. Until Saint Archer there was never a beer specifically marketed for this crowd and its fans, and this was something that Josh wanted to fix. He paired up with 12 world-class athletes, coined "ambassadors," and they set out to create world-class beer for their people. On top of the cast of athletes, Josh also hired esteemed brewer Yiga Miyashiro from Port Brewing/The Lost Abbey and Pizza Port and Kim Lutz of Maui Brewing Company to drive the 30 BBL brewhouse.

Saint Archer Brewery is in a huge facility located in the Miramar brewery district. The building is massive, leaving them plenty of room for growth. The entrance is small, but as you cross the threshold into the tasting room, you'll see exactly how big the operation really is. The taps are at the far end of the entrance to the left. In

Beer Lover's Pick

Saint Archer Pale Ale
Style: Pale Ale
ABV: 5.2%
Availability: Year-round
Saint Archer Pale Ale is a great example of the classic style somewhat modified for West Coast San Diego drinkers. It's more hop-forward than a normal pale and employs some of the hops—Simcoe, Cascade, and Chinook—that are more prevalent in the San Diego–style IPAs. The result is a piney-citrus pale ale that clocks in at a sessional 5.2%. It's flavorful and not incredibly bitter. The light cara-

mel maltiness pairs nicely with the hops, but doesn't detract from the complex floral aroma. This beer is geared towards those new to craft, but does a very good job of being something that those well-versed would drink, too.

front of them is a wooden bar that extends the length of the cold box and wraps its way to the right towards the entrance. There are no tables, just standing room, but this makes it perfect for large groups to congregate and enjoy good beer. Behind the bar, patrons can easily see the fermentors and brewhouse. Bright, shiny, new stainless tanks dominate the room and tower above. Saint Archer Brewery is very focused on presentation and image, which is why the layout is the way it is. Picturesque.

Saint Archer beers are straightforward. Not only are they brewed to style, but they are also available in 12- and 22-ounce bottles. This was something very intentional to get the beer into wide distribution as soon as possible. Growlers are also available for takeaway. There are three beers currently available: Blonde Ale, Pale Ale, and IPA. The **Blonde Ale** is a classic German-style Kölsch—light, crisp, and approachable. The **Pale Ale** is a medium-bodied, citrusy light beer, while the **IPA** is more hop-forward with dank, doggy notes. The beers are made to be approachable to a wide range of people and they succeed.

SOCIETE BREWING COMPANY

8262 Clairemont Mesa Blvd., San Diego, CA 92111; (858) 598-5409; societebrewing.com; @SocieteBrewing
Founded: 2012 **Founder:** Travis Smith and Doug Constantiner **Brewer:** Travis Smith and Doug Constantiner **Flagship Beer:** N/A **Year-round Beers:** The Pupil, The Harlot, Debutante, The Widow, The Publican, The Apprentice, The Butcher **Seasonals/Special Releases:** Single Hop "Bachelor" Series, The Roustabout, The Miser **Tours:** Free public tours Sat at 2 and 4 p.m. **Taproom:** Yes

It's easy to drive past the small street leading to Societe Brewing off Clairemont Mesa Boulevard, but this is definitely one brewery you don't want to miss. Founded in May of 2012 by pro craft-beer friends Doug Constantiner and Travis Smith, Societe Brewing Company is one of the hottest new breweries in San Diego. Their focus above all else is to create quality, focused beer that unites people of all walks of life. Both brewers, though young, have an impressive brewing history. Travis was Vinnie Cilurzo's first hire at Russian River, and Doug worked at Green Flash, Oggi's, and Pizza Port. Both brewers worked at Orange County's The Bruery, where they originally met, which ultimately led to their starting up Societe.

Societe Brewing Company has a beautifully large tasting room with high-seated wooden tables, a medium-size wooden bar, and an intimate view of the impressive brewhouse and barrel room. The entire place has an old-style late 1800s/early 1900s feel to it with rustic wood, eclectic beer names like the Harlot and Butcher, and a focus on communing with fellow guests. The 20 BBL JV Northwest brewhouse is a

The Harlot
Style: Belgian Extra (Single)
ABV: 6.0%
Availability: Year-round

Pages could be spent fawning over Societe Brewing's beers, but one beer sticks out above the rest in both complexity and flavor profile. The Harlot is an uncommon Belgian style blending elements from both pale and blonde varieties. It pours a clear straw gold with a clean white head. The Harlot has an incredibly spicy yeast character, which cannot be overstated. It's crisp, dry, and fruity on the nose, with subtle notes of pepper and fresh-baked bread. It shares malt elements with a Czech-style pilsner, but with the added Belgian yeast notes. Crisp hopping is present and adds a touch of bitterness, which is followed up with pleasant lively carbonation. It's often called "More-ish" as in you want to drink "More" of it. This is definitely the beer you want to start out with before you wreck your palate on their wonderfully hoppy offerings and is the go-to beer for the other local brewers.

sight to behold and propels their 3,500 BBL annual production. The Barrel Room is off to the side and includes an impressive lineup of wine barrels that are full of currently unreleased beer. Tours are available on Saturdays, but space is limited and you'll need to sign up at the bar or call ahead.

The beer is the main focus at Societe and what beer it is. Societe Brewing currently focuses on three different areas: hoppy American styles, Belgians, and "dark" beers. Each one is expertly crafted, and in the case of the Belgians, achieves a complexity in flavor I have not experienced before in unspiced beer. Travis and Doug use reverse osmosis and treat all of the water to achieve the exact profile they want, which is a difference that can be tasted. The **Pupil** and **Apprentice** are widely sought-after IPAs and employ dank aroma-intense hops like Amarillo and Simcoe. The **Butcher** is an imperial stout that's simplicity turns into a massive symphony of layered, complex malt flavors reminiscent of both fresh dark breads and decadent chocolate ganache. When you've had your fill of the beer at the bar, you can snag a slick stainless growler and take more home with you. Stay tuned because 750 ml bottled beer is slated for sometime in 2014.

STONE BREWING CO.—STONE BREWING WORLD BISTRO & GARDENS—LIBERTY STATION

2816 Historic Decatur Rd., #116, San Diego, CA 92106; (619) 269-2100; stonelibertystation.com; @StoneBistro
Founded: 2013 **Founder:** Greg Koch and Steve Wagner **Brewer:** Kris Ketcham **Flagship Beer:** N/A **Year-round Beers:** N/A **Seasonals/Special Releases:** All Stone Brewing World Bistro & Gardens—Liberty Station beers are considered one-off special releases
Tours: No **Taproom:** Yes

In 2011 Stone Brewing Co. co-founders Greg Koch and Steve Wagner announced they would be expanding their empire by adding Stone Company Stores in key hot spots in Southern California, taking over an organic methods farm and renaming it Stone Farms, and creating another farm-to-table restaurant, Stone Brewing World Bistro & Gardens—Liberty Station. The Liberty Station location would not only serve as a new hangout for beer fans, but would also incorporate a 10 BBL brewhouse for experimental batches in a 23,500-square-foot space. It's no surprise that Liberty Station was the chosen spot. Located in the San Diego neighborhood of Point Loma, Stone World Bistro & Gardens—Liberty Station opened in May of 2013 to a crowd of thirsty fans.

You can enter Stone Brewinig World Bistro & Gardens—Liberty Station through the main dining room entrance or through the Stone Company Store entrance in the back. As soon as you get to the taproom, you'll start to realize how truly massive this place is. The taproom sports more than 50 taps pouring great beer. It is really nice, with a bar that wraps around the center stone tap sculpture. Bocce courts are located adjacent to the dining room. A banquet hall lies to the right, and the shiny new 10 BBL pilot system is to the left. Continuing on, you'll walk into a massive courtyard with sand floors, flaming rock fountain sculptures, and crowds upon crowds. A large bar in the back acts as the pouring destination for this area of the restaurant. This place is beautiful, amazing, and huge.

The taps flowing at Stone Brewing World Bistro & Gardens—Liberty Station are a mix of Stone Brewing Co. beers and craft beer from around the world. You'll find local breweries like Societe Brewing Company on tap, along with Los Angeles–area breweries like El Segundo Brewing. Bear Republic, Rogue, Green Flash, Dogfish, Ommegang, and other craft beer establishments are represented, too. Stone Brewing World Bistro & Gardens—Liberty Station brews its own beers and puts them on tap, and they are definitely worth trying. The brewhouse makes limited one-off varieties ranging from low-ABV English IPAs and Scottish exports to high-ABV imperial Hefeweizens and double IPAs. If you aren't sure what to get, grab a tasting flight and try all the beers brewed on-site—there's a good chance you'll never see them again. You'll find the same great food options as at the Escondido location, like spiced quail knots, duck tacos, and farm-to-table salads, on the menu. This location also offers an impressive selection of more than 100 bottles. Make sure to fill your growler on the way out.

Beer Lover's Pick

Commander in the Crosshairs
Style: English Pale Ale
ABV: 4.5%
Availability: Limited
Stone Brewing Co. is known for their
heavy-hitting, hoppy, strong beers, so
it's nice to see some experimental low-
ABV options coming out of Stone Brewing World Bistro & Gardens—Liberty
Station. Commander in the Crosshairs
is a malt-forward, lightly balanced,
English-style pale ale. The base malt,
Maris Otter, gives the beer that super-
biscuity signature maltiness, and the
lighter hop bill saves the palate. The
beer pours a clear golden orange with
a tiny, fluffy white head. It is very
light-bodied and is incredibly sessionable. This beer isn't available in wide release, so
you'll likely only find it at one of the Stone restaurants or Stone Company Stores.

THORN STREET BREWERY

3176 Thorn St., San Diego, CA 92104; (619) 501-2739;thornstreetbrew.com;
@ThornStBrewery
Founded: 2012 **Founder:** Dennis O'Connor, Dan Carrico, and Eric O'Connor
Brewer: Dennis O'Connor, Dan Carrico, and Eric O'Connor **Flagship Beer:** N/A **Small-
Batch Rotating Beers:** Solstice Session IPA, Bad Moon Hefeweizen, Saison du South
Park, Hammersmith Bitter, The Dark Tsar, Golden Hills Pils, Foreplay, Santos Coffee Stout,
North Park Pale, Relay IPA, The Menace, Chilecabra, Just Chuck, Smugglers, Red Headed
Hop Child, O'Connors Oatmeal Stout, Switzer Canyon Blond, Fornication **Tours:** No formal
tours offered. Call for private tour availability. **Taproom:** Yes

Thorn Street Brewery, a boutique neighborhood microbrewery, is located at the
cross of the North Park, Colonial Court, and Altadena districts of San Diego
on Thorn Street between Herman Avenue and 32nd Street. The neighborhood is

Santos Coffee Stout
Style: Coffee Stout
ABV: 5.9%
Availability: Limited year-round

As stated earlier, Thorn Street Brewery beers are limited, so most are rotated in and out and some may never return. That being said, the beers are constantly well made, so you can't go wrong. Santos Coffee Stout is a mid-ABV session stout with impressive vanilla, caramel, and coffee flavors. The balance is spot on, with no flavor being too intense, although the coffee, as it should be, is the main event. The beer pours a nice ruby black with a light tan head. Santos is served on nitro so carbonation is low, but creaminess and silky smooth chocolate are high. This is a terrific beer and would be a great pairing with some homemade ice cream.

phenomenal and something that you don't see very often in California. Founded by Dennis O'Connor, who previously owned the Home Brew & Gardens shop at the same location, with the help of fellow home brewers Dan Carrico and Eric O'Connor, Thorn Street Brewery is a craft brew bastion right in the middle of the suburbs. Dennis realized that he liked making beer a lot more than he liked selling home brew equipment, and the jump to manufacturing was an easy choice.

Thorn Street Brewery is located in an eclectic artist area of San Diego's suburbs. Walking up to the brewery, you'll likely see random art in front lawns, paintings, and local farmers' markets. Right next door is an open-air plant nursery, and there are usually food trucks pulled up in front. Due to the area's popularity, parking can be a bit of an issue, but a little walk never hurt anyone. The building's facade is beautiful, with dark wood planks and stainless lettering. Inside they take a minimalist rustic approach with hardwood floors, gray paint, and a stainless line of taps at the bar. The space is pretty modestly sized and gets busy, but the popular open-air back area is incredibly spacious and is available most days of the week. Because it's set in a neighborhood, it's relatively family-friendly. Locals living in the area visit with their kids, strollers, dogs, and bikes to grab growlers and taste brews. The 7 BBL brewhouse is in the back and not currently viewable to the public, but that may change in the future.

Thorn Street Brewery makes an impressive lineup of beers. It's clear that the home brew quality and creativity was not sacrificed in the move to commercial brewing. Dennis has a long history of brewing, so the beers he and his team make are well made, clean, and tasty. They consider themselves a boutique brewery, so the idea of flagship, year-round, and seasonal beers is not really a concern. They brew what they want, they repeat batches when they want, and they make consistently good beer. Some beers like the **Santos Coffee Stout** can be found more often than others, and there is usually a spiced saison as well as a team of hoppy and double hoppy beers on tap. The best recommendation would be to grab a flight. They make it easy for you by giving out flight cards where you can write the beers you want on them, hand them to the bartender, and they give you those beers. This also makes it easier to remind you which is which. Beer is available for takeaway in 64-ounce growler form if you want to bring some home.

WHITE LABS TASTING ROOM
9495 Candida St., San Diego, CA 92126; (858) 693-3441; whitelabs.com/white-labs-tasting-room; @whitelabs
Founded: 2012 **Founder:** Chris White **Brewer:** Joe Korowski **Flagship Beer:** Hansen IPA **Year-round Beers:** Hansen IPA, Leeuwenhoek Saison, Buchner Pale Ale, Pasteur Porter **Seasonals/Special Releases:** 32 constantly changing taps **Tours:** Yes; Mon through Thurs, no specific times; Fri and Sat, hourly from 2:30 to 6:30 p.m. **Taproom:** Yes

If you're a home brewer or a professional brewer, White Labs is mostly likely a name you are familiar with. Something you may not know is that they have their own tasting room where you can try beers brewed with their enormous yeast catalogue. The White Labs Tasting Room, located off Candida (Yeast) Street, officially opened in June of 2012 and has received wide acclaim. The lab, headed by founder Chris White, has seen incredible success since its opening in 1995. It was recently reported that over 79 percent of the winning beers in the 2012 Great American Beer Festival were brewed with White Labs yeast, and with their yeast being shipped from Brazil to Canada, it's easy to see why.

The White Labs tasting room is medium-size but can accommodate groups with larger numbers, too. Walking in, the bar is immediately to the right, with its 32

Hansen IPA
Style: IPA
ABV: 6.46%
Availability: Year-round

The main focus of this tasting room is to taste many beers side by side, which is ultimately what I would suggest. That being said, they do brew four beers regularly, each named after a prominent yeast scientist. Hansen IPA is a medium-bodied West Coast–style IPA that clocks in at 6.46% on the dot. It's brewed with WLP075, which is a proprietary IPA blend ale yeast.

The yeast's fruity notes help to accentuate the dominant hop aromas. It pours a golden amber color, with heavy notes of citrus. If you start with this beer, definitely try another similar to it with a different yeast strain. You'll be surprised at what you find.

constantly changing taps meticulously lined up waiting to pour. The lab is located to the left, and if you're lucky, you may even see lab techs testing out various QC'ed beers. Brewers typically send in their beers to White Labs to catalogue their yeast and run quality-control tests. The lab-meets-taproom is a unique mix, and it makes for a very enjoyable experience. Tours are free and run fairly often on the weekend. They are worth going on if you've never been to the facility, and the tour guides are very knowledgeable, so ask questions.

The tasting room operates a nanobrewhouse, which brews 80-gallon batches of wort that is then split up and fermented with different types of yeast. Beers are served in 4-ounce increments, and it's important to realize that the primary purpose

of this taproom is to show drinkers how yeast affects the flavor of beer. These 80-gallon batches are split up into anywhere from 8 to 16 different kegs and then inoculated with different strains of yeast. The result is a unique, educational side-by-side tasting experience. Find out how different Belgian yeast strains affect fruity profiles or which English ale strain gives off the most diacetyl—it's all very fun.

Brewpubs

AMPLIFIED ALE WORKS

4150 Mission Blvd., #208, San Diego, CA 92109; (858) 270-5222; amplifiedales.com; @AmplifiedAles

Founded: 2012 **Founder:** JC Hill and Alex Pierson **Brewer:** Cy Henley and JC Hill
Flagship Beer: Leggy Blonde **Nano Releases:** Electrocution IPA, Leggy Blonde, Pig Nose Pale, Rare Form, Dry School Hop Out **Tours:** No formal tours offered. Call for private tour availability. **Taproom:** Yes

Amplified Ale Works is a nanobrewery located inside the California Kebab & Beer Garden restaurant near Pacific Beach. Owners JC Hill and Alex Pierson opened up the original California Kebab location near SDSU, but then moved the entire operation to Pacific Beach. In November of 2012, inspired by JC's home brew fascination, they opened up a nanobrewery within the restaurant, and today it operates pretty much as a separate entity. The team is very passionate about both fresh food

Dry School Hop Out
Style: Double IPA
ABV: 10.5%
Availability: Limited

The focus at Amplified is on the session, but that doesn't mean they don't have larger beers. Dry School Hop Out is their San Diego–style double IPA, and it clocks in at an impressive 10.5%. For how big it is, it's not boozy, and it incorporates a subtle maltiness that contributes a slight caramel and vanilla sweetness at the back end of the tasting. Falconer's Flight 7 C's dominate the aroma and main hop flavor, so expect some dank citrus zestiness along with a lingering pine resin. You'll also find a pleasant note of white grapes and will likely be surprised that it's as alcoholic as it is, because it definitely doesn't drink like a 10.5%.

and fresh beer, so not only do they have a nanobrewery in the restaurant, but they also carry 23 rotating drafts, 4 of which are usually Amplified Ale's. This form of nanobrewery functions very differently than the brewpub model and is becoming more popular in beer towns like San Diego.

Amplified Ales can be difficult to find if you are using Google Maps, so it's best to search for California Kebab in Pacific Beach if you are using any sort of GPS. It's on the upstairs floor of a strip mall that overlooks the beach. The restaurant itself is very modern beachy and is extremely laid-back. It hosts mixed ages that congregate for lunch and dinner and gets packed as the night draws on. Because of their impressive local draft lineup, California Kebab/Amplified Ale Works is a perfect hangout after a day of surfing or beach activities. The Amplified portion is fueled completely by a 3 BBL nano system, which is run about three times a month by JC and local celeb brewer Cy Henely, who coincidentally also works at Saint Archer. There are plenty of seats, and you can also pull up a chair next to the bar.

The Amplified team loves music, and as such their beer labels look like record jackets. Because of its nano status, they brew often and variously, so there aren't as many year-round beers as there are rotating styles. You'll likely see **Leggy Blonde, Electrocution IPA, Rare Form,** or **Pig Nose Pale** when you visit, but be prepared for something different just in case. As with many San Diego breweries, there is an emphasis on hops and so IPA is a big focus here. The other emphasis is on the session and the food-friendly. Amplified prefers people buying multiple pints while enjoying California Kebab rather than getting ripped up on a barleywine. That being said, **Rare Form** is a 13.0% bourbon-barrel-aged dark strong ale, so you'll still find the bigger beers here. Growlers are available and you can find Amplified on draft at select beer bars, but there are no bottles yet.

BLIND LADY ALE HOUSE & AUTOMATIC BREWING COMPANY

3416 Adams Ave., San Diego, CA 92116; (619) 255-2491; blindladyalehouse.com; automaticbrewingco.com; @blindladyale; @automaticbrewco

Founded: 2009 **Founder:** Lee and Jenniffer Chase, Jeff Motch, and Clea Hantman **Brewer:** Lee Chase **Flagship Beer:** N/A **Year-round Beers:** N/A **Seasonals/Special Releases:** Saison De Lyla, Mustan 15 IPA, Handlebar Double IPA, I Pity the Pale, Will Powered IPA **Tours:** No

Blind Lady Ale House, comically referred to BLAH (it's anything but blah), opened its doors in January of 2009 in San Diego's Normal Heights/North Park bar district. Not only is it one of the most popular beer bars in the area, but it's also the home of Automatic Brewing Company, run by Lee Chase, Stone Brewing Co.'s original brewer. Together with the help of Jenniffer Chase, Jeff Motch, and Clea Hantman, the group runs a successful gastropub offering seasonal organic food, a community-oriented atmosphere, and nanobrewed beer. The group also runs the popular Tiger!Tiger!, which is located not too far from BLAH.

Blind Lady Ale House is a medium-size gastropub with repurposed wood walls, high-seated bar tables, and communal seating. The mix of seating types and areas makes it easy to pick a place for a large group or find a private nook to enjoy with close friends. They have an impressive lineup of vintage cans in the back, all coming from the personal collection of Ben Davidson, famed Oakland Raider from the Lite Beer commercials. It makes Blind Lady even more eclectic. To the left of the entrance

Saison De Lyla

Style: Belgian Saison

ABV: 5.3%

Availability: Limited

Saison De Lyla has a spicy Belgian yeast nose with upfront farmhouse funk. The beer is light, effervescent, and pours a hazy straw. It has an intense tropical fruitiness to it, along with a very dry finish. Saison De Lyla is unfiltered, which makes it slightly hazy. It's perfect for the style, and goes very well with some of the organic greens on the menu at BLAH.

is a large backlit sign with the Automatic Brewing Company logo on it. Food and beer is ordered at the bar, and a hostess brings it out to your table. It's highly recommended that you try one of the special Neapolitan-style pizzas; the Egg & Bacon Pizza and House Chorizo Pizza are especially good.

In addition to the Automatic beers (there are usually two or three), Blind Lady Ale House showcases some 24 taps of mostly San Diego craft beer. Definitely try the Automatic first because this is the only place, other than Tiger!Tiger!, that you can get them. Automatic Brewing beers are usually one-offs; some make their way into production again, but not too often. Brewed by renowned beer master Lee Chase, it's hard to go wrong, and since you usually only have two or three choices, order them all. All styles are fair game. From hoppy IPAs to beers that use salt and fruit, Lee tends to brew more experimental beers. You can even take home the beer in 1-liter and 64-ounce growlers. Blind Lady Ale House is a great San Diego destination bar and should be at the top of your list while in North Park.

San Diego and East

CORONADO BREWING COMPANY

170 Orange Ave., Coronado, CA 92118; (619) 437-4452; coronadobrewingcompany.com; @coronadobrewing

Founded: 1996 **Founder:** Rick Chapman and Ron Chapman **Brewer:** Ryan Brooks, Daniel Drayne (brewpub only) **Flagship Beer:** Mermaid's Red **Year-round Beers:** Coronado Golden, Orange Ave Wit, Islander IPA, Mermaid's Red, Blue Bridge Coffee Stout **Seasonals/Special Releases:** Idiot IPA, Hoppy Daze, Red Devil, Frog's Breath IPA, Stupid Stout, Coronado Collection—Barrel-Aged Beers **Tours:** No formal tours offered. Call for private tour availability.

Coronado Brewing Company's original brewery and brewpub is located on Coronado Island, and it's still alive and kicking. Before founders Rick and Ron Chapman opened their massive production facility on the mainland, all production was done in-house at the brewpub on the 10 BBL brewhouse. That means that if you were drinking a Coronado brew outside of San Diego before 2012, you were drinking beer that was made on this system, which is amazing when you consider that the system was not only driving the externally distributed kegs and bottles, but also servicing the pub itself. That's dedication.

The brewpub itself is a beautiful classic and classy establishment. With a well-lit and warmly atmospheric interior and open-air patio in the front, Coronado is the perfect place to enjoy a nice summer's day lunch. The menu is expansive and curated by Ron Chapman's son, Kasey, who recently won a local link sausage competition with a handmade Vietnamese sausage, which you can find on the menu in the *báhn mì* sandwich. Chicken wings, wood-fired pizzas, pastas, rich desserts—you name it, they have it, but whereas some brewpubs sacrifice quality for quantity, Coronado seems to have found the right balance. If you are just interested in the beer, the bar is the place to be, and it's right past the front door. It gets busy, though, so get there early.

Coronado's brewpub serves the same beers as their newer production facility, with an emphasis on the flagships and some more experimental beers. They frequently have casks, which also make their way to neighboring beer bars. How about a **Blue Bridge Coffee Stout** cask with Peanut Butter Crunch?! Amazing. The base beer itself is one of the smoothest, most well-balanced coffee stouts there is, and it's one that, at 5.4%, won't slow you down. If you want something bigger, try their imperial **Stupid Stout** or **Idiot IPA.** Both are seasonal, but you'll likely find one or the other on tap when you visit. It's a brewpub, so get a flight of tasters and pair them with some food. When you're done, take a growler and a monikered Coronado pint glass home.

Beer Lover's Pick

Mermaid's Red
Style: American Amber Ale
ABV: 5.7%
Availability: Year-round

This day and age, with the elevated popularity of IPAs, ambers have seen a bit of a decline. That being said, the American amber ale is alive and well at Coronado Brewing Company. Mermaid's Red is a rich, biscuity American amber with notes of toasted bread and caramel and a hint of citrus. The hopping profile, although at 50 IBUs, is generally pretty balanced and does well with the malty characters. This is a great beer to order a pint of at the brewpub while enjoying any number of items off the menu. The hoppy character isn't enough to blow out your palate, but it does lend a bit of a kick accompanying some of the spicier items on the menu like the chicken wings. This is a solid, food-friendly beer.

HILLCREST BREWING COMPANY

1458 University Ave., San Diego, CA 92103; (619) 269-4323; hillcrestbrewingcompany
.com; @QueensOfBeer
Founded: 2012 **Founder:** David White **Brewer:** David White **Flagship Beer:** Banana
Hammock **Year-round Beers:** Perle Necklace Pale Ale, Brain Lubricant Imperial IPA,
Crotch Rocket Irish Red, Banana Hammock Scotch Ale, Lucy American Brown Ale,
Long and Stout Russian Imperial Stout, U-Hawle Hefe Wheat Beer, Hoppy Endings IPA
Seasonals/Special Releases: '13 Pride Xtra Pale Ale **Tours:** No

Hillcrest Brewing Company is a brewpub located in the LGBT University Heights district of San Diego. It is the world's first and only "Out and Proud LGBT Brewery." Owner and brewmaster David White started the brewery in 2012 and since has seen tremendous success. Prior to opening Hillcrest, he was an animal trainer in

Vegas. His favorite pet, a raccoon, even aided him in creating one of his flagship beer recipes, Lucy American Brown Ale. Prior to taking on the Hillcrest name, the brewery's intended name was Scooter Brewing, which was later changed to pay homage to the area the facility was being opened in. Today Hillcrest is a fully functioning brewpub offering a wide selection of food options as well as great beer.

The brewpub is located in an upscale district with lots of walkable shops, cafes, and restaurants. The Hillcrest-area rainbow pride flag is located right on the corner and can be seen from the outside patio. The restaurant is modern, chic, and has a warm vibe. A bottle chandelier hangs in the middle of the circular bar in the center

Beer Lover's Pick

Pride '13 Xtra Pale Ale
Style: XPA
ABV: 4.0%
Availability: Limited seasonal
Pride '13 Xtra Pale Ale was originally made as an anniversary beer for Hillcrest's one-year anniversary party. This incredibly low-ABV session ale hits all the right marks and is a great pairing to a classic Margherita pizza and/or spicy chicken wings. It has a light body with delicate notes of citrus, pine, and orange sherbet. Falconers Flight and Chinook hops shine through nicely, giving Pride '13 a very pleasant floral aroma. It pours a light golden orange and has a subtle malt straw grainy

finish. Pride '13 is an incredibly well-made session XPA and does an excellent job of redefining the style with a West Coast spin.

of the establishment. The brewhouse is tucked back to the right as you walk in, and one of the fermentors is adorned with a tiger head. The crowd is mixed ages, and the staff is incredibly friendly. They specialize in pizzas, but have other bar options like chicken wings and salads available as well. All in all it's a great place for lunch, dinner, or evening drinks. It does get busy on the weekends, so make sure you go early if you want a seat.

Hillcrest beers are impressive. David offers a wide selection of classic styles along with some interesting and creative ones as well. Their flagship best seller is a classic clove-forward Bavarian Hefeweizen called **Banana**

Hammock. The most interesting beer they have on tap, though, was made from a recipe devised by David's beloved pet, Lucy, a raccoon. Lucy was trained to pick out various malts and ingredients she liked from an ice-cube tray, and the resulting beer, **Lucy American Brown Ale,** is a brownish ale that defies classic style. It's dark in color with a light body and incorporates bitter hops and brown bread flavors. This beer is definitely the most fun. You really can't go wrong with any of the Hillcrest beers, so if you can't decide, order a flight for $10 and then take home a growler of your favorite.

MONKEY PAW PUB AND BREWERY

805 16th St., San Diego, CA 92101; (619) 358-9901; monkeypawbrewing.com;
@MonkeyPawPub

Founded: 2011 **Founder:** Scot Blair **Brewer:** Cosimo Sorrentino **Flagship Beer:**
None, but Bonobos, Low and Slow, and Sweet Georgia Brown are popular **Small-Batch
Rotating Beers:** Monkey Paw 15, Jimbo's Ale, Lovelike Beer, Low and Slow Rauchbier,
Mandrill IPA, Pineapple X-Press, Rich Man's IPA, Satanic Chimp, Sweet Georgia Brown, Live
Wire Caramel Coffee Milk Stout, Live Wire Caramel Coffee Milk Stout with Vanilla, 16th and
F, Bonobos IPA/SD Pale, Brainfood, Cornelius IIPA, Free Ken Allen Robust Rye, Great Ape
Nectar, Hooked on Chinook, Howler IPA, Jerry's Farewell Mocha Porter, Kong Barleywine,
Low and Slow Rauchbier with Serrano, Mighty Joe Young, Missing Link Belgian Pale with
Kaffir, Monkey Gose Bananas, Monkey Gose with Tart Cherry, Oatmeal Pale, Patas Pale Ale,
Rhesus Chocolate/Peanut Butter Porter, Santa's Pet Monkey, Summer Honey Citrus, Sweet
Tea Session IPA, Thatcher in the Rye, The Downs Family Irish Stout, Tiger Bomb Uakari
Wit, Valentine's Ale, Waypoing 730, collaboration beers **Tours:** No formal tours offered.
Call for private tour availability.

Monkey Paw Pub and Brewery is one of the most unique stops on the San Diego beer trail. They specialize in crazy eclectic beer and cheesesteaks—a great combination. The pub as it is today was opened in 2011 by beer guru Scot Blair, of Hamiltons Tavern fame. Before it became Monkey Paw, it was a well-known dive bar called the Jewel Box, but craft beer demand presented a great opportunity to take the old space and modernize it. When Scot first opened Monkey Paw, it was just a pub with great food, with a brewery coming soon. He hired brewer Derek Freese, who made Monkey Paw beers until he recently moved over to the new brewery Modern Times. His shoes were filled by Cosimo Sorrentino, an Italian South Park native with a creative passion to brew great beer.

Monkey Paw is an award-winning boutique brewery located in the East Village directly next to the 94 off-ramp. It's easy to pass, so look for the bright yellow rectangular sign. Inside you'll find a sort of revamped Euro-style pub with monkey tchotchkes everywhere. One of the definite highlights of the place is the giant stained-glass window to the right of the entrance depicting a monkey paw reaching towards the sky with a banana peel wrapped between the fingers. The place has a really cool vibe, and it's a fantastic place to enjoy craft beer in the company of friends. Check out the cool chalk drawings in the back. The bar to the left offers some 30 craft taps, usually California local, with at least one cast pouring. The menu offers incredibly rich cheesesteak sandwiches and amazing waffle-cut fries. Order the Blair Steak, Monkey Bones, and a side of Naughty Monkey Sauce.

Monkey Paw beers are inspired. Cosimo brews on a 5 BBL system with five 10 BBL fermentors. Everything served at Monkey Paw is limited release, which is why they have so many seasonals, but they do repeat crowd favorites like **Sweet Georgia Brown** and **Bonobos IPA/SD Pale.** The focus is on creative uniqueness, so don't be surprised if you see a peanut butter beer or an Anzac, an Australian coconut-treacle cookie beer. It is San Diego, though, so expect to find pales and IPAs. Monkey Paw only distributes to local bars as far north as Los Angeles, which makes their kegs and casks even more limited. You can't really go wrong with any of their beers, so order a flight or take a chance and order something you've never had before. Growlers are available for takeaway in 64-ounce format.

Beer Lover's Pick

Sweet Georgia Brown
Style: Brown Ale
ABV: 5.8%
Availability: Limited year-round

Ain't nobody got time for that! Well, make time for Monkey Paw's Sweet Georgia Brown. It's based on a Southern English brown recipe, but it's really its own unique take. You'll notice up-front notes of malty roast, chocolate, and a touch of smoke in the aroma. The body is incredibly creamy, with a chocolate Ovaltine quality. As it warms it begins to smell and taste like oatmeal cookies with a hint of marshmallow. The beer pours brown/black with a tan head and clocks in at a sessionable 5.8%. It's a great dessert-pairing beer and goes surprisingly well with cheesesteak. This beer, although limited, is made fairly regularly so you'll more than likely see it on the menu. It's a great example of what Monkey Paw has to offer.

SAN DIEGO BREWING COMPANY

10450 Friars Rd., San Diego, CA 92120; (619) 284-2739; sandiegobrewing.com; @SanDiegoBrewing

Founded: 1993 **Founder:** Scott Stamp and Lee Doxtader **Brewer:** Jeff Drum **Flagship Beer:** Infinitude IPA **Year-round Beers:** El 'Hefe' weizen, GranTVille Gold, Infinitude IPA, San Diego Amber, Old Town Nut Brown **Seasonals/Special Releases:** Monster Mash, Peep Show, Old 395, Patriot Extra Pale Ale, Lakshmi Imperial Red, Silver Strand Stout **Tours:** No

The original San Diego Brewing Company opened in 1896 and was able to produce 75,000 BBLs of beer. The company was shut down in 1942, being replaced by a naval base. The new San Diego Brewing Company opened up in 1993 during the '90s brewery boom and is currently owned and operated by the same restaurant team that runs Callahan's Pub & Brewery. It's located in a restaurant strip mall off Friar's road in San Diego's GranTVille very close to Qualcomm Stadium.

San Diego Brewing Company resembles a classic '90s-style brewpub. The interior is dark wood, large, and open with a few arcade machines in the back. The L-shaped bar wraps around the back left corner of the restaurant, and directly left lives the brewhouse. Behind the bar you'll find 46 taps with the addition of 4 casks; 9 of those taps are house San Diego Brewing Company beers. The beer list is kept up to date on a chalkboard, but there are also menus. An impressive lineup of beers include locals like Societe Brewing, Stone, Karl Strauss, and Modern Times. The menu at SDBC is large and varied, with everything from salads to burgers to pizza—even breakfast. One menu item to consider, for sheer novelty, is the Hop Infused Hummus. Slightly bitter, but very tasty. San Diego Brewing is family-friendly and has enough room for large groups.

Callahan's Pub & Brewery

Callahan's Pub & Brewery, located in Mira Mesa, opened in 1989 and the team behind it now also runs San Diego Brewing Company. The experience at both places is very similar, although Callahan's focuses more on the Irish pub side of things. They have 24 taps; 7 of those are house beers, which focus mostly on Irish, macro, and domestic beers, but there are some craft options available, too. Food ranges from traditional American fare to Irish-inspired offerings like Irish stew and fish-and-chips. It's a family-friendly restaurant offering a wide selection of options to have something for everyone.

Infinitude IPA
Style: IPA
ABV: 6.8%
Availability: Year-round

Patriot Extra Pale Ale is an incredible fresh beer and should be ordered if you see it on the menu. It's a seasonal, though, so if it's not around, go for the Infinitude IPA. Infinitude IPA is a hop-forward caramel-colored beer that showcases Cascade, Centennial, and Columbus hops. It has a refreshing resiny citrus taste that is sure to please hop heads. The beer is sticky and would pair well with the spicy chicken wings, but is also great just by itself. It has moderately high carbonation with a thick white head. Infinitude is very hoppy in aroma and flavor but not overly bitter or sweet. Malt plays second fiddle in this beer, so order it for the hops. Feel free to session.

Beer from San Diego Brewing tends to fall into classic-style categories, and they are very well made. It's recommended to order a tasting flight while you wait for your food—that way you can figure out which pint you want. The bar staff is incredibly friendly and knowledgeable and can point you in the right direction if you aren't sure what to order. The **GranTVille Gold,** their blonde ale, is the lightest option and usually sells out fast. Their list of rotating seasonals will entice hop heads and more eclectic beer drinkers, showcasing roasty stouts, XPAs, and imperial reds. The **Infinitude IPA,** a classic West Coast IPA, is one of the most popular items on the menu and is a solid option if you like forward classic hops. You can't go wrong with the beers here, and if you want more, growlers are available.

Beer Bars & Bottle Shops

BOTTLECRAFT

Little Italy: 2161 India St., San Diego, CA 92101; (619) 487-9493
North Park: 3007 University Ave., San Diego, CA 92104; (619) 501-1177; bottlecraftbeer
.com @Bottlecraft
Draft Beers: 2 taps (Little Italy only) **Bottled/Canned Beers:** 700+ bottles

Bottlecraft is a high-end bottle shop specializing in craft beer and craft beer merchandise. Owned and operated by craft beer evangelist Brian Jensen, Bottlecraft serves both the Little Italy and North Park areas of San Diego. The Little Italy shop, located in an art gallery district, has a bottle shop on one side and fully functioning tasting room on the other. Guests can purchase bottles and then share them with

Little Italy

The Bottlecraft Little Italy location, like North Park, is very walkable. Surrounded by galleries, the shop is also across the street from hip restaurants and bars. Like the North Park Location, Bottlecraft Little Italy has an impressive 700+ bottle line up with a few rotating taps as well. A nice spot to stop for a drink or to pick up some great craft on the way home.

Nearby you'll find some excellent restaurants, galleries, and The 98-Bottles beer bar and bottle shop, which is located across the street.

friends on-site. The Little Italy location also offers two unique rotating draft lines. Bottlecraft's mission is to elevate craft beer and educate people about the wonders of the drink. They've branded themselves with a modern minimalist approach, which works harmoniously with the overall craft movement.

Brian opened the original Little Italy shop in 2011 to wide praise and followed up in February of 2013 with the North Park location right in the middle of walkable University Avenue. While North Park does not offer on-site tastings, it still has one of the most complete and impressive lineups of amazing local, domestic, and international craft beer around. It's also walking distance from Hess's new North

Park brewery. Both shops are sparse in decoration and focus on showcasing the unique artwork of each beer bottle, letting the labels do the work. Bottlecraft offers a complete online experience and entrance into a beer club that yields six bottles of hand-curated beer, with tasting notes, in a carryout package. Club membership can be purchased in 1- to 12-month increments ranging from $35 to $350. It's clear that Bottlecraft cares about craft beer and seeks to educate the masses, while offering a fun and memorable experience for enthusiasts.

CLEM'S BOTTLE HOUSE & DELI AND CLEM'S TAP HOUSE
4100 Adams Ave., San Diego, CA 92116; (619) 284-2485; clemsbottlehouse.com; @ClemsBottleHous, @ClemsTapHouse
Bottle House—Bottled/Canned Beers: 1,500 bottles **Tap House:** 16 taps

Located in the Kensington district of San Diego, Clem's Bottle House has been family owned and operated since 1987. Not only is it host to some 1,500 bottles, but it's also the home of a small deli where beer lovers can get salads, sandwiches, and fresh bread. The space is located on the corner of Adams Avenue and Kensington Drive. There is a small outdoor patio with Boar's Head umbrellas where you can enjoy your food if you order at the deli. The inside of the store is open and well organized, showcasing craft beer, spirits, and great wine. When you are done picking your bottles, head over to Clem's Tap House.

Clem's Tap House, located in the same corner complex just a few doors down, opened in July of 2012. Above it are residential apartments. Clem's Tap House is a favorite of actor Will Ferrell, a fact Clem's is proud of. They offer 16 taps of regularly rotating curated beer and put together predetermined tasting flights to showcase specific varieties. Flights come in tiny long-stemmed tulip glasses and range in price. There is a definite educational spin on everything being served, so the staff is incredibly knowledgeable. Wine flights are also offered. Next time you're in Kensington, stop off at Clem's.

HAMILTONS TAVERN
1521 30th St., San Diego, CA 92102; (619) 238-5460; hamiltonstavern.com; @hamiltons
Draft Beers: 28 taps **Bottled/Canned Beers:** 200+ bottles

Among the great San Diego beer bars, Hamiltons is one of the most well-known. Owned by Monkey Paw founder Scot Blair, Hamiltons is named after a South Park resident, patriot Herman Hamilton. The neighborhood alehouse opened in 2006 in the spot of local dive bar Sparky's, and has since become one of the premier craft beer spots in San Diego. Hamiltons is located on 30th Street in a heavy residential area, and is the oldest in the famed 30th Street craft beer corridor. It's hard to miss the big green tavern building, and if it's nighttime, look for the trees with Christmas lights. Inside is a classic redux Euro-style tavern. The bar is located to the left, with pool tables and seating to the right. Beer signs and paraphernalia line the walls, and a massive tap handle graveyard covers the entire ceiling—accompanied by blue Christmas lights.

Hamiltons features 2 real ale beer engines, 28 craft taps, and over 200 bottles. Beers from Scot's other establishment, Monkey Paw, can also be found on tap. Hamiltons gets busy during drinking hours and can get super-crowded at night, so be prepared. Happy hour is a great time to visit if you haven't been here before and tends to be less crowded. Food can be ordered at the bar from a menu including everything from potato patty sandwiches to hop sausages to spicy buffalo wings. Friday nights are for Firkin cask tapping, and you can find out what's on tap by going to the website. Hamiltons is a classic tavern updated for modern times and has a great old-style vibe.

THE NEIGHBORHOOD
777 G St., San Diego, CA 92101; (619) 446-0002; neighborhoodsd.com; @Neighborhood SD
Draft Beers: 27 taps **Bottled/Canned Beers:** 50 bottles

Where would Jesus eat a hamburger if he were here today? The Neighborhood in San Diego's Gas Lamp district. The Gas Lamp area is well known for its nightlife hot spots and is frequented by college kids and the young craft crowd. The Neighborhood is right in the middle of it all on G Street, walking distance from the Bootlegger, J Wok, Smashburger, and Best Damn Beer Shop. It showcases 27 local craft taps, 50 assorted craft bottles, and a simple, "straightforward" menu that is easily paired with beer and other drinks. Deviled eggs, eclectic burgers, salads, and a large assortment of house-made sauces sum up the menu. They even have authentic malt shakes, so if you are interested in finding out what barley sugar tastes like prior to fermentation, give these a whirl. They also feature a full bar with handmade cocktails as well as wine.

The Neighborhood has a hip, young vibe with outdoor seating and large open windows that give it a spacious, breezy feel. Inside, subway tiles, stainless steel, taxidermy, and comical paintings of famous icons holding hamburgers—hence the Jesus reference—can be found. For those that like adventure, try going straight to the back of the restaurant near the restrooms. There is an impressive wall of kegs that when pushed on reveals a hidden speakeasy. Titled Noble Experiment, this speakeasy does not feature beer, but it does have incredibly high-end spirits that are fashioned into amazing cocktails under low light and a wall of skulls. Worth a visit.

O'BRIEN'S AMERICAN PUB
4646 Convoy St., San Diego, CA 92111; (858) 715-1745; obrienspub.net; @ObriensPubSD
Draft Beers: 20+ taps plus 2 casks **Bottled/Canned Beers:** 150 bottles with 10 meads

Located in Kearny Mesa is one of San Diego's friendliest and best beer bars, O'Brien's. O'Brien's refers to itself as an American pub to differentiate itself from the traditional Irish variety. Originally opened in 1994 by founder Tom Nichol, O'Brien's is a host to over 20 craft taps showcasing mostly local but also some regional delicacies. O'Briens frequently brings in jockey boxes to expand their already great taplist. The pub is located in a small strip mall and has a medium-size patio in front. Walking in, you'll immediately notice the beer paraphernalia decorating the

walls, the mismatched '80s office chairs, and the lineup of Cheers-style mugs hanging behind the bars. These mugs are actually part of a mug club Beer Ambassador program. O'Brien's offers a full menu of sandwiches, salads, grilled meats, and sides. If you don't know what to order and you're hungry, order Tom's Torta, an amazingly huge sandwich piled high with goodness.

Patrons that visit regularly make it a point to be friendly while promoting craft beer, and those who generally show that they deserve an ambassador mug are awarded one. There is a long waiting list. If you see someone sitting at the bar with one of these mugs, you can bet that they've earned it. A well-known regular, Bill Snyder, a jolly older gentleman, is one such mug club member, and he will be more than happy to tell you of his beer adventures. So sit down and stay a while. The O'Brien's vibe is incredibly community-oriented and worth experiencing. It's a unique side trip that'll net you some great beer, a full stomach, and memorable conversation.

TIGER!TIGER!
3025 El Cajon Blvd., San Diego, CA 92104; (619) 487-0401; tigertigertavern.com; @TigerTigerTav
Draft Beers: 23 taps, including 3 Automatic Brewing taps

Tiger!Tiger! is located in the North Park district of San Diego about 1 mile away from Blind Lady Ale House. This well-known beer bar is owned by the same crew that owns BLAH, which is why 3 of the 23 taps are designated Automatic Brewing Company lines. Opened in 2011 by Lee Chase, Jenniffer Chase, Jeff Motch, and Clea Hantman, Tiger!Tiger! is a hip craft beer bar frequented by younger craft drinkers. The location also offers a tasty assortment of wood-fired sandwiches like the *bánh mì,* house-made sausages, and wood-fire roasted pork, all using fresh local ingredients. Also worth noting: Tiger!Tiger! is 100 percent draft, from beer to wine to soda.

Tiger!Tiger! is pretty easy to spot. It's on El Cajon Boulevard and has a lit wooden facade. A tavern sign hangs over the entrance depicting a tiger in a tuxedo. Upon walking in, you'll notice a pretty open space with a longer line to the bar. Communal seating at wooden picnic tables is offered along with standing room. A large repurposed backlit Automatic Brewing Company sign hangs in the back to remind everyone that Lee Chase is in control of the beer. The vibe is chill and very similar to Blind Lady Ale House. It's the perfect craft beer hangout spot after a hard day at the office or for one of the frequent beer events Tiger!Tiger! holds. It's also part of the monthly North Park Drink About (sddrinkabout.com) beer tour along with Blind Lady. Stop for a draft beer and meet the coolest tiger in a tuxedo.

TORONADO
4026 30th St., San Diego, CA 92104; (619) 282-0456; toronadosd.com; @ToronadoSD
Draft Beers: 56 taps plus 3 casks **Bottled/Canned Beers:** 500+ bottles

Toronado, located in North Park, is a serious craft beer bar. Like its counterpart in San Francisco, Toronado San Diego offers an incredible tap lineup of some 56 beers along with 3 casks and over 500 bottles to choose from. If you are in the mood for craft beer and you want to go to a place that does it right, look no further than Toronado. The famous beer bar can be found off 30th Street between Lincoln and Polk Avenue. It's advised that you park on a side street, but pay attention to parking enforcement rules as they vary on each street. Finding the bar is easy; the blacked-out glass windows in front are hard to miss with the red logo holding a pint glass, and the large Toronado sign above the door beckons you to enter. There's also usually a chalkboard outside detailing daily specials.

Once inside and your eyes adjust to the dim bar lighting, you'll see a long bar to the right and neon beer signs on the walls. It gets crowded early on, so it can be hard to find a seat at the bar, but there are tables to the left and a back patio area in case the crowds are too dense. Bar food like fries, burgers, and sausages are also available to order at the bar. Toronado is a well-known craft beer spot and as such has frequent and exclusive events showcasing some of the rarest beers in the US. It's definitely worth a visit.

The San Diego Drink About

The San Diego Drink About is a celebration of great craft beer spots in North Park and is held on the third Wednesday of every month. This list of bars is a living list, so expect it to change periodically. To stay up to date, visit their website, sddrinkabout.blogspot.com. The Drink About features some of the bars from the San Diego pub crawl along with others. The main perk here is that there is a bus circuit. The Drink About features over 10 (depending on the week) craft beer bars and eateries, such as Blind Lady, Small Bar, Live Wire, Toronado, Ritual Tavern, Sea Rocket, The Station, Hamiltons, Bar Eleven, and Tiger!Tiger! The event provides buses the third Wednesday of every month with rigid drop-off and pickup times at each location. This is a great opportunity to see some fantastic spots and remove the driving from the equation.

Pub Crawl

North to South Park

San Diego's North Park is full to the brim with craft beer bars. It's advised to take public transportation to get to a few of these places, as the entire walk covers a 5-mile span. You could also break this tour into a few days if you want, as all of these places deserve your time and attention. The crawl starts at Blind Lady Ale House and ends at Hamiltons, the oldest beer establishment on 30th Street. This trail is also featured on the San Diego Drink About (see sidebar), which highlights over 10 popular North Park beer locations with scheduled bus pickup times.

Blind Lady Ale House, 3416 Adams Ave., San Diego, CA 92116.blindladyalehouse .com. One of the best beer bars in San Diego, Blind Lady Ale House features a great lineup of craft beer as well as their own brand brewed by brewmaster Lee Chase of Automatic Brewing Company. They feature an organic, seasonal, and locally sourced menu including some amazing pizzas. This is definitely a great place to fuel up on food before commencing the long walk.

Head west on Adams Avenue to 30th Street for about 0.6 mile and then go south on 30th for another 0.6 mile to Tiger!Tiger!

Tiger!Tiger! 3025 El Cajon Blvd., San Diego, CA 92104; tigertigertavern.blogspot .com. Brought to you by the same crew that runs the Blind Lady, Tiger!Tiger! offers more craft beer, more Automatic Brewing Company, and more great food. The focus here is on beer, community, and craft sandwiches. Like the Blind Lady, you'll need to wait in line and order at the counter, but when you get to the front of the line, you'll have 23 craft taps to choose from!

Right around the corner, almost next door, and little farther south on 30th Street is the Belching Beaver tasting room.

Belching Beaver North Park, 4223 30th St., San Diego, CA 92104; belchinbeaver .com/north-park. One of the newest additions to North Park is the satellite tasting room from Vista brewery Belching Beaver. The Beaver is located off 30th Street and includes the full line of Belching Beaver beers. It's not often that you get to include a brewery tasting room in a craft beer walking crawl.

Toronado is about 0.3 mile away, a couple-minute walk down 30th Street.

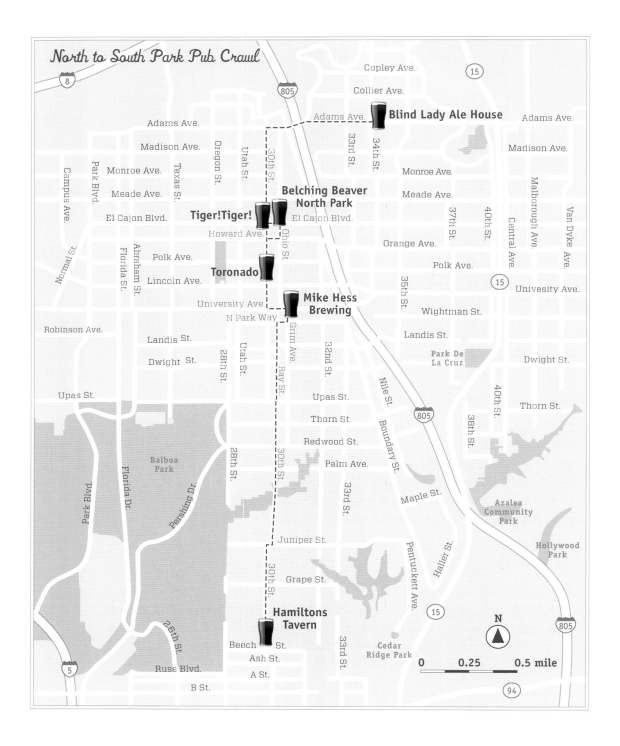

North to South Park Pub Crawl

Blind Lady Ale House

Belching Beaver North Park

Tiger!Tiger!

Toronado

Mike Hess Brewing

Hamiltons Tavern

N

0   0.25   0.5 mile

Toronado, 4026 30th St., San Diego, CA 92104; toronadosd.com. On to one of the most well-known craft beer bars in San Diego, Toronado has over 53 taps to choose from and a massive bottle list including some of the rarest beers around. The place is easy to find and usually has a chalkboard sign out front. Food is available at the counter, and they have an average of three casks on at all times. Toronado also has an equally well-known sister location in San Francisco, and both spots frequently hold beer events and carry hard-to-find craft.

Keep heading south on 30th Street to Mike Hess Brewing.

Mike Hess Brewing, 3812 Grim Ave., San Diego, CA 92126; hessbrewing.com. The newest brewery to hit North Park is Mike Hess's entry into large-format commercial brewing. Up until August of 2013, Mike and his team were brewing nano batches in their Miramar-area tasting room. This new space prominently features a 30 BBL brewhouse set into the floor, with an awesome catwalk that goes through the brewing equipment and leads to the tasting room. Visit, have a few tastings, and then come back again because this space is really cool and the beer is great.

At this point you may want to cab it. Hamiltons is about 2 miles south on 30th, which is 8 minutes by car but obviously a lot longer on foot.

Hamiltons Tavern, 1521 30th St., San Diego, CA 92102; hamiltonstavern.com. End your crawl at the oldest beer bar on 30th Street, Hamiltons. The bar as it is now is a revamped concept and was originally a dive bar. The spot's collective history makes it one of the oldest places to serve alcohol in the area. It's set against the backdrop of a neighborhood and has a lit tavern-style front facade, which makes it easy to see. There are usually people outside hanging out and enjoying tobacco products. When you go inside, you'll be met with a crowd unless you go at happy hour. Enjoy some of the same awesome food you'll find at Monkey Paw along with 28 taps that include Monkey Paw beers. Hamiltons also has a large assortment of bottles, over 200, to choose from and share with your friends.

San Diego and East

Multilocation Beer Spots

BACKSTREET BREWERY + LAMPPOST PIZZA

lamppostpizza.com/backstreet; @backstreetbrew
Founded: 1976 **Founder:** Tom, Dan, and Angelo Baro **Brewmaster:** Chris Gort **Year-round Beers:** Heritage Hefeweizen, Jagged Little Pilsner, Hep Kat Pale Ale, Rita Red

The Lamppost Pizza and Backstreet Brewery chain can be found in several places in Southern California, Northern California, and Nevada. In SoCal, the Lamppost Pizza side has 18 locations, of which 10 are co-branded with Backstreet Brewery, though only 5 of those locations actually have brewhouses in them. Only the brewery locations are listed here. Backstreet Brewery is a very classic '90s-style brewpub experience with a full run of brewed-to-style beer offerings. The Lamppost chain was originally founded in 1976 by Tom, Dan, and Angelo Baro. Tom and Dan still manage

the restaurants to this day. The Backstreet Brewery subbrand was added in the late '90s and is currently managed by Chris Gort, who brews at all five locations.

Backstreet Brewery offers a classic brewpub experience with a large menu, seasonal beers, guest taps, and a sports bar vibe. The walls are decked out in brick with industrial lanterns hanging over each table, while the 10 BBL brewpub systems are tucked away behind the seating areas and also occupy the mezzanine above in some locations. As it is technically part of Lamppost Pizza, the specialty and recommended order is pizza. If you aren't super-hungry you can order the Teaser, which is basically small pizzas cut up into bite-size pieces meant to be shared—think cheesy bread. It's not exactly elevated dining, but it is a great place to hang out and it's very family-friendly. Most of these locations are tucked into outdoor malls next to movie theaters and retail shopping.

Backstreet Brewery beer is pretty straightforward. Their mainstays, **Heritage Hefeweizen, Jagged Little Pilsner, Hep Kat Pale Ale,** and **Rita Red,** are brewed to style and pair well with the food menu. Their seasonal beers are more interesting and modern. **Lil' Tommy** is a session IPA version of one of their regular seasonals called Tomahawk, which, as you would guess, is brewed with Tomahawk hops. **Tomahawk** is a double IPA showcasing a very classic West Coast hop. Both of these beers are pine and citrus forward with very little dankness. Bitter on the back end with a slight breadiness on the palate, they'll go well with spicy food like chicken wings. Growlers are available for takeaway, and Backstreet Brewery beers can be found at Lamppost Pizza restaurants as well as the Backstreet Brewery Tap House locations.

Backstreet Brewery Locations with Microbreweries

Corona, 300 N. Main St., Corona, CA 91720; (951) 371-1471

Irvine, 14450 Culver Dr., Irvine, CA 92604; (949) 857-0160

Ladera Ranch, 27702 Crown Valley Pkwy., Ladera Ranch, CA 92694; (949) 388-7260

La Quinta, 78-772 Hwy. 111, La Quinta, CA 92253; (760) 564-4568

Vista, 15 Main St., Ste. #100, Vista, CA 92084; (760) 407-7600

KARL STRAUSS BREWING COMPANY—BREWPUBS

karlstrauss.com; @Karl_Strauss

Founded: 1989 **Founder:** Chris Cramer and Matt Rattner **Brewer:** Paul Segura **Year-round Beers:** Tower 10 IPA, Red Trolley Ale, Karl Strauss Amber, Pintail Pale Ale
Seasonals/Special Releases: Brewer-specific beers different at each location

Karl Strauss Brewing Company originally opened in 1989 in its initial downtown San Diego location off of Columbia Street. The original location, founded by Chris Cramer and Matt Rattner, is an iconic piece of San Diego history. Named after world-renowned German brewmaster Karl M. Strauss, who emigrated to America from Germany in 1932, the brewpub carries on his legacy of high-quality flavor-consistent beer. Karl originally brewed at Pabst Brewing Company and was responsible for reformulating the classic recipe in the 1950s. He was also cofounder Chris Cramer's cousin, hence his involvement in the brewpub chain. Karl passed away in 2006 but left behind an amazing legacy of quality beer, with which both Chris and Matt continue on at their seven Karl Strauss Brewing Company brewpubs.

Karl Strauss Brewing Company restaurants are classic-style brewpubs, but due to the advanced demand of craft beers and their developing tastes, Karl Strauss has sought to revamp some of its classic ways. While they have a large menu, you'll

Karl Strauss Brewing Company Locations

Carlsbad, 5801 Armada Dr., Carlsbad, CA 92008; (760) 431-2739; karlstrauss
.com/PAGES/Eats/Carlsbad. Year opened: 2000; Equipment: 7-barrel brewery;
Brewer: John Hunter

Costa Mesa, 901 S. Coast Dr., Costa Mesa, CA 92626; (714) 546-2739;
karlstrauss.com/PAGES/Eats/CostaMesa. Year opened: 2002; Equipment:
20-barrel brewery; Brewer: Matt Dale

La Jolla, 1044 Wall St., La Jolla, CA 92037; (858) 551-2739; karlstrauss
.com/PAGES/Eats/LaJolla. Year opened: 1996; Equipment: 7-barrel brewery;
Brewer: Lyndon Walker

San Diego—Downtown, 157 Columbia St., San Diego, CA 92101; (619) 234-
2739; karlstrauss.com/PAGES/Eats/Downtown. Year opened: 1989; Equipment: 10-barrel brewery; Brewer: Sean Albrecht

San Diego—4S Ranch, 10448 Reserve Dr., San Diego, CA 92127; (858) 376-
2739; karlstrauss.com/PAGES/Eats/4SRanch. Year opened: 2012; Equipment:
7-barrel brewery; Brewer: Nolan Clark

San Diego—Sorrento Mesa, 9675 Scranton Rd., San Diego, CA 92121; (858)
587-2739; karlstrauss.com/PAGES/Eats/SorrentoMesa. Year opened: 1994;
Equipment; $\frac{1}{2}$-barrel brewery (test batches); Brewer: Matt Johnson

Universal Citywalk, 1000 Universal Studios Blvd., Universal City, CA 91608;
(818) 753-2739; karlstrauss.com/PAGES/Eats/CityWalk. Year opened: 2000;
Equipment: 7-barrel brewery; Brewer: Austin Pinder

find high-end gourmet gastropub food. The chicken wings and blackened wahoo
are two very popular orders. There is really something for everyone at Karl Strauss
in both the food and beer arenas. Each Karl Strauss location has a different brewer,
and while they do brew some of the classic Karl Strauss offerings from time to
time, those beers are mainly left up to the main brewery to produce. That means
that each brewpub has a different lineup of custom location-specific beers that get
shared within the Karl Strauss network. They also frequently do beer dinners, cask
nights, and special beer events, so be sure to check back frequently. Growlers and
merchandise are available at each location, and Karl Strauss beer is widely available
in Southern California.

OGGI'S PIZZA AND BREWING COMPANY

oggis.com; @oggis

Founded: 1991 **Founder:** George, Dora, and John Hadjis **Flagship Beer:** California Gold, Torrey Pines IPA **Year-round Beers:** California Gold, Duck Dive Hefeweizen, Paradise Pale Ale, Torrey Pines IPA, Double Up Double IPA, Sunset Amber Ale, McGarvey's Scottish Ale, Black Magic Stout **Seasonals/Special Releases:** Big Tease Baltic Porter, White Rose, Ambers Ale, Ten Barrel Scottish, 1492 Discovery Ale, 1492 Barley Wine, Sweet Spot Hefeweizen, Oggi's Light

Oggi's Pizza and Brewing Company was originally founded in 1991 by George, Dora, and John Hadjis. The successful pizza and beer chain has since spawned 15 franchised locations across Southern California and a production brewery, Left Coast Brewing Company. Oggi's was named Best Small Brewing Company at the 2004 World Beer Cup and has won over 50 medals in commercial beer competitions. The Del Mar Oggi's location was the very first to become a brewpub in 1995, and six others took up brewing between then and 2004. In 2004 Left Coast Brewing began large-scale production of beers unique to Left Coast as well as the full Oggi's lineup. Today only two Oggi's restaurants continue to brew beer on-site: the Carmel Mountain Ranch and Mission Valley locations.

Oggi's restaurants have a sports bar vibe. They are low-lit with a focus on the flat-screen TVs showing any number of professional sports. They continue to be a great hangout for easygoing food, approachable beers, and a view of the big game. High-seated bar tables, larger tables for groups, booths, and a relatively medium-size bar are common, although each of the 15 locations is slightly different. The most popular Oggi's pizza is the Oggi's Special, which is basically the works. There's also a meat-centric pizza called Heavy Weight. **California Gold** and **Torrey Pines IPA** are the biggest-selling beers across all locations, and they continue to be the flagships for the brand. Both the Carmel Mountain Ranch and Mission Valley locations

Oggi's Pizza and Brewing Company Locations with Microbreweries

Carmel Mountain Ranch, 10155 Rancho Carmel Dr., San Diego, CA 92128; (858) 592-7883; cmr.oggis.com; @oggisCMR

Mission Valley, 2245 Fenton Pkwy., #101, San Diego, CA 92108; (619) 640-1072; missionvalley.oggis.com; @oggisMV

brew the Oggi's flagship beers along with seasonal varieties that can only be found at those pubs. Oggi's has a long history in Southern California as a great pizza restaurant and brewpub and is definitely a great stop for sports-minded craft beer enthusiasts.

ROCK BOTTOM BREWERY

rockbottom.com; @rockbottom

Founded: 1994 **Founder:** Frank Day **Brewer:** Location Specific **Flagship Beer:** Kölsch, Red Ale **Beers:** India Pale Ale, Kölsch, Red Ale, White Ale **Seasonals/Special Releases:** Brewmaster's Choice, Summer Honey Ale, Specialty Dark

Rock Bottom Brewery's first location opened in downtown Denver, CO, in 1994. Since then the rapidly expanding brewpub chain has opened a total of 38 locations in 17 different states. Three of those 38 locations are right here in Southern California. The Rock Bottom concept is simple: It's a classic '90s-style brewpub that has somewhat evolved with time. They have an expansive menu, a full lineup of regular house beers, and then special beers brewed in each specific location. Think about it as the Cheesecake Factory of beer. The restaurants are usually very large, with massive logo work out front. Plenty of seating makes them a perfect place for large groups, birthdays, and other celebrations. The brewery chain is actually owned and managed by a larger corporate entity called CraftWorks Restaurants and Breweries, which also owns brewpub chains such as Gordon Biersch Brewery Restaurants, Chophouse & Brewery, and Old Chicago Pizza & Taproom.

Despite the big corporate vibe of Rock Bottom Brewery, they have good beer. In fact, not only do they have special beers at each location, but they also have unique brewers at each location. Rock Bottom Brewery tends to get overlooked in terms of creativity, but the reality is that these brewers making Rock Bottom beer are very talented and have a lot to offer the craft beer scene in Southern California. So before you write it off as a giant corporate fixture, be sure to check in and try the beer. Rock Bottom has a mug club that is free to join and nets you discounts and monthly e-mail blasts.

Rock Bottom beer runs though the classic styles with the addition of rotating seasonal beers. Among their classic lineup are an IPA, Kölsch, red ale, white ale, and a rotating seasonal dark ale that changes frequently. There is also a Brewmaster's Choice, a beer specifically created for each Rock Bottom brewpub by its resident brewmaster. Tasting sets are a great way to get a lay of the land, and when you do figure out what you like, you can order beer in glasses small to large.

Rockbottom Brewery Locations

La Jolla—San Diego, 8980 Villa La Jolla Dr., La Jolla, CA 92037; (858) 450-9277; rockbottom.com/locations/la-jolla. Brewmaster: Marty Mendiola

Long Beach, 1 Pine Ave., Long Beach, CA 90802; (562) 308-2255; rockbottom.com/locations/long-beach. Brewmaster: Thomas Mercado

San Diego, 401 G St., San Diego, CA 92101; (619) 231-7000; rockbottom.com/locations/san-diego. Brewmaster: Jason Stockburger

STONE COMPANY STORES

stonebrewing.com

Stone Brewing Co.'s expanse into greatness has spawned Stone Brewing World Bistro & Gardens, a second restaurant and brewing location in Liberty Station, Stone Farms, and multiple Stone Company Stores. The Stone Company Stores serve as satellite taprooms where you can enjoy Stone beers, buy Stone merchandise, and refill Stone-branded growlers with whatever beer is on tap. So good news: If you are miles away from Escondido and need your Stone Brewing Co. fix, you can now get über-fresh beers by visiting the Stone Company Store near you. Each store has a similar setup with a large cracked gray stone bar, merchandise shelves, bottle cooler, and around 20 taps serving roughly 9 year-round beers and up to 11 specialty beers.

Stone Company Store Locations

Escondido, 1999 Citracado Pkwy., Escondido, CA 92029; (760) 471-4999

Liberty Station, 2816 Historic Decatur Rd., #116, San Diego, CA 92106; (619) 269-2200

Oceanside, 310 N. Tremont St., Oceanside, CA 92054; (760) 529-0002

Pasadena, 220 S. Raymond Ave., Ste. 103, Pasadena, CA 91105; (626) 440-7243

South Park, 2215 30th St., San Diego, CA 92104; (619) 501-3342

Patrons can enjoy tasting flights or full pints at varying prices at various locations. Keg purchase, with deposit, is also available at each location, but be sure to call for availability. There is a high likelihood that more Stone Company Stores are on their way so check the website as locations are added all over Southern California.

BYOB: Brew Your Own Beer

One of the best ways to learn and appreciate beer is to take the power into your own hands. Home brewing can be one of the most rewarding skills a beer drinker can learn, and regardless of the outcome, you'll definitely appreciate the craft more after you've done it. I've been home brewing for 5 years now and know people who have been doing it for 20 to 40, and the most important thing you can learn as a home brewer is that you will never know everything. As the incredibly inspirational documentary *Jiro Dreams of Sushi* teaches us, a true craftsman is humble and learns something new every day. So what are you waiting for? Grab a brewing book, get some equipment, and start brewing!

Okay, hold on, put on the brakes. There are a few things you can do as a home brewer that will ensure, but not guarantee, you have a successful first batch. Here they are.

Reading and Notes: Few things are more valuable than a good set of home-brewing books by your side. Wise home brewers still refer back to them, and even the authors themselves find themselves flipping through their books for guidance. Not all humans have the capacity for photographically memorizing everything, so you'll need some good books to reference and you want to write down everything you do during your process.

Tasting Beer **by Randy Mosher:** A great complement to *Radical Brewing,* Tasting Beer will run you through how to properly taste beers side by side. This is invaluable when trying to understand brewing classic styles and also will help you train your tongue to identify off flavors in your own beer.

Home Brew Stores: After you've done your reading online or in book form, you'll want to find your nearest home brew shop. There are many in Southern California to choose from and also plenty of online retailers that have a wide array of malts, hops, yeasts, and equipment. Don't forget, home brewing is "in" right now, so it's easier than ever to find the ingredients and help you need to make great-tasting home brew. Check out the "Home Brew Stores" section in this chapter to find the one that's nearest to you.

Sanitation: Now that you have your books and have read up on the subject, you have your starting brew kit from your local home brew store, and you have your ingredients ready, what do you do? Follow the directions in your recipe. If this is your first time brewing, just follow your favorite book, the home brew store's recipe,

Building Your Library

How to Brew **by John Palmer:** A classic book that should be on every brewer's shelf. John is a gifted engineer and home brewer, and when he's not brewing or writing about beer stuff, he's working on the space station ensuring the air locks are nice and tight. This book will prove to be an invaluable resource—read it cover to cover with some coffee by your side. Also look for John Palmer's newest book *Water: A Comprehensive Guide for Brewers,* if you are looking to learn even more.

Radical Brewing **by Randy Mosher:** One of the best books to read when studying the history of beer style. *Radical Brewing* is a complete guide through historical methods of brewing, ingredients, and what they do when you use them in beer, and will most definitely spark creativity you never knew you had. After you're done with the book, you'll see that these methods are less radical and more historical. I have this book marked up like crazy and constantly look up ingredient profiles, recipe bases, and general information.

The Complete Guide to Home Brewing **by Charlie Papazian:** This is a staple brewing book for beginners, written by a well-respected home brewer and president of the Brewers Association.

Brewing Classic Style **by Jamil Zainacheff and John Palmer:** Heretic Brewery Brewmaster Jamil Zainacheff and John Palmer team up to talk about the nitty-gritty in the classic-style realm. In here you'll find 80 classic-style recipes that are great jumping-off points for your own beer recipes. Refine your brew techniques and expand on them.

The Everything Home Brew Book **by Drew Beechum:** Another invaluable resource from a local SoCal home brew celebrity and Maltose Falcon, Drew Beechum. This is a great beginner book, and there are some pretty handy tidbits covering oak-aging beer and saison in here as well.

or the recipe your friend gave you. All the books listed in "Building Your Library" cover the basic process. One thing you'll want to pay extra-special attention to is sanitization. There are a couple sanitizers out there that most people use, including iodine-based sanitizers and my favorite, the phosphoric acid–based Star San. Using these will help reduce unwanted microbes in your beer.

There are two stages in brewing: the hot side and the cold side. Cleanliness is important throughout. I recommend PBW (Powdered Brewers Wash), available at your local home brew store, to keep everything the beer touches clean. Pay extra attention to sanitization on the cold side. You've just spent an hour boiling your beer to coagulate proteins and kill all possible infectors, and you need to keep those same infectors out of your beer as you cool it down. You can never be too sanitary. Make sure everything is clean, soaked, and sanitized.

Temperature Control: Yeasts work best at their intended fermentation temperature. You can find this temperature by looking up the yeast profile online. If you are using White Labs yeast, for example, going to whitelabs.com will provide you with helpful information, including pitching rates, ideal temperatures for fermentation, and flavors created by the yeast strain. Fermenting a beer in warmer-than-ideal temperatures can lead to off flavors that can destroy an otherwise good beer—band-aid, umami, meat, or sourness are possible side effects. By fermenting the beer at the right temperature, you'll be more likely to only get the intended flavors from the yeast you are using.

How do you control temperature? Most home brewers buy kegerators. Normally used for serving beer, kegerators provide the ideal fermentation environment for beer. By outfitting a kegerator with a Ranco temperature controller, you'll ensure that the temp is just the way you want it. Some home brewers recondition used refrigerators, freezers, or air conditioners to create their own custom kegerators. The sky is the limit. You can also outfit your fermentors with thermowells to dial in the temperature even more.

Yeast Starter: We are back to yeast again. Keeping yeast happy is the key to good beer. Adding yeast—or pitching, as brewers call it—in insufficient quantities can overstress it and lead to off flavors. For this reason, home brewers create yeast starters. Yeast starters can be a pain to make, but they are invaluable and necessary. By creating a small unhopped batch of beer, usually with dry malt extract, you can grow your yeast up, make it healthy, and pitch necessary amounts into your beer to ensure a healthy fermentation. This helps to prevent fermentation lag, underattenuation, and off flavors.

Wrap-Up: These are clearly high-level explanations of aspects of the brewing process that have quite a bit of research behind them. You'll likely want to do research on methods and best practices, which can all be found in the books recommended. By prioritizing the items listed above, you can ensure your first, second, third, and brews beyond are worthy of your own palate and those of your friends. Remember,

Local Home Brew Clubs

*Larger Classic Clubs

Los Angeles
The Arroyo Brewery
Carbon Nation
Crude Brew Crew
FERM
*Long Beach Home Brewers
*Maltose Falcons Home Brewing
Society
*Pacific Gravity Home Brewers Club
*Strand Brewers Club
Western Federation QUAFF and
Belch
What Ales You
*YeastSide Brewers

Orange County
*AHP Brew Club
*Barley Bandits
Beer Masters Tasting Society
*BrewCommune
Fear No Beer Brewclub
The Fermenters
Los Flores Brew Club
Meisters of the Brewniverse
Surf City Brewers
West Coast Brewer
Yeast of Eden

Inland Empire & Antelope Valley
Brewing Enthusiasts of the Antelope
Valley Region
Cervesa Cevada Club
Coachella Valley Homebrew Club
Empire Brewing Club

Fear No Beer
Hops Unlimited
*Inland Empire Brewers
Ripperside Brewpunx
*Riverside Homebrew Crew Club
*Temecula Valley Homebrewers
Association

San Diego
Barley Literates Homebrew Club
CHUG
Foam on the Brain
Hoppy Trails Brew Club
Julian Homebrewers Association
The League of Extraordinary Brewers
*Mash Heads
Mother Earth Brew Crew
*North County Home Brewers Asso-
ciation
*QUAFF
*San Diego–Orange County Brewers
Alliance
*Society of Barley Engineers
*Symposium

Santa Barbara & Ventura
The Beer Necessities
Big Wave Homebrew Club
Carpinteria and Rincon Point (CARP)
Homebrewers
Hollister Hoppers Homebrew Club
Lompoc Brew Crew
Thousand Oaks Home Brewers
*Valley Brewers
*Ventura Independent Beer Enthusi-
asts (VIBE)

your friends may be your greatest fans, but some may not be comfortable telling you the truth if your beer sucks. Do them a favor and make sure it's good when you give it to them, unless it's a prank or you are testing their honesty.

Beer Judging & Competitions: When you brew your first beer, you may consider submitting it to a beer competition. You can get a list of competitions in your area online and/or from your local home brew club. Competitions usually require you to send two to three unlabeled/umarked 12 ounce bottles along with a nominal entry fee of $5 to $10 per entry. After the competition is held you'll receive feedback in the form of BJCP (Beer Judge Certification Program) score sheets and maybe even a medal, if you scored high enough. The BJCP is both a program for brewers that want to learn more about beer and a set of advanced beer style guidelines that specify what each beer style is. You'll find details on everything from aroma, mouthfeel, and ingredients to commercial examples in the BJCP style guidelines. To learn more about the program check out BJCP.org.

Home Brew Clubs: Join a home brew club as soon as you can. One of the biggest mistakes I made when I started brewing was not joining Pacific Gravity, my local home brew club. Remember that it's okay to geek out on beer. Home brew clubs have in them some of the most seasoned and classic brewers around. From people that have just begun to people that have been brewing for most of their lives, there is a fountain of information that can be consumed.

Have club members taste your beers to offer objective critical feedback—something that is hard to attain from family and friends. Also try others' beers, offering the same constructive criticism. You can train your palate and mind, and learn new brewing methods in a home brew club. They also have frequent parties, style focus nights, and brewing demonstrations that are incredibly fun to attend.

Home Brew Recipes

If you are like me, you'll probably want to build your recipe from scratch, but in order to do that, you need to know where to start. Brewers from around the world hone their craft so that we can drink amazing beer. Here is a collection of five great clone recipes that you can try at home distilled down to 5 gallons.

BLIND AMBITION ABBEY ALE

Brewmaster David Griffiths comes from an extensive beer background and has an impressive brewing resume, including BJ's Brewhouse. He currently creates globally inspired beers of all styles with Ladyface proprietor Cyrena Nouzille. Together they make everything from Belgian farmhouse ales to dank American IPAs. This recipe is one of their most well known, a dark strong ale called Blind Ambition Abbey Ale.

YIELD: 5 GALLONS

Grain:

    10 pounds Pilsner Two-Row
    4 ounces Caravienne (20L)
    4 ounces Aromatic Malt
    4 ounces Special B
    2 ounces Chocolate Malt
    1.15 lbs Dark Belgian Candi Sugar/Syrup

Hops:

    0.25 ounce Apollo (pellet) at 60 minutes (20 IBU)
    0.5 ounce Galena (pellet) at 20 minutes (10 IBU)

Additions:

    Yeast Nutrient—as needed (typically 2 grams per 5 gallons)
    Kettle Finings—as needed (typically 2 grams per 5 gallons)

Yeast:

    White Labs 510 or similar Trappist ale yeast

    OG: 1.068, FG: 1.017, IBU: 29, SRM: 28

Incorporate crushed grain into 3 gallons of 158°F water. Stabilize temp at 152°F for 1 hour. Slowly raise temp to 180°F. Sparge with enough 180°F water to collect 6 gallons total in kettle.

Add sugar and Apollo hops and bring to a boil. Boil time is 60 minutes total. With 20 minutes remaining, add Galena hops, yeast nutrient, and kettle finings. At end of boil, remove as much kettle trub as possible; chill to 68°F and pitch yeast.

Ferment for 3 weeks at 70°F then transfer to secondary holding tank for 2 weeks. Bottle with priming sugar, wait 2 to 3 weeks for carbonation, and enjoy.

COURTESY OF CYRENA NOUZILLE AND DAVID GRIFFITHS, LADYFACE ALE COMPANIE—
ALEHOUSE & BRASSERIE (PAGE 27)

SOLIDARITY BLACK MILD

Eagle Rock Brewery is the first manufacturing/packaging craft brewery to open within the Los Angeles city limits in over 30 years. Piloted by brewmaster Jeremy Raub; his father, Steve Raub; and Jeremy's women's beer advocate wife, Ting Su, this family-run operation has become synonymous with LA craft. Eagle Rock Brewery focuses on beers of all styles, but has become known for their session ales. Solidarity Black Mild is a beer well known in Los Angeles and is one of the only milds available on the market.

YIELD: 5 GALLONS

Grain:

4.25 pounds Maris Otter (53.3%)
1.5 pounds German Munich (18.8%)
9 ounces Pale Wheat Malt (7.1%)
7 ounces Chocolate Malt (5.5%)
5 ounces Crystal Malt 60°L (3.9%)
5 ounces Crystal Malt 80°L (3.9%)
3.5 ounces Smoked Malt (2.7%)
3.5 ounces British Black Patent (2.7%)
1.25 ounces Roast Barley (1.0%)
1.25 ounces Carafa Type II (1.0%)

Hops:

3.76 AAU Willamette Hop Pellets (boiled 60 minutes)

Additions:

Calcite (Chalk)—add to mash to achieve residual alkalinity of 85–95 (amount will depend on your local water profile)
Yeast Nutrient—as needed (typically 2 grams per 5 gallons)
Kettle Finings—as needed (typically 2 grams per 5 gallons)

Yeast:

British Ale Yeast

OG: 1.042, FG: 1.013, IBU: 17, SRM: 25

Incorporate grains into 1.25 quarts of water per pound. This is a single-infusion mash. Rest at 153°F for 60 minutes. (Assumed mash efficiency of 75% used in this recipe.)

Add calcite (chalk) to your mash to achieve a residual alkalinity of 85–95. Make sure to do this addition after adding the grains. (The amount of mineral additions will vary depending on your local brewing water.)

Collect a pre-boil volume of 6 gallons.

Conduct a 1-hour boil adding hops at recipe specified times.

Ferment at 69°F with British ale yeast for 10 to 14 days and secondary ferment for 7 to 14 days. Bottle with priming sugar, wait 2 to 3 weeks for carbonation, chill, and enjoy.

COURTESY OF JEREMY AND STEVE RAUB, EAGLE ROCK BREWERY (PAGE 74)

BREAKER PALE ALE

Beachwood BBQ originally opened in Seal Beach as an upscale beer bar and gastropub. When they opened their second location in Long Beach, owner Gabriel Gordon decided to partner with a brewer, Julian Shrago, and open a brewery as well. Beachwood BBQ & Brewing has become one of LA's favorite breweries and brewpubs. Julian's passion for the craft has won him medals at GABF and the hearts of locals. He brews constantly, and the beers on tap are always changing. Here's one of his favorites, a West Coast pale called Breaker.

YIELD: 6 GALLONS

Grain:

11.9 pounds Pale Malt (Two-Row) (92.7%)

0.5 pound Crystal 45L (4.0%)

0.45 pound Cara-Pils Dextrine Malt (3.4%)

Hops:

0.8 ounce Columbus Pellet 17.00 56.0 (60 minutes)

0.4 ounce Centennial Pellet 10.50 9.1 (30 minutes)

0.3 ounce Columbus Pellet 17.00 4.2 (10 minutes)

0.5 ounce Cascade Pellet 6.50 2.2 (1 minute)

2 ounces Cascade Pellet 6.50 0.0 (Dry Hop)

2 ounces Pellet 17.00 0.0 (Dry Hop)

Additions:

1 unit Whirlfloc Fining 10 minutes (boil)

Yeast:

White Labs WLP001 California Ale

OG: 1.054, FG: 1.012, IBU: 71, SRM: 5.7

This is a single-step infusion recipe using a ratio of 1.3 quarts of water per pound of grain. The infusion should be at 153°F for 60 minutes, followed by a mash out at 167°F for 10 minutes. The sparge temperature should be 167°F and should be slow—60 minutes long. Follow the hopping profile above, cool, and then add yeast. Ferment at selected yeast's ideal fermentation temperature for 7 to 10 days. Secondary fermentation for additional 7 to 14 days. Bottle with priming sugar, wait 2 to 3 weeks for carbonation, chill, and enjoy.

COURTESY OF JULIAN SHRAGO, BEACHWOOD BBQ & BREWING (PAGE 117)

MERMAID'S RED

Coronado Brewing Company is one of the most well-known brewpubs in San Diego. From their quaint brewpub on Coronado Island to their new, flashy tasting room on the mainland, Coronado is making some seriously great beer. Mermaid's Red is one of their original flagships and is an amazingly straight-ahead amber. In the days of super-hop bombs and ultra-bourbon-barrel-aged beers, a simple well-made amber is a great thing. Mermaid's Red is a perfect example of the style—both approachable and complex.

YIELD: 5 GALLONS

Grain:

7.5 pounds American Two-Row or 6.5 Light Dry Malt Extract

0.5 pound Crystal 10L

0.75 pound Crystal 15L

0.75 pound Crystal 45L

0.75 pound Crystal 80L

0.10 pound English Chocolate Malt

Hops:

1.25 ounces Northern Brewer Hops 9.6% AA (60-minute addition)

1 ounce Cascade Hops 7% AA (10-minute addition)

1 ounce Cascade Hops 7% AA (flameout addition)

1 ounce Cascade Hops 7% AA (dry hop addition)

Additions:

1 Whirlfloc Tablet or 1 teaspoon Irish Moss

Yeast:

WLP 001 Yeast Starter

OG: 1.056, FG: 1.012, IBU: 50 IBS, SRM: 16

Mash at 152°F with 1.3 quarts of water per pound of grain, so 13.3 quarts or 3.3 gallons. Let the mash rest for 60 minutes, then vorlauf prior to sparge.

Sparge with 5.3 gallons of 170°F water and gather 6.4 gallons preboil. Bring wort to a boil and follow hop addition schedule. After boil, cool wort to 65°F, pitch yeast, and oxygenate your wort.

Ferment for 2 weeks at 67°F then add 1 ounce of Cascade for the dry hop that lasts for 7 days. Bottle with priming sugar, wait 2 to 3 weeks for carbonation, chill, and enjoy.

COURTESY OF DANIEL DRAYNE, CORONADO BREWING COMPANY (PAGE 281)

GAMS-BART BAVARIAN ROGGENBIER

Founded by local USC grads John Rockwell and Kristofor Barnes, Los Angeles Ale Works (aka LAAW) is a brewery start-up in the City of Angels. LAAW launched their first beer in February 2013 during their successful Kickstarter campaign. The style, Roggenbier, is one of their favorites—a long-dead but baffling, delicious traditional beer from Bavaria. This recipe is from their home brew days and is the recipe that won them a third place in the final round of the National Home Brew Competition.

YIELD: 6 GALLONS

Grain:

   3.5 pounds (30.4%) Pale Ale Malt; Weyermann

   1.5 pounds (13.0%) German Dark Munich

   1.5 pounds (13.0%) German Light Munich

   0.25 pound (2.2%) German CaraMunich I

   3.75 pounds (32.6%) Rye Malt; Weyermann

   0.75 pound (6.5%) Roasted Rye; Weyermann

   0.25 pound (2.2%) Rice Hulls

Hops:

   1 ounce Tettnanger 4.5% (whole)—added during boil, boiled 60 minutes

   0.5 ounce Hallertau Mittelfruh -4.5% (whole)—added during boil, boiled 15 minutes

Additions

   $^1/_2$ teaspoon Gypsum—added to mash

   1 Whirlfloc Tablet—added during boil, boiled 20 minutes

   Wyeast Nutrient—added during boil, boiled 15 minutes

Yeast:

   Wyeast 3638 Bavarian Wheat

   OG: 1.051, TG: 1.014, IBU: 19, SRM: 14.8

This is a multistep mash with a water-to-grain ratio of 1.5 quarts/pound. The first rest is at 122°F for 20 minutes. This protein rest will help make the large portion of rye malt more manageable.

Raise the temp slowly to 148°F and then rest for 20 minutes. Mash out at 168°F for 10 minutes and then sparge for 45 to 60 minutes.

Primary fermentation should be held at 62 to 64°F for 10 days, with a long secondary at 65°F for 14 days. Bottle with priming sugar, wait 2 to 3 weeks for carbonation, chill, and enjoy.

COURTESY OF KRISTOFOR BARNES AND JOHN ROCKWELL, LOS ANGELES ALE WORKS (PAGE 50)

Home Brew Stores

If you are going to make beer, you are going to need ingredients. With the boom in craft beer there has also been an increase in home brewers. Here are some of the top home brew shops.

VENTURA

Surf Brewery Home Brew Shop

4561 Market St., Ventura, CA 93003; (805) 644-2739; surfbrewery.com

NEAR LANCASTER

The Bearded Brewer

4855 W. Ave. M (Columbia Way), Quartz Hill, CA 93536; (661) 418-6348

LOS ANGELES AND SOUTH BAY

Culver City Home Brewing Supply

4234 Sepulveda Blvd., Culver City, CA 90230; (310) 397-3453; brewsupply.com

Eagle Rock Home Brewing Supply

4981 Eagle Rock Blvd., Los Angeles 90041; (323) 258-2107; brewsupply.com

South Bay Brewing Supply Co.

1311 Post Ave., Torrance, CA 90501; (310) 328-2133; southbaybrewingsupply.com

Steinfillers

4160 N. Norse Way, Long Beach, CA 90808; (562) 425-0588; steinfillers.com

The Home Wine, Beer, and Cheesemaking Shop

22836 Ventura Blvd., Woodland Hills, CA 91364; (818) 884-8586; homebeerwine cheese.com

INLAND EMPIRE

More Beer—Riverside

1506 Columbia Ave., #12, Riverside, CA 92507; (951) 779-9974; morebeer.com/riverside (see photo right)

So Cal Homebrew Supply

2170 Arrow Hwy., La Verne, CA 91762; (909) 593-4249; socalhomebrew.com

Recommended Online Resources

If you can't find what you need from a local store, you can always shop online. Amazon.com is a great resource, but so are the following:

Brewhemoth—brewhemoth.com

Midwest Brewing Supply—midwestsupplies.com

More Beer—morebeer.com

Northern Brewer—northernbrewer.com

White Labs—whitelabs.com

TEMECULA

Vintner's Vault

27941 Diaz Rd., Temecula, CA 92590; (951) 587-8900; thevintnervault.com (see photo right)

SAN DIEGO

Home Brew Mart—San Diego

5401 Linda Vista Rd., San Diego, CA 92110; (619) 295-2337; homebrewmart.com

Mother Earth Brew Co. Homebrew Store

206 Main St., Vista, CA 92084; (760) 726-2273; motherearthbrewco.com

American Home Brewing Supply

9535 Kearny Villa Rd., #104, San Diego, CA 92126; (858) 268-3024; redkart.com/ahbs

The Homebrewer

2911 El Cajon Blvd., #2, San Diego, CA 92104; (619) 450-6165; thehomebrewersd.com

Best Damn Beer Shop

1036 Seventh Ave., San Diego, CA 92101; (619) 232-6367; bestdamnbeershop.com

In the Kitchen

Beer is an incredible pleasure to both drink and pair with food, but it's also fantastic used as an ingredient. The craft beer movement has resulted a plethora of amazing breweries opening in SoCal and culinary minded fans of those local breweries have taken it upon themselves to catalogue tasty recipes online and in print form. In this section you'll find a great assortment of food recipes from local SoCal chefs, restaurants, and beer bloggers, which will tantalize your palate.

Cooking with Beer

From salad dressing to grilled cheese to beer shortcakes, beer, and its wide rainbow of style types, has an incredible versatility in the kitchen. Sours, porter, stouts, and IPAs can be used to amplify flavors in specific dishes and make a great accompaniment to your favorite brew.

ARUGULA SALAD WITH FLANDERS PLUM VINAIGRETTE

This incredibly refreshing vinaigrette recipe was prepared for us by the lovely Jessica Christensen from well-known West LA craft beer hot spot City Tavern in Culver City. Jessica runs the culinary program at the restaurant, starting out as chef de cuisine but now overseeing the entire Kaufman Restaurant Group's menus along with co-chef Dave Northrup. Jessica focuses on gourmet comfort foods with a Southern flair. This recipe uses sour ale to impart an amazing tanginess to this tasty salad dressing.

SERVES SALAD PLATTER FOR 4

For the vinaigrette:
 $^1/_2$ cup orange juice
 $^3/_4$ cup sour ale, Flanders red is best
 $^1/_4$ cup rice wine vinegar
 $^1/_4$ cup sliced shallots
 $^1/_4$ cup honey
 1 teaspoon salt
 1 teaspoon black pepper
 2 $^1/_4$ cups grapeseed or blend oil
 1 stem rosemary, leaves only, chopped
 $^1/_4$ cup chiffonade basil

For the salad:
 1 $^1/_2$ cups plum scraps and plums
 $^1/_4$ cup chiffonade basil
 Olive oil
 1 (7–8 ounce) bag organic arugula
 Sea salt to taste
 2 balls burrata, cut in quarters or halves

Blend the first 7 vinaigrette ingredients in a blender, then slowly add oil to slightly emulsify. Stir in rosemary and basil.

For the salad, halve plums (or pluots) and rub lightly with olive oil. On a clean grill, char plum halves, then toss with chiffonade basil while still warm. Place on a plate or platter and drizzle with vinaigrette. Toss arugula with vinaigrette and sea salt and place on top of plums. Finish with burrata halves, sprinkled with sea salt.

COURTESY OF EXECUTIVE CHEF JESSICA CHRISTENSEN, CITY TAVERN (PAGE 88)

LADYFACE FRENCH ONION SOUP

This recipe comes from popular craft microbrewery and brasserie Ladyface Ale Companie. Their executive chef, Adrian Gioia, focuses on seasonal menus and using beer as an ingredient in his dishes. Adrian has prepared two recipes for us. First is an amazing French onion soup that utilizes both cognac and Ladyface's Picture City Porter in the broth. Second, Coq-à-la-Bière, or "Chicken with Dark Beer," is a savory dish utilizing Ladyface's dark Belgian beer, Blind Ambition. Ladyface is well known for their creative and delicious food, so enjoy these two amazing recipes.

SERVES 8–10

> 5 pounds yellow onions, thinly sliced
> 5 cloves garlic, minced
> 1 bunch thyme, picked and finely chopped
> 1 ounce cognac or brandy
> 1 gallon water, vegetable stock, or chicken stock. (Ladyface uses a broth made from the same roasted malts used in brewing beer called "wort" that adds body to the soup, but you can use water or stock with great results. Adding water only or vegetable stock will keep this soup entirely vegetarian.)
> 1 (12-ounce) bottle dark beer (Ladyface uses its Picture City Porter in this recipe, but an amber, porter, or any sweeter beer will do. Avoid hoppier beers that will tend to go bitter with cooking.)
> Salt and freshly ground pepper to taste
> A few chunks of crusty bread, preferably a little stale or lightly toasted
> Sliced Gruyère cheese

In a wide-bottomed, heavy pot, bring a few tablespoons of olive oil just to the point of smoking and add all of the onions at once. Stir occasionally until the onions are a deep brown color and well caramelized, about 10 minutes. This is the most important part of the cooking process. The onions need to get very dark without burning. Turn the heat down towards the end to give them a chance to really caramelize. This is where all of the complex, sweet, meaty flavors are going to come from.

Add the garlic and thyme and continue to cook for another 2 minutes. Add the cognac, but use caution as the alcohol may catch fire briefly. Add the water or stock and the beer and simmer the soup for 20 minutes, adding salt and freshly ground pepper to taste.

To serve, ladle the soup into tall bowls and add some of the bread chunks to cover the top. Lay 2 slices of Gruyère over the top, making sure that the cheese covers the rim of the bowl. This will keep it from sinking into your soup. Place the bowls under the broiler element of your oven for about 30 seconds or until the cheese is nicely browned and bubbling hot. Serve immediately.

COURTESY OF EXECUTIVE CHEF ADRIAN GIOIA, LADYFACE ALE COMPANIE & BRASSERIE (PAGE 27)

LADYFACE COQ-À-LA-BIÈRE
SERVES 8

2 tablespoons olive oil
8 chicken thighs
Flour for dusting
1 pound bacon, cut into thin strips or lardons
1 pound button mushrooms, sliced
1 yellow onion, diced
3 cloves garlic
1 (22-ounce or 750 ml) bottle strong dark Belgian beer (While Ladyface might use
    its Blind Ambition or La Trappistine, a dubbel would work great with this recipe.)
1 bunch thyme, picked and chopped
1 bay leaf

In a large heavy-bottomed pot, add oil and heat almost to smoking. Season and lightly dust the chicken thighs in flour and lay them skin-side down in the pan. Turn the heat down to medium and sauté the thighs until they are golden brown, turning them over as necessary.

Remove the thighs from the pan and add the bacon. Cook bacon, stirring to break the pieces up, until it is nicely browned and crispy and most of the fat has rendered out. Remove the bacon from the pan and set aside.

Add the mushrooms to the bacon fat and cook over high heat until they are browned. Lower heat to medium, add the onions and garlic, and let cook another 5 minutes or until they are softened.

Add the beer, then add the reserved bacon, thyme, and bay leaf, and return the thighs to the pan. The liquid should almost cover the thighs. Add more beer, water, or chicken stock if you need it. Bring to a simmer, cover the pan tightly with a lid or aluminum foil, and put into a 325°F oven for 2 ½ hours.

When the thighs are done, remove them from the liquid. Adjust the seasoning and discard the bay leaf. The flour serves to thicken the sauce a bit, but if you prefer your sauce on the thicker side, you can whisk a bit of extra flour into the sauce to give it more body. Just be sure to bring it back to a simmer to cook the raw flour taste out. Season to taste.

Serve over simple mashed potatoes or on its own with a baguette to scoop up the sauce.

COURTESY OF CHEF ADRIAN GIOIA, LADYFACE ALE COMPANIE & BRASSERIE (PAGE 27)

CHOCOLATE BEER SHORTCAKES WITH HEFEWEIZEN-SOAKED STRAWBERRIES & BEER WHIPPED CREAM

Food blogger and beer lover Jackie Dodd, better known as "The Beeroness," is one of LA's most talented beer chefs. Her website includes a large collection of incredible gourmet recipes utilizing beer as a main ingredient, along with vibrant food photography. Jackie recently released an amazing recipe book called *The Craft Beer Cookbook*, which details 100 artisanal recipes for cooking with beer. Jackie brings us a decadent dessert recipe for Chocolate Beer Shortcakes!

SERVES 8

For the strawberries:
$^1/_3$ *cup Hefeweizen beer*
$^2/_3$ *cup powdered sugar*
1 cup fresh strawberries, diced

For the shortcakes:
1 $^1/_2$ cups flour
$^1/_2$ *cup cocoa powder*
2 tablespoons espresso powder
$^1/_2$ *teaspoon sea salt*
1 $^1/_2$ teaspoons baking powder
$^1/_2$ *teaspoon baking soda*
$^1/_2$ *cup granulated sugar*
$^1/_2$ *cup butter, cut into small cubes*
$^1/_4$ *cup heavy cream*
$^1/_2$ *cup dark beer*

For the whipped cream:
> *1 cup heavy cream, chilled*
> *1/3 cup powdered sugar*
> *1 tablespoon Hefeweizen*

In a small bowl, whisk the Hefeweizen and the powdered sugar until well combined. Add the strawberries and allow to soak at room temperature for 2 hours.

In a food processor, add the flour, cocoa powder, espresso powder, salt, baking powder, baking soda, and sugar and pulse to combine. Add the butter and process until the butter is well incorporated. Add the cream and beer and process until just combined. The dough will be very soft.

On a baking sheet that has been covered with parchment paper (or sprayed with cooking spray), drop about 1/3 cup of dough into a fairly round ball. Repeat until all dough is used (about 8 shortcakes). Chill dough for 20 minutes.

Preheat the oven to 350°F. Bake for 18–20 minutes or until shortcakes spring back when touched. Allow to cool to room temperature.

In the bowl of a stand mixer, add the whipped cream ingredients. Beat on high until soft peaks form, about 3 minutes.

Split the shortcakes. Fill with strawberries and whipped cream.

Notes: For the whipped cream and berries, I (Jackie Dodd) used Golden Road Hefeweizen; its notes of wheat malt and citrus go well with this recipe. For the chocolate shortcakes, I used Eagle Rock Solidarity, which is an English black mild style. The notes of coffee and malt work well with a chocolate dessert, and the carbonation level is higher than most dark beers, giving a little extra leavening to these cakes. If you can't find an English black mild beer, look for a porter or stout with notes of coffee and cocoa.

COURTESY OF JACKIE DODD, THE BEERONESS, THEBEERONESS.COM

THE BEER BARON: PORTER PULLED PORK AND
PICKLED ONION GRILLED CHEESE

Aften Detwiler, better known as "The Beerista" to the LA beer community, has been blogging about her adventures in beer since the beginning of the Los Angeles beer boom. Her website not only covers beer events and tastings, but also focuses on cooking with the bubbly stuff. On her site you'll find countless amazing recipes ranging from beer-steamed mussels to rye ale soft pretzels. Aften was also recently crowned champion of LA's 2012 Grilled Cheese Invitational for her delicious "Beer Baron" grilled cheese sandwich. Aften, who was recently promoted to LA Events Manager at Sierra Nevada Brewing Co., was nice enough to share her award-winning recipe with us. Enjoy!

Note: Also see Aften's Spent Grain Bread with Brown Ale recipe (page 367).

MAKES 6 SANDWICHES

> 1 ^{1}/$_2$ pounds pork shoulder or pork butt
> Your favorite spice rub
> 1 (750 ml) bottle porter (Aften uses Telegraph Brewing Co.)
> 8–9 ounces good-quality BBQ sauce
> ^{1}/$_2$ cup red wine vinegar or apple cider vinegar
> ^{1}/$_2$ cup water
> 1 teaspoon sugar
> Kosher salt
> 1 medium red onion, thinly sliced (about 1 cup)
> 18 ounces Vermont white cheddar cheese, sliced
> 12 slices hearty bread
> 6 tablespoons butter

Begin by making your porter pulled pork. Coat the pork with a moderate layer of the spice rub on all sides. Place the pork into a slow cooker and pour ^{1}/$_2$ of the bottle of porter over the pork. It should be a little more than half-submerged in the beer. Cover the slow cooker and turn it on low for 8–10 hours.

When the pork is finished cooking in the slow cooker, remove it and flake it apart with a fork. Move the pork into a large skillet with high sides. Pour the rest of the beer over the pork and add the BBQ sauce. Mix the pork to combine and turn the heat on high to bring to a boil. When the liquid starts to boil, lower the heat and simmer the pork for about 15–20 minutes or until most of the liquid is gone.

Next, make the pickled onions by putting the vinegar and water in a saucepan. Add the sugar and a few sprinkles of salt. Heat the mixture on medium until it begins to simmer. Put your sliced onions in a sealable container and pour the hot liquid over them. Let stand for 30 minutes, then put the container in the fridge. Allow onions to cool completely before using. (These can be made up to 3 days ahead of time.)

To make the sandwiches, assemble by placing a few slices of cheese, a layer of pork, and pickled onions on a slice of bread. Top with one more layer of cheese and another slice of bread. Put a tablespoon of butter in a pan and heat on medium. Once your butter is melted, carefully place the assembled sandwich in the pan and grill for 3–4 minutes. Once it is crisp and the cheese begins to melt, flip and grill for an additional 3–4 minutes on the other side. Repeat until all the sandwiches are made.

COURTESY OF AFTEN DETWILER, THE BEERISTA, THEBEERISTA.COM

BREWHOUSE FISH N' CHIPS WITH LEMON-CAPER REMOULADE

Coronado Brewing Company is a well-known fixture on San Diego's Coronado Island. Their expansive menu includes traditional pub staples as well as incredible seasonal and locally sourced gourmet delicacies. Executive Chef Kasey Chapman's culinary expertise led to his recently being crowned Sausage King at the San Diego Sausage Festival. Kasey is also no stranger to brewing and frequently helps prepare herbal infusions for special-release beers at the Coronado pub. He brings us a classic recipe for beer-battered fish-and-chips using Coronado Brewing Company's classic beer, Mermaid's Red Ale.

SERVES 4

For the remoulade:
- 1/4 cup mayonnaise
- 1 teaspoon Dijon mustard
- 1 tablespoon capers, rinsed and chopped
- 1 tablespoon fresh lemon juice
- 1/4 teaspoon dry dill
- 1/2 teaspoon salt
- ½ teaspoon pepper

For the fish and chips:

> *4 cups canola oil*
>
> *4 russet potatoes, cut ¼-inch thick and soaked in cold water for 30 minutes*
>
> *1 ½ cups Mermaid's Red Ale*
>
> *1 ½ cups all-purpose flour, plus ¼ cup for dredging*
>
> *1 teaspoon Old Bay Seasoning, plus ¼ teaspoon for dredging*
>
> *1 tablespoon baking powder*
>
> *½ teaspoon salt*
>
> *½ teaspoon pepper*
>
> *2 pounds firm whitefish (cod, tilapia, pollock), cut into 4-ounce pieces*

Mix all the remoulade ingredients and refrigerate until ready to use.

In a cast-iron pot or Dutch oven, heat oil to 325°F. Pat the potatoes dry and slowly add to oil. Cook 6 minutes. Using a slotted spoon, extract from oil and raise temperature to 375°F. Again, slowly add potatoes and cook thoroughly until golden brown and crisp. Keep fried potatoes on a paper towel–lined sheet pan in a 200°F oven.

Whisk the beer, 1½ cups flour, 1 teaspoon Old Bay, baking powder, salt, and pepper together until smooth.

Combine ¼ cup flour and ¼ teaspoon Old Bay. Dredge fish fillets in flour mixture, then dip in beer batter and add to hot oil 1 piece at a time without overcrowding. Cook fish 8 minutes, turning fillets about halfway through. Note: Cook fish in small batches to help retain oil temperature.

Serve with lemon wedges, remoulade, and malt vinegar. Enjoy!

COURTESY OF KASEY CHAPMAN, EXECUTIVE CHEF, CORONADO BREWING COMPANY (PAGE 312)

Cooking with Spent Grain

It's becoming more and more common to reduce waste in the brewing industry. Brewers are donating their spent grain and yeast to local farmers for cattle feed, but they save some of that grain for us. Spent grain isn't garbage—it's a rich source of fiber and an amazing ingredient to cook with. Some brewpubs have embraced the spent grain cooking phenomenon, but definitely not enough. If you are a home brewer, be sure to check out these recipes. Reuse your spent grain, and don't be afraid to experiment. Your friends will thank you for your fiber-full gift and will ask you for more on a REGULAR basis.

Spent Grain Recipe Research

Be sure to check the Spent Grain Chef at brooklynbrewshop.com for some truly inspired ways to use spent grain. Once you learn how to use it, you'll never forget. The Spent Grain Burger is one of the best veggie burgers I have ever had. It is incredible versatile, easy to make, and the base can be used for burgers, meatloaf, and stuffed peppers. You'll never go to the frozen section again.

SPENT GRAIN BREAD WITH BROWN ALE

Another stellar recipe from The Beerista, Aften Detwiler, this recipe for Spent Grain Bread with Brown Ale is the counterpart to the Beer Baron sandwich in the previous section. If you want to make your own bread, this is how you do it. If you like cooking with spent grain, make sure you visit her website to find more delicious ways to use the stuff.

MAKES 2 LOAVES

> 1 package (2 ½ teaspoons) active dry yeast
> ¾ cup brown ale, room temperature
> 3 cups cool water
> 1 cup spent grain flour (dried spent grain processed to a fine powder in a food processor)
> 5 ½ cups all-purpose flour, divided
> 1 cup spent grain
> 1 tablespoon sea salt

Start by making what is called "the sponge." To do this, in a large bowl combine the yeast, beer, water, spent grain flour, and 2½ cups of the all-purpose flour. Whisk them all together until combined, then cover the bowl with plastic wrap and let it sit overnight or for 8 hours at room temperature. The sponge will grow in size and look like, um, a sponge when ready—light and airy with some holes in it.

When the sponge is ready, add the remaining flour, spent grain, and salt to the bowl. Mix with a wooden spoon until it comes together. Scrape the dough out of the bowl onto a well-floured work surface. Knead the dough until it is smooth and elastic, about 5–7 minutes. Continue to flour the dough as needed to prevent it from sticking.

PHOTO COURTESY OF AFTEN DETWILER

Form the dough into a ball and place it in a lightly oiled bowl. Cover the bowl with plastic wrap and let the dough rise in a warm, draft-free place until it doubles in size (about 2 hours). After 2 hours, dust your counter and a sheet pan with flour.

Punch the dough down in the bowl, then scrape it out of the bowl onto the floured counter. Shape it into a large, round loaf. Put the loaf on the floured baking sheet, cover it with a towel, and let it rest in a warm, draft-free location for 30–45 minutes.

In the meantime move a rack in your oven to the lower third and preheat it to 400°F. When the bread is finished rising, sprinkle the top with all-purpose flour and use a sharp knife to cut the loaf in half. Separate the halves and turn them a quarter turn so that the cut side is now facing up. You will end up with 2 oval-shaped loaves. Space the loaves apart on the baking sheet and bake until they are brown and hollow-sounding, 35–45 minutes.

When they are done, turn the oven off and let the bread sit for 10 minutes without opening the door. Allow the bread to cool before cutting.

COURTESY OF AFTEN DETWILER, THE BEERISTA, THEBEERISTA.COM

SPENT GRAIN GRANOLA

This recipe for Spent Grain Granola was created using a lot of Web research. There are some pretty good sources online if you are looking for ways to cook with spent grain. This recipe is incredibly flexible and can be altered at will. Don't be afraid to throw in more ingredients, and please experiment. Spent Grain Granola is an amazing breakfast treat. It goes great on yogurt and ice cream, and has many other uses. This recipe makes quite a bit of granola.

MAKES 8 QUARTS OF LOOSELY PACKED GRANOLA

The solids:

8 cups dried spent grain
1 cup wheat germ
1–1 1/2 cups organic rolled oats, barley, or wheat
1 cup organic flaxseeds
1 cup organic chia seeds
1–2 cups organic cashews (or) raw cashews (pre-soaked)
1 cup shredded organic coconut

The binders/liquids:

12–16 ounces raw organic honey

2 teaspoons bourbon vanilla extract

¼ cup coconut oil

1 cup boiling water

The finishing touch:

16 ounces dried fruit, to be added after granola is dry (dried cranberries, apricots, strawberries, cherries, raisins, prunes, apples, and blackberries are a great start)

Preheat the oven to 350°F. Mix the solid dry ingredients together (minus the dried fruit) in a large mixing bowl. In a separate bowl, mix the binders/liquids together. Make sure that the honey is completely dissolved. Pour the liquid mixture over the dry ingredients and mix thoroughly with a spoon. Make sure everything is combined.

On 2 or 3 parchment paper–covered baking sheets, evenly disperse the granola mixture, making about a 1-inch layer. Bake at 350°F for 15 minutes. Turn the oven temperature down to 200°F and let sit for 5–8 hours or until dry, stirring every 1–2 hours. Once granola is dry, add the dried fruit, mix, and bake for an additional 20 minutes. Cool granola, place in a large container, and store in the fridge.

Note: The refrigerator step at the end solidifies the granola. This will make the granola crunchy and will keep it fresh.

COURTESY OF KRISTOFOR BARNES, BIERKAST.COM/LOS ANGELES ALE WORKS (PAGE 50)

SPENT GRAIN PIZZA DOUGH

This recipe is brought to you by Katie McKissick, Bierkast editor and resident Internet biology expert. Katie is also my lovely and supportive wife, and was creatively inspired when I started using spent grain. When she isn't teaching people about science on her website, beatricebiologist.com, she's experimenting in the kitchen with spent grain while sipping on saison. Everyone likes pizza dough, and this one is packed with fiber! Making your own dough is actually easier than you think, and it's a great way to impress your friends, especially if they home brew. Toppings are your choice, but seasonal ingredients like heirloom tomatoes are some of the best choices.

MAKES 1 LARGE OR 2 MEDIUM SIZED PIZZAS

1 package active dry yeast
$^1/_2$ cup warm water (around 110°F)
1 $^1/_2$ cups flour
$^3/_4$ cups spent grain, wetted with $^3/_4$ cup water
1 $^1/_2$ teaspoons salt
Olive oil

Add the yeast to the warm water and swirl to combine. Let it sit for 5 minutes.

In a large bowl, mix the flour, spent grain, and salt. Add the yeast mixture to the dry ingredients and mix it together with a spoon or your clean hands.

Prepare a floured work surface. Place the dough on the surface and knead it for 10 minutes.

Place the olive oil in a bowl and place the dough on top, turning it over to cover it in the olive oil. Place the bowl in a warm place, cover it with a towel, and let the dough rise for 2 hours.

Punch the dough, re-cover with the towel, and let it rise for another 30 minutes.

Roll the dough out on a floured work surface until it is about $^1/_4$ inch thick. Bake it at 350°F for 10 minutes on a pizza stone or pan.

Add desired sauce and toppings and bake again for 12 more minutes.

COURTESY OF KATIE MCKISSICK—BIERKAST.COM/BEATRICE THE BIOLOGIST

Beer Festivals

Beer festivals are a perfect way to spend a weekend while enjoying craft beer, local music, and crowds of revelers. With the huge explosion in craft beer in Southern California and in the US in general, there's been a massive flood of beer festivals. Keep in mind that quantity is not necessarily quality, though. While some beer festivals aim to elevate craft and educate, others are just an expensive excuse to get sloshed. There is a time and place for everything, but if you want to remember your experience, do your research on each event so you know exactly what to expect when you get there.

ALPINE VILLAGE OKTOBERFEST & ALPINE KRAFT BIERFEST
alpinevillagecenter.com

Alpine Village, located in Torrance, CA, has been throwing massive Oktoberfest celebrations since 1968. It's one of the few places where you can get a traditional Oktoberfest experience in SoCal, complete with massive event space, communal beer tables, a giant tent, and oompa bands. The Alpine Oktoberfest is held September 15 through October 26. Admission is $10 and you pay for your pretzels, sausages, and beer inside the tent. Oktoberfest offers three traditional German beers, a selection of local craft, and wine. For a more crafty experience, visit Alpine Village in November for their annual Alpine Village Kraft Bierfest, which showcases some 30 to 50 craft beers on tap. Both of these events are fun, but can get extremely crowded. Be prepared to have fun.

DRINK EAT PLAY
drinkeatplay.com

Drink Eat Play focuses on large-scale beer festivals in the major cities. They have annual and seasonal beer fests that draw incredibly large crowds. The Los Angeles event is held at Paramount Studios, the Orange County fest is at Irvine Lake, and the San Diego gathering takes place at Liberty Station. Tickets range from $40 to $50, and there are usually a couple sessions each running for about four hours. These events, although fun, are more focused on drinking as much as possible than tasting. That being said, you can still find some pretty good beers on tap, as many breweries attend. Be prepared for large crowds.

Beer Fest Tips

Transportation: Before going to a beer fest, figure out how you are getting there and also how you are getting back. Select a designated driver, use public transportation, or call a taxi.

Know Your Limit: Most beer fests supply a 2- to 6-ounce taster glass, the most common being 4-ounce. While this seems like a relatively small amount, beer fests, depending on breweries present, pour a large selection of different beer styles, all with varying alcohol percentages. Keep in mind that you don't have to obliterate yourself to have a good time.

Eat: Eat before you go and while you are there. This cannot be understated. Make sure you get a full meal before you start drinking, and plan to eat during the festival if it's four hours or longer.

Hydration: All festivals are required to have water stations—use them. Between fills of bubbly goodness, drink plenty of water. If you're a beer purist and like to rinse glasses between tastings, drink that water. Depending on the festival venue and whether or not you are outside in the hot sun, this may be even more important. Fests like the Firestone Walker Invitational can approach 100 degrees or over, so it's important to stay hydrated while you enjoy yourself.

Respect Others: Don't be that guy. Be aware of your special constraints and the crowds, and be courteous. Have a good time, but remember hundreds if not thousands of other people who also want to have a good time surround you.

Keep the Line Moving: Nothing is worse than standing in line forever while the guy in front of you gets multiple refills and talks the server's ear off. Get your taster and move on. If you like the brewery and the beer, make a note of it and research them when you get home. Beer festivals, depending on the venue, may not be the best opportunity to catch up with your favorite brewer and/or brewery staff members.

Tasting Beer: Let's just say that not all beer fests are the best medium for actually tasting beer critically, and that's okay. If you want to critically taste beer, just keep note of the breweries and beers you liked, and taste them again at a later time. Hoppy beers, although delicious, will wreck your palate faster than other beers. If you have a long day ahead of you, you may want to save them for last. Don't take notes at a fest, take pictures.

Blogging: The OC Beer Blogger, Greg Nagel, had a really good tip that has helped me: "Never finish your glass at a tasting." If you are writing about the event, you'll more than likely need to stay more sober, while at the same time tasting the beers. People will expect a review of the event detailing your experience so they can look out for the next one. Fests also use these reviews/articles as advertising when they plan their next event. Make sure you cover the basics well and supply feedback if anything was out of the ordinary.

Support Local Beer: The brewers are there for you to have a good time and are also interested in raising awareness about their product, so if you like it, support them and buy their beer outside of the fest.

FIRESTONE WALKER INVITATIONAL BEER FEST

firestonebeer.com/mingle/fw-invitational-beer-fest

The Firestone Walker Invitational Beer Fest, although not technically in Southern California, is one of the most incredible beer festivals around. It draws fans from across the US and in some cases from around the world. The concept is simple: Firestone invites around 40 breweries to pour their most rare and amazing beers and limits the number of tickets sold. It's a beer geek's paradise. What's even better, food is included. Along with the large selection of breweries, there are over 20 local food vendors serving some of the most delicious food around. The all-inclusive ticket is a heavy-hitting $75, but is well worth it. The event lasts five hours, is held in Paso Robles near the brewery on the fairgrounds, and includes live music. It cannot be stated enough how cool this event is.

FOOD GPS EVENTS

foodgps.com

World traveler and food journalist Joshua Lurie runs an amazing food and beer blog called Food GPS with the help of Beer Search Party beer enthusiast Sean Inman, who covers the beer side of things. In addition to operating Food GPS, Joshua holds regular events aimed at elevating both craft food and craft beer. His events are usually smaller in scale, with limited tickets, and feature an incredibly focused selection of drinks and restaurant vendors. From a Father's Day event featuring coffee beers and brunch to a Fried Chicken Festival showcasing over 10 types of gourmet-fried chicken, these events are intimate, memorable, and always have great beer. The focus is on pairing the two. Be sure to sign up for event listings and/or their weekly newsletter detailing LA and regional craft food and beverage.

LA BEER WEEK

labeerweek.com

Los Angeles's beer scene is still in its infancy, but the beer bug is biting at a regular rate. To celebrate LA beer and the developing scene, a group of LA beer personalities have assembled a weeklong event held in September called LA Beer Week. It typically begins and/or ends with a gala or festival at Union Station, and throughout the week special events are held all over the city. Local breweries, brewpubs, and beer bars can register their events on the website, and craft beer drinkers can view the calendar to choose which ones they want to go to. It's an amazing week for craft beer, and as with any special event, expect special beer releases, rare beers, incredible beer opportunities, and a ton of fun.

Anniversary Parties

With the rapid increase in beer fests, it can be hard to know which one to go to. A simple suggestion would be to stay close to home and focus on your favorite craft breweries and watering holes. Every craft beer bar and brewery has an anniversary party. The beers pouring at these parties are usually rare and special, and always good. You'll attend with like-minded fans while supporting businesses that you truly care about. From the airfields of Redlands celebrating Hangar 24 to the backyard patio of Verdugo Bar reveling in Eagle Rock Brewery, these anniversary gatherings are some of the most unique and memorable events you can go to. Stone Brewing Co.'s anniversary party is always a worthwhile event and showcases lots of San Diego breweries on tap. Ballast Point Brewing's 17th-anniversary party was held on the water at the Maritime Museum of San Diego, where fest-goers enjoyed craft beer on boats in the marina. Fun!

LA VEGAN BEER & FOOD FESTIVAL
losangelesvegan.com

The Los Angeles Vegan Beer & Food Festival is held in May and was inspired by outspoken craft beer advocate and vegan Tony Yanow. The festival features vegan food and beer along with live music and eclectic crowds. The event is typically held on Sunset Boulevard in West Hollywood. Fest-goers can expect large crowds, 40 or so breweries, and a slew of restaurants serving vegan-friendly food. This event is very Los Angeles and is worth going to if you're in the area. Tickets are $40 to $50.

OC BREW HA HA
ocbrewhaha.com

The OC Brew Ha Ha started its annual festival routine in 2010 and has been pleasing Orange County beer lovers ever since. The festival is typically held in September near Irvine Lake. What's different about this festival is the option to camp. Fest-goers can get a camping space, which mitigates the risk of people driving under the influence. This is a larger festival, but it's one that is run very well. Fest-goers are given 4-ounce tasters and have the option to taste 175-plus craft and import beers from over 70 breweries. The festival also includes presentations given by craft beer personalities like Greg Koch, who has spoken at the event in the past. The event is partnered with the Local 3631 Firefighters Union, so it's for a good cause. The Brew Ha Ha also has a winter fest called the Brew Ho Ho, so watch out for this one as well.

SAN DIEGO BEER WEEK
sdbw.org

San Diego Beer Week runs from November 1 to 10 and showcases some of the best San Diego has to offer. The weeklong festivities are managed by the San Diego Brewers Guild, which also has a festival-style event happening on the first two days of the Beer Week. San Diego beer establishments can register their events on the website, and beer lovers can view them via the calendar. As San Diego currently has over 85 breweries, it's a good assumption that there is a lot to do. Most breweries hold special keg and cask tappings as well as partnering with gastropubs for pint nights.

SAN DIEGO INTERNATIONAL BEER FESTIVAL
sdfair.com/index.php?fuseaction=festivals.beer_festival

Also known as the San Diego County Fair, the San Diego International Beer Festival showcases both local and international beers. In 2013 they had 407 different beers represented. The fest runs from June 21 to 23 and is held in the Del Mar Arena. Along with being a large beer venue, the festival also judges beers, awarding medals to the best in their category.

STONE BREWING CO. BEER FESTIVALS
stonebrewing.com/festivals

It goes without saying that Stone Brewing Co. is an amazing brewery. They are currently the 10th-largest brewery in the US, and with that great size comes great responsibility—the responsibility to preach the gospel of craft, which they frequently do in many forms, including events. Stone has some of the most amazing events in Southern California. From their anniversary party in August, where they debut their newest anniversary beer, to their Stone Pour It Black in October where nothing but dark beers are poured, each event has its own theme.

Other events include the Stone Winter Storm, a festival that features a massive catalogue of Stone beers, some years and years old. From barrel-aged to tea-infused, this event is incredible. Another event worth noting is the Stone Sour Fest featuring tart and sour beers—get ready for Cantilion bottles, beer geeks. Events are constant and constantly changing, so be sure to check the website and get on the mailing list. Tickets are $45 and up, depending on the event and type of ticket.

Get Informed

A big part of craft beer is being enthusiastic, evangelizing, and documenting experiences. If you're traveling somewhere new, why not take the advice of the local experts? Many people have taken up the great cause of putting their thoughts to paper to better inform the masses of the greatness that is craft beer. In Southern California we have a massive cast of talented folks who cover events, interview the pros, review beers, produce festivals, and expose new fans to the greatest beverage on earth. Here are some of the best SoCal beer blogs and beer news sites, in alphabetical order.

THE BEER CHICKS
thebeerchicks.com

Christina Perozzi and Hallie Beaune are both beer sommeliers who run the popular site The Beer Chicks. Together they've written two books on beer and have actively worked on elevating craft beer in SoCal in general and for women in particular. Their website covers everything from beer tastings and events to beer news to beer cooking recipes. Christina and Hallie are local celebrities and make a point to be as active in the local beer scene as possible. They are also cohosts of the annual LA Craft Beer Crawl.

BEER GUY LA
beerguyla.com

Beer Guy LA, run by seasoned beer taster Jeff Proser, is an LA beer site that covers beer reviews and local themed events. You'll frequently find Jeff in LA-area bars during new beer release events. A fellow beer enthusiast, David Willis, also writes for Jeff's site in a column called Dave Hates Your Beer, where he intentionally subjects himself to comical craft beer experiments. It's tongue in cheek along with being informative.

BEER OF TOMORROW
beeroftomorrow.com

Headed by local LA beer writers John and Julie Verive, Beer of Tomorrow focuses on critical issues, advice, and a more journalistic approach to the beer scene. John also writes for the *LA Times'* online Daily Dish and *Beer Paper LA*. Beer of Tomorrow is a great resource for local beer enthusiasts looking to expand their knowledge and learn more about how to enjoy beer to its fullest.

BEER PAPER LA
beerpaperla.com

The first beer-centered newspaper to be printed for Los Angeles, *Beer Paper LA* comes out in monthly editions covering the greater LA area. It's an impressive collection of articles from seasoned local beer writers specifically about the LA beer scene. Founders Aaron Carroll and Rob Wallace are passionate about LA beer and wanted to create something unique to the city to inform the masses. *Beer Paper LA,* found in most local beer spots, is a great resource for learning about local craft beer stars, the beers they make, and the amazing places that serve them.

BEERQWEST
beerqwest.com

Created by Bryan Hardyman, one of the original co-founders of another beer site BierBuzz.com, BeerQwest.com is made up of an altruistic team of writers who cover not only the greater LA area, but also beer in other cities like Portland and Seattle. BeerQwest is a top-notch looking site with great articles, beer hot-spot reviews, and beer ratings.

BEERS IN PARADISE
beersinparadise.com

Voted as most valuable beer blog in *LA Weekly*'s Best of the Web, Beers in Paradise covers the greater LA area along with extended events in San Diego. Articles both critical and enthusiastic are what you'll find, along with Instagrams depicting great craft beer in picturesque locals.

BIERBUZZ
bierbuzz.com

If you prefer to watch your craft beer coverage, BierBuzz.com produces regular video content highlighting the rise of craft beer in the Inland Empire and greater Los Angeles area. Headed by BierBuzz CEO and founder, Jason Torres, the team recently paired up with playboy radio to expand their reach and have hosted several craft beer festivals. If you are looking to party, look no further than BierBuzz.com.

BIERKAST
bierkast.com

Bierkast, founded by Kristofor Barnes, started out as a home brew blog and now covers Los Angeles beer with extended coverage in San Diego by Derek Springer. Bierkast focuses primarily on stories concerning beer issues, interesting places to enjoy beer, and beer celeb interviews. Bierkast hosts a collection of writers including Brett Padelford, who covers a national baseball and beer tour he does every year.

THE *CELEBRATOR*
celebrator.com

Touted as the nation's oldest craft beer publication, the *Celebrator* is a monthly magazine covering the national craft beer scene. Including the writings of some of SoCal's most talented writers like Tomm Carroll and Brandon Hernandez, the *Celebrator* is a more traditional approach to beer news and can be found online or in paper form.

FOOD GPS/BEER SEARCH PARTY
foodgps.com and beersearchparty.com

Food GPS, the food-centric blog started by Joshua Lurie, has exploded in recent years. Its highly polished interface not only details LA-area food, but also covers professionals, chefs, brewers, and hot spots from all around. Josh accompanies his articles with incredible food photography, and there is also a beer section written by local blogger Sean Inman of Beer Search Party. Sean writes several columns that cover weekly craft advice, local interviews, and monthly happenings around town. This is a great resource for craft beer/foodies.

THE FULL PINT
thefullpint.com

Recently celebrating their sixth year, the Full Pint crew, Dan and Jon, have been spreading the beer gospel around Southern California and beyond. On their site you'll find beer news, reviews, press releases, events, and a blog by Franny Fullpint of Golden Road. The Full Pint is one of the most well-known sites in the area and holds an annual anniversary party that includes some of the rarest beers on tap available anywhere.

Let the Bloggers Be Your Guide

Some great information can also be found on brewery blog pages, but restrictions due to Alcohol Beverage Control laws limit the amount of info that can be posted on social media outlets. Subscribing to a few local beer blogs can be a great way to get a lay of the land so you can generate a game plan for how to best tackle your intended area.

Freelance Writers

You'll find that a lot of these writers, like Daniel Drennon, Randy Clemens, Erika Bolden, Sarah Bennett, Brandon Hernandez, and Farley Elliott, to name a few, write for multiple publications. Figure out which writers you enjoy, and stick with them. Sometimes the best information is in multiple places, so you may have to follow a writer through several publications as they write about craft beer.

GIRLS WHO LIKE BEER
girlswholikebeer.com

Founded by graphic designer Kelly Erickson, Girls Who Like Beer covers most of LA, with a focus on Echo Park and East LA. Touted as a "Rustic Girl's Guide to LA," Kelly covers everything from great beer spots to beer reviews. You can always find good event advice and great photos on her site. Kelly also manages the blog Echo Park Now.

HOP HEAD SAID
hopheadsaid.com

A blog from Craftbeer.com writer Curtis Taylor, Hop Head Said covers the Ventura area and also features a craft beer and football section. Curtis also runs the *Happy Hour with Joby and Curtis* podcast, which interviews SoCal and beyond beer experts.

LA—BEER—BLOG
www.la-beer-blog.com

Managed by the charismatic duo Josh Sellers and Craig Berry, the LA Beer Blog covers everything from press releases to event reviews. You'll find opinion pieces, punch-happy comic relief, and useful tips about navigating the LA beer scene. Josh and Craig aren't afraid to give you their honest opinion about what's going on in town and you'll thank them for it.

LA BEER BLOGGERS
labeerbloggers.org

The LA Beer Bloggers group established itself in 2012 with its first summit meeting at Eagle Rock Brewery. The group brings together media types from all blogs and walks of life to celebrate beer while focusing on professional development, guest speakers, and networking. If you are a beer enthusiast looking to connect with the online writing community, look no further. A full listing of participating members and suggested beer blogs can be located on the main website.

LA WEEKLY—SQUID INK
blogs.laweekly.com/squidink

The online publication for *LA Weekly* enjoys a number of talented writers covering LA's burgeoning beer scene. Check out the Squid Ink portion to read writers like Sarah Bennett, Erika Bolden, and Farley Elliott, local beer experts who recommend amazingly awesome spots to enjoy some of the best LA has to offer.

OC BEER BLOG
blog.ocbeerblog.com

Run by a passionate OC native Greg Nagel, OC Beer Blog covers all things Orange County beer. Greg posts frequently to social media outlets like Facebook and Twitter, getting the word out about local hot spots and noteworthy beer people. OC Beer Blog recently won the title of best Beer Blog in Orange County in the 2013 Best of OC Weekly Awards. Greg is also a regular writer for *Beer Paper LA* and *West Coaster*.

WEST COASTER—SOCAL AND SAN DIEGO
westcoastersocal.com, westcoastersd.com

Originally a San Diego–specific magazine, the *West Coaster* recently expanded its coverage throughout SoCal. Founded by Ryan Lamb and Mike Shess, the *West Coaster* has two magazines, SoCal and San Diego. SoCal prominently features the greater Los Angeles area, highlighting important people and events, while the San Diego edition is specific to San Diego. *West Coaster* is well known for its quality articles and is a great addition to the craft beer scene in SoCal. Quarterly issues are printed for the greater LA area and monthly issues are printed for San Diego, with availability in most local beer spots.

Conclusion

Southern California has a massive amount of beer to offer beer lovers from around the world. There is so much going on in this area that it's a bit hard to keep up with, which makes it incredibly exciting. There are dozens of breweries in planning, many of which will be newly opened by the time this book is published. Use this guide to jump-start your search for new beer, new food pairings, and perhaps even your favorite brewery. Take an active role and get involved with home brewing and educating those around you about the exciting world of craft beer. And, hey, if you find a new brewery in SoCal that blows your mind that isn't in the book, don't be afraid to let me know. Enjoy yourself out there! Cheers!

PHOTO COURTESY OF GEOFF KOWALCHUCK

Index